Neoliberalism's War on Higher Education

Neoliberalism's War on Higher Education

Henry A. Giroux

Between the Lines
Toronto

Neoliberalism's War on Higher Education
Copyright © 2014 Henry A. Giroux

First published in Canada in 2014 by
Between the Lines
401 Richmond Street West, Studio 277
Toronto, Ontario M5V 3A8
1-800-718-7201
www.btlbooks.com

Library and Archives Canada Cataloguing in Publication
Giroux, Henry A., author
Higher education after neoliberalism / Henry A. Giroux.

Includes bibliographical references and index. Issued in print and electronic formats. Co-published by: Haymarket.
ISBN 978-1-77113-112-4 (pbk.).
ISBN 978-1-77113-113-1 (epub).
ISBN 978-1-77113-114-8 (pdf)

1. Education, Higher--Political aspects--United States.   2. Education, Higher--Economic aspects--United States. 3. Neoliberalism--United States. I. Title.
LC89.G45 2013   378.73   C2013-907416-3
                                                C2013-907417-1

Printed in Canada by union labor.

Between the Lines gratefully acknowledges assistance for its publishing activities from the Canada Council for the Arts, the Ontario Arts Council, the Government of Ontario through the Ontario Book Publishers Tax Credit program, and the Government of Canada through the Canada Book Fund.

RECYCLED
Paper made from
recycled material
FSC
www.fsc.org   FSC® C103567

Table of Contents

For Wendy Simon

*To those brave and committed teachers who are struggling
to educate young people for a more just and democratic
world*

ACKNOWLEDGMENTS

This book could not have been completed without the help of many people. My late dear friend Roger Simon provided a range of insightful ideas regarding the Quebec student protest. I will miss his friendship and the many conversations we had. Susan Searls Giroux, Brad Evans, and Michael Peters all contributed greatly to the articles we co-authored and shared. Grace Pollock once again provided editorial advice and skills that continually improve the quality of my writing. My colleague David L. Clark was enormously generous in reading some chapters and offering a range of insightful ideas. Through his kindness, patience, and professional insight, Dr. Bruno Salena contributed greatly to the conditions that allowed me to write this book. Lynn Worsham has always been a wonderful colleague, and I want to thank her for publishing earlier versions of "Intellectual Violence in the Age of Gated Intellectuals" and "Universities Gone Wild" in *JAC*. I especially want to thank my administrative assistant, Danielle Martak, for reading and editing every word of this book. Her interventions were invaluable, and her insights, editorial help, and administrative skills have greatly improved the quality of the manuscript. This book was written mostly in Hamilton and Toronto, Ontario, during a difficult time in my life—a time made much easier by the continued presence of my two canine companions, Miles and Kaya.

INTRODUCTION

Neoliberalism's War on Democracy

It is certain, in any case, that ignorance, allied with power, is the most ferocious enemy justice can have.

—**James Baldwin**

Four decades of neoliberal policies have resulted in an economic Darwinism that promotes privatization, commodification, free trade, and deregulation. It privileges personal responsibility over larger social forces, reinforces the gap between the rich and poor by redistributing wealth to the most powerful and wealthy individuals and groups, and it fosters a mode of public pedagogy that privileges the entrepreneurial subject while encouraging a value system that promotes self-interest, if not an unchecked selfishness.[1] Since the 1970s, neoliberalism or free-market fundamentalism has become not only a much-vaunted ideology that now shapes all aspects of life in the United States but also a predatory global phenomenon "that drives the practices and principles of the International Monetary Fund, the World Bank, and World Trade Organization, trans-national institutions which largely determine the economic policies of developing countries and the rules of international trade."[2]

With its theater of cruelty and mode of public pedagogy, neoliberalism as a form of economic Darwinism attempts to undermine all forms of solidarity capable of challenging market-driven values and social relations, promoting the virtues of an unbridled individualism almost pathological in its disdain for community, social responsibility, public values, and the public good. As the welfare state is dismantled and spending is cut to the point where government becomes unrecognizable—*except* to promote policies that benefit the rich, corporations, and the defense industry—the already weakened federal and state governments are increasingly replaced by what João Biehl has called proliferating "zones of social abandonment" and "terminal exclusion."[3]

One consequence is that social problems are increasingly criminalized while social protections are either eliminated or fatally weakened. Not only are public servants described as the new "welfare queens" and degenerate freeloaders but young people are also increasingly subjected to harsh disciplinary measures both in and out of schools, often as a result of a violation of the most trivial rules.[4] Another characteristic of this crushing form of economic Darwinism is that it thrives on a kind of social amnesia that erases critical thought, historical analysis, and any understanding of broader systemic relations. In this regard, it does the opposite of critical memory work by eliminating those public spheres where people learn to translate private troubles into public issues. That is, it breaks "the link between public agendas and private worries, the very hub of the democratic process."[5] Once set in motion, economic Darwinism unleashes a mode of thinking in which social problems are reduced to individual flaws and political considerations collapse into the injurious and self-indicting discourse of character. Many Americans are preoccupied less with political and moral outrage over a country whose economic and political system is in the hands of a tiny, exorbitantly rich elite than they are with the challenges of being isolated and surviving at the bottom of a savage neoliberal order. This makes it all the simpler for neoliberalism to convince people to remain attached to a set of ideologies, values, modes of governance, and policies that generate massive suffering and hardships. Neoliberalism's "best trick" is to persuade individuals, as a matter of common sense, that they should "imagine [themselves] as . . . solitary agent[s] who can and must live the good life promised by capitalist culture."[6]

As George Lakoff and Glenn Smith argue, the anti-public philosophy of economic Darwinism makes a parody of democracy by defining freedom as "the liberty to seek one's own interests and well-being, without being responsible for the interests or well-being of anyone else. It's a morality of personal, but not social, responsibility. The only freedom you should have is what you can provide for yourself, not what the Public provides for you to start out."[7] Put simply, we alone become responsible for the problems we confront when we can no longer conceive how larger forces control or constrain our choices and the lives we are destined to lead.

Yet the harsh values and practices of this new social order *are* visible—in the increasing incarceration of young people, the modeling of public schools after prisons, state violence waged against peaceful student protesters, and state policies that bail out investment bankers but leave the middle and working classes in a state of poverty, despair, and insecurity. Such values are also evident in the Republican Party's social Darwinist budget plans that reward the rich and cut aid for those who need it the most. For instance, the 2012 Romney/Ryan budget plan "proposed to cut the taxes of households earning over $1 million by an average of $295,874 a year,"[8] at a cruel cost to those most disadvantaged populations who rely on social programs. In order to pay for tax reductions to benefit the rich, the Romney/Ryan budget would have cut funds for food stamps, Pell grants, health care benefits, unemployment insurance, veterans' benefits, and other crucial social programs.[9] As Paul Krugman has argued, the Ryan budget

> isn't just looking for ways to save money [it's] also trying to make life harder for the poor—for their own good. In March [2012], explaining his cuts in aid for the unfortunate, [Ryan] declared, "We don't want to turn the safety net into a hammock that lulls able-bodied people into lives of dependency and complacency, that drains them of their will and their incentive to make the most of their lives."[10]

Krugman rightly replies, "I doubt that Americans forced to rely on unemployment benefits and food stamps in a depressed economy feel that they're living in a comfortable hammock."[11] An extremist version of neoliberalism, Ryanomics is especially vicious toward US children, 16.1 million of whom currently live in poverty.[12] Marian Wright Edelman captures the harshness and savagery of the Ryan budget passed by the House of Representatives before being voted down in the Senate. She writes:

Ryanomics is an all out assault on our poorest children while asking not a dime of sacrifice from the richest 2 percent of Americans or from wealthy corporations. Ryanomics slashes hundreds of billions of dollars from child and family nutrition, health, child care, education, and child protection services, *in order* to extend and add to the massive Bush tax cuts for millionaires and billionaires at a taxpayer cost of $5 trillion over 10 years. On top of making the Bush tax cuts permanent, the top income bracket would get an additional 10 percent tax cut. Millionaires and billionaires would on average keep at least an additional quarter of a million dollars each year and possibly as much as $400,000 a year according to the Citizens for Tax Justice.[13]

As profits soar for corporations and the upper 1 percent, both political parties are imposing austerity measures that punish the poor and cut vital services for those who need them the most.[14] Rather than raising taxes and closing tax loopholes for the wealthy and corporations, the Republican Party would rather impose painful spending cuts that will impact the poor and vital social services. For example, the 2013 budget cuts produced by sequestration slash $20 million from the Maternal, Infant, and Early Child Home Visiting Program, $199 million from public housing, $6 million from emergency food and shelter, $19 million from housing for the elderly, $116 million from higher education, and $96 million from homeless assistance grants—and these are only a small portion of the devastating cuts enacted.[15] Seventy thousand children will be kicked off of Head Start, ten thousand teachers will be fired, and "the long-term unemployed will see their benefits cut by about 10 percent."[16] Under the right-wing insistence on a politics of austerity, Americans are witnessing not only widespread cuts in vital infrastructures, education, and social protections but also the emergence of policies produced in the spirit of revenge aimed at the poor, the elderly, and others marginalized by race and class. As Robert Reich, Charles Ferguson, and a host of recent commentators have noted, this extreme concentration of power in every commanding institution of society promotes predatory practices and rewards sociopathic behavior. Such a system creates an authoritarian class of corporate and hedge-fund swindlers that reaps its own profits by

placing big bets with other people's money. The winners in this system are top Wall Street executives and traders, private-equity managers and hedge-fund moguls, and the losers are most of the rest of us. The system is largely responsible for the greatest concentration of the nation's income and wealth at the very top since the Gilded Age of the nine-teenth century, with the richest 400 Americans owning as much as the bottom 150 million put together. And these multimillionaires and bil-lionaires are now actively buying . . . election[s]—and with [them], American democracy.[17]

Unfortunately, the US public has largely remained silent, if not also complicit in the rise of a neoliberal version of authoritarianism. While workers in Wisconsin, striking teachers in Chicago, and young people across the globe have challenged this politics and machinery of corruption, war, brutality, and social and civil death, they represent a small and mar-ginalized part of the larger movement that will be necessary to initiate mas-sive collective resistance to the aggressive violence being waged against all those public spheres that further the promise of democracy in the United States, the United Kingdom, France, and a host of other countries. The ac-tions of teachers, workers, student protesters, and others have been crucial in drawing public attention to the constellation of forces that are pushing the United States and other neoliberal-driven countries into what Hannah Arendt called "dark times"or what might be described as an increasingly authoritarian public realm that constitutes a clear and present danger to democracy. The questions now being asked must be seen as the first step toward exposing the dire social and political costs of concentrating wealth, income, and power into the hands of the upper 1 percent. What role higher education will play in both educating and mobilizing students is a crucial issue that will determine whether a new revolutionary ideal can take hold in order to address the ideals of democracy and its future.

Neoliberal Ideology and the Rhetoric of Freedom

In addition to amassing ever-expanding amounts of material wealth, the rich now control the means of schooling and other cultural apparatuses in the United States. They have disinvested in critical education while repro-ducing notions of "common sense" that incessantly replicate the basic values, ideas, and relations necessary to sustain the institutions of economic Dar-winism. Both major political parties, along with plutocrat "reformers," sup-port educational reforms that increase conceptual and cultural illiteracy.

Critical learning has been replaced with mastering test-taking, memorizing facts, and learning how *not* to question knowledge or authority. Pedagogies that unsettle common sense, make power accountable, and connect class-room knowledge to larger civic issues have become dangerous at all levels of schooling. This method of rote pedagogy, heavily enforced by mainstream educational reformists, is, as Zygmunt Bauman notes, "the most effective prescription for grinding communication to a halt and for [robbing] it of the presumption and expectation of meaningfulness and sense."[18] These radical reformers are also attempting to restructure how higher education is organized. In doing so, they are putting in place modes of governance that mimic corporate structures by increasing the power of administrators at the expense of faculty, reducing faculty to a mostly temporary and low-wage workforce, and reducing students to customers—ripe for being trained for low-skilled jobs and at-risk for incurring large student loans.

This pedagogy of market-driven illiteracy has eviscerated the notion of freedom, turning it largely into the desire to consume and invest exclusively in relationships that serve only one's individual interests. Losing one's individuality is now tantamount to losing one's ability to consume. Citizens are treated by the political and economic elite as restless children and are "invited daily to convert the practice of citizenship into the art of shopping."[19] Shallow consumerism coupled with an indifference to the needs and suffering of others has produced a politics of disengagement and a culture of moral irresponsibility. At the same time, the economically Darwinian ethos that places individual interest at the center of everyday life undercuts, if not removes, moral considerations about what we know and how we act from larger social costs and moral considerations. In media discourse, language has been stripped of the terms, phrases, and ideas that embrace a concern for the other. With meaning utterly privatized, words are reduced to signifiers that mimic spectacles of violence, designed to provide entertainment rather than thoughtful analysis. Sentiments circulating in the dominant culture parade either idiocy or a survival-of-the-fittest ethic, while anti-public rhetoric strips society of the knowledge and values necessary for the development of a democratically engaged and socially responsible public.

In such circumstances, freedom has truly morphed into its opposite. Neoliberal ideology has construed as pathological any notion that in a healthy society people depend on one another in multiple, complex, direct, and indirect ways. As Lewis Lapham observes, "Citizens are no longer held in thoughtful regard . . . just as thinking and acting are removed from acts of public conscience."[20] Economic Darwinism has produced a legitimating ideology in which the conditions for critical inquiry, moral responsibility, and social and economic justice disappear. The result is that neoliberal ideology increasingly resembles a call to war that turns the principles of democracy against democracy itself. Americans now live in an atomized and pulverized society, "spattered with the debris of broken interhuman bonds,"[21] in which "democracy becomes a perishable commodity"[22] and all things public are viewed with disdain.

Neoliberal Governance

At the level of governance, neoliberalism has increasingly turned mainstream politics into a tawdry form of money-laundering in which the spaces and registers that circulate power are controlled by those who have amassed large amounts of capital. Elections, like mainstream politicians, are now bought and sold to the highest bidder. In the Senate and House of Representatives, 47 percent are millionaires—the "estimated median net worth of a current US senator stood at an average of $2.56 million while the median net worth of members of Congress is $913,000."[23] Elected representatives no longer even purport to do the bidding of the people who elect them. Rather, they are now largely influenced by the demands of lobbyists, who have enormous clout in promoting the interests of the elite, financial services sector, and megacorporations. In 2012, there were just over fourteen thousand registered lobbyists in Washington, DC, which amounts to approximately twenty-three lobbyists for every member of Congress. Although the number of lobbyists has steadily increased by about 20 percent since 1998, the Center for Responsive Politics found that "total spending on lobbying the federal government has almost tripled since 1998, to $3.3 billion."[24] As Bill Moyers and Bernard Weisberger succinctly put it, "A radical minority of the superrich has gained ascendency over politics, buying the policies, laws, tax breaks, subsidies, and rules that consolidate a permanent state of vast inequality by which they can further help themselves to America's wealth and resources."[25] How else to explain that the 2013 bill designed to regulate the banking and financial sectors was drafted for legislators by Citigroup lobbyists?[26] There is more at stake here than legalized corruption, there is the arrogant dismantling of democracy and the production of policies that extend rather than mitigate human suffering, violence, misery, and everyday hardships. Democratic governance has been replaced by the sovereignty of the market, paving the way for modes of governance intent on transforming democratic citizens into entrepreneurial agents. The language of the market and business culture have now almost entirely supplanted any celebration of the public good or the calls to enhance civil society characteristic of past generations. Moreover, authoritarian governance now creeps into every institution and aspect of public life. Instead of celebrating Martin Luther King for his stands against poverty, militarization, and racism, US society holds him up as an icon denuded of any message of solidarity and social struggle. This erasure and depoliticization of history and politics is matched by the celebration of a business culture in which the US public transforms Bill Gates into a national hero. At the same time, civil rights heroine Rosa Parks cedes her position to the Kardashian sisters, as the prominence of civic culture is canceled out by herd-like public enthusiasm for celebrity culture, reality TV, and the hyper-violence of extreme sports. The older heroes sacrificed in order to alleviate the suffering of others, while the new heroes drawn from corporate and celebrity culture live off the suffering of others.

Clearly, US society is awash in a neoliberal culture of idiocy and illiteracy. It produces many subjects who are indifferent to others and are thus incapable of seeing that when the logic of extreme individualism is extended into the far reaches of the national security state, it serves to legitimate the breakdown of the social bonds necessary for a democratic society and reinforces a culture of cruelty that upholds solitary confinement as a mode of punishment for thousands of incarcerated young people and adults.[27] Is it any wonder that with the breakdown of critical education and the cultural apparatuses that support it, the American public now overwhelmingly supports state torture and capital punishment while decrying the necessity of a national health care system? Fortunately, there are signs of rebellion among workers, young people, students, and teachers, indicating that the US public has not been entirely colonized by the bankers, hedge fund managers, and other apostles of neoliberalism.

For example, in Connecticut, opponents of public-school privatization replaced three right-wing, pro-charter school board members. In Chicago, reform efforts prevented the city from outsourcing the lease of Midway Airport and breast cancer screening for uninsured women. And, in Iowa, as a result of pressure from progressives, the governor rejected corporate bids to purchase Iowa's statewide fiber-optics network.

Neoliberal governance has produced an economy and a political system almost entirely controlled by the rich and powerful—what a Citigroup report called a "plutonomy," an economy powered by the wealthy.[28] I have referred to these plutocrats as "the new zombies": they are parasites that suck the resources out of the planet and the rest of us in order to strengthen their grasp on political and economic power and fuel their exorbitant lifestyles.[29] Power is now global, gated, and driven by a savage disregard for human welfare, while politics resides largely in older institutions of modernity such as nation states. The new plutocrats have no allegiance to national communities, justice, or human rights, just potential markets and profits. The work of citizenship has been set back decades by this new group of winner-take-all global predators.[30] Policies are now enacted that provide massive tax cuts to the rich and generous subsidies to banks and corporations—alongside massive disinvestments in job creation programs, the building of critical infrastructures, and the development of crucial social programs ranging from health care to school meal programs for disadvantaged children.

Neoliberalism's massive disinvestment in schools, social programs, and an aging infrastructure is not about a lack of money. The real problem stems from government priorities that inform both how the money is collected and how it is spent.[31] More than 60 percent of the federal budget goes to military spending, while only 6 percent is allocated toward education. The United States spends more than $92 billion on corporate subsidies and only $59 billion on social welfare programs.[32] John Cavanagh has estimated that if there were a tiny tax imposed on Wall Street stock and derivatives transactions, the government could raise $150 billion annually.[33] In addition, if the tax code were adjusted in a fair manner to tax the wealthy, another $79 billion could be raised. Finally, Cavanagh notes that $100 billion in tax income is lost annually through tax haven abuse; proper regulation would make it costly for corporations to declare "their profits in overseas tax havens like the Cayman Islands."[34]

At the same time, the financialization of the economy and culture has resulted in the poisonous growth of monopoly power, predatory lending, abusive credit card practices, and misuses of CEO pay. The false but central neoliberal tenet that markets can solve all of society's problems grants unchecked power to money and has given rise to "a politics in which policies that favor the rich ... have allowed the financial sector to amass vast economic and political power."[35] As Joseph Stiglitz points out, there is more at work in this form of governance than a pandering to the wealthy and powerful: there is also the specter of an authoritarian society "where people live in gated communities," large segments of the population are impoverished or locked up in prison, and Americans live in a state of constant fear as they face growing "economic insecurity, healthcare insecurity, [and] a sense of physical insecurity."[36] In other words, the authoritarian nature of neoliberal political governance and economic power is also visible in the rise of a national security state in which civil liberties are being drastically abridged and violated.

As the war on terror becomes a normalized state of existence, the most basic rights available to American citizens are being shredded. The spirit of revenge, militarization, and fear now permeates the discourse of national security. For instance, under Presidents Bush and Obama, the idea of habeas corpus, with its guarantee that prisoners have minimal rights, has given way to policies of indefinite detention, abductions, targeted assassinations, drone killings, and an expanding state surveillance apparatus. The Obama administration has designated forty-six inmates for indefinite detention at Guantánamo because, according to the government, they can be neither tried nor safely released. Moreover, another "167 men now confined at Guantanamo . . . have been cleared for release yet remain at the facility."[37]

With the passing of the National Defense Authorization Act in 2012, the rule of legal illegalities has been extended to threaten the lives and rights of US citizens. The law authorizes military detention of individuals who are suspected of belonging not only to terrorist groups such as al-Qaida but also to "associated forces." As Glenn Greenwald illuminates, this "grants the president the power to indefinitely detain in military custody not only accused terrorists, but also their supporters, all without charges or trial."[38] The vagueness of the law allows the possibility of subjecting to indefinite detention US citizens who are considered to be in violation of the law. Of course, that might include journalists, writers, intellectuals, and anyone else who might be accused because of their dealings with alleged terrorists. Fortunately, US district judge Katherine Forrest of New York agreed with Chris Hedges, Noam Chomsky, and other writers who have challenged the legality of the law. Judge Forrest recently acknowledged the unconstitutionality of the law and ruled in favor of a preliminary barring of the enforcement of the National Defense Authorization Act.[39] Unfortunately, on July 17, 2013, an appeals court in New York ruled in favor of the Obama administration, allowing the government to detain indefinitely without due process persons designated as enemy combatants.

The antidemocratic practices at work in the Obama administration also include the US government's use of state secrecy to provide a cover for practices that range from the illegal use of torture and the abduction of innocent foreign nationals to the National Security Association's use of a massive surveillance campaign to monitor the phone calls, e-mails, and Internet activity of all Americans. A shadow mass surveillance state has emerged that eschews transparency and commits unlawful acts under the rubric of national security. Given the power of the government to engage in a range of illegalities and to make them disappear through an appeal to state secrecy, it should come as no surprise that warrantless wiretapping, justified in the name of national security, is on the rise at both the federal and state levels. For instance, the New York City Police Department "implemented surveillance programs that violate the civil liberties of that city's Muslim-American citizens [by infiltrating] mosques and universities [and] collecting information on individuals suspected of no crimes."[40] The US public barely acknowledged this shocking abuse of power. Such antidemocratic policies and practices have become the new norm in US society and reveal a frightening and dangerous move toward a twenty-first-century version of authoritarianism.

Neoliberalism as the New Lingua Franca of Cruelty

The harsh realities of a society defined by the imperatives of punishment, cruelty, militarism, secrecy, and exclusion can also be seen in a growing rhetoric of insult, humiliation, and slander. Teachers are referred to as "welfare queens" by right-wing pundits; conservative radio host Rush Limbaugh claimed that Michael J. Fox was "faking" the symptoms of Parkinson's disease when he appeared in a political ad for Democrat Claire McCaskill; and the public is routinely treated to racist comments, slurs, and insults about Barack Obama by a host of shock jocks, politicians, and even a federal judge.[41] Poverty is seen not as a social problem but as a personal failing, and poor people have become the objects of abuse, fear, and loathing. The poor, as right-wing ideologues never fail to remind us, are lazy—and, for that matter, how could they truly be poor if they own TVs and cell phones? Cruel, racist insults and the discourse of humiliation are now packaged in a mindless rhetoric as unapologetic as it is ruthless—this has become the new lingua franca of public exchange.

Republican presidential candidate Mitt Romney echoed the harshness of the new lingua franca of cruelty when asked during the 2012 campaign about the government's responsibility to the 50 million Americans who don't have health insurance. Incredibly, Romney replied that they already have access to health care because they can go to hospital emergency rooms.[42] In response, a *New York Times* editorial stated that emergency room care "is the most expensive and least effective way of providing care" and such a remark "reeks of contempt for those left behind by the current insurance system, suggesting that they must suffer with illness until the point where they need an ambulance."[43] Indifferent to the health care needs of the poor and middle class, Romney also conveniently ignores the fact that, as indicated in a Harvard University study, "more than 62% of all personal bankruptcies are caused by the cost of overwhelming medical expenses."[44] The new lingua franca of cruelty and its politics of disposability are on full display here. To paraphrase Hannah Arendt, we live in a time when revenge has become the cure-all for most of our social and economic ills.

Neoliberalism and the Retreat from Ethical Considerations

Not only does neoliberal rationality believe in the ability of markets to solve all problems, it also removes economics and markets from ethical considerations. Economic growth, rather than social needs, drives politics. Long-term investments are replaced by short-term gains and profits, while compassion is viewed as a weakness and democratic public values are derided. As Stanley Aronowitz points out, public values and collective action have given way to the "absurd notion the market should rule every human activity," including the "absurd neoliberal idea that users should pay for every public good from parks and beaches to highways [and] higher education."[45] The hard work of critical analysis, moral judgments, and social responsibility have given way to the desire for accumulating profits at almost any cost, short of unmistakably breaking the law and risking a jail term (which seems unlikely for Wall Street criminals). Gordon Gekko's "Greed is good" speech in the film *Wall Street* has been revived as a rallying cry for the entire financial services industry, rather than seen as a critique of excess. With society overtaken by the morality of self-interest, profit-seeking weaves its way into every possible space, relationship, and institution. For example, the search for high-end profits has descended upon the educational sector with a vengeance, as private bankers, hedge fund elites, and an assortment of billionaires are investing in for-profit and charter schools while advocating policies that disinvest in public education. At the same time the biotech, pharmaceutical, and defense industries and a range of other corporations are investing in universities to rake in profits while influencing everything from how such institutions are governed and define their mission to what they teach and how they treat faculty members and students. Increasingly, universities are losing their power not only to produce critical and civically engaged students but also to offer the type of education that enables them to refute the neoliberal utopian notion that paradise amounts to a world of voracity and avarice without restrictions, governed by a financial elite who exercise authority without accountability or challenge. Literacy, public service, human rights, and morality in this neoliberal notion of education become damaged concepts, stripped of any sense of reason, responsibility, or obligation to a just society.

In this way, neoliberalism proceeds, in zombie-like fashion, to impose its values, social relations, and forms of social death upon all aspects of civic life. This is marked by not only a sustained lack of interest in the public good, a love of inequitious power relations, and a hatred of democracy. There is also the use of brutality, state violence, and humiliation to normalize a neoliberal social order that celebrates massive inequalities in income, wealth, and access to vital services. This is a social Darwinism without apology, a ruthless form of casino capitalism whose advocates have suggested, without irony, that what they do is divinely inspired.[46] Politics has become an extension of war, just as state-sponsored violence increasingly finds legitimation in popular culture and a broader culture of cruelty that promotes an expanding landscape of selfishness, insecurity, and precarity that undermines any sense of shared responsibility for the well-being of others. Too many young people today learn quickly that their fate is solely a matter of individual responsibility, legitimated through market-driven laws that embrace self-promotion, hypercompetitiveness, and surviving in a society that increasingly reduces social relations to social combat. Young people today are expected to inhabit a set of relations in which the only obligation is to live for oneself and to reduce the obligations of citizenship to the demands of a consumer culture.

Gilded Age vengeance has also returned in the form of scorn for those who are either failed consumers or do not live up to the image of the United States as a white Christian nation. Reality TV's overarching theme, echoing Hobbes's "war of all against all," brings home the lesson that punishment is the norm and reward the exception. Unfortunately, it no longer mimics reality, it is the new reality. There is more at work here than a flight from social responsibility. Also lost is the importance of those social bonds, modes of collective reasoning, and public spheres and cultural apparatuses crucial to the construction of the social state and the formation of a sustainable democratic society. Nowhere is the dismantling of the social state and the transformation of the state into a punishing machine more evident than in the recent attacks on youth, labor rights, and higher education being waged by Republican governors in a number of key states such as Michigan, Wisconsin, Florida, and Ohio.

What is often missed in discussions of these attacks is that the war on the social state and the war on education represent part of the same agenda of destruction and violence. The first war is being waged for the complete control by the rich and powerful of all modes of wealth and income while the second war is conducted on the ideological front and represents a battle over the very capacity of young people and others to imagine a different and more critical mode of subjectivity and alternative mode of politics. If the first war is on the diverse and myriad terrain of political economy the second is being waged though what C. Wright Mills once called the major cultural apparatuses, including public and higher education. This is a struggle to shape indentities, desires, and modes of subjectivity in accordance with market values, needs, and relations. Both of these wars register as part of a larger effort to destroy any vestige of a democratic imaginary, and to relegate the value of the ethical responsibility and the social question to the wasteland of political thought. Paul Krugman is on target in arguing that in spite of massive suffering caused by the economic recession—a recession that produced "once-unthinkable levels of economic distress"— there is "growing evidence that our governing elite just doesn't care."[47] Of course, Krugman is not suggesting that if the corporate and financial elite cared the predatory nature of capitalism would be transformed. Rather, he is suggesting that economic Darwinism leaves no room for compassion or ethical considerations, which makes its use of power much worse than more liberal models of a market-based society.

Politics of Disposability and the Attack on Higher Education

The not-so-hidden order of politics underlying the second Gilded Age and its heartless version of economic Darwinism is that some populations, especially those marginalized by class, race, ethnicity, or immigration status, are viewed as excess populations to be removed from the body politic, relegated to sites of terminal containment or exclusion. Marked as disposable, such populations become targets of state surveillance, violence, torture, abduction, and injury. Removed from all vestiges of the social contract, they have become the unmentionables of neoliberalism. For them, surviving— not getting ahead—marks the space in which politics and power converge. The politics of disposability delineates these populations as unworthy of investment or of sharing in the rights, benefits, and protections of a substantive democracy.[48] Pushed into debt, detention centers, and sometimes prison, the alleged human waste of free-market capitalism now inhabits zones of terminal exclusion—zones marked by forms of social and civil death.[49] Particularly disturbing is the lack of opposition among the US public to this view of particular social groups as disposable—this, perhaps more than anything else, signals the presence of a rising authoritarianism in the United States. Left unchecked, economic Darwinism will not only destroy the social fabric and undermine democracy; it will also ensure the marginalization and eventual elimination of those intellectuals willing to fight for public values, rights, spaces, and institutions not wedded to the logic of privatization, commodification, deregulation, militarization, hypermasculinity, and a ruthless "competitive struggle in which only the fittest could survive."[50] This new culture of cruelty and disposability has become the hallmark of neoliberal sovereignty, and it will wreak destruction in ways not yet imaginable—even given the horrific outcomes of the economic and financial crisis brought on by economic Darwinism. All evidence suggests a new reality is unfolding, one characterized by a deeply rooted crisis of education, agency, and social responsibility.

The current assault threatening higher education and the humanities in particular cannot be understood outside of the crisis of economics, politics, and power. Evidence of this new historical conjuncture is clearly seen in the growing number of groups considered disposable, the collapse of public values, the war on youth, and the assault by the ultra-rich and megacorporations on democracy itself. This state of emergency must take as its starting point what Tony Judt has called "the social question," with its emphasis on addressing acute social problems, providing social protections for the disadvantaged, developing public spheres aimed at promoting the collective good, and protecting educational spheres that enable and deepen the knowledge, skills, and modes of agency necessary for a substantive democracy to flourish.[51] What is new about the current threat to higher education and the humanities in particular is the increasing pace of the corporatization and militarization of the university, the squelching of academic freedom, the rise of an ever increasing contingent of part-time faculty, the rise of a bloated manegerial class, and the view that students are basically consumers and faculty providers of a saleable commodity such as a credential or a set of workplace skills. More striking still is the slow death of the university as a center of critique, vital source of civic education, and crucial public good.

Or, to put it more specifically, the consequence of such dramatic transformations is the near-death of the university as a democratic public sphere. Many faculties are now demoralized as they increasingly lose rights and power. Moreover, a weak faculty translates into one governed by fear rather than by shared responsibilities, one that is susceptible to labor-bashing tactics such as increased workloads, the casualization of labor, and the growing suppression of dissent. Demoralization often translates less into moral outrage than into cynicism, accommodation, and a retreat into a sterile form of professionalism. Faculty now find themselves staring into an abyss, unwilling to address the current attacks on the university or befuddled over how the language of specialization and professionalization has cut them off from not only connecting their work to larger civic issues and social problems but also developing any meaningful relationships to a larger democratic polity.

As faculties no longer feel compelled to address important political issues and social problems, they are less inclined to communicate with a larger public, uphold public values, or engage in a type of scholarship accessible to a broader audience.[52] Beholden to corporate interests, career building, and the insular discourses that accompany specialized scholarship, too many academics have become overly comfortable with the corporatization of the university and the new regimes of neoliberal governance. Chasing after grants, promotions, and conventional research outlets, many academics have retreated from larger public debates and refused to address urgent social problems. Assuming the role of the disinterested academic or the clever faculty star on the make, endlessly chasing theory for its own sake, these so-called academic entrepreneurs simply reinforce the public's perception that they have become largely irrelevant. Incapable, if not unwilling, to defend the university as a crucial site for learning how to think critically and act with civic courage, many academics have disappeared into a disciplinary apparatus that views the university not as a place to think but as a place to prepare students to be competitive in the global marketplace.

This is particularly disturbing given the unapologetic turn that higher education has taken in its willingness to mimic corporate culture and ingratiate itself to the national security state.[53] Universities face a growing set of challenges arising from budget cuts, diminishing quality of instruction, the downsizing of faculty, the militarization of research, and the revamping of the curriculum to fit the interests of the market, all of which not only contradicts the culture and democratic value of higher education but also makes a mockery of the very meaning and mission of the university as a place both to think and to provide the formative culture and agents that make a democracy possible. Universities and colleges have been largely abandoned as democratic public spheres dedicated to providing a public service, expanding upon humankind's great intellectual and cultural achievements, and educating future generations to be able to confront the challenges of a global democracy.

Higher education increasingly stands alone, even in its attenuated state, as a public arena where ideas can be debated, critical knowledge produced, and learning linked to important social issues. Those mainstream cultural apparatuses that once offered alternative points of view, challenged authority, and subordinated public values to market interests have largely been hijacked by the consolidation of corporate power. As Ashley Lutz, Bob McChesney, and many others have noted, approximately 90 percent of the media is currently controlled by six corporations.[54] This is a particularly important statistic in a society in which the free circulation of ideas is being replaced by ideologies, values, and modes of thought managed by the dominant media. One consequence is that dissent is increasingly met with state repression, as indicated by the violence inflicted on the Occupy Wall Street protesters, and critical ideas are increasingly viewed or dismissed as banal, if not reactionary. For many ultra-conservatives, reason itself is viewed as dangerous, along with any notion of science that challenges right-wing fundamentalist world views regarding climate change, evolution, and a host of other social issues.[55] As Frank Rich has observed, the war against literacy and informed judgment is made abundantly clear in the populist rage sweeping the country in the form of the Tea Party, a massive collective anger that "is aimed at the educated, not the wealthy."[56] This mode of civic illiteracy is rooted in racism and has prompted a revival of overtly racist language, symbols, and jokes. Confederate flags are a common feature of Tea Party rallies, as are a variety of racially loaded posters, barbs, and derogatory, racist shouting aimed at President Obama.

Democracy can only be sustained through modes of civic literacy that enable individuals to connect private troubles to larger public issues as part of a broader discourse of critical inquiry, dialogue, and engagement. Civic literacy, in this context, provides a citizenry with the skills for critical understanding while enabling them to actually intervene in society. The right-wing war on education must be understood as a form of organized irresponsibility; that is, it represents a high-intensity assault on those cultures of questioning, forms of literacy, and public spheres in which reason and critique merge with social responsibility as a central feature of critical agency and democratization. As the political philosopher Cornelius Castoriadis insists, for democracy to be vital "it needs to create citizens who are critical thinkers capable of putting existing institutions into question so that democracy again becomes '. . . a new type of regime in the full sense of the term."[57]

The right-wing war on critical literacy is part of an ongoing attempt to destroy higher education as a democratic public sphere that enables intellectuals to stand firm, take risks, imagine the otherwise, and push against the grain. It is important to insist that as educators we ask, again and again, how higher education can survive in a society in which civic culture and modes of critical literacy collapse as it becomes more and more difficult to distinguish opinion and emotive outbursts from a sustained argument and logical reasoning. Equally important is the need for educators and young people to take on the challenge of defending the university. Toni Morrison gets it right:

> If the university does not take seriously and rigorously its role as a guardian of wider civic freedoms, as interrogator of more and more complex ethical problems, as servant and preserver of deeper democratic practices, then some other regime or ménage of regimes will do it for us, in spite of us, and without us.[58]

Defending the humanities, as Terry Eagleton has recently argued, means more than offering an academic enclave for students to learn history, philosophy, art, and literature. It also means stressing how indispensable these fields of study are for all students if they are to be able to make any claim whatsoever to being critical and engaged individual and social agents. But the humanities do more. They also provide the knowledge, skills, social relations, and modes of pedagogy that constitute a formative culture in which the historical lessons of democratization can be learned, the demands of social responsibility can be thoughtfully engaged, the imagination can be expanded, and critical thought can be affirmed. As an adjunct of the academic-military-industrial complex, however, higher education has nothing to say about teaching students how to think for themselves in a democracy, how to think critically and engage with others, and how to address through the prism of democratic values the relationship between themselves and the larger world. We need a permanent revolution around the meaning and purpose of higher education, one in which academics are more than willing to move beyond the language of critique and a discourse of both moral and political outrage, however necessary to a sustained individual and collective defense of the university as a vital public sphere central to democracy itself.

We must reject the idea that the university should be modeled after "a sterile Darwinian shark tank in which the only thing that matters is the bottom line."[59] We must also reconsider how the university in a post-9/11 era is being militarized and increasingly reduced to an adjunct of the growing national security state. The public has apparently given up on the idea of either funding higher education or valuing it as a public good indispensable to the life of any viable democracy. This is all the more reason for academics to be at the forefront of a coalition of activists, public servants, and others in both rejecting the growing corporate management of higher education and developing a new discourse in which the university, and particularly the humanities, can be defended as a vital social and public institution in a democratic society.

Beyond Neoliberal Miseducation

As universities turn toward corporate management models, they increasingly use and exploit cheap faculty labor. Many colleges and universities are drawing more and more upon adjunct and nontenured faculty, many of whom occupy the status of indentured servants who are overworked, lack benefits, receive little or no administrative support, and are paid salaries that qualify them for food stamps.[60] Students increasingly fare no better in sharing the status of a subaltern class beholden to neoliberal policies and values. For instance, many are buried under huge debt, celebrated by the collection industry because it is cashing in on their misfortune. Jerry Aston, a member of that industry, wrote in a column after witnessing a protest rally by students criticizing their mounting debt that he "couldn't believe the accumulated wealth they represent—for our industry."[61] And, of course, this type of economic injustice is taking place in an economy in which rich plutocrats such as the infamous union-busting Koch brothers each saw "their investments grow by $6 billion in one year, which is three million dollars per hour based on a 40-hour 'work' week."[62] Workers, students, youth, and the poor are all considered expendable in this neoliberal global economy. Yet the one institution, education, that offers the opportunities for students to challenge these antidemocratic tendencies is under attack in ways that are unparalleled, at least in terms of the scope and intensity of the assault by the corporate elite and other economic fundamentalists.

Casino capitalism does more than infuse market values into every aspect of higher education; it also wages a full-fledged assault on the very notion of public goods, democratic public spheres, and the role of education in creating an informed citizenry. When Rick Santorum argued that intellectuals were not wanted in the Republican Party, he was articulating what has become common sense in a society wedded to narrow instrumentalist values and various modes of fundamentalism. Critical thinking and a literate public have become dangerous to those who want to celebrate orthodoxy over dialogue, emotion over reason, and ideological certainty over thoughtfulness.[63] Hannah Arendt's warning that "it was not stupidity but a curious, quite authentic inability to think"[64] at the heart of authoritarian regimes is now embraced as a fundamental tenet of Republican Party politics.

Right-wing appeals to austerity provide the rationale for slash-and-burn policies intended to deprive governmental social and educational programs of the funds needed to enable them to work, if not survive. Along with health care, public transportation, Medicare, food stamp programs for low-income children, and a host of other social protections, higher education is being defunded as part of a larger scheme to dismantle and privatize all public services, goods, and spheres. But there is more at work here than the march toward privatization and the neverending search for profits at any cost; there is also the issue of wasteful spending on a bloated war machine, the refusal to tax fairly the rich and corporations, and the draining of public funds in order to support the US military presence in Iraq, Afghanistan, and elsewhere. The deficit argument and the austerity policies advocated in its name are a form of class warfare designed largely for the state to be able to redirect revenue in support of the commanding institutions of the corporate-military-industrial complex and away from funding higher education and other crucial public services. The extent of the budget reduction assault is such that in 2012 "states reduced their education budgets by $12.7 billion."[65] Of course, the burden of such reductions falls upon poor minority and other low-income students, who will not be able to afford the tuition increases that will compensate for the loss of state funding.

What has become clear in light of such assaults is that many universities and colleges have become unapologetic accomplices to corporate values and power, and in doing so increasingly regard social problems as either irrelevant or invisible.[66] The transformation of higher education both in the United States and abroad is evident in a number of registers. These include decreased support for programs of study that are not business oriented, reduced support for research that does not increase profits, the replacement of shared forms of governance with business management models, the ongoing exploitation of faculty labor, and the use of student purchasing power as the vital measure of a student's identity, worth, and access to higher education.[67]

As I point out throughout this book, one consequence of this ongoing disinvestment in higher education is the expansion of a punishing state that increasingly criminalizes a range of social behaviors, wages war on the poor instead of poverty, militarizes local police forces, harasses poor minority youth, and spends more on prisons than on higher education.[68] The punishing state produces fear and sustains itself on moral panics. Dissent gives way to widespread insecurity, uncertainty, and an obsession with personal safety. Political, moral, and social indifference is the result, in part, of a public that is increasingly constituted within an educational landscape that reduces thinking to a burden and celebrates civic illiteracy as a prerequisite for negotiating a society in which moral disengagement and political corruption go hand in hand.[69] The assault on the university is symptomatic of the deep educational, economic, and political crisis facing the United States. It is but one lens through which to recognize that the future of democracy depends on the educational and ethical standards of the society we inhabit.[70]

This lapse of the US public into a political and moral coma is induced, in part, by an ever-expanding, mass-mediated celebrity culture that trades in hype and sensation. It is also accentuated by a governmental apparatus that sanctions modes of training that undermine any viable notion of critical schooling and public pedagogy. While there is much being written about how unfair the Left is to the Obama administration, what is often forgotten by these liberal critics is that Obama has aligned himself with educational practices and policies as instrumentalist and anti-intellectual as they are politically reactionary, and therein lies one viable reason for not supporting his initiatives and administration.[71] What liberals refuse to entertain is that the Left is correct in attacking Obama for his cowardly retreat from a number of progressive issues and his dastardly undermining of civil liberties. In fact, they do not go far enough in their criticisms. Often even progressives miss that Obama's views on education are utterly reactionary and provide no space for the nurturance of a radically democratic imagination. Hence, while liberals point to some of Obama's progressive policies—often in a New Age discourse that betrays their own supine moralism—they fail to acknowledge that Obama's educational policies do nothing to contest, and are in fact aligned with, his weak-willed compromises and authoritarian policies. In other words, Obama's educational commitments undermine the creation of a formative culture capable of questioning authoritarian ideas, modes of governance, and reactionary policies. The question is not whether Obama's policies are slightly less repugnant than those of his right-wing detractors. On the contrary, it is about how the Left should engage politics in a more robust and democratic way by imagining what it would mean to work collectively and with "slow impatience" for a new political order outside of the current moderate and extreme right-wing politics and the debased, uncritical educational apparatus that supports it.[72]

The Role of Critical Education

One way of challenging the new authoritarianism is to reclaim the relationship between critical education and social change. The question of what kind of subjects and modes of individual and social agency are necessary for a democracy to survive appears more crucial now than ever before, and this is a question that places matters of education, pedagogy, and culture at the center of any understanding of politics. We live at a time when too few Americans appear to have an interest in democracy beyond the every-four-years ritual performance of voting, and even this act fails to attract a robust majority of citizens. The term "democracy" has been emptied of any viable meaning, hijacked by political scoundrels, corporate elites, and the advertising industry. The promise that democracy exhibits as an ongoing struggle for rights, justice, and a future of hope has been degraded into a misplaced desire to shop and to fulfill the pleasure quotient in spectacles of violence, while the language of democracy is misappropriated and deployed as a rationale for racist actions against immigrants, Muslims, and the poor. Of course, while more and more nails are being put into the coffin of democracy, there are flashes of resistance, such as those among workers in Wisconsin, the Occupy Wall Street movement, and the more recent strike by Chicago teachers. Public employees, fast food workers, Walmart employees, disaffected youth, and others are struggling to expose the massive injustices and death-dealing machinations of the 1 percent and the pernicious effects of casino capitalism. But this struggle is just beginning and only time will tell how far it goes.

The time has come not only to redefine the promise of democracy but also to challenge those who have poisoned its meaning. We have already witnessed such a challenge by protest movements both at home and abroad in which the struggle over education has become one of the most powerful fulcrums for redressing the detrimental effects of neoliberalism. What these struggles, particularly by young people, have in common is the attempt to merge the powers of persuasion and critical, civic literacy with the power of social movements to activate and mobilize real change. They are recovering a notion of the social and reclaiming a kind of humanity that should inspire and inform our collective willingness to imagine what a real democracy might look like. Cornelius Castoriadis rightly argues that "people need to be educated for democracy by not only expanding the capacities that enable them to assume public responsibility but also through active participation in the very process of governing."[73]

As the crucial lens through which to create the formative culture in which politics and power can be made visible and held accountable, pedagogy plays a central role. But as Archon Fung notes, criticism is not the only public responsibility of intellectuals, artists, journalists, educators, and others who engage in critical pedagogical practices. "Intellectuals can also join citizens—and sometimes governments—to construct a world that is more just and democratic. One such constructive role is aiding popular movements and organizations in their efforts to advance justice and democracy."[74] In this instance, understanding must be linked to the practice of social responsibility and the willingness to fashion a politics that addresses real problems and enacts concrete solutions. As Heather Gautney points out,

> We need to start thinking seriously about what kind of political system we really want. And we need to start pressing for things that our politicians did NOT discuss at the conventions. Real solutions—like universal education, debt forgiveness, wealth redistribution, and participatory political structures—that would empower us to decide together what's best. Not who's best.[75]

Critical thinking divorced from action is often as sterile as action divorced from critical theory. Given the urgency of the historical moment, we need a politics and a public pedagogy that make knowledge meaningful in order to make it critical and transformative. Or, as Stuart Hall argues, we need to produce modes of analysis and knowledge in which "people can invest something of themselves . . . something that they recognize is of them or speaks to their condition."[76] A notion of higher education as a democratic public sphere is crucial to this project, especially at a time in which the apostles of neoliberalism and other forms of political and religious fundamentalism are ushering in a new age of conformity, cruelty, and disposability. But as public intellectuals, academics can do more.

First, they can write for multiple audiences, expanding public spheres, especially online, to address a range of social issues including, importantly, the relationship between the attack on the social state and the defunding of higher education. In any democratic society, education should be viewed as a right, not an entitlement, and this suggests a re-ordering of state and federal priorities to make that happen. For instance, the military budget could be cut by two-thirds and those funds invested instead in public and higher education. There is nothing utopian about this demand, given the excess of military power in the United States, but addressing this task requires a sustained critique of the militarization of American society and a clear analysis of the damage it has caused both at home and abroad. Brown University's Watson Institute for International Studies, with the efforts of a number of writers such as Andrew

Bacevich, has been doing this for years and offers a treasure trove of information that could be easily accessed and used by public intellectuals in and outside of the academy. A related issue, as Angela Davis, Michelle Alexander, and others have argued, is the need for public intellectuals to become part of a broader social movement aimed at dismantling the prison-industrial complex and the punishing state, which drains billions of dollars in funds to put people in jail when such funds could be used to fund public and higher education or other social supports that may help prevent criminalized behaviors in the first place. The punishing state is a dire threat not only to public and higher education but also, more broadly, to democracy itself. It is the pillar of the authoritarian state, undermining civil liberties, criminalizing a range of social behaviors related to concrete social problems, and intensifying the legacy of Jim Crow against poor people of color. The US public does not need more prisons; it needs more schools.

Second, academics, artists, journalists, and other cultural workers need to connect the rise of subaltern, part-time labor in the university as well as the larger society with the massive inequality in wealth and income that now corrupts every aspect of American politics and society. Precarity has become a weapon both to exploit adjuncts, part-time workers, and temporary laborers and to suppress dissent by keeping them in a state of fear over losing their jobs. Insecure forms of labor increasingly produce "a feeling of passivity born of despair."[77] Multinational corporations have abandoned the social contract and any vestige of supporting the social state. They plunder labor and perpetuate the mechanizations of social death whenever they have the chance to accumulate capital. This issue is not simply about restoring a balance between labor and capital, it is about recognizing a new form of serfdom that kills the spirit as much as it depoliticizes the mind. The new authoritarians do not ride around in tanks; they have private jets, they fund right-wing think tanks, and they lobby for reactionary policies that privatize everything in sight while filling their bank accounts with massive profits. They are the embodiment of a culture of greed, cruelty, and disposability.

Third, academics can fight for the rights of students to get a free education, a formidable and critical education not dominated by corporate values, to have a say in its shaping, and to experience what it means to expand and deepen the practice of freedom and democracy. Young people have been left out of the discourse of democracy. They are the new disposable individuals, a population lacking jobs, a decent education, and any hope of a future better than the one their parents inherited. They are a reminder of how finance capital has abandoned any viable vision of the future, including one that would support future generations. This is a mode of politics and capital that eats its own children and throws their fate to the vagaries of the market. If a society is in part judged by how it views and treats its children, US society by all accounts has truly failed in a colossal way and, in doing so, provides a glimpse of the heartlessness at the core of the new authoritarianism.

Last, public intellectuals should also address and resist the ongoing shift in power relations between faculty and the managerial class. Too many faculty are now removed from the governing structures of higher education and as a result have been abandoned to the misery of impoverished wages, excessive class loads, no health care, and few, if any, social benefits. This is shameful and is not merely an issue of the education system but a deeply political matter, one that must address how neoliberal ideology and policy have imposed on higher education an antidemocratic governing structure that mimics the broader authoritarian forces now threatening the United States.[78]

I want to conclude by quoting from James Baldwin, a courageous writer who refused to let the hope of democracy die in his lifetime, and who offered that mix of politics, passion, and courage that deserves not just admiration but emulation. His sense of rage was grounded in a working-class sensibility, eloquence, and heart that illuminate a higher standard for what it means to be a public and an engaged intellectual. His words capture something that is missing from the US cultural and political landscape, something affirmative that needs to be seized upon, rethought, and occupied by intellectuals, academics, artists, and other concerned citizens—as part of both the fight against the new authoritarianism and its cynical, dangerous, and cruel practices, and the struggle to reclaim a belief in justice and mutuality that seems to be dying in all of us. In *The Fire Next Time*, Baldwin writes:

> One must say Yes to life, and embrace it wherever it is found—and it
> is found in terrible places. . . . For nothing is fixed, forever and forever,

it is not fixed; the earth is always shifting, the light is always changing, the sea does not cease to grind down rock. Generations do not cease to be born, and we are responsible to them because we are the only witnesses they have. The sea rises, the light fails, lovers cling to each other, and children cling to us. The moment we cease to hold each other, the moment we break faith with one another, the sea engulfs us and the light goes out.

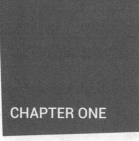

CHAPTER ONE

Dystopian Education
in a Neoliberal Society

I n the United States and abroad, public and higher education is under
assault by a host of religious, economic, ideological, and political fundamentalists. As regards public schools, the most serious attack is
being waged by religious conservatives and advocates of neoliberalism
whose reform efforts focus narrowly on high-stakes testing, skill-based
teaching, traditional curriculum, and memorization drills.[1] Ideologically,
the pedagogical emphasis is the antithesis of a critical approach to teaching and learning, emphasizing a pedagogy of conformity and a curriculum marked by a vulgar "vocationalist instrumentality."[2] At the level of
policy, the assault is driven by an aggressive attempt to disinvest in public
schools, replace them with charter schools, and remove state and federal
governments completely from public education in order to allow education to be organized and administered by a variety of privatizing, market-driven forces and for-profit corporations.[3] In this instance, public
schools are defined through practices of repression, removed from any
larger notion of the public good, reduced to "simply another corporate
asset bundled in credit default swaps," valuable solely for their rate of exchange and trade value on the open market.[4] Clearly, public education
should not be harnessed to the script of cost-benefit analyses, the national

security state, or the needs of corporations, which often leads to the loss of egalitarian and democratic values, ideals, and responsibilities.

At the same time, a full-fledged assault is also being waged on higher education in North America, the United Kingdom, and various European countries. While the nature of the assault varies across countries, there is a common set of assumptions and practices driving the transformations of higher education into an adjunct of corporate power and values. The effects of the assault are not hard to discern. Universities are being defunded, tuition fees are skyrocketing, faculty salaries are shrinking as workloads are increasing, and faculty are being reduced to a subaltern class of migrant laborers. Corporate management schemes are being put in place, "underpinned by market-like principles, based on metrics, control, and display of performance."[5] The latter is reinforcing an audit culture that mimics the organizational structures of a market economy. In addition, class sizes are ballooning, curriculum is stripped of liberal values, research is largely assessed for its ability to produce profits, administrative staffs are being cut back, governance has been handed over to paragons of corporate culture, and valuable services are being either outsourced or curtailed.

The neoliberal paradigm driving these attacks on public and higher education abhors democracy and views public and higher education as a toxic civic sphere that poses a threat to corporate values, power, and ideology. As democratic public spheres, colleges and universities are allegedly dedicated to teaching students to think critically, take imaginative risks, learn how to be moral witnesses, and procure the skills that enable one to connect to others in ways that strengthen the democratic polity, and this is precisely why they are under attack by the concentrated forces of neoliberalism.[6] Self-confident citizens are regarded as abhorrent by conservatives and evangelical fundamentalists who, traumatized by the campus turmoil of the sixties, largely view dissent, if not critical thought itself, as a dire threat to corporate power and religious authority.[7] Similarly, critical thought, knowledge, dialogue, and dissent are increasingly perceived with suspicion by the new corporate university that now defines faculty as entrepreneurs, students as customers, and education as a mode of training.[8]

Welcome to the dystopian world of corporate education, in which learning how to think, appropriate public values, and become an engaged critical citizen is viewed as a failure rather than a success. Instead of producing "a generation of leaders worthy of the challenges,"[9] the dystopian mission of public and higher education is to produce robots, technocrats, and trained workers. There is more than a backlash at work in these assaults on public and higher education; there is a sustained effort to dismantle education from the discourse of democracy, public values, critical thought, social responsibility, and civic courage. Put more bluntly, the dystopian shadow that has fallen on public and higher education reveals the coming darkness of a counterrevolution that is putting into place a mode of corporate sovereignty constituting a new, updated form of authoritarianism. During the Cold War, US officials never let us forget that authoritarian countries put their intellectuals into prison. While such practices do not prevail in the United States or other capitalist democracies, the fate of critical intellectuals today is no better, since they are either fired or denied tenure for being too critical, or relegated to an intolerable state of dire poverty and existential impoverishment in part-time appointments that pay low wages.[10]

Education within the last three decades has been removed from its utopian possibilities of educating young people to be reflective, critical, and socially engaged agents. The post-WWII Keynesian period up to the civil rights movement and the campus uprisings in the 1960s witnessed an ongoing expansion of public and higher education as democratic public spheres. Democratic ideals were never far from the realms of public and higher education, though they often lacked full support of both the public and the university administration. While not all educators willingly addressed matters of equity, inclusion, racism, and the role of education as a public good, such issues never disappeared from public view. Under neoliberal regimes, however diverse, the notion of public and higher education, as well as the larger notion of education as the primary register of the greater culture, are viewed as too dangerous by the apostles of free-market capitalism. Critical thought and the imaginings of a better world present a direct threat to a neoliberal paradigm in which the future replicates the present in an endless circle, with capital and the identities that legitimate it merging with each other into what might be called the dead zone of casino capitalism. This dystopian impulse thrives on producing myriad forms of violence embracing the symbolic and the structural as part of a broader attempt to define education in purely instrumental and anti-intellectual terms. It is this replacement of educated hope with an aggressive dystopian project in particular that characterizes the current assault on higher education in various parts of the globe extending from the United States and the United Kingdom to Greece and Spain.

In light of this dystopian attempt to remove education from any notion of critique, dialogue, and empowerment, it would be an understatement to suggest that there is something very wrong with US public and higher education. For a start, this counterrevolution is giving rise to punitive evaluation schemes, harsh disciplinary measures, and the ongoing deskilling of many teachers that together are reducing many excellent educators to the debased status of technicians and security personnel. Additionally, as more and more wealth is distributed to the richest Americans and corporations, states are drained of resources and are shifting the burden of their deficits onto public schools and other vital public services. With 40 percent of wealth going to the top 1 percent, public services are drying up from lack of revenue, and more and more young people find themselves locked out of the dream of getting a decent education or a job, robbed of any hope for the future.[11]

While the nation's schools and infrastructure suffer from a lack of resources, right-wing politicians are enacting policies that lower the taxes of the rich and megacorporations. For the elite, taxes are seen as constituting a form of class warfare waged by the state against the rich, who view the collection of taxes as a form of state coercion. What is ironic in this argument is the startling fact that not only are the rich not taxed fairly but they also receive billions in corporate subsidies. But there is more at stake here than untaxed wealth and revenue; there is also the fact that wealth corrupts and buys power. And this poisonous mix of wealth, politics, and power translates into an array of antidemocratic practices that have created an unhealthy society in every major index ranging from infant mortality rates to a dysfunctional political system.[12]

Hidden in this hollow outrage by the wealthy is the belief that the real enemy is any form of government that needs to raise revenue in order to build and maintain infrastructures, provide basic services for those who need them, and develop investments such as a transportation system and schools that are not tied to the logic of the market. One consequence of this vile form of actual class warfare is a battle over crucial resources, a battle that has dire political and educational consequences especially for the poor and middle classes, if not democracy itself. This battle in the United States is particularly fierce over the issue of taxes. As David Theo Goldberg points out, neoliberal ideology makes clear—as part of its project of hollowing out public institutions—that "paying taxes has devolved from a central social responsibility to a game of creative work-arounds. Today, taxes are not so much the common contribution to cover the costs of social benefits and infrastructure relative to one's means, as they are a burden to be avoided."[13]

Money no longer simply controls elections; it also controls policies that shape public education, if not practically all other social, cultural, and economic institutions.[14] One indicator of such corruption is that hedge fund managers now sit on school boards across the country, doing everything in their power to eliminate public schools and punish union-ized teachers who do not support charter schools. In New Jersey hundreds of teachers have been sacked because of alleged budget deficits. Not only is Governor Christie using the deficit argument to fire teachers, he also uses it to break unions and balance the budget on the backs of students and teachers. How else to explain Christie's refusal to endorse reinstitut-ing the "millionaires' taxes," or his craven support for lowering taxes on the top twenty-five hedge fund officers in New Jersey, who in 2009 raked in $25 billion, enough to fund 658,000 entry-level teachers?[15]

In this conservative right-wing reform culture, the role of public and higher education, if we are to believe the Heritage Foundation and bil-lionaires such as Bill Gates, is to produce students who laud conformity, believe job training is more important than education, and view public values as irrelevant. While Gates, former DC education chancellor Michelle Rhee, and secretary of education Arne Duncan would argue they are the true education reformers, the fact of the matter is that education in their view is tied to job training, quantitative measurements, and the development of curricula to prepare students for particular occupations. Teaching to the test, undercutting the power of teachers, and removing subjects such as art, literature, music, and critical thinking from the school curriculum are at the core of their conservative vision for reform. More-over, their relentless attempts to turn public schools into charter schools are in direct opposition to their claims that their policies serve the public good and empower young people, especially poor minorities. Students in this corporate-driven world view are no longer educated for democratic citizenship. On the contrary, they are being trained to fulfill the need for human capital.[16] At the same time, this emphasis on defining schools through an audit culture and various accountability regimes conveniently allows the financial elite to ignore those forces that affect schools such as poverty, unemployment, poor health care, inequality, and other important social and economic forces. Removing matters of equity from issues of excellence and learning also makes it easier for right-wing foundations and conservative foundations to blame teachers and unions for the failure of schools, making it all the easier to turn public schools, universities, and colleges over to for-profit forces.

What is lost in this approach to schooling is what Noam Chomsky describes as "creating creative and independent thought and inquiry, challenging perceived beliefs, exploring new horizons and forgetting external constraints."[17] At the same time, public schools and colleges are under assault not because they are failing (though some are) but because they are one of the few public spheres left where people can learn the knowledge and skills necessary to allow them to think critically and hold power and authority accountable. It is worth repeating that not only are the lines between the corporate world and public and higher education blurring, but all modes of education (except for the elite) are being reduced to what Peter Seybold calls a "corporate service station," in which the democratic ideals at the heart of public and higher education are up for sale.[18] At the heart of this crisis of education are larger questions about the formative culture necessary for a democracy to survive, the nature of civic education and teaching in dark times, the role of educators as civic intellectuals, and what it means to understand the purpose and meaning of education as a site of individual and collective empowerment.

This current right-wing emphasis on low-level skills distracts the US public from examining the broader economic, political, and cultural forces that bear down on schools. Matters concerning the influence on schools of corporations, textbook publishers, commercial industries, and the national security state are rendered invisible, as if schools and the practices they promote exist in a bubble. At work here is a dystopian pedagogy that displaces, infantilizes, and depoliticizes both students and large segments of the US public. Under the current regime of neoliberalism, schools have been transformed into a private right rather than a public good. Students are being educated to become consumers rather than thoughtful, critical citizens. Increasingly, as public schools are put in the hands of for-profit corporations, hedge fund elites, and other market-driven sources, their value is derived from their ability to turn a profit and produce compliant students eager to join the workforce.[19]

What is truly scandalous about the current dismantling of and disinvestment in public schooling is that those who advocate such changes are called the new education reformers. They are not reformers at all. They are reactionaries and financial mercenaries, and resemble dystopian zombies in spewing toxic educational gore. In their wake, teaching is turned into the practice of conformity, and curricula are driven by an anti-intellectual obsession with student test scores. In addition, students are educated to be active consumers and compliant subjects, increasingly unable to think critically about themselves and their relationship to the larger world. This virus of repression, conformity, and instrumentalism is turning public and higher education into a repressive site of containment, devoid of poetry, critical learning, or soaring acts of curiosity and imagination. As Diane Ravitch sums it up, what is driving the current public school reform movement is a profoundly anti-intellectual project that promotes "more testing, more privately managed schools, more deregulation, more firing of teachers, [and] more school closings."[20]

At the level of higher education, the script is similar with a project designed to defund higher education, impose corporate models of governance, purge the university of critical thinkers, turn faculty into a low-wage army of part-time workers, and allow corporate money and power to increasingly decide course content and determine what faculty get hired. As public values are replaced by corporate values, students become clients, faculty are deskilled and depoliticized, tuition rises, and more and more working-class and poor minority students are excluded from the benefits of higher education. There are no powerful and profound intellectual dramas in this view of schooling, just the noisy and demonstrative rush to make schools another source of profit for finance capital with its growing legion of bankers, billionaires, and hedge fund scoundrels.

Public schooling and higher education are also increasingly harnessed to the needs of corporations and the warfare state. One consequence is that many public schools, especially those occupied by poor minority youth, have become the equivalent of factories for dumbing down the curricula and turning teachers into what amounts to machine parts. At the same time, such schools have become increasingly militarized and provide a direct route for many youth into the prison-industrial complex via the "school-to-prison pipeline."[21] What is buried under the educational-reform rhetoric of hedge fund and casino capitalism is the ideal of offering public school students a civic education that provides the capacities, knowledge, and skills that enable students to speak, write, and act from a position of agency and empowerment. At the college level, students are dazzled with a blitz of spaces that now look like malls, while in between classes they are endlessly entertained by a mammoth sports culture that is often as debasing as it is dangerous in its hypermasculinity, racism, and overt sexism.[22]

Privatization, commodification, militarization, and deregulation are the new guiding categories through which schools, teachers, pedagogy, and students are defined. The current assaults on public and higher education are not new, but they are more vile and more powerful than in the past. Crucial to any viable resistance is the need to understand the historical context in which education has been transformed into an adjunct of corporate power as well as the ways in which the current right-wing reform operates within a broader play of forces that bear down in antidemocratic ways on the purpose of schooling and the practice of teaching itself. Making power visible is important but only a first step in understanding how it works and how it might be challenged. But recognizing such a challenge is not the same thing as overcoming it. Part of this task necessitates that educators anchor their own work in classrooms, however diverse, in projects that engage the promise of an unrealized democracy against its existing, often repressive forms. And this is only a first step.

Public and higher education, along with the pedagogical role of the larger culture, should be viewed as crucial to any viable notion of democracy, while the pedagogical practices they employ should be consistent with the ideal of the good society. This means teaching more than the knowledge of traditional canons. In fact, teachers and students need to recognize that as a moral and political practice pedagogy is about the struggle over identity just as much as it is a struggle over what counts as knowledge. At a time when censorship is running amok in public schools and dissent is viewed as a distraction or unpatriotic, the debate over whether we should view schools as political institutions seems not only moot but irrelevant. Pedagogy is a mode of critical intervention, one that endows teachers with a responsibility to prepare students not merely for jobs but for being in the world in ways that allow them to influence the larger political, ideological, and economic forces that bear down on their lives. Schooling is an eminently political and moral practice because it is directive of and also actively legitimates what counts as knowledge, sanctions particular values, and constructs particular forms of agency.

One of the most notable features of contemporary conservative reform efforts is the way in which they increasingly position teachers as a liability and in doing so align with modes of education that are as demeaning as they are deskilling. These reforms are not innocent and actually promote failure in the classroom. And when that is successful, they open the door for more public schools to be closed, provide another chance at busting the union, and allow such schools to be taken over by private and corporate interests. Under the influence of market-based pedagogies, public school teachers are subjected to what can only be described as repressive disciplinary measures in the school and an increasing chorus of verbal humiliation from politicians outside of the classroom. Academics do not fare much better and are often criticized for being too radical, for not working long hours, and for receiving cushy paychecks— a position at odds with the fact that more than 70 percent of academic labor is now either part-time or on a non-tenure track. Many contingent faculty earn so little income that they are part of the growing new class of workers who qualify for food stamps. With no health insurance and lacking other crucial benefits, they are truly on their own.

Teachers and academics are not only on the defensive in the neoliberal war on schools, they are also increasingly pressured to assume a more instrumentalist and mercenary role. Such approaches leave them with no time to be creative, use their imagination, work with other teachers, or develop classroom practices that are not wedded to teaching to the test and other demeaning empirical measures. Of course, the practice of disinvesting in public schools and higher education has a long history, but it has strengthened since the election of Ronald Reagan in 1980 and intensified in the new millennium. How else to explain that many states invest more in building prisons than educating students, especially those who are poor, disabled, and immersed in poverty? What are we to make of the fact that there are more black men in prison than in higher education in states such as Louisiana and California?[23] The right-wing makeover of public education has resulted in some states, Texas for example, banning the teaching of critical thinking in their classrooms, while in Arizona legislation has been passed that eliminates all curricular material from the classroom that includes the histories of Mexican Americans. The latter case is particularly loathsome. Masquerading as legislation designed to teach students how— no irony intended—to value each other and eliminate the hatred of other ethnic groups and races, Bill HB2281 bans ethnic studies. According to the bill, it is illegal for a school district to have any courses or classes that will "promote the overthrow of the U.S. government, promote resentment of a particular race or class of people, are designed primarily for students of a particular ethnic group or advocate ethnic solidarity instead of the treatment of pupils as individuals."[24] Schools that do not comply with this racist law will lose 10 percent of their monthly share of state aid.

It gets worse. In addition to eliminating the teaching of the history and culture of those ethnic groups considered a threat or disposable, the Arizona Department of Education "began telling school districts that teachers whose spoken English it deems to be heavily accented or ungrammatical must be removed from classes for students still learning English."[25] The targets here include not only ethnic studies but also those educators who inhabit ethnic identities. This is an unadulterated expression of educational discrimination and apartheid, and it is as disgraceful as it is racist. It is worth noting that these states also want to tie the salaries of faculty in higher education to performance measures based on a neoliberal model of evaluation. In this case, these racist reforms share an unholy alliance with neoliberal reforms that make teachers voiceless, if not powerless, to reject them by preoccupying them with modes of pedagogy as repressive as they are anti-intellectual and depoliticized.

Fighting for democracy as an educational project means encouraging a culture of questioning in classrooms, one that explores both the strengths and weaknesses of the current era. This notion of questioning is not simply about airing conflicting points of view, nor is it about substituting dogma for genuine dialogue and critical analysis. Most importantly, it is about a culture of questioning that raises ideas to the status of public values and a broader encounter with the larger social order. At issue here are pedagogical practices that are not only about the search for the truth but also about taking responsibility for intervening in the world by connecting knowledge and power, learning and values to interrelated modes of commitment and social engagement. I think Zygmunt Bauman is right in arguing that "if there is no room for the idea of *a wrong* society, there is hardly much chance for the idea of a good society to be born, let alone make waves."[26] The relevant question in this instance is what kind of future do our teachings presuppose? What forms of literacy and agency do we make available to our students through our pedagogical practices? How do we understand and incorporate in classroom pedagogies the ongoing search for equity and excellence, truth and justice, knowledge and commitment? I believe that this broader project of addressing democratization as a pedagogical practice should be central to any worthwhile attempt to engage in classroom teaching. And this is a political project. As educators, we have to begin with a vision of schooling as a democratic public sphere, and then we have to figure out what the ideological, political, and social impediments are to such a goal and organize collectively to derail them. In other word, educators need to start with a project, not a method. They need to view themselves through the lens of civic responsibility and address what it means to educate students in the best of those traditions and knowledge forms we have inherited from the past and also in terms of what it means to prepare them to be in the world as critically engaged agents.

Educators need to be more forceful and committed to linking their overall investment in democracy to modes of critique and collective action that address the presupposition that democratic societies are never too just or just enough. Moreover, such a commitment suggests that a viable democratic society must constantly nurture the possibilities for self-critique, collective agency, and forms of citizenship in which teachers and students play a fundamental role. Rather than being forced to participate in a pedagogy designed to raise test scores and undermine forms of critical thinking, students must be involved pedagogically in critically discussing, administrating, and shaping the material relations of power and ideological forces that structure their everyday lives. Central to such an educational project is the continual struggle by teachers to connect their pedagogical practices to the building of an inclusive and just democracy, which should be open to many forms, offers no political guarantees, and provides an important normative dimension to politics as an ongoing process that never ends. Such a project is based on the realization that a democracy open to exchange, question, and self-criticism never reaches the limits of justice; it is never just enough and never finished. It is precisely the open-ended and normative nature of such a project that provides a common ground for educators to share their resources with a diverse range of intellectual pursuits while refusing to believe that such struggles in schools ever come to an end.

In order to connect teaching with the larger world so as to make pedagogy meaningful, critical, and transformative, educators will have to focus their work on important social issues that connect what is learned in the classroom to the larger society and the lives of their students. Such issues might include the ongoing destruction of the ecological biosphere, the current war against youth, the hegemony of neoliberal globalization, the widespread attack by corporate culture on public schools, the relentless attack on the welfare system, the increasing rates of incarceration of people of color, the dangerous growth of the prison-industrial complex, the increasing gap between the rich and the poor, the rise of a generation of students who are laboring under the burden of debt, and the increasing spread of war globally.

Once again, educators need to do more than create the conditions for critical learning for their students; they also need to responsibly assume the role of civic educators willing to share their ideas with other educators and the wider public. This suggests writing and speaking to a variety of audiences through a host of public means of expression including the lecture circuit, Internet, radio interviews, alternative magazines, and the church pulpit, to name only a few. Such writing needs to become public by crossing over into spheres and avenues of expression that speak to more general audiences in a language that is clear but not theoretically simplistic. Capitalizing on their role as intellectuals, educators can address the challenge of combining scholarship and commitment through the use of a vocabulary that is neither dull nor obtuse, while seeking to reach a broad audience. More importantly, as teachers organize to assert the importance of their role and that of public schooling in a democracy, they can forge new alliances and connections to develop social movements that include and also expand beyond working with unions.

Educators also need to be more specific about what it means to be self-critical as well as attentive to learning how to work collectively with other educators through a vast array of networks across a number of public spheres. This might mean sharing resources with educators in a variety of fields and sites, extending from other teachers to community workers and artists outside of the school. This also suggests that educators become more active in addressing the ethical and political challenges of globalization. Public schools, teachers, and higher education faculties need to unite across the various states and make a case for public and higher education. At the very least, they could make clear to a befuddled American public that the deficit theory regarding school cutbacks is a fraud.

There is plenty of money to provide quality education to every student in the United States—and this certainly holds true for the United Kingdom and Canada as well. As Salvatore Babones points out, "The problem isn't a lack of money. The problem is where the money is going."[27] The issue is not about the absence of funds as much as it is about where funds are being invested and how more revenue can be raised to support public education in the United States. The United States spends around $960 billion on its wars and defense-related projects.[28] In fact, the cost of war over a ten-year period "will run at least $3.7 trillion and could reach as high as $4.4 trillion, according to the research project "Costs of War" by Brown University's Watson Institute for International Studies."[29] Military spending seems to know no bounds. The United States could spend as much as a trillion dollars for a fleet of F-35 fighter planes with stealth technology. Each plane costs $90 million, and the military is "spending more on this plane than Australia's entire GDP ($924 billion)."[30] Many military experts urged the Pentagon to ditch the project because of cost overruns and a series of technological problems that more recently have resulted in the Pentagon grounding all F-35s. In just this one example, billions are being wasted on faulty military planes when the money could be used to fund food programs for needy children, scholarships for low-income youth, and shelter for the homeless. As Barbones argues, the crucial recognition here is that research consistently shows that education spending creates more jobs per dollar than any other kind of government spending. A University of Massachusetts study ranked military spending worst of five major fiscal levers for job creation. The UMass study ranked education spending the best. A dollar spent on education creates more than twice as many jobs than a dollar spent on defense. Education spending also outperforms health care, clean energy and tax cuts as a mechanism for job creation.[31]

Surely, this budget could be trimmed appropriately to divert much-needed funds to education, given that a nation's highest priority should be investing in its children rather than in the production of organized violence. As capital, finance, trade, and culture become extraterritorial and increasingly removed from traditional political constraints, it becomes all the more pressing to put global networks and political organizations into play to contend with the reach and power of neoliberal globalization. Engaging in intellectual practices that offer the possibility of alliances and new forms of solidarity among public school teachers and cultural workers such as artists, writers, journalists, academics, and others who engage in forms of public pedagogy grounded in a democratic project represents a small, but important, step in addressing the massive and unprecedented reach of global capitalism.

Educators also need to register and make visible their own subjective involvement in what they teach, how they shape classroom social relations, and how they defend their positions within institutions that often legitimate educational processes based on narrow ideological interests and political exclusions. This suggests making one's authority and classroom work the subject of critical analysis with students but taken up in terms that move beyond the rhetoric of method, psychology, or private interests. Pedagogy in this instance can be addressed as a moral and political discourse in which students are able to connect learning to social change, scholarship to commitment, and classroom knowledge to public life. Such a pedagogical task suggests that educators speak truth to power, exercise civic courage, and take risk in their role as public intellectuals. Theodor Adorno is insightful here in arguing that "the undiminished presence of suffering, fear and menace necessitates that thought that cannot be realized should not be discarded."[32] This suggests, in part, that academics must overcome an intense obsession with the demands of their own circumscribed professional pursuits, rejecting the privatized notion of scholarship and agency that dominates academic life. Too many academics are willing to depoliticize their work by insulating theory, teaching, and research from the discourse, structures, and experiences of everyday life. This is not merely a matter of intellectuals selling out but of standing still, refusing to push against the grain to address the crimes and rubbish of the new Gilded Age. Of course, there are many academics, teachers, and right-wing pundits who argue that the classroom should be free of politics and hence a space where matters of power, values, and social justice should not be addressed. The usual object of scorn in this case is the charge that teachers who believe in civic education indoctrinate students. In this ideologically pure world, authority in the classroom is reduced to a transparent pedagogy in which nothing controversial can be stated and teachers are forbidden to utter one word related to any of the major problems facing the larger society. Of course, this position is as much a flight from responsibility as it is an instance of a dreadful pedagogy.

One useful approach to embracing the classroom as a political site but at the same time eschewing any form of indoctrination is for educators to think through the distinction between a *politicizing pedagogy*, which insists wrongly that students think as we do, and a *political pedagogy*, which teaches students by example and through dialogue about the importance of power, social responsibility, and of taking a stand (without standing still) while rigorously engaging the full range of ideas about an issue.

Political pedagogy offers the promise of nurturing students to think critically about their understanding of classroom knowledge and its relationship to the issue of social responsibility. Yet it would also invoke the challenge of educating students not only to engage the world critically but also to be responsible enough to fight for those political and economic conditions that make democratic participation in both schools and the larger society viable. Such a pedagogy affirms the experience of the social and the obligations it evokes regarding questions of responsibility and transformation. In part, it does this by opening up for students important questions about power, knowledge, and what it might mean for them to critically engage the conditions under which life is presented to them. In addition, the pedagogy of freedom would provide students with the knowledge and skills to analyze and work to overcome those social relations of oppression that make living unbearable for those who are poor, hungry, unemployed, deprived of adequate social services, and viewed under the aegis of neoliberalism as largely disposable. What is important about this type of critical pedagogy is the issue of responsibility as both a normative issue and a strategic act. Responsibility not only highlights the performative nature of pedagogy by raising questions about the relationship that teachers have to students but also the relationship that students have to themselves and others.

Central here is the importance for educators to encourage students to reflect on what it means for them to connect knowledge and criticism to becoming agents of social change, buttressed by a profound desire to overcome injustice and a spirited commitment to social agency. Political education teaches students to take risks, challenge those with power, and encourage them to be reflexive about how power is used in the classroom. Political education proposes that the role of the teacher as public intellectual is not to consolidate authority but to question and interrogate it, and that teachers and students should temper any reverence for authority with a sense of critical awareness and an acute willingness to hold it accountable for its consequences. Moreover, political education foregrounds education not within the imperatives of specialization and professionalization but within a project designed to expand the possibilities of democracy by linking education to modes of political agency that promote critical citizenship and address the ethical imperative to alleviate human suffering.

On the other hand, politicizing education silences in the name of orthodoxy and imposes itself on students while undermining dialogue, deliberation, and critical engagement. Politicizing education is often grounded in a combination of self-righteousness and ideological purity that silences students as it enacts "correct" positions. Authority in this perspective rarely opens itself to self-criticism or for that matter to any criticism, especially from students. Politicizing education cannot decipher the distinction between critical teaching and pedagogical terrorism because its advocates have no sense of the difference between encouraging human agency and social responsibility and molding students according to the imperatives of an unquestioned ideological position and sutured pedagogical script. Politicizing education is more religious than secular and more about training than educating; it harbors a great dislike for complicating issues, promoting critical dialogue, and generating a culture of questioning.

If teachers are truly concerned about how education operates as a crucial site of power in the modern world, they will have to take more seriously how pedagogy functions on local and global levels to secure and challenge the ways in which power is deployed, affirmed, and resisted within and outside traditional discourses and cultural spheres. In this instance, pedagogy becomes an important theoretical tool for understanding the institutional conditions that place constraints on the production of knowledge, learning, and academic labor itself. Pedagogy also provides a discourse for engaging and challenging the production of social hierarchies, identities, and ideologies as they traverse local and national borders. In addition, pedagogy as a form of production and critique offers a discourse of possibility, a way of providing students with the opportunity to link meaning to commitment and understanding to social transformation—and to do so in the interest of the greatest possible justice. Unlike traditional vanguardist or elitist notions of the intellectual, critical pedagogy and education should embrace the notion of rooting the vocation of intellectuals in pedagogical and political work tempered by humility, a moral focus on suffering, and the need to produce alternative visions and policies that go beyond a language of sheer critique.

I now want to shift my frame a bit in order to focus on the implications of the concerns I have addressed thus far and how they might be connected to developing an academic agenda for teachers as public intellectuals, particularly at a time when neoliberal agendas increasingly guide social policy.

Once again, in opposition to the privatization, commodification, commercialization, and militarization of everything public, educators need to define public education as a resource vital to the democratic and civic life of the nation. At the heart of such a task is the challenge for teachers, academics, cultural workers, and labor organizers to join together in opposition to the transformation of public education into a commercial sector—to resist what Bill Readings has called a consumer-oriented corporation more concerned about accounting than accountability.[33] As Bauman reminds us, schools are one of the few public spaces left where students can learn the "skills for citizen participation and effective political action. And where there is no [such] institution, there is no 'citizenship' either."[34] Public education may be one of the few sites available in which students can learn about the limits of commercial values, address what it means to learn the skills of social citizenship, and learn how to deepen and expand the possibilities of collective agency and democratic life.

Defending education at all levels of learning as a vital public sphere and public good rather than merely a private good is necessary to develop and nourish the proper balance between democratic public spheres and commercial power, between identities founded on democratic principles and identities steeped in forms of competitive, self-interested individualism that celebrate selfishness, profit-making, and greed. This view suggests that public education be defended through intellectual work that self-consciously recalls the tension between the democratic imperatives and possibilities of public institutions and their everyday realization within a society dominated by market principles. If public and higher education are to remain sites of critical thinking, collective work, and thoughtful dialogue, educators need to expand and resolutely defend how they view the meaning and purpose of their work with young people. As I have stressed repeatedly, academics, teachers, students, parents, community activists, and other socially concerned groups must provide the first line of defense in protecting public education as a resource vital to the moral life of the nation, open to people and communities whose resources, knowledge, and skills have often been viewed as marginal. This demands not only a revolutionary educational idea and concrete analysis of the neoliberal and other reactionary forces at work in dismantling public education but also the desire to build a powerful social movement as a precondition to real change and free quality education for everyone.

Such a project suggests that educators develop a more inclusive vocabulary for aligning politics and the task of leadership. In part, this means providing students with the language, knowledge, and social relations to engage in the "art of translating individual problems into public issues, and common interests into individual rights and duties."[35] Leadership demands a politics and pedagogy that refuses to separate individual problems and experience from public issues and social considerations. Within such a perspective, leadership displaces cynicism with hope, challenges the neoliberal notion that there are no alternatives with visions of a better society, and develops a pedagogy of commitment that puts into place modes of critical literacy in which competency and interpretation provide the basis for actually intervening in the world. Leadership invokes the demand to make the pedagogical more political by linking critical thought to collective action, human agency to social responsibility, and knowledge and power to a profound impatience with a status quo founded upon deep inequalities and injustices.

One of the crucial challenges faced by educators is rejecting the neoliberal collapse of the public into the private, the rendering of all social problems as biographical in nature. The neoliberal obsession with the private not only furthers a market-based politics that reduces all relationships to the exchange of money and the accumulation of capital, it also depoliticizes politics itself and reduces public activity to the realm of utterly privatized practices and utopias, underscored by the reduction of citizenship to the act of purchasing goods. Within this discourse all forms of solidarity, social agency, and collective resistance disappear into the murky waters of a politics in which the demands of privatized pleasures and ready-made individual choices are organized on the basis of market mentalities and moralities that cancel out all modes of social responsibility, commitment, and action. This is a reactionary public pedagogy that finds its vision in the creation of atomized individuals who live in a moral vacuum and regress to sheer economic Darwinism or infantilism. One of the major challenges now facing educators, especially in light of the current neoliberal attack on public workers, is to reclaim the language of the social, agency, solidarity, democracy, and public life as the basis for rethinking how to name, theorize, and strategize a new kind of education as well as more emancipatory notions of individual and social agency, as well as collective struggle.

This challenge suggests, in part, positing new forms of social citizenship and civic education that have a purchase on people's everyday lives and struggles. Teachers and faculty bear an enormous responsibility in opposing neoliberalism—the most dangerous ideology of our time—by bringing democratic political culture back to life. Part of this effort demands creating new locations of struggle, vocabularies, and values that allow people in a wide variety of public spheres to become more than they are now, to question what it is they have become within existing institutional and social formations, and "to give some thought to their experiences so that they can transform their relations of subordination and oppression."[36] One element of this struggle could take the form of resisting attacks on existing public spheres, such as schools, while creating new spaces in clubs, neighborhoods, bookstores, trade unions, alternative media sites, and other places where dialogue and critical exchanges become possible. At the same time, challenging neoliberalism means fighting against the state's ongoing reconfiguration into the role of an enlarged police precinct, designed to repress dissent, regulate immigrant populations, incarcerate youth who are considered disposable, and safeguard the interests of global investors. It also means shifting spending priorities in favor of young people and a sustainable democracy.

Revenue for investing in young people, social services, health care, crucial infrastructures, and the welfare state has not disappeared. It has simply been moved into other spending categories or used to benefit a small percentage of the population. As mentioned above, military spending is bloated and supports a society organized for the mass production of violence. Such spending needs to be cut to the bone and could be done without endangering the larger society. In addition, as John Cavanagh has suggested, educators and others need to fight for policies that provide a small tax on stocks and derivatives, eliminate the use of overseas tax havens by the rich, and create tax policies in which the wealthy are taxed fairly.[37] Cavanagh estimates that the enactment of these three policies could produce as much as $330 billion in revenue annually, enough to vastly improve the quality of education for all children throughout the United States.[38]

As governments globally give up their role of providing social safety nets, maintaining public services, and regulating corporate greed, capital escapes beyond the reach of democratic control, leaving marginalized individuals and groups at the mercy of their own meager resources to survive. In such circumstances, it becomes difficult to create alternative public spheres that enable people to become effective agents of change. Under neoliberalism's reign of terror, public issues collapse into privatized discourses and a culture of personal confessions, greed, and celebrity worship emerges to set the stage for depoliticizing public life and turning citizenship and governance into a form of consumerism. Celebrity has become the principal expression of value in a society in which only commodified objects have any value. The rich and the powerful dislike public education as much as they despise any real notion of democracy and they will do all in their power to defend their narrow ideological and economic interests.

The growing attack on public and higher education in American society, as well as in the United Kingdom and many other neoliberal countries, may say less about the reputed apathy of the populace than about the bankruptcy of old political languages and orthodoxies and the need for new vocabularies and visions for clarifying our intellectual, ethical, and political projects, especially as they work to reabsorb questions of agency, ethics, and meaning back into politics and public life. In the absence of such a language and the social formations and public spheres that make democracy and justice operative, politics becomes narcissistic and caters to the mood of widespread pessimism and the cathartic allure of the spectacle. In addition, public service and government intervention are sneered at as either bureaucratic or a constraint upon individual freedom. Any attempt to give new life to a substantive democratic politics must address the issue of how people learn to be political agents as well as what kind of educational work is necessary within what kind of public spaces to enable people to use their full intellectual resources to provide a profound critique of existing institutions and to undertake a struggle to make the operation of freedom and autonomy achievable for as many people as possible in a wide variety of spheres.

As engaged educators, we are required to understand more fully why the tools we used in the past feel inadequate in the present, often failing to respond to problems now facing the United States and other parts of the globe. More specifically, educators face the challenge posed by the failure of existing critical discourses to bridge the gap between how society represents itself and how and why individuals fail to understand and critically engage such representations in order to intervene in the oppressive social relationships they often legitimate.

Against neoliberalism, educators, students, and other concerned citizens face the task of providing a language of resistance and possibility, a language that embraces a militant utopianism while constantly being attentive to those forces that seek to turn such hope into a new slogan or punish and dismiss those who dare to look beyond the horizon of the given. Hope is the affective and intellectual precondition for individual and social struggle, the mark of courage on the part of intellectuals in and out of the academy who use the resources of theory to address pressing social problems. But hope is also a referent for civic courage that translates as a political practice and begins when one's life can no longer be taken for granted, making concrete the possibility for transforming politics into an ethical space and a public act that confronts the flow of everyday experience and the weight of social suffering with the force of individual and collective resistance and the unending project of democratic social transformation.

There is a lot of talk among educators and the general public about the death of democratic schooling and the institutional support it provides for critical dialogue, nurturing the imagination, and creating a space of inclusiveness and critical teaching. Given that educators and others now live in a democracy emptied of any principled meaning, the ability of human beings to imagine a more equitable and just world becomes more difficult. I would hope educators, of all groups, would be the most vocal and militant in challenging this assumption by making clear that at the heart of any notion of a substantive democracy is the assumption that learning should be used to expand the public good, create a culture of questioning, and promote democratic social change. Individual and social agency become meaningful as part of the willingness to think in oppositional, if not utopian, terms "in order to help us find our way to a more human future."[39] Under such circumstances, knowledge can be used for amplifying human freedom and promoting social justice, not for simply creating profits. The diverse terrains of critical education and critical pedagogy offer some insights for addressing these issues, and we would do well to learn as much as possible from them in order to expand the meaning of the political and revitalize the pedagogical possibilities of cultural politics and democratic struggles. The late Pierre Bourdieu has argued that intellectuals need to create new ways for doing politics by investing in political struggles through a permanent critique of the abuses of authority and power, especially under the reign of neoliberalism. Bourdieu wanted educators to use their skills and knowledge to break out of the microcosm of academia and the classroom, combine scholarship with commitment, and "enter into sustained and vigorous exchange with the outside world (especially with unions, grassroots organizations, and issue-oriented activist groups) instead of being content with waging the 'political' battles, at once intimate and ultimately, and always a bit unreal, of the scholastic universe."[40]

At a time when our civil liberties are being destroyed and public institutions and goods all over the world are under assault by the forces of a rapacious global capitalism, there is a concrete urgency on the horizon that demands not only the most engaged forms of political opposition on the part of teachers but also new modes of resistance and collective struggle buttressed by rigorous intellectual work, social responsibility, and political courage. The time has come for educators to distinguish caution from cowardice and recognize the need for addressing the dire crisis public education is now facing. As Jacques Derrida reminds us, democracy "demands the most concrete urgency . . . because as a concept it makes visible the promise of democracy, that which is to come."[41] We have seen glimpses of such a promise among those brave students and workers who have demonstrated in Montreal, Paris, London, Athens, Toronto, Mexico City, and many other cities across the globe.

As engaged intellectuals, teachers can learn from such struggles by turning the colleges and public schools into vibrant critical sites of learning and unconditional spheres of pedagogical and political resistance. The power of the existing dominant order does not merely reside in the economic or in material relations of power, but also in the realm of ideas and culture. This is why educators must take sides, speak out, and engage in the hard pedagogical work of debunking corporate culture's assault on teaching and learning, orient their teaching for social change, and connect learning to public life. At the very least, educators can connect knowledge to the operations of power in their classroom, providing a safe space for students to address a variety of important issues ranging from the violation of human rights to crimes against humanity. Assuming the role of public intellectual suggests being a provocateur in the classroom; it means asking hard questions, listening carefully to what students have to say, and pushing teaching against the grain. But it also means stepping out of the classroom and working with others to create public spaces where it becomes possible not only to "shift the way people think about the moment but potentially to energize them to do something differently in that moment," to link one's critical imagination with the possibility of activism in the public sphere.[42] This is, of course, a small step, but if we do not want to repeat the present as the future or, even worse, become complicit in the workings of dominant power, it is time for educators to collectively mobilize their energies by breaking down the illusion of unanimity that dominant power propagates while working diligently, tirelessly, and collectively to reclaim the promises of a truly global, democratic future. There is no room for a dystopian pedagogy in a democratic society because it destroys the foundation for a formative culture necessary to provide the modes of shared sociality and social agents who possess the knowledge, skills, and values that support an ongoing collective struggle for democratization. In light of the current neoliberal assault on all democratic public spheres, along with the urgency of the problems faced by those marginalized because of their class, race, age, or sexual orientation, I think it is all the more crucial to imagine a politics that both challenges and rejects the dystopian "dreamworlds" of consumption, privatization, deregulation, and the neverending search for accumulating profits. At the heart of such a struggle is the need for a new radical imagination—in this case, one that is willing to develop new social movements, a fresh language for politics, an intense struggle to preserve the democratic educational possibilities of higher education, and alternative public spheres. All of which are crucial to sustain a democratic formative culture to challenge the neoliberal authoritarianism that generates massive social inequality, deepens market savagery, promotes massive privatization, and unleashes a global war against any viable notion of social citizenship and critical education.

CHAPTER TWO

At the Limits of Neoliberal Higher Education:
Global Youth Resistance and the American/British Divide

We need a wholesale revision of how a democracy both listens to and treats young people.

—Andy Mycock

The global reach and destructiveness of neoliberal values and disciplinary controls are not only evident in the widespread hardships and human suffering caused by the economic recession of 2008, they are also visible in the ongoing and ruthless assault on the social state, workers, unions, higher education, students, and any vestige of the social at odds with neoliberal values. Under the regime of market fundamentalism, institutions that were meant to limit human suffering and misfortune and protect the public from the excesses of the market have been either weakened or abolished, as have been many of those public spheres where private troubles can be understood as social problems and addressed as such.[1] Government institutions and policies to protect workers' rights and regulate corporations have been weakened just as the institutional basis of

the welfare state has been undermined along with "the ideas of social provision that supported it."[2] Many programs inaugurated during FDR's New
Deal and Lyndon Johnson's Great Society eras have either been eliminated
or are now under attack by conservative politicians, especially Texas senator
Ted Cruz and other adherents of the Tea Party. One startling example of
growing inequality is the reinstatement of ability grouping in public
schools, which is a blatant return to the old forms of tracking students by
class and race.[3] Such tracking already exists in higher education by virtue
of the correlation between a student's opportunity to get a quality education and the ability to pay soaring tuition rates at the best public and private schools. Under neoliberalism, privatization has run rampant,
engulfing institutions as different in their goals and functions as public
schools and core public services, on the one hand, and prisons, on the
other. This shift from the social contract to savage forms of corporate sovereignty is part of a broader process of "reducing state support of social
goods [and] means that states—the institutions best placed to defend the
gains workers and other popular forces have made in previous struggles—
are instead abandoning them."[4] In this brave new world, there is rapidly
growing inequality in income and wealth, the financial sector now occupies an unprecedented position in the economy, and one consequence is
a "scale of worldwide misery not seen since the 1930s."[5]

Faced with massive deficits, the US federal government, along with
that of many states, is refusing to raise taxes either on the rich or on
wealthy corporations while at the same time enacting massive cuts in
everything from Medicaid programs, food banks, and worker retirement
funds to higher education and health care programs for children. As one
example, Florida governor Rick Scott has

> proposed slashing corporate income and property taxes, laying off
> 6,700 state employees, cutting education funding by $4.8 billion, and
> cutting Medicaid by almost $4 billion. Scott's ultimate plan is to phase
> the Sunshine state's corporate income tax out entirely. He [wants] to
> gut Florida's unemployment insurance system, leaving unemployed
> workers "with much less economic protection than unemployed work-
> ers in any other state in the country."[6]

As social problems are privatized and public spaces are commodified,
there has been an increased emphasis on individual solutions to socially
produced problems, while at the same time market relations and the

commanding institutions of capital are divorced from matters of politics, ethics, and responsibility. Free market ideology, with its emphasis on the privatization of public wealth, the elimination of social protections, and its deregulation of economic activity, now shapes practically every commanding political and economic institution in the United States. In these circumstances, notions of the public good, community, and the obligations of citizenship are replaced by the overburdened demands of individual responsibility and an utterly privatized ideal of freedom.

In the current market-driven society, with its ongoing uncertainties and collectively induced anxieties, core public values that safeguard the common good have been abandoned under a regime that promotes a survival-of-the-fittest economic doctrine. As Jeffrey Sachs points out, "Income inequality is at historic highs, but the rich claim they have no responsibility to the rest of society. They refuse to come to the aid of the destitute, and defend tax cuts at every opportunity. Almost everybody complains, almost everybody aggressively defends their own narrow, short-term interests, and almost everybody abandons any pretense of looking ahead or addressing the needs of others."[7] Shared sacrifice and shared responsibilities now give way to shared fears and a disdain for investing in the common good or, for that matter, the security of future generations of young people. Conservatives and liberals alike seem to view public values as either a hindrance to the profit-seeking goals of the allegedly free market or as an enervating drain on society. Espousing a notion of the common good is now treated as a sign of weakness, if not a dangerous pathology.[8]

Public spheres that once offered at least the glimmer of progressive ideas, enlightened social policies, noncommodified values, and critical exchange have been increasingly commercialized—or replaced by private spaces and corporate settings whose ultimate fidelity is to expanding profit margins. For example, higher education is increasingly defined as an adjunct of corporate power and culture. Public spaces such as libraries are detached from the language of public discourse and viewed increasingly as a waste of taxpayers' money. No longer vibrant political spheres and ethical sites, public spaces are reduced to dead spaces in which it becomes almost impossible to construct those modes of knowledge, communication, agency, and meaningful interventions necessary for an aspiring democracy. What has become clear is that the neoliberal attack on the social state, workers, and unions is now being matched by a full-fledged assault on higher education. Such attacks are not happening just in the United States but in the many other parts of the globe where neoliberalism is waging a savage battle to eliminate all of those public spheres that might offer a glimmer of opposition to and protection from market-driven policies, institutions, ideology, and values. Higher education is being targeted by conservative politicians and governments because it embodies, at least ideally, a sphere in which students learn that democracy, as Jacques Rancière suggests, entails rupture, relentless critique, and dialogue about official power, its institutions, and its never-ending attempts to silence dissent.[9]

The Neoliberal Attack on Higher Education

As Ellen Schrecker observes, "Today the entire enterprise of higher education, not just its dissident professors, is under attack, both internally and externally."[10] In England and the United States, universities and businesses are forming stronger ties, the humanities are being underfunded, student tuition is rising at astronomical rates, knowledge is being commodified, and research is valued through the lens of an audit culture. In England, the Browne Report—an ostensibly independent review of British higher education, released in 2009—has established modes of governance, financing, and evaluation that for all intents and purposes make higher education an adjunct of corporate values and interests.[11] Delivering improved employability has reshaped the connection between knowledge and power while rendering faculty and students as professional entrepreneurs and budding customers. The notion of the university as a center of critique and a vital democratic public sphere that cultivates the knowledge, skills, and values necessary for the production of a democratic polity is giving way to a view of the university as a marketing machine essential to the production of neoliberal subjects.[12] This is completely at odds with the notion that higher education, in particular, is wedded to the presupposition that literacy in its various economic, political, cultural, and social forms is essential to the development of a formative culture that provides the foundation for producing critically engaged and informed citizens.

Clearly, any institution that makes a claim to literacy, critical dialogue, informed debate, and reason is now a threat to a political culture in which ignorance, stupidity, lies, misinformation, and appeals to common sense have become the dominant, if not most valued, currency of exchange. And this seems to apply as well to the dominant media. How else to explain the widespread public support for politicians in the United States such as Herman Cain, who is as much a buffoon as he is an exemplar of illiteracy and ignorance in the service of the political spectacle? In fact, one can argue reasonably that the entire slate of 2012 presidential Republican Party candidates, extending from Cain to Rick Santorum to Rick Perry and Michele Bachmann, embodied not simply a rejection of science, evidence, informed argument, and other elements associated with the Enlightenment but a deep-seated disdain and hatred for any vestige of a critical mind. During the 2012 campaign, almost every position taken by the Republican primary candidates harked back to a pre-Enlightenment period when faith and cru elty ruled the day and ignorance was the modus operandi for legitimating political and ethical impotence. Mitt Romney, the eventual Republican Party front-runner, not only supported such views but also appeared to have little regard for the truth, as he constantly changed his positions on a number of issues to simply fit the demands of his various audiences. Even the post-election attempt by the Republican Party to find new faces of leadership, such as Florida senator Marco Rubio, perpetuated the legacy of ignorance and denial that plagues the party. For example, Rubio, in his response to Obama's state of the union address, "dismissed the idea that the U.S. government could do anything to combat climate change," crassly implying that climate change was not man-made and was not a vital political and environmental issue.[13] Rubio has also made comments about hearing what he called "reasonable debate" from both sides about whether climate change is man-made. In this regressive, neoliberal worldview, ignorance and scientific evidence are weighed equally, as if one balances the other. This type of ideological fundamentalism buttressed by a willful ignorance is especially disingenuous in light of a large number of scientific studies that affirm the existence of man-made global warming. "In fact, a study, published in 2010 in the *Proceedings of the National Academy of Sciences*, surveyed 1,372 climate researchers and found that 97 to 98 percent of them agree that climate change is anthropogenic."[14]

Beneath the harsh rule of a neoliberal sovereignty, education, if not critical thought itself, is removed from its civic ties and rendered instrumental, more closely tied to the production of ignorance and conformity than informed knowledge and critical exchange. Under such circumstances, it is not surprising that higher education, or for that matter any other critical public sphere in the United States and increasingly in England, occupies a high-profile target for dismantlement and reform by neoliberal and right-wing politicians and other extremists. While there is ample commentary on the dumbing down of the culture as a result of the corporate control of the dominant media, what is often missed in this argument is how education has come under a similar attack, and not simply because there is an attempt to privatize or commercialize such institutions.

Under casino capitalism, higher education matters only to the extent that it promotes national prosperity and drives economic growth, innovation, and transformation. But there is more at stake here in turning the university into an adjunct of the corporation: there is also an attempt to remove it because it is one of the few remaining institutions in which dissent, critical dialogue, and social problems can be critically engaged. Young people in the United States now recognize that the university has become part of a Ponzi scheme designed to impose on students an unconscionable amount of debt while subjecting them to the harsh demands and power of commanding financial institutions for years after they graduate. Under this economic model of subservience, there is no future for young people, there is no time to talk about advancing social justice, addressing social problems, promoting critical thinking, cultivating social responsibility, or engaging noncommodified values that might challenge the neoliberal world view.

One of the most flagrant examples of how the university as a place to think is being dismantled can be seen in the Browne Report. Chaired by Lord Browne of Madingley, the former chief executive of BP, the Browne Report recommended a series of deeply conservative changes to British higher education, including raising the cap on fees that universities could charge students. The report's guiding assumptions suggest that "student choice," a consumer model of pedagogy, an instrumentalist culture of auditing practices, and market-driven values are at the core of the new neoliberal university. Like most neoliberal models of education, higher education matters only to the extent that it promotes national prosperity and drives economic growth, innovation, and transformation.[15] Tuition will be tripled in some cases. Numerous schools will be closed. Higher education will be effectively remade according to the dic-. tates of a corporate culture.

On March 26, 2011, students in London joined with labor union activists, public service employees, and others in a massive demonstration protesting the savage cuts in jobs, services, and higher education proposed by the Conservative-Liberal Democratic coalition government formed in May 2010. Yet the government appears indifferent to the devastating consequences its policies will produce. Simon Head has suggested that the Browne policies represent a severe threat to academic freedom. In actuality, the neoliberal policies outlined in the report represent a fundamental threat to the future of democracy as well as the university—one of the few remaining institutions left in which dissent, critical dialogue, and social problems can be critically engaged.[16] What is often lost in critiques of the neoliberal university is the connection to broader society. Democracy necessitates a culture of questioning and a set of institutions in which complicated ideas can be engaged, authority challenged, power held accountable, and public intellectuals produced.

In the United States, the neoliberal model takes a somewhat different form since states control the budgets for higher education. Under the call for austerity, states have begun the process of massively defunding public universities while simultaneously providing massive tax breaks for corporations and the rich. At the same time, higher education in its search for funding has "adopted the organizational trappings of medium-sized or large corporations."[17] University presidents are now viewed as CEOs, faculty as entrepreneurs, and students as consumers. In some universities, college deans are shifting their focus beyond the campus in order to take on "the fund-raising, strategic planning, and partner-seeking duties that were once the bailiwick of the university president."[18] Academic leadership is now defined in part through the ability to partner with corporate donors. In fact, deans are increasingly viewed as the heads of complex businesses, and their job performance is rated according to their fundraising capacity.

College presidents now willingly and openly align themselves with corporate interests. The *Chronicle of Higher Education* has reported that "presidents from 19 of the top 40 research universities with the largest operating budges sat on at least one company board."[19] As business culture permeates higher education, all manner of school practices—from food service and specific modes of instruction to the hiring of temporary faculty—is now outsourced to private contractors. In the process of adopting market values and cutting costs, classes have ballooned in size, matched only by a top-heavy layer of managerial elites, who now outnumber faculty at American universities. For faculty and students alike, there is an increased emphasis on rote learning and standardized testing. Tuition fees have skyrocketed, making it impossible for thousands of working-class youth to gain access to higher education. Moreover, the value of higher education is now tied exclusively to the need for credentials. Disciplines and subjects that do not fall within the purview of mathematical utility and economic rationality are seen as dispensable.

Among the most serious consequences facing faculty in the United States under the reign of neoliberal austerity and disciplinary measures is the increased casualization of academic labor. As universities adopt models of corporate governance, they are aggressively eliminating tenure positions, increasing part-time and full-time positions without the guarantee of tenure, and attacking faculty unions. In a number of states such as Ohio and Utah, legislatures have passed bills outlawing tenure, while in Wisconsin the governor has abrogated the bargaining rights of state university faculty.[20] At a time when higher education is becoming increasingly vocationalized, the ranks of tenure-track faculty are being drastically depleted in the United States, furthering the loss of faculty as stakeholders. Currently, only 27 percent of faculty are either on a tenure track or in a full-time tenure position.[21] As faculty are demoted to contingency forms of labor, they lose their power to influence the conditions of their work; they see their work load increase; they are paid poorly, deprived of office space and supplies, and refused travel money; and, most significantly, they are subject to policies that allow them to be fired at another's will.[22] The latter is particularly egregious because, when coupled with an ongoing series of attacks by right-wing ideologues against left-oriented and progressive academics, many nontenured faculty begin to censor themselves in their classes. At a time when critical faculty might be fired for their political beliefs, have their names posted on right-wing web sites, be forced to turn over their e-mail correspondence to right-wing groups,[23] or face harassment by the conservative press, it is crucial that protections be put in place that safeguard their positions and enable them to exercise the right of academic freedom.[24]

Neoliberal and right-wing political attacks on higher education and the rise of student protests movements in England and the United States, in particular, must be viewed within a broader political landscape that goes far beyond a critique of massive increases in student tuition. A broader analysis is needed to provide insights into how neoliberal policies and modes of resistance manifest themselves in different historical contexts while also offering possibilities for building alliances among different student groups across a range of countries. What both the United Kingdom and the United States share is a full-fledged attack by corporate and market-driven forces to destroy higher education as a democratic public sphere, despite the ongoing "desirability of an educated population to sustain a vibrant democracy and culture that provides a key component of the good life."[25]

Students Against Neoliberal Authoritarianism

In the face of the mass uprisings in England, Europe, Canada, and the Middle East, many commentators have raised questions about why comparable forms of widespread resistance did not take place earlier among US youth. Before the California student movement of 2009–2010 and the Occupy Wall Street protests, everyone from left critics to mainstream radio commentators voiced surprise and disappointment that US youth appeared unengaged by the collective action of their counterparts in other countries. In a wave of global protests that indicted the lack of vision, courage, and responsibility on the part of their elders and political leaders, young people in London, Paris, Montreal, Tunis, Quebec, and Athens were taking history into their own hands, fighting not merely for a space to survive but also for a society in which matters of justice, dignity, and freedom are objects of collective struggle. These demonstrations have created a new stage on which young people once again are defining what John Pilger calls the "theater of the possible."[26] Signaling a generational and political crisis that is global in scope, young people sent a message to the world that they refuse to live any longer under repressive authoritarian regimes sustained by morally bankrupt market-driven policies and repressive governments. Throughout Europe, students protested the attack on the social state, the savagery of neoliberal policies, and the devaluation of higher education as a public good. In doing so, they defied a social order in which they could not work at a decent job, have access to a quality education, or support a family—a social order that offered them a meager life stripped of self-determination and dignity. In London, students have been at the forefront of a massive progressive movement protesting against a Cameron-Clegg government that has imposed, under the ideological rubric of austerity-driven slash-and-burn policies, drastic cuts to public spending. These draconian policies are designed to shift the burden and responsibility of the recession from the rich to the most vulnerable elements of society, such as the elderly, workers, lower-income people, and students.

While young people in the United States did not take to the streets as quickly as their European counterparts, they have embraced the spirit of collective protests with the Occupy Wall Street movement. In the United States young people are not simply protesting tuition increases, the defunding of academia, and the enormous debt many of them are laboring under, they are also situating such concerns within a broader attack on the fundamental institutions and ideology of casino capitalism in its particularly virulent neoliberal form. Claiming that they are left out of the discourse of democracy, student protesters have not only made clear that inequality is out of control but that power largely resides in the hands of the top 1 percent, who control almost every aspect of society, from the government and the media to the schools and numerous cultural apparatuses. The Occupy Wall Street movement, taking a lesson from the Quebec student movement, is leading the move away from a focus on isolated issues in an attempt to develop a broader critique as the basis for an energized social movement less interested in liberal reforms than in a wholesale restructuring of US society under more radical and democratic values, social relations, and institutions of power. Ironically, very few progressives saw this movement coming and had for all intents and purposes written off the possibility of a new youth movement protesting against the savage policies of neoliberalism.

Some commentators, including Courtney Martin, a senior correspondent for *The American Prospect*, suggested that the problem is one of privilege. In a 2010 article for the magazine titled "Why Class Matters in Campus Activism," Martin argues that US students are often privileged and view politics as something that happens elsewhere, far removed from local activism.[27]

> Many of us from middle- and upper-income backgrounds have been socialized to believe that it is our duty to make a difference, but undertake such efforts abroad—where the "real" poor people are. We found nonprofits aimed at schooling children all over the globe while rarely acknowledging that our friend from the high school football team can't afford the same kind of opportunities we can. Or we create Third World bicycle programs while ignoring that our lab partner has to travel two hours by bus, as he is unable to get a driver's license as an undocumented immigrant. We were born lucky, so we head to the bars—oblivious to the rising tuition prices and crushing bureaucracy inside the financial aid office.[28]

This theme is taken up in greater detail in Martin's latest book, *Do It Anyway: A New Generation of Activists*. Sadly, however, the analysis Martin provides in that book suffers, like her piece in *The American Prospect*, from the same sort of privilege it critiques. It suggests not only that privileged middle-class kids are somehow the appropriate vanguard of change for this generation but also that they suffer from both a narcissistic refusal to look inward and a narrow, ego-driven sense of politics that is paternalistic and missionary in focus. This critique is too simplistic, overlooks complexity, and ignores social issues in a manner as objectionable as the attitudes it purports to find so misguided.

The other side of the overprivileged youth argument is suggested by longtime activist Tom Hayden, who argues that many students are so saddled with financial debt and focused on what it takes to get a job that they have little time for political activism.[29] According to Hayden, student activism in the United States, especially since the 1980s, has been narrowly issues-based, ranging from a focus on student unionization and gender equity to environmental topics and greater minority enrollment, thus circumscribing in advance youth participation in larger political spheres.[30] While Martin and Hayden both offer enticing narratives to explain the belated onslaught of student resistance, Simon Talley, a writer for *Campus Progress*, may be closer to the truth in claiming that students in the United States have had less of an investment in higher education than European students because for the last thirty years they have been told that higher education neither serves a public good nor is a valuable democratic public sphere.[31]

These commentators, however much they sometimes got it right, still underestimated the historical and current impacts of the conservative political climate on American campuses and the culture of youth protest. This conservatism took firm hold with the election of Ronald Reagan and the emergence of both neoconservative and neoliberal disciplinary apparatuses since the 1980s. Youth have in fact been very active in the last few decades, but in many instances to deeply conservative ends. As Susan Searls Giroux has argued, a series of well-funded, right-wing campus organizations have made much use of old and new media to produce bestselling screeds as well as interactive websites for students to report injustices in the interests of protesting the alleged left-totalitarianism of the academy. In her book *Between Race and Reason: Violence, Intellectual Responsibility and the University to Come*, Susan Searls Giroux writes:

> Conservative think tanks provide $20 million annually to the campus Right, according to the People for the American Way, to fund campus organizations such as Students for Academic Freedom, whose credo is "You can't get a good education if they're only telling you half the story" and boasts over 150 campus chapters. Providing an online complaint form for disgruntled students to fill out, the organization's website monitors insults, slurs and claims of more serious infractions that students claim to have suffered. Similarly, the Intercollegiate Studies Institute, founded by William F. Buckley, funds over 80 right-wing student publications through its Collegiate Network, which has produced such media darlings as Dinesh D'Souza and Ann Coulter. There is also the Leadership Institute, which trains, supports and does public relations for 213 conservative student groups who are provided with suggestions for inviting conservative speakers to campus, help starting conservative newspapers, or training to win campus elections. Or the Young Americans for Freedom, which sponsors various campus activities such as "affirmative action bake sales" where students are charged

variously according to their race or ethnicity, or announcements of "whites only" scholarships.[32]

Resistance among young people has not always been on the side of freedom and justice. Many liberal students for the past few decades, for their part, have engaged in forms of activism that also tend to mimic neoliberal rationalities. The increasing emphasis on consumerism, immediate gratification, and the narcissistic ethic of privatization took its toll in a range of student protests developed over issues such as "a defense of the right to consume alcohol."[33] As Mark Edelman Boren points out in his informative book on student resistance, alcohol-related issues caused student uprisings on a number of American campuses. He recounts one telling example: "At Ohio University, several thousand students rioted in April 1998 for a second annual violent protest over the loss of an hour of drinking when clocks were officially set back at the beginning of daylight savings time; forced out of area bars, upset students hurled rocks and bottles at police, who knew to show up in full riot gear after the previous year's riot. The troops finally resorted to shooting wooden 'knee-knocker' bullets at the rioters to suppress them."[34]

Widening the Lens

All of these explanations have some merit in accounting for the lack of resistance among American students until the Occupy Wall Street movement, but I'd like to shift the focus of the analysis. Student resistance in the United States should be viewed within a broader political landscape, especially for what it might tell us about the direction the current Wall Street protests might take; yet, with few exceptions, this landscape still remains unexamined. First, we have to remember that students in England, in particular, were faced with a series of crises that were more immediate, bold, and radical in their assault on young people and the institutions that bear down heavily on their lives than those in the United States. In the face of the economic recession, educational budgets were and continue to be cut in an extreme, take-no-prisoners fashion; the social state is being radically dismantled; tuition costs have spiked exponentially; and unemployment rates for young people are far higher than in the United States (with the exception of youth in poor minority communities). Students in England have experienced a massive and bold assault on their lives, educational opportunities, and their future. Moreover, these students live in a society where it becomes more difficult to collapse public life into largely private considerations. Students in these countries have access to a wider range of critical public spheres, politics in many of these countries has not collapsed entirely into the spectacle of celebrity/commodity culture, left-oriented political parties still exist, and labor unions have more political and ideological clout than they do in the United States. Alternative newspapers, progressive media, and a profound sense of the political constitute elements of a vibrant, discerning formative culture within a wide range of public spheres that have helped nurture and sustain the possibility to think critically, engage in political dissent, organize collectively, and inhabit public spaces in which alternative and critical theories can be developed.

In the United States, by contrast, the assault on colleges and universities has been less uniform. Because of the diverse nature of how higher education is financed and governed, the cuts to funding and services have been differentially spread out among community colleges, public universities, and elite colleges, thus US students are lacking a unified, oppressive narrative against which to position resistance. Moreover, the campus "culture wars" narrative fueled by the Right has served to galvanize many youth around a reactionary cultural project while distancing them from the very nature of the economic and political assault being waged against their future. All this raises another set of questions. The more important questions, ones that do not reproduce the all-too-commonplace demonization of young people as merely apathetic, are twofold. First, the issue should not be why there have been no student protests until recently, but why previous protests have been largely ignored. Evidence of such nascent protests, in fact, has been quite widespread. The student protests against the draconian right-wing policies attempting to destroy the union rights and collective bargaining power of teachers, promoted by Republican governor Scott Walker in Wisconsin, is one example indicating that students were in fact engaged and concerned. There were also smaller student protests taking place at various colleges, including Berkeley, CUNY, and other campuses throughout the United States. Until recently, student activists constituted a minority of US students, with very few enrolled in professional programs. Most student activists have come from the arts, social sciences, and humanities (the conscience of the college). Second, there is the crucial issue regarding what sort of disabling conditions young people have inherited in American society. What political and cultural shifts have worked together to undermine their ability to be critical agents capable of waging a massive protest movement against the growing injustices they face on a daily basis? After all, the assault on higher education in the United States, while not as severe as in Europe, still provides ample reason for students to be in the streets protesting.

Close to forty-three states have pledged major cuts to higher education in order to compensate for insufficient state funding. This means an unprecedented hike in tuition rates is being implemented, enrollments are being slashed, salaries are being reduced, and need-based scholarships are being eliminated in some states. Pell grants, which enable poor students to attend college, are also being cut. Robert Reich has chronicled some of the specific impacts on university budgets, which include cutting state funding for higher education by $151 million in Georgia, reducing student financial aid by $135 million in Michigan, raising tuition by 15 percent in Florida's eleven public universities, and increasing tuition by 40 percent in just two years in the University of California system.[35] As striking as these increases are, tuition has been steadily rising over the past several decades, becoming a disturbingly normative feature of postsecondary education in the United States.

A further reason that US students took so long to begin to mobilize may be because by the time the average US student now graduates, he or she has not only a degree but also an average debt of about $23,000.[36] As Jeffrey Williams points out in a 2008 article for *Dissent,* "Student Debt and the Spirit of Indenture," this debt amounts to a growing form of indentured servitude for many students. Being burdened by excessive debt upon graduation only to encounter growing rates of unemployment— "unemployment for recent college graduates rose from 5.8 percent to 8.7 percent in 2009"[37]—surely undercuts the opportunity to think about, organize, and engage in social activism. In other words, crippling debt plus few job prospects in a society in which individuals are relentlessly held as being solely responsible for the problems they experience leaves little room for rethinking the importance of larger social issues or the necessity for organized collective action against systemic injustice. In addition, as higher education increasingly becomes a fundamental requirement for employment, many universities have been able to justify the reconfiguration of their mission exclusively in corporate terms. They have replaced education with training while defining students as consumers, faculty as a cheap form of subaltern labor, and entire academic departments as revenue-generating units.[38] No longer seen as a public good or a site of social struggle, higher education is increasingly viewed as a credential mill for success in the global economy.

Meanwhile, not only have academic jobs been disappearing, but given the shift to an instrumentalist education that is decidedly technicist in nature, the culture of critical thinking has been slowly disappearing on US campuses as well. As universities and colleges emphasize market-based skills, students are learning neither how to think critically nor how to connect their private troubles with larger public issues. The humanities continue to be downsized, eliminating some of the most important opportunities many students will ever have to develop a commitment to public values, social responsibilities, and the broader demands of critical citizenship. Moreover, critical thinking has been devalued as a result of the growing corporatization of higher education. Under the influence of corporate values, thought in its most operative sense loses its modus operandi as a critical mediation on "civilization, existence, and forms of evaluation."[39]

It has become increasingly difficult for students to recognize how their formal education and social development in the broadest sense have been systematically devalued, and how this not only undercuts their ability to be engaged critics but contributes to the further erosion of what is left of US democracy. How else to explain the reticence of students within the last decade toward protesting against tuition hikes? The forms of instrumental training they receive undermine any critical capacity to connect the fees they pay to the fact that the United States puts more money into the funding of wars, armed forces, and military weaponry than the next twenty-five countries combined—money that could otherwise fund higher education.[40] The inability to be critical of such injustices and to relate them to a broader understanding of politics suggests a failure to think outside of the prescriptive sensibilities of a neoliberal ideology that isolates knowledge and normalizes its own power relations. In fact, one recent study by Richard Arum and Josipa Roksa found that "45 percent of students show no significant improvement in the key measures of critical thinking, complex reasoning and writing by the end of their sophomore years."[41]

The corporatization of schooling and the commodification of knowledge over the last few decades have done more than make universities into adjuncts of corporate power. They have produced a culture of critical illiteracy and further undermined the conditions necessary to enable students to become truly engaged, political agents. The value of knowledge is now linked to a crude instrumentalism, and the only mode of education that seems to matter is that which enthusiastically endorses learning marketable skills, embracing a survival-of-the-fittest ethic, and defining the good life solely through accumulation and disposal of the latest consumer goods. Academic knowledge has been stripped of its value as a social good. To be relevant, and therefore adequately funded, knowledge has to justify itself in market terms or simply perish.

Enforced privatization, the closing down of critical public spheres, and the endless commodification of all aspects of social life have created a generation of students who are increasingly being reared in a society in which politics is viewed as irrelevant, while the struggle for democracy is being erased from social memory. This is not to suggest that Americans have abandoned the notion that ideas have power or that ideologies can move people. Progressives pose an earnest challenge to right-wing ideologies and policies, but they seem less inclined to acknowledge the diverse ways in which the pedagogical force of the wider culture functions in the production, distribution, and regulation of both power and meaning. By contrast, the conservative willingness to use the educational force of the culture explains in part both the rapid rise of the Tea Party movement and the fact that it seemed to have no counterpart among progressives in the United States, especially young people. This is now changing, given the arrogant, right-wing attacks being waged on unions, public sector workers, and public school educators in Wisconsin, Florida, Ohio, New Jersey, and other states where Tea Party candidates have come to power.[42]

Progressives, largely unwilling to engage in a serious manner the educational force of the larger culture as part of their political strategy, have failed to theorize how conservatives successfully seize upon this element of politics in ways that far outstrip its use by the left and other progressive forces. Missing from their critical analyses is any understanding of how public pedagogy has become a central element of politics itself.

Public pedagogy in this sense refers to the array of different sites and technologies of image-based media and screen culture that are reconfiguring the very nature of politics, cultural production, knowledge, and social relations. Market-driven modes of public pedagogy now dominate major cultural apparatuses such as mainstream electronic and print media and other elements of screen culture, whose one-sided activities, permeated by corporate values, proceed more often than not unchallenged. Left to their own devices by progressive movements, which for decades have largely refused to take public pedagogy seriously as part of their political strategy, the new and old media with their depoliticized pedagogies of consumption may finally be encountering some resistance from the rising student protests around the globe.

Higher Education and the Erasure of Critical Formative Cultures

In a social order dominated by the relentless privatization and commodification of everyday life and the elimination of critical public spheres, young people find themselves in a society in which the formative cultures necessary for a democracy to exist have been more or less eliminated, or reduced to spectacles of consumerism made palatable through a daily diet of talk shows, reality TV, and celebrity culture. What is particularly troubling in US society is the absence of the vital formative cultures necessary to construct questioning persons who are capable of seeing through the consumer come-ons, who can dissent and act collectively in an increasingly imperiled democracy. Sheldon Wolin is instructive in his insistence that the creation of a democratic formative culture is fundamental to enabling both political agency and a critical understanding of what it means to sustain a viable democracy. According to Wolin,

Democracy is about the conditions that make it possible for ordinary people to better their lives by becoming political beings and by making power responsive to their hopes and needs. What is at stake in democratic politics is whether ordinary men and women can recognize that their concerns are best protected and cultivated under a regime whose actions are governed by principles of commonality, equality, and fairness, a regime in which taking part in politics becomes a way of staking out and sharing in a common life and its forms of self-fulfillment. Democracy is not about bowling together but about managing together those powers that immediately and significantly affect the lives and circumstances of others and one's self.[43]

Instead of public spheres that promote dialogue, debate, and arguments with supporting evidence, US society offers young people a conservatizing, consumer-driven culture through entertainment spheres that infantilize almost everything they touch, while legitimating opinions that utterly disregard evidence, reason, truth, and civility. The "Like" button has replaced the critical knowledge and the modes of education needed for long-term commitments and the search for the good society. Intimate and committed social attachments are short-lived, and the pleasure of instant gratification cancels out the interplay of freedom, reason, and responsibility. As a long-term social investment, young people are now viewed in market terms as a liability, if not a pathology. No longer a symbol of hope and the future, they are viewed as a drain on the economy, and if they do not assume the role of functioning consumers, they are considered disposable.

Within the last thirty years, the United States under the reign of market fundamentalism has been transformed into a society that is more about forgetting than learning, more about consuming than producing, more about asserting private interests than democratic rights. In a society obsessed with customer satisfaction and the rapid disposability of both consumer goods and long-term attachments, US youth are not encouraged to participate in politics. Nor are they offered the help, guidance, and modes of education that cultivate the capacities for critical thinking and engaged citizenship. As Zygmunt Bauman points out, in a consumerist society, "the tyranny of the moment makes it difficult to live in the present, never mind understand society within a range of larger totalities."[44] Under such circumstances, according to Theodor Adorno, thinking loses its ability to point beyond itself and is reduced to mimicking existing certainties and modes of common sense. Thought cannot sustain itself and becomes short-lived, fickle, and ephemeral. If young people do not display a strong commitment to democratic politics and collective struggle, then, it is because they have lived through thirty years of what I have elsewhere called "a debilitating and humiliating disinvestment in their future," especially if they are marginalized by class, ethnicity, and race.[45]

What sets this generation of young people apart from past generations is that today's youth have been immersed since birth in a relentless, spreading neoliberal pedagogical apparatus with its celebration of an unbridled individualism and its near pathological disdain for community, public values, and the public good. They have been inundated by a market-driven value system that encourages a culture of competitiveness and produces a theater of cruelty that has resulted in what Bauman calls "a weakening of democratic pressures, a growing inability to act politically, [and] a massive exit from politics and from responsible citizenship."[46] And, yet, they refuse to allow this deadening apparatus of force, manufactured ignorance, and ideological domination to shape their lives. Reclaiming both the possibilities inherent in the political use of digital technologies and social media, US students are now protesting in increasing numbers the ongoing intense attack on higher education and the welfare state, refusing a social order shaped by what Alex Honneth describes as "an abyss of failed sociality," one in which "the perceived suffering [of youth] has still not found resonance in the public space of articulation."[47]

Young people, students, and other members of the 99 percent are no longer simply enduring the great injustices they see around them, they are now building new public spaces, confronting a brutalizing police apparatus with their bodies, and refusing to put up with the right-wing notion that they are part of what is often called a "failed generation." Young people, especially, have flipped the script and are making clear that the failures of casino capitalism lie elsewhere, pointing to the psychological and social consequences of growing up under a neoliberal regime that goes to great lengths to enshrine ignorance, privatize hope, derail public values, and reinforce economic inequality and its attendant social injustices. What the Occupy Wall Street protesters, like their counterparts in London, Montreal, Athens, Cairo, and elsewhere, have made clear is that not only is casino capitalism the site of political corruption and economic fraud, but it also reproduces a "failed sociality" that hijacks critical thinking and agency along with any viable attempt of democracy to deliver on its promises.

In the face of a politically organized ignorance on the part of right-wing anti-public intellectuals, think tanks, media organizations, and politicians, the Occupy Wall Street protesters have refused to provide recipes and blueprints about a longed-for utopian future. Instead, they have resurrected the most profound elements of a radical politics, one that recognizes that critical education, dialogue, and new modes of solidarity and communication serve as conditions for their own autonomy and for the sustainability of democratization as an ongoing social movement. This is evident in their embrace of participatory democracy, a consensus model of leadership, the call for direct action, the development of co-op food banks, free health care clinics, and the development of a diverse model of multimedia communication, production, and circulation. What terrifies the corporate rich, bankers, media pundits, and other bloviators about this movement is not that it has captured the attention of the broader public but that it constantly hammers home the message that a substantive democracy requires citizens capable of self-reflection and social criticism, and that such citizens, through their collective struggles, are the products of a critical formative culture in which people are provided with the knowledge and skills to participate effectively in developing a radically democratic society. And this fear on the part of ruling classes and the corporate elite has gone global.

When we see fifteen-year-olds battling against established oppressive orders in the streets of Montreal, Paris, Cairo, and Athens in the hope of forging a more just society, we are being offered a glimpse of what it means for youth to enter "modernist narratives as trouble."[48] This expression of "trouble" exceeds the dominant society's eagerness to view youth as a pathology, as monsters, or as a drain on the market-driven order. Instead, trouble in this sense speaks to something more suggestive of what John and Jean Comaroff call the "productive unsettling of dominant epistemic regimes under the heat of desire, frustration, or anger."[49] The expectations that frame market-driven societies are losing their grip on young people, who can no longer be completely seduced or controlled by the tawdry promises and failed returns of corporate-dominated and authoritarian regimes.

What is truly remarkable about this movement is its emphasis on connecting learning to social change and its willingness to do so through new and collective modes of education. Equally encouraging is that this movement views its very existence and collective identity as part of a larger struggle for the economic, political, and social conditions that give meaning and substance to what it means to make democracy possible. In the United States, the Occupy Wall Street protests have made clear that the social visions embedded in casino capitalism and deeply authoritarian regimes have lost both their utopian thrust and their ability to persuade and intimidate through manufactured consent, threats, coercion, and state violence. Rejecting the terrors of the present along with the modernist dreams of progress at any cost, young people have become, at least for the moment, harbingers of democracy, fashioned through the desires, dreams, and hopes of a world based on the principles of equality, justice, and freedom. One of the most famous slogans of May 1968 was "Be realistic, demand the impossible." The spirit of that slogan is alive once again. But what is different this time is that it appears to be more than a slogan—it now echoes throughout the United States and abroad as both a discourse of critique and as part of a vocabulary of possibility and long-term collective struggle. The current right-wing politics of illiteracy, exploitation, and cruelty can no longer hide in the cave of ignorance, legitimated by their shameful accomplices in the dominant media. The lights have come on all over the United States and young people, workers, and other progressives are on the move. Thinking is no longer seen as an act of stupidity, acting collectively is no longer viewed as unimaginable, and young people are no longer willing to be viewed as disposable. Of course, how this movement plays out over time remains to be seen.

In the United States, the most important question to be raised about US students is no longer why they do not engage in massive protests or why have they not continued the massive protests that characterized the first year of the Occupy Wall Street protest movement, but *when will they join* their youthful counterparts protesting in London, Montreal, Athens, Istanbul, and elsewhere in building a global democratic order in which they can imagine a future different from the present? The test of these movements will be their ability to develop national associations and international alliances that can be sustained for the long run. But this will only happen when young people and others begin to organize collectively in order to develop the formative cultures, public spheres, and institutions that are crucial to helping them confront neoliberalism and the threats it poses to the environment, public goods, and those dispossessed by race, class, and age. Only then will they join together in individual and collective efforts to reclaim higher education as a public good vital for creating new imaginaries and democratic social visions.

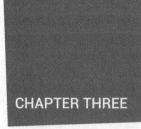

CHAPTER THREE

Intellectual Violence in the Age of Gated Intellectuals:
Critical Pedagogy and a Return to the Political

BRAD EVANS AND HENRY A. GIROUX

> *The more radical the person is, the more fully he or she enters into reality so that, knowing it better, he or she can transform it. This individual is not afraid to confront, to listen, to see the world unveiled. This person is not afraid to meet the people or to enter into a dialogue with them. This person does not consider himself or herself the proprietor of history or of all people, or the liberator of the oppressed; but he or she does commit himself or herself, within history, to fight at their side.*
> **—Paulo Freire**

Introduction

Proverbial wisdom warns that while sticks and stones shall inflict pain, words will never kill us. Yet nothing is further from the truth: inflammatory rhetoric has *always* been a strategic precursor to the drums of warfare. This was perhaps most obvious in recent years in the discursive violence used by the Bush administration to justify the invasions of Iraq and Afghanistan. Moreover, the periodic militaristic pronouncements employed by Israel and the United States as a precursor for a potential attack on Iran demonstrate that discourse can continually authenticate the meaning of violent encounters and produce organized violence. Intellectual discourse is also a veritable minefield littered with the corpses of radical pioneers who dared to venture into uncharted fields. One does not have to look too far to find the most sophisticated regimes of truth being used to offer the surest moral backbone to the most reasoned forms of human atrocities. Recent memory provides sufficient testimony here: we only have to look to the gradual buildup for each of the so-called wars on terror for evidence of "discursive creep." As we seamlessly moved through the various stages of securitization, civil liberties were shredded, terrorism became a term that justified the most violent actions, and the seemingly impossible became the altogether inevitable state of affairs. Among both academic and public intellectuals the paths to recognition, resources, and credibility have become dependent upon one's willingness to shamefully compromise with the utility of force and its compulsion to embed all things potentially subversive.

The university has not in any way been immune to these strategies of absorption, as the lines between the times of civic peace and militarism have become increasingly blurred to the latter's normalization. Increasingly, research and the production of knowledge within the university have become militarized as the role of the university has in fact given way to various methods of intellectual policing, with the main strategic function becoming the need to think how to wage war better. For such reasons academics occupy a somewhat (in)enviable position when it comes to the study of intellectual violence. We remain empirical objects and principal stakeholders due to the political stakes. Drawing upon personal experiences, many critical scholars in the post-9/11 moment have publically attested to and critiqued deeply embedded institutional forms of intellectual violence that have shaped their everyday working relations. They have also been highly critical of what they perceive as state violence around the world, a mode of violence that provides cover for the role that higher education often plays in legitimating such violence. Consequently, various critical scholars, such as Ward Churchill, Patricia Adler,

Norman Finklestein, Abu-Manneh, Terri Ginsburg, David Graeber, and, more recently, Samer Shehata, have been refused promotions, or, more severely, denied tenure.[1]

All too frequently positions of academic authority have been awarded to opportunistic careerists who remain completely untroubled by the burdens of complicated thought and the fight for ethical and political responsibility. While it is somewhat easier to come to terms with the usual suspects, who remain openly hostile to any form of post-1968 criticality as it challenges the simple comforts of rehearsed orthodoxy, it is the institutionally sanctioned violence that tends to take more subtle forms, frequently masked by the collegiate language of "consensus," "playing the game," and "majoritarianism," that is of greater concern. Such consensus-building majorities brazenly offer the most fantastic appropriation of democratic terms. What passes for the majority here is not a numeric expression but a particularistic relation of force that provides a sure glimpse into the authoritarian personality so apt to Theodor Adorno's sense of inquiry.[2] Some may invariably call this leadership. The dark and poisonous influence of authoritarianism often wraps itself in the discourse of patriotism, rights, duty, and —most shamefully—the mantle of democracy. Yet if leadership is to reclaim its political and ethical standing and have any collegiate relevance whatsoever, it must be afforded by those who are meant to be inspired by the example and not made to feel coerced into submission.

We are not suggesting a uniform experience. Nor do we refuse to acknowledge the many forms of resistance to this mode of creeping academic authoritarianism. Some schools, faculties, and globally reputable institutions still take great pride in their commitment to the opening of possibilities for thinking the political anew and reclaiming a link between the production of knowledge and social change. Such resistance needs to be celebrated and vigorously defended. And so do the principles of a significant number of scholars who still recognize that the essential function of the university is to continue to hold power to account. The neoliberal assault on global academia is, however, now so pervasive and potentially dangerous in its effects that it is must be viewed as more than a "cause for concern." While the system in the United States has been at the forefront of policies that have tied academic merit to market-driven performance indicators, the ideologically driven transformations under way in the United Kingdom point in an equally worrying direction as the need for policy entrepreneurship increasingly becomes the norm.

The closures of entire philosophy programs signify the most visible shift away from reflective thinking to the embrace of a dumbed-down approach to humanities education with no time for anything beyond the objectively neutralizing and politically compromising deceit of pseudo-scientific paradigms that replace education with training and emphasize teaching to the test. Instrumentalism in the service of corporate needs and financial profit now dominates university modes of governance, teaching, research, and the vocabulary used to describe students and their relationship to each other and the larger world. What is most disturbing about the hyper-militarization of the university and of knowledge is the militarization of pedagogy itself. No longer viewed as a political and ethical practice that provides the conditions for critical thought and engaged modes of democratic action, pedagogy has become repressive. That is, this market-driven pedagogy "mobilizes people's feelings primarily to neutralize their senses, massaging their minds and emotions so that the individual succumbs to the charisma of vitalistic power,"[3] if not the normalization of violence itself. Increasingly within the university, thinking critically and embracing forceful new angles of vision are all too frequently viewed as heresy. One consequence is that those who dare challenge institutional conformity through a commitment to academic freedom and intellectual inquiry often find that insightful ideas emerge only to die quickly.

Discourses, ideas, values, and social relations that push against the grain, redefine the boundaries of the sensible, and reclaim the connection between knowledge and power in the interest of social change too often not only become inconvenient but also rapidly accelerate to being viewed as dangerous. If the dissent is pressed too far, it can lead to being fired, prison time, and possibly death. As Gilles Deleuze once maintained, nobody is ever intellectually put into prison for powerlessness or pessimism. It is the courage to articulate the truth that so perturbs. For thought to be "meaningful," then, it has to become empty, inhabiting a "no-fly" space utterly policed by the apologists for conformity. Any pedagogy that aims at turning out informed citizens makes one immediately suspect.

And it is not simply academics but all cultural workers who now suffer under this rising tide of ignorance that has become a hallmark of a repressive neoliberal ideology. This leaves us, in part, wondering how any author or artist in the current climate could ever create anything remotely comparable to oft-cited historical masterpieces that were not subjected to intellectually compromised performance deadlines. But we are also left to question whether the term "university" itself is appropriate for certain institutions that declare open hostility to the very academic discipline and forms of intellectual inquiry that gave original meaning to the idea of public education.

Despite their provocative intentions, our concerns take us beyond those all-too-familiar vitriolic forms of extremism that seek to publicly shut down points of difference through good old-fashioned bullying techniques. However abhorrent they appear, it is better that such inflammatory thoughts are put into the public arena so that nothing is subject to misinterpretation or counterfactual claims of misrepresentation. Indeed, although it is undoubtedly the case that the center ground for global politics more generally has moved to the extreme right of the spectrum in all its various ontotheological, faith-based expressions, the symbolic violence of the vitriolic leaves enough visible traces to be openly condemned with an even greater degree of intellectual effort. Yet our concern is with the more sophisticated forms of intellectual violence that, although sometimes openly condescending in their patronizing churlishness, nevertheless present a formidable challenge due to the weight of their reasoning. Such violence is a familiar neoliberal deceit. It emanates from a progressive constituency that draws upon the virtues of enlightened praxis and its normalizing tendencies to make us desire that which even the most momentary forms of conscious and reflective political thought will deem particularly intolerable. These normalizing tendencies can be seen in the support of progressives for the wars in Iraq and Afghanistan, indifference to the corporatization of higher education, and utter silence about the status of the United States as "one of the biggest open-air prisons on earth."[4] And such intellectual violence occasions with either personal displays of utmost courteousness or talks to a much wider claim of humanitarianism.

There is a bankrupt civility at work here, disingenuous in its complicity with violence and disillusioned about the social costs it promotes and the moral coma it attempts to impose on those considered rudely uncivil, code for those who take intellectual risks and are willing to think critically and hold power accountable. The very notion that the university might have a role to play in either promoting or resisting authoritarian politics, state and corporate-sponsored violence, and war is often met with a condescending lifting of the head or wave of the hand that bespeaks the violence and deep order of politics lurking beneath this banalized appropriation of civility as code for a flight from moral, political, and pedagogical responsibility. This is the civility of authoritarians who flee from open conflict and mask their intellectual violence with weak handshakes, forced smiles, and mellowed voices. Like the punishment dished out to a recalcitrant child, however, through reason of seductive persuasion or reason of a more brutal force, more "mature" (the authoritarian default) ways of thinking about the world must eventually be shown to be the natural basis for authority and rule.

The concept of violence is not taken lightly here. Violence remains poorly understood if it is accounted for simply in terms of how and what it kills, the scale of its destructiveness, or any other element of its annihilative power. Intellectual violence is no exception as its qualities point to a deadly and destructive conceptual terrain. As with all violence, there are two sides to this relation. There is the annihilative power of nihilistic thought that seeks, through strategies of domination and practices of terminal exclusion, to close down the political as a site for differences. Such violence appeals to the authority of a peaceful settlement, though it does so in a way that imposes a distinct moral image of thought that already maps out what is reasonable to think, speak, and act. Since the means and ends are already set out in advance, the discursive frame is never brought into critical question. And there is an affirmative counter that directly challenges authoritarian violence. Such affirmation refuses to accept the parameters of the rehearsed orthodoxy. It brings into question that which is not ordinarily questioned. Foregrounding the life of the subject as key to understanding political deliberation, it eschews intellectual dogmatism with a commitment to the open possibilities in thought. However, as we shall argue in this chapter, rather than countering intellectual violence with a "purer violence" (discursive or otherwise), there is a need to maintain the language of critical pedagogy. By "criticality," we insist upon a form of thought that does not have war or violence as its object. If there is destruction, this is only apparent when the affirmative is denied. And by criticality we also insist upon a form of thought that does not offer its intellectual soul to the seductions of militarized power. Too often we find that while the critical gestures toward profane illumination, it is really the beginning of violence that amounts to a death sentence for critical thought. Our task is to avoid this false promise and demand a politics that is dignified and open to the possibility of nonviolent ways of living.

The Tyranny of Reason

Michel Foucault introduced the concept of the biopolitical to denounce the illusion of institutional peace and the inevitability of freedom despite the existence of free-flowing power relations. As he put to question, "When, how and why did someone come up with the idea that it is a sort of uninterrupted battle that shapes peace, and that the civil order— its basis, its essence, its essential mechanisms—is basically an order of battle?"[5] There are two important aspects to deal with here. First, when Foucault refers to "killing" in a biopolitical sense he does not simply refer to the vicious and criminal act of physically taking a life: "When I say 'killing,' I obviously do not mean simply murder as such, but also every form of indirect murder: the fact of exposing someone to death, increasing the risk of death for some people, or, quite simply, political death, expulsion, rejection and so on."[6] And second, despite any semblance of peace, it is incumbent upon the critical cartographer to bring into question normalized practices so as to reveal their scars of battle:

> [My methodology] is interested in rediscovering the blood that has dried in the codes, and not, therefore, the absolute right that lies beneath the transience of history; it is interested not in referring the relativity of history to the absolute of law, but in discovering beneath the stability of the law or the truth, the indefiniteness of history. It is interested in the battle cries that can be heard beneath the formulas of right.[7]

This represents an important shift in our understanding of violence. No longer simply content with exploring extrajuridical forms of violent abuse, attentions instead turn toward those forms of violence that take place in the name of human progress and the emancipatory subject. This type of violence takes place through a hidden order of politics concealed beneath the circuits of discursive regimes of truth, civility, and representations of a commodified culture that is fully and uncritically absorbed in the modernist notion of progress.

The dominant institutions for social progress today are no longer sovereign in any popular sense of the term. State sovereignty has been compromised by corporate sovereignty just as state power now more closely resembles the workings of a carceral state. At the same time, politics has become local and power is now global, unrestricted by the politics of the nation-state and indifferent to the specificity of its practices and outcomes. Power and violence have been elevated into the global space of flows.[8] The most evident development of this has been the veritable "capitalization of peace" in which the global ravages of poverty, war, and violence are tied to neoliberal policies that, proceeding in the name of human togetherness/progress/unity, conceal an inner logic of biopolitical separation and social containment.[9]

As politics is emptied of its ability to control global power, the bankruptcy of biocapitalism becomes evident in the hollowing out of the social state and the increasing force of the dominant discourses and policies that legitimate its extinction. For example, when the Bush and Obama administrations argued that the banks were too big to fail, we were presented with more than another neoliberal conceit regarding supply-side economics and its practice of distributing wealth and income away from the already impoverished to the already enriched. The more dangerous conceit paved the way for the destruction of even the most minimal conditions for a sustainable democracy. This subterfuge at one level argues that the victims of casino capitalism are guilty of waging class warfare while at the same time the ruling elite destroy all those public spheres capable of providing even minimal conditions for individuals to engage the capacities to think, feel, and act as engaged and critical citizens. And they do it in the midst of a decrepit and weakened state of politics that holds corporate power unaccountable, while endlessly repeating the poisonous mantra of deregulation, privatization, and commodification. The banking elite and the mega-financial services openly serve the rich while engaging in widespread ecological devastation as well as destroying the safety nets that serve the poor and the middle class. But since the banking sector is seen to be integral to the vision of planetary peace, its survivability is morally tied to humanity's potential for self-ruination.

The ruinous logic of militarization now provides global finance with the mad machinery of violence in order to dispense with the power of reason and the demands of global social responsibility. To put it another way, since global finance is openly presented to be central to the neoliberal security *dispositif*, we should be under no illusions where military allegiance lies. George W. Bush certainly didn't send troops into Iraq and Afghanistan for the betterment of the victims of market fundamentalism at home or those Iraqis suffering under the ruthless dictatorship of Saddam Hussein. Neither was the more recent securitization of the London Olympics carried out to protect immigrant populations living on the margins in the capital's run-down areas. There is therefore no hegemonic discourse in any conventional sovereign geo-strategic sense of the term. Instead, what appears is a neoliberal will to rule that is upheld by a formidable school of intellectual thought and takes direct aim at the critically minded as a dangerous community to be vanquished. Reason in this sense is unmoored from its emancipatory trappings, reduced to a legitimating discourse for a notion of progress that embraces a mode of technological rationality that operates in the service of repression and the militarization of thought itself.[10]

The contemporary tyranny of reason is not exclusively tied to state power and now works within modes of sovereignty constructed through the logics of biocapitalism and its growing banking and financial sectors. Reason embraces such tyranny through an ossified logic of the market and its principle of risk. It is most revealing to find that economic agencies are at the forefront of this policy that has made economic questions of prime political significance. During the 1990s organizations such as the World Bank increasingly became interested in political concerns as the focus of their work (along with economics more generally) changed from the managed recoveries of national crises to the active promotion of better lives.[11] Transforming their remit from economic management to security governance, such organizations became moral agents in their own right, advocating economic solutions to the ravages of civil wars, criminality, shadow economies, poverty, endemic cultural violence, and political corruption. This was matched by a particular revival in the ideas of political economists such as Friedrich Von Hayek and Milton Friedman, who long equated neoliberalism with marketable freedoms. Neoliberalism in this case becomes a source of political and moral legitimacy, determined not only to institute market-based structural reforms but also to establish the conditions for producing particular types of agency, subjects, and social relations that are said to thrive by embracing a logic of risk that promotes insecurity as a principal design for existence.

The unchecked celebration of a neoliberal subject willing to take market-based risks—either financial or through acts of consumption—does more than provide a rationale for the corrupt trading practices of investment bankers and hedge fund power brokers, it also points to the closer connection between those considered the producers of capital and those who are now the new at-risk, disposable populations. The financial elite now view themselves as corporate missionaries promoting policies, practices, and ideas that are not only designated as universal but take their inspiration from God. How else to interpret Goldman Sachs's chief executive Lloyd Blankfein's comment that he is just a banker "doing God's work."[12] Needless to say, those individuals and populations who are outside the accumulation, possession, and flow of capital are considered the new parasites, excess, and global human waste. That is, those considered failed consumers—"enemy combatants," unpatriotic dissidents, poor minority youth, low-income white kids, immigrants, and others inhabiting the margins of global capital and its intellectual ecosystem of vast inequality and ruthless practices of disposability. Capital is not only wedded to the production of profits, it is also invested in a form of intellectual violence that legitimates its savage market-driven practices and the exercise of ruthless power. When applied to the intellectual terrain, to paraphrase C. Wright Mills, we are seeing the breakdown of democracy, the disappearance of critical thought, and "the collapse of those public spheres which offer a sense of critical agency and social imagination."[13] Since the 1970s, we have seen the forces of market fundamentalism strip education of its public values, critical content, and civic responsibilities as part of its broader goal of creating new subjects wedded to the logic of privatization, efficiency, flexibility, consumerism, and the destruction of the social state.

Tied largely to instrumental purposes and measurable paradigms, many institutions of higher education are now committed almost exclusively to economic growth, instrumental rationality, and the narrow civically deprived task of preparing students strictly for the workforce. The question of what kind of education is needed for students to be informed and active citizens is now rarely asked.[14] Hence, it is no surprise, for example, to read that "Thomas College, a liberal arts college in Maine, advertises itself as Home of the Guaranteed Job!"[15] Within this discourse, faculty are largely understood as a subaltern class of low-skilled entrepreneurs, removed from the powers of governance and subordinated to the policies, values, and practices within a market model of the university that envisages pure instrumentality.[16]

Within both higher education and the educational force of the broader cultural apparatus—with its networks of knowledge production in the old and new media—we are witnessing the emergence and dominance of a form of a powerful and ruthless, if not destructive, market-driven notion of governance, teaching, learning, freedom, agency, and responsibility. Such modes of education do not foster a sense of organized responsibility central to a democracy. They corrupt any commitment to critical pedagogy. As David Harvey insists, "The academy is being subjected to neoliberal disciplinary apparatuses of various kinds [while] also becoming a place where neoliberal ideas are being spread."[17]

Not only does neoliberalism undermine civic education and public values as well as confuse education with training, it also treats knowledge as a product, promoting a neoliberal logic that views schools as malls, students as consumers, and faculty as entrepreneurs. Just as democracy appears to be fading throughout the liberal world, so is the legacy of higher education's faith in and commitment to democracy. As the humanities and liberal arts are downsized, privatized, and commodified, higher education finds itself caught in the paradox of claiming to invest in the future of young people while offering them few intellectual, civic, and ethical supports. One such measure of the degree to which higher education has lost its ethical compass can be viewed in the ways in which it disavows any relationship between equity and excellence, eschews the discourse of democracy, and reduces its commitment to learning to the stripped-down goals of either preparing students for the workforce or teaching them the virtues of measurable utility. While such objectives are not without vocational merit, they have little to say about the role that higher education might play in influencing the fate of future citizens and the state of democracy itself, nor do they say much about what it means for academics to be more than technicians or hermetic scholars.

Gated Academics

Giorgio Agamben came to prominence during the immediate aftermath of 9/11 as his work on the state of exception seemed to strike a precise chord.[18] Central then to Agamben's work was his concern with the spatial figuration of the camp and how sites such as Guantánamo Bay removed any semblance of political, legal, and ethical rights. Bare life thus became a defining critical motif for many who were concerned with the perceived lawlessness of the US administration and its allies as they deployed excessive force against enemies real or newly provoked. We have never been entirely convinced by Agamben's understanding of the modern *nomos* or stripping away of political agency for the globally oppressed. Neither have we been content to focus our attentions simply on the violence that takes place in distinct sites of social abandonment as if all things within law (especially violence) are devoid of complementary relations.

While we do accept that policies of containment are sometimes a preferred method for dealing with troublesome populations who need to be curtailed, along with disposable populations that have nothing meaningful to exploit, encamped life has always been situated within a much wider terrain of market-driven processes that give secondary consideration to surplus lives. What is more, as neoliberal governmentality faces a global crisis of its own making, we are in fact encountering a logical inversion to Agamben's modeling as the politically *included* are increasingly being forced into fortified compounds and gated protectorates that link together the nodal points of a privatized sovereignty within the global space of flows. Having said this, Agamben's insistence that biopolitical marks of separation reveal a distinct violence has merit. It is not, however, that the human condition needs violence in order to resolve its differences. Imposed universality takes hold of difference to produce a violent cartography of human separation.

It is often said that the days when intellectuals could live in an ivory tower are gone. While this is true (and is partly driven by the market's need to have a distinct intellectual identity), contemporary intellectuals, mirroring the world of which they are part, increasingly inhabit a radically interconnected world in which corporate-driven, networked, structured relations define how they mediate their relationship both to the university and the broader world of global flows. A number of critical scholars and academics have been dismayed by this development, as the pursuit of knowledge once central to the creation of epistemic communities gives way to various risk-based assessments. Others openly embrace the idea of "the gated intellectual."[19] Replicating the structural logic of privately owned, fortified strongholds evident in all global megacities, gated intellectuals—walled off from growing impoverished populations—are also cut loose from any ethical mooring or sense of social responsibility as understood in a reciprocal sense of the term. Instead they voice their support for what might be called gated or border pedagogy—one that establishes boundaries to protect the rich, isolates citizens from each other, excludes those populations considered disposable, and renders invisible young people, especially poor youth of color, along with others marginalized by class and race. Such intellectuals play no small role in legitimating what David Theo Goldberg has called a form of neoliberalism that promotes a "shift from the caretaker or pastoral state of welfare capitalism to the 'traffic cop' or 'minimal' state, ordering flows of capital, people, goods, public services and information."[20]

Gated intellectuals and the privately funded institutions or marketed forms of finance that support them believe in societies that stop questioning themselves, engage in a history of forgetting, and celebrate the progressive "decomposition and crumbling of social bonds and communal cohesion."[21] Policed borders, surveillance, state secrecy, targeted assassinations, armed guards, and other forces provide the imprimatur of dominant power and containment, making sure that no one can trespass onto gated property, domains, sites, protected global resources, and public spheres. On guard against any claim to the common good, the social contract, or social protections for the underprivileged, gated intellectuals spring to life in universities, news programs, print media, charitable foundations, churches, think tanks, and other cultural apparatuses, aggressively surveying the terrain to ensure that no one is able to do the crucial pedagogical work of democracy by offering resources and possibilities for resisting the dissolution of sociality, reciprocity, and social citizenship itself. Such guarded consolidation and retrenchment of positions does not entertain paranoiac entropy. It has already amassed an arsenal of pre-emptive intellectual strikes that allegedly document the demise of the public intellectual as an unfortunate side effect or collateral damage to a wider war effort into which we are all openly recruited. If gated communities are the false registers of safety, gated intellectuals have become the new registers of conformity.

The gated mentality of market fundamentalism has walled off, if not disappeared, those spaces where dialogue, critical reason, and the values and practices of social responsibility can be engaged. The armies of antipublic intellectuals who appear daily on television, radio talk shows, and other platforms work hard to create a fortress of indifference and manufactured stupidity. They ask that intellectualism remain a private affair. Public life is therefore reduced to a host of substanceless politicians, embedded experts, and gated thinkers who pose a dire threat to those vital public spheres that provide the minimal conditions for citizens who can think critically and act responsibly. Higher education is worth mentioning because, for engaged and public intellectuals, it is one of the last strongholds of democratic action and reasoning and one of the most visible targets along with the welfare state.

As is well known, higher education is increasingly being removed from the discourse of public values and the ideals of a substantive democracy at a time when it is most imperative to defend the institution against an onslaught of forces that are as anti-intellectual as they are antidemocratic in nature. Many of the problems in higher education can be linked to the evisceration of funding, the intrusion of the security apparatus of the state, the lack of faculty self-governance, and a wider culture that appears increasingly to view education as a private right rather than a public good. Within the wider sociopolitical environment, corporate power and interests are all too willing to define higher education as a business venture, students as consumers and investors, and faculty as a cheap source of labor. Left to the logic of the market, education is something that consumers and investors now purchase for the best price, deal, and profit. All of these disturbing trends, left unchecked, are likely to challenge the very meaning and mission of the university as a democratic public sphere.

Gated intellectualism points to new forms of intellectual violence—violence(s) that is/are markedly different from the old colonial pursuit of "redeeming savages" through brutalizing subservience, the suppression of women's rights, and the often violent attacks on homosexuals. Although it is fully appreciated that the outside can no longer be left to chance, the veritable distancing between the gated intellectual and his or her precarious surroundings points to a form of inclusive exclusion whose violence employs the preferred technologies of the time. Not only is drone violence the preeminent technology for contemporary forms of violence in which war is seldom declared, it is also the apt metaphor for the twenty-first-century intellectual violence of the gated intellectual.

Abandoning any attempts at making the world more enlightened, what takes its place is a short, sharp, and speedy intellectual attack that points to a purely immanent conception of thought. Such thinking has no time to reflect upon the significance of events. It has no patience for contested memories or excavating the complex histories that make our present. Neither does it entertain the possibility that the world may be thought and lived otherwise. What remains is a politically settled intellectual environment that deems everything alternative to be potentially hostile. There is nothing in this relationship that suggests any reciprocal attempt at establishing better ethical relations among the world of peoples. Instead, fully removed from the realities of contested political spaces, neoliberal risk assessment measures, along with their highly biotechnologized performance indicators, become the surest way to create alternative conditions of the real. This is nothing but simulacrum. It proposes nothing but a manufactured reality that is virtually conceived within the highly policed nodal protectorates of neoliberal governance without any concern to experience the world.

Violence to Memory

History remains the biggest casualty of intellectual violence. The past is written so that the present course of action appears both natural and timeless. What is at stake here is the question of memorialization and how this relates to a politics of events. We have no concern here with those various speculative attempts at offering a definitive philosophical proof for the meaning of events in order to stupefy publics with another form of intellectual violence. There is no poetic joy to reading such hyperstructural technicism, whose language is akin to a perpetual motion machine whose only purpose is its own activity. Political events are now framed in order to debunk any notion of critical analyses on account of the fact that they break open what false semblance of peace exists to the creation of new ways of thinking and relating to the world. Not, of course, to suggest that the conditions that give rise to a revolutionary impetus cannot be critically understood as we seek to explain systemic oppression. But it is to acknowledge that political events have to be understood in terms of their own specificity, and that they forever appear *untimely* (to echo Nietzsche's claim) to us at their moment of arising. Who, for instance, could have anticipated the impact of Rosa Parks's simple yet profound disruption of elements that sent into permanent flux the conventional order of things? Or that the first visible signs of resistance to the New World Order would come from the Zapatistas—an incredibly poor indigenous population in an unknown land?

Our concern with intellectual violence brings us directly to the closing down of the historical space as the multiple experiences of political events are subsumed within the one "true" narrative. September 11, 2001, showed how imposing a uniform truth on the event represented a profound failure of the political imaginary. Judith Butler accounts for this in terms of the framing of the problem:

> The "frames" that work to differentiate the lives we can apprehend from those we cannot (or that produce lives across a continuum of life) not only organize visual experience but also generate specific ontologies of the subject. Subjects are constituted through norms which, in their reiteration, produce and shift the terms through which subjects are recognized.[22]

Importantly, for Butler, since what matters here is the subsequent production of certain truthful subjectivities out of the ashes of devastation, we must bring into question the framing of life as a seemingly objective ontological and epistemological fact:

> To call the frame into question is to show that the frame never quite contained the scene it was meant to limn, that something was already outside, which made the very sense of the inside possible, recognizable. The frame never quite determined precisely what it is we see, think,

recognize, and apprehend. Something exceeds the frame that troubles our sense of reality; in other words, something occurs that does not conform to our established understanding of things.[23]

This call to break with the dominating content of the time is more than an attempt to draw attention to the multiplicity of the experiences of events. It is to open up the space of the political by breaking apart the myth that there is a universal experience of truth. In the hours and days that followed the tragic events of September 11, 2001, the unfolding sense of trauma and loss drew people together in a fragile blend of grief, shared responsibility, compassion, and a newfound respect for the power of common purpose and commitment.[24] The translation of such events into acts of public memory, mourning, and memorializing are ambivalent and deeply unsettling. They offered no certainty. We must recall that they do not only bring about states of emergency and the suspension of civil norms and order: they can, and did, give birth to enormous political, ethical, and social possibilities. Yet, such enlightened moments proved fleeting. A society has to move with deliberate speed from the act of witnessing to the responsibility of just memorializing; put simply, to the equally difficult practice of reconfiguring what politics, ethics, and civic engagement should mean after 9/11. On the tenth anniversary of that tragic day, the struggle to remember and reclaim those moments in good faith was constantly challenged, and in ways that few of us would dare to have imagined a decade later. Public memory became the enemy of a state immersed in a culture of fear as dissent and civil liberties were sacrificed on the altar of security, and ethics and justice gave way from the state legitimation of torture under George W. Bush to the state's right, under President Obama, to murder those considered an enemy of the state, regardless of the due process of law.[25]

The events of 9/11 show how loss, memory, and remembrance share an uneasy, if not unsettled, embrace. Remembrance can become dysfunctional, erasing the most important elements of history and trivializing what survives of the event through either crass appeals to an untroubled celebration of patriotism or a crass commercialization of 9/11 as just another commodity for sale. But remembrance can also recover what is lost to this historical amnesia. It can both produce difficult thoughts, bringing forth not only painful memories of personal loss and collective vulnerability but also new understandings of how specific events infuse the present, and become a force for how one imagines the future, including, to quote Roger Simon, how "one imagines oneself, one's responsibility to others, and one's civic duty to a larger democratic polity and range of diverse communities."[26] Memory can be an instigator of both despair and hope, often in ways in which the division between desperation and hope becomes blurred. For instance, the spectacular shock and violence of 9/11 ruptured an arrogant and insular period in American history that had proclaimed the triumph of progress and the end of ideology, history, and conflict, all the while imposing an unbearable experience of loss, grief, sorrow, and shock on large segments of the world's population.

The collective fall from grace is now well known. Instead of being a threshold to a different future and a register for a restored democratic faith, the decade following 9/11 became an era of buried memories and monumentalization. Rather than initiating a period of questioning and learning, the war on terror morphed into a war without end, producing abuses both at home and abroad, all of which resembled an unending fabric of normalizing violence. America's particular status as a symbol of freedom that elicited worldwide respect was fatefully diminished, giving way to a culture of fear, mass hysteria, and state secrecy. At the same time that the Bush administration waged war overseas, it unleashed ruthless market forces at home, along with a virulent propaganda machine in which public issues collapsed into private concerns, and the future—like the futures market that drove it—was detached from any viable notion of ethical and social responsibility. Finance capital replaced human capital, economics was detached from ethics, youth were viewed as *a* risk rather than *at* risk, and the formative culture necessary for a democracy collapsed into a rampaging commercialism as citizens became defined exclusively as consumers and the notion of the social along with collaborative social bonds were viewed as a liability rather than as a public good central to any viable notion of civic engagement and democracy itself. Finance capital replaced the social debt—based on the obligations we owe to each other—with financial debt, in which creditors now savagely rule a generation of debtors chained to contractual relations marked by persistent deficits, hardships, surveillance, and subordination.[27]

Shared trauma of violence doesn't, however, necessarily translate into discourses of revenge. Counter-violence is simply the option most preferred by certain political ways of thinking. Undoubtedly the history of modern politics has been marked out by the normality of violence. Therefore, what the United States and its allies did in the immediate aftermath of 9/11 was not in any way exceptional. Doing nothing violent in response would have been exceptional. Instead, the response followed the all-too-familiar conventional norm of using violence to reason the world, serve justice, and avert future catastrophes. But it *must* be remembered that none of this is inevitable. Indeed, despite this violent weight of historical reasoning, at the human level it is increasingly clear that the experience of the tragedy was far more complex. What 9/11 made apparent is that memory as a moral, critical, and informed practice requires those elements of counter-memory that challenge the official narratives of 9/11 in order to recover the most valuable and most vulnerable elements of democratic culture too often sacrificed in tragedy's aftermath.

In the hours and days that bled out from the tragic events of 9/11, the unfolding sense of trauma and loss drew us together in a fragile blend of grief, shared responsibility, compassion, and a newfound respect for the power of common purpose and commitment. Hence, if we truly wished to honor the victims of 9/11, we should not be reluctant to engage in a public dialogue about both the legacy and the politics that precipitated and emerged from the events that took place on that tragic day. Such uncomfortable moments of consciousness provide the basis for a form of witnessing that refuses the warmongering, human rights violations, xenophobia, and violations of civil liberties that take shape under the banner of injury and vengeance. Simon Critchley dared to think the "impossible":

> What if the government had simply decided to turn the other cheek and forgive those who sought to attack it, not seven times, but seventy times seven? What if the grief and mourning that followed 9/11 were allowed to foster a nonviolent ethics of compassion rather than a violent politics of revenge and retribution? What if the crime of the Sept. 11 attacks had led not to an unending war on terror, but the cultivation of a practice of peace — a difficult, fraught and ever-compromised endeavour, but perhaps worth the attempt?[28]

Critchley's provocation offers more than a warning against the political ruination of violent responses. He is challenging us to think how we may have a political ethics adequate to such events. This shift toward a politics of forgiveness is no doubt a remarkable task. Perhaps that is the precise point. Ours remains a history marked by a violent humanism so often masquerading under the name of security, peace, and justice. Advocating a politics of forgiveness when faced with such crises is that which passes for something truly exceptional—an affirmative politics of real exceptionalism. Critchley's affinity with Derridean ethics is striking here. As Jacques Derrida maintained, an act of forgiveness worthy of the name must be offered in event of something altogether unforgiveable: "It *should not be* normal, normative, normalizing. It should remain exceptional and extraordinary, in the face of impossible: as if it interrupted the ordinary course of historical temporality."[29] This forgiveness as we currently see it presents itself as an aporia of the impossibility of forgiving unforgivable acts.

And yet, as Derrida reminds us, it is precisely when the aporetic moment arrives that it becomes both possible and necessary. He writes: "It only becomes possible from the moment that it appears impossible."[30] The fact that such a proposition still appears altogether impossible is indicative of the continuum of violence. And yet, the normalized alternative, so common to the history of modern life, illustrates with devastating and politically debilitating surety why Nietzsche was insistent that nihilistic behavior was tied to a spirit of revenge. Once we begin to act out of resentment, so the catastrophic cycle of violence continues to the evacuation of political alternatives. At a time when neoliberalism has turned governance into a legitimation for war, surveillance, and terror, the spirit of revenge and a culture of cruelty do more than permeate everyday lives; the discourse of revenge also reinforces the power of the national security state and contributes to the expansion of its punishing apparatuses, extending from the prison to the schoolroom. And increasingly, the punitive nature of the practices produced by the national security state bear down heavily on those intellectuals now labeled as whistle blowers, "unprivileged enemy belligerents," unpatriotic critical academics, and so on. In the midst of the production of such violence, collective fear serves to silence intellectuals, force them into gated and safe citadels where they do not have to fear being wiretapped, targeted, kidnapped, or subject to state of emergency laws such as the Patriot Act or the National Defense

Authorization Act (NDAA). Or it seduces them into either silence or complicity with the rewards of power, regardless of how tainted ethically and politically such rewards might be.

Radical Criticality

One of the consequences of thinking about threats in global terms has been the collapse of the space/time continuum that once held together the linear world of sovereign reasoning.[31] While we may rejoice, in part, at the breaking open of the former Westphalia semblance of peace that effectively served already established colonial powers by rewriting the rules in their favor, its displacement by a full-spectrum catastrophic imaginary of endangerment has been politically disastrous. As times of war and times of peace merge without any meaningful distinction, so there has been a collapse of the private into the public, the militaristic into the civic, and the authoritarian into the humanitarian. An intellectual casualty of this has been the merger between the radical and the fundamental. While each of these terms once retained a very distinct and oppositional meaning, their coming together is indicative of a social terrain that is violently hostile to political difference. Any thought that seeks to affirm alternative ways of thinking or service to the world is treated as either some immature posturing (the unreason of youth) or the surest indication of a pathological dysfunction (reasoned hostility). So our question therefore becomes, How may we reclaim the terms of radical criticality without succumbing to a violent reasoning that propels us to mimic dominant ways of thinking politics?

We need to learn to live with violence less through the modality of the sacred than through the critical lens of the profane. By this we mean that we need to appreciate our violent histories and how our subjectivities have been formed through a history of physical bloodshed. This requires more of a willingness to interrogate violence in a variety of registers (ranging from the historical and concrete to the abstract and symbolic) than it does a bending to the neoliberal discourses of fate and normalization. We need to acknowledge our own shameful compromises with the varied forces of violence. And we need to accept that intellectualism shares an intimate relationship with violence both in its complicity with violence and as an act of violence. There is an echo of the pornographic here not just in the ethical detachment that now accompanies state violence, particularly with drone technologies, but also in the recuperation of the pleasure principle in the increasing maximization of the spectacle of violence. We need then to reject what Leo Lowenthal has called the imperative to believe that "thinking becomes a stupid crime."[32] This does not require a return to the language of Benjamin's idea of divine violence as a pure expression of force regardless of its contestable claims to non-violent violence.[33] We prefer instead to deploy the oft-abused term "critical pedagogy" as a meaningful political counter to vicissitudes of intellectual violence.

Intellectuals are continually forced to make choices (sometimes against our better judgments). The truth, of course, is that there are no clear lines drawn in the sand neatly separating what is left from what is right. And yet as Paulo Freire insisted, one is invariably drawn into an entire history of struggle the moment our critical ideas are expressed as force and put out into the public realm to the disruption of orthodox thinking. There is, however, a clear warning from history: our intellectual allegiances should be less concerned with ideological dogmatism. There is, after all, no one more micro-fascist or intellectually violent than the authenticating militant whose self-imposed vanguardism compels allegiance through the stupidity of unquestioning loyalty and political purity. To the charges here that critical pedagogy merely masks a retreat into cultural relativism, we may counter that there is no reciprocal relationship with that which doesn't respect difference while at the same time recognizing that pedagogy is an act of intervention. Pedagogy always represents a commitment to the future, and it remains the task of educators to make sure that the future points the way to a more socially just world, a world in which the discourses of critique and possibility in conjunction with the values of reason, freedom, and equality function to alter, as part of a broader democratic project, the grounds upon which life is lived. This is hardly a prescription for either relativism or political indoctrination, but it is a project that gives education its most valued purpose and meaning, which in part is "to encourage human agency, not mould it in the manner of Pygmalion."[34]

Critical pedagogy has a responsibility to mediate the tension between a respect for difference and the exercise of authority that is directive, that is, a mode of authority capable of taking a position while not standing still. Central to its understanding as a moral and political practice, pedagogy as a form of cultural politics contests dominant forms of symbolic production while constantly opening a space to question its own authority and the ever-present danger of fetishizing its own practices. An ethics of difference is central to such a pedagogy, especially at a historical conjuncture in which neoliberalism arrogantly proclaims that there are no alternatives. Within this regime of common sense, neoliberalism eliminates issues of contingency, struggle, and social agency by celebrating the inevitability of economic laws in which the ethical ideal of intervening in the world gives way to the idea that we "have no choice but to adapt both our hopes and our abilities to the new global market."

An ethics of difference, as Foucault critically maintained, requires waging an ongoing fight against fascism in all its forms: "not only historical fascism, the fascism of Hitler and Mussolini—which was able to use the desire of the masses so effectively—but also the fascism in us all, in our heads, and in our everyday behaviour, the fascism that causes us to love power, to desire the very thing that dominates and exploits us."[35] Or as Deleuze once put it, "In every modernity and every novelty, you find conformity and creativity; an insipid conformity, but also 'a little new music'; something in conformity with the time, but also something untimely—separating the one from the other is the task of those who know how to love, the real destroyers and creators of our day."[36]

Academics then are required to speak a kind of truth, but as Stuart Hall points out, "maybe not truth with a capital T, but . . . some kind of truth, the best truth they know or can discover [and] to speak that truth to power."[37] Implicit in Hall's statement is the awareness that to speak truth to power is not a temporary and unfortunate lapse into politics on the part of academics: it is central to opposing all those modes of ignorance, whether they are market-based or rooted in other fundamentalist ideologies that make judgments difficult and democracy dysfunctional. Our view is that academics have an ethical and pedagogical responsibility not only to unsettle and oppose all orthodoxies, to make problematic the commonsense assumptions that often shape students' lives and their understanding of the world, but also to energize them to come to terms with their own power as individual and social agents. Higher education, in this instance, as Pierre Bourdieu, Paulo Freire, Edward Said, Stanley Aronowitz, Susan Searls Giroux, and other intellectuals have reminded us, cannot be removed from the hard realities of those political, economic, and social forces that both support it and consistently, though in diverse ways, attempt to shape its sense of mission and purpose.[38] Politics is not alien to higher education but central to comprehending the institutional, economic, ideological, and social forces that give it meaning and direction. Politics also references the outgrowth of historical conflicts that mark higher education as an important site of struggle. Rather than the scourge of either education or academic research, politics is a primary register of their complex relation to matters of power, ideology, freedom, justice, and democracy.

Talking heads who proclaim that politics have no place in the classroom can, as Jacques Rancière points out, "look forward to the time when politics will be over and they can at last get on with political business undisturbed," especially as it pertains to the political landscape of the university.[39] In this discourse, education as a fundamental basis for engaged citizenship, like politics itself, becomes a temporary irritant to be quickly removed from the hallowed halls of academia. In this stillborn conception of academic labor, faculty and students are scrubbed clean of any illusions about connecting what they learn to a world "strewn with ruin, waste and human suffering."[40] As considerations of power, politics, critique, and social responsibility are removed from the university, balanced judgment becomes code, as C. Wright Mills suggests, for "surface views which rest upon the homogeneous absence of imagination and the passive avoidance of reflection. A vague point of equilibrium between platitudes."[41] Under such circumstances, the university and the intellectuals who inhabit it disassociate higher education from larger public issues, remove themselves from the task of translating private troubles into social problems, and undermine the production of those public values that nourish a democracy. Needless to say, pedagogy is always political by virtue of the ways in which power is used to shape various elements of classroom identities, desires, values, and social relations, but that is different from being an act of indoctrination.

Instead of accepting the role of the gated intellectual, there is an urgent need for public intellectuals in the academy, art world, business sphere, media, and other cultural apparatuses to move from negation to hope. Now more than ever we need reasons to believe in this world. This places renewed emphasis on forms of critical pedagogy that move across different sites—from schools to the alternative media—as part of a broader attempt to construct a critical formative culture in the Western world that enables citizens to reclaim their voices, speak out, exhibit ethical outrage and create the social movements, tactics, and public spheres that will reverse the growing tide of neoliberal fascism. Such intellectuals are essential to democracy, even as social well-being depends on a continuous effort to raise disquieting questions and challenges, use knowledge and analytical skills to address important social problems, alleviate human suffering where possible, and redirect resources back to individuals and communities who cannot survive and flourish without them. Engaged public intellectuals are especially needed at this time to resist the hollowing out of the social state, the rise of a governing-through-crime complex, and the growing gap between the rich and poor that is pushing all liberal democracies back into the moral and political abyss of the Gilded Age—characterized by what David Harvey calls the "accumulation of capital through dispossession," which he claims is "is about plundering, robbing other people of their rights" through the dizzying dreamworlds of consumption, power, greed, deregulation, and unfettered privatization that are central to a neoliberal project.[42]

Under the present circumstances, it is time to remind ourselves that critical ideas are a matter of critical importance. Ideas are not empty gestures, and they do more than express a free-floating idealism. Ideas provide a crucial foundation for assessing the limits and strengths of our senses of individual and collective agency and what it might mean to exercise civic courage in order to not merely live in the world but to shape it in light of democratic ideals that would make it a better place for everyone.

Critical ideas and the technologies, institutions, and public spheres that enable them matter because they offer us the opportunity to think and act otherwise, challenge common sense, cross over into new lines of inquiry, and take positions without standing still—in short, to become border-crossers who refuse the silos that isolate the privileged within an edifice of protections built on greed, inequitable amounts of income and wealth, and the one-sided power of neoliberal governance. Gated intellectuals refute the values of criticality. They don't engage in debates; they simply offer already rehearsed positions in which unsubstantiated opinion and sustained argument collapse into each other. Yet, instead of simply responding to the armies of gated intellectuals and the corporate money that funds them, it is time for critical thinkers with a public interest to make pedagogy central to any viable notion of politics. It is time to initiate a cultural campaign in which the positive virtues of radical criticality can be reclaimed, courage to truth defended, and learning connected to social change. The current attack on public and higher education by the armies of gated intellectuals is symptomatic of the fear that reactionaries have of critical thought, quality education, and the possibility of a generation emerging that can both think critically and act with political and ethical conviction. Our task is to demand a return to the political as a matter of critical urgency.

CHAPTER FOUR

Universities Gone Wild:
Big Sports, Big Money, and the Return
of the Repressed in Higher Education

HENRY A. GIROUX AND SUSAN SEARLS GIROUX

The ever-expanding, ever-deepening nature of the scandal that took place at Pennsylvania State University in 2012 reveals a broad constellation of forces that contributed to the lurid events that sent shock waves through Happy Valley. Comprehending all of the factors that enabled Jerry Sandusky to perpetrate the decade-long serial sexual abuse of young boys is very challenging to say the least—like finding an intellectual foothold in a bottomless pit. One thing is certain, the sordid details constituting the evidence of abuse, the subsequent cover-up and the firing of legendary coach Joe Paterno, along with a number of high-ranking administrators including the university's president, add credence to the rising concern among many Americans that political democracy and the institutions and values that support it are in jeopardy. Although influential media commentators, including journalists such as Paul Krugman of the *New York Times*, have sounded alarms about the collapse of public values, few have connected this horrific scandal to the larger war on youth in America and the continuing collapse of higher education as a democratic public sphere.

This absence of concern regarding youth represents more than a failure of the imagination, particularly given the growing numbers of young people across the United States who are calling attention to a national crisis in education—one that cannot be separated from the radical retreat from social responsibility by an adult citizenry charged with the dual guardianship of its children and the institutions that sustain democratic public life. When placed in this broader context, the Penn State scandal must be seen as a tragic, but not an isolated, incident. Rather, the conditions that have made this revolting series of events possible are replicated on university campuses across the country, derailing the academic mission that has historically defined the enterprise of higher education and compromising the moral leadership and integrity of many postsecondary institutions. Young people have suffered not only the degradation of quality education at all levels but also its increasing inaccessibility for much of their generation. Tuition hikes have gone fist in glove with the defunding of public education, and those who attend university are more often than not saddled with massive debt. In fact, "student private loan debt topped 1 trillion dollars, beating out credit card debt as the highest form of consumer debt, with the exception of mortgage loans."[1] States, in turn, have used their dwindling financial resources as an effective alibi to abet the transformation of universities into commodified knowledge factories or refashion them into extensions of the military-industrial complex.[2] The corporatization and militarization of higher education are not new processes, but they were sharply accelerated during the decade that followed the September 11, 2001, terrorist attacks and have continued unchecked through the recession that commenced with the global financial crisis of 2008.

When students, such as those recently on the campus of University of California, Davis, organized peacefully to challenge these processes and their objectionable impacts on higher education, they have directly experienced—or have borne witness to their friends and peers—being arrested, pepper-sprayed at point-blank range, and assaulted by baton-wielding police on a number of campuses across the country. All the while, the very politicians who support permanent war whatever the costs—and refuse to fund job programs for young people facing record unemployment as they slash financial aid for higher education—taunt the student protesters to take showers and find work. In an irony that invariably escapes the notice of the "liberal media," peaceful protesters are now criminalized and subject to the ruthless dictates of the punishing state, while Wall Street executives and bankers who engaged in various forms of financial fraud, causing savage and ruinous injury to many Americans, roam free and unscathed by the criminal justice system. Given that young people will bear the burden of a multitrillion-dollar deficit, disappearing social safety nets, stagnant job growth, and decrepit educational institutions at all levels, it is no longer hyperbolic to suggest that the war effort has come home—and its primary targets are youth, especially the most vulnerable.[3]

Consider that the conservative politician and former Republican Party presidential candidate Newt Gingrich advocates rewarding the rich with generous tax cuts while exploiting young people by revoking child labor laws in order to allow them to work as janitors in their own schools. He has justified this ludicrous plan by alleging that poor young people grow up in neighborhoods where they are not taught much-needed work habits, and they don't know how to show up for work on Monday. Encouraged by this line of thought, an expansive Gingrich proclaims that poor Black kids don't have to become "pimps, prostitutes, or drug dealers"; to the contrary, they can learn good work habits when they go to school by mopping floors and cleaning toilets. That such youth would take over the unionized janitorial jobs of members of their communities is an added bonus in Gingrich's eyes. One of the few to condemn his racist logic was Comedy Central's Larry Wilmore, whose satirical skit on *The Daily Show* sums up Gingrich's position with the comment: "Dream big, black people! You don't have to be a pimp, prostitute or drug dealer, just clean toilets." In mock juxtaposition with Obama's 2008 "campaign of hope," a banner appears across the Republican candidate's bully pulpit reading "Yes, We Clean!"[4] There is no room in Gingrich's benevolent racism for the concept of the *working* poor, nor for policy reforms calling for job creation for young people, decent employment for their parents, adequate childcare, a living wage, or quality schools for all children. In fact, Gingrich is also against extending unemployment insurance because, as he says, "I am opposed to giving people money for doing nothing."[5] And yet many of the wealthy today have made their fortunes not by creating jobs but by destroying them—a charge he did not fail to level at his arch-rival for the 2012 Republican nomination, Mitt Romney.

As the 2012 Republican presidential candidate race made clear, the poisonous values and power relations that animated the corrupt Wall Street financiers and bankers who produced the financial meltdown and subsequent recession have been embraced by those vying for political leadership in this country.[6] But these market-driven values and power relations have also seeped into a range of public institutions, including higher education. Challenging the pervasive influence of unfettered capitalism across a variety of social institutions has become a central tenet of the student protesters, who argue that such institutions no longer serve the educational, intellectual, economic, and social interests of young people. Too many universities are now beholden to big business, big sports, and big military contracts. And it is within this set of contexts that we must read the Penn State scandal. Much media attention has been drawn to the fact that Penn State pulls in tens of millions of dollars in football revenue annually, but nothing has been said of the fact that it also receives millions from Defense Department contracts and grants, ranking sixth among universities and colleges receiving funds for military research.

The lure of such lucrative partnerships is all the more irresistible given the cumulative consequences of decades of ever-receding state financial support for higher education. The drivers for the cuts in governmental support arise not only from the neoliberal desire to defund all things public, but also from certain demographic shifts that exacerbate such pressures, like the population's changing age distribution, which pits the young and the aged, along with the institutions and policies that serve them, against one another. Consider that "by 2030, for every retired person there will be only two persons in the labor force. When Social Security was introduced in the 1930s, the ratio was 20:1."[7] The postsecondary sector has also been losing the competition for state funding given the increased demand for health care and other forms of care for an aging population. The criminal justice system has been another beneficiary of increased state support, the fiscal consequences of which have been particularly felt in the state of California. But these shifts only account for part of the financial challenges confronting the postsecondary sector. Indeed, higher education now faces a wave of revolutionary changes similar to those in the period of significant upheaval from 1940–1970.

These are the result of the increasing internationalization of higher education and new competition for students coming from Asia, India, and elsewhere. In addition, the proliferation of digital technologies, which has in turn enabled the phenomenon of online universities, has brought with it greater competition for students from the for-profit educational sector. In large part, the result of these considerable financial pressures has been that the academic mission of the university is now less determined by internal criteria established by faculty researchers with knowledge, expertise, and a commitment to the public good than by external market forces concerned with achieving fiscal stability and, if possible, increasing profit margins. One has only to look closely at the tragedy at Penn State University to understand the potentially catastrophic consequences of this decades-long transformation in higher education.

The Penn State crisis may well prove one of the most serious scandals in the history of college athletics and university administration, while it also reinforces the claim by Paul Krugman that "democratic values are under siege in America."[8] Jerry Sandusky, who coached the Nittany Lions for more than thirty years, used his position of authority at the university as well as at his Second Mile Foundation, a foster home, to lure vulnerable minors into situations in which he preyed on them sexually, having gained unfettered access to male youths through a range of voluntary roles.[9] Sandusky was charged with sexually abusing at least a dozen boys, all of whom were twelve years old or younger when they were attacked. In fact, his adopted son announced during the trial that he was also abused by Sandusky.

On at least three occasions, extending from 1998 to 2002, Sandusky was caught abusing young boys on the Penn State campus. These incidents have been the consistent focus of media attention. In 1998, a distraught mother of a boy who had showered with Sandusky reported the incident to the campus police. A janitor also observed Sandusky performing oral sex on a young boy in a Penn State gym in 2000. Finally, according to the grand jury report in the Sandusky case, Mike McQueary, then a twenty-eight-year-old graduate assistant for the Penn State football team, alleged that in 2002 he saw Sandusky raping a young boy in the shower in the Lasch Football Building on the University Park campus. It therefore took nine years for the police to investigate and finally arrest Sandusky, who was eventually charged with and convicted of forty-five charges of sexual abuse. In October 2012, Judge John Cleland ruled Sandusky a dangerous sexual offender and sentenced him to thirty to sixty years in prison for sexually abusing ten boys—"all of the boys were from disadvantaged homes"—over a fifteen-year period.[10]

As tantalizingly sensational as the media have found these events, the scandal is about much more than a person of influence using his power to sexually assault young boys. This tragic narrative is as much about the shocking lengths to which rich and powerful people and institutions will go in order to cover up their complicity in the most horrific crimes, and to refuse responsibility for egregious violations that threaten their power, influence, and brand names.[11] The desecration of public trust is all the more vile when the persons and institution in question have been assigned the intellectual and moral stewardship of generations of youth. Nor is this the first time that Penn State's senior administration and their beloved Coach Paterno have been guilty of inaction when confronted with evidence of escalating harassment and actual threats to young people's lives on campus—and subsequent efforts to conceal such events.

Beginning in 2000, coterminous with the unfolding Sandusky affair but an altogether separate incident, Black students and football players on the main campus in the town of State College began receiving hate mail and actual death threats. The team's Black quarterback was singled out (it was assumed) for much of the vitriol because he had been arrested off-season for assaulting a white police officer in his home town of Hoboken, New Jersey.[12] The events came to a painful head when the body of a Black male was found near the main campus by police, as one of the death threats had warned. Very little was known about the threats to students on campus—though many appeared at their May 2001 graduation ceremony wearing bullet-proof vests—because neither Penn State officials nor its legendary coach would risk the negative publicity such media attention would inevitably bring.

More than ten years later, when news of the coach's firing broke, the former president of the campus's Black Student Caucus, LaKeisha Wolf, recalled a chilling 2001 meeting with Paterno in which she and other students asked him to talk with the players who were concerned for their safety. Paterno's reply to the students was that he would never do anything to risk the university's reputation. Wolf recalled, "To me that said that even if he had specific knowledge of football players' or students' lives in danger that he wouldn't allow that to risk Penn State's image being tainted and that this is something that has stuck in my mind for the last ten years."[13]

The most recent cover-up appears to have begun in 1998 when the Centre County district attorney, Ray Cricar, did not file charges against Sandusky, in spite of obtaining credible evidence that Sandusky had molested two young boys in a shower at Penn State. Then, in 2000, the janitor who witnessed similar abuse and his immediate superior whom he told about it both failed to report the incident to the police for fear of losing their jobs, only to reveal the story years later. But the cover-up that has attracted the most attention took place in 2003 after Mike McQueary reported to celebrated coach Joe Paterno that he saw Sandusky having anal intercourse with a ten-year-old boy in one of the football facility's showers. Paterno reported the incident to his athletic director, Tim Curley, who then notified Gary Schultz, a senior vice president for finance and business. Both informed President Spanier about the incident. In light of the seriousness of a highly credible and detailed report alleging that a child had been raped, the Penn State administration simply responded by barring Sandusky from bringing young boys onto the university campus. At the end of the day, neither Paterno nor any of the highly positioned university administrators reported the alleged assault of a minor to the police and other proper authorities. Within a week after the story broke in the national media eight years later, Paterno, Schultz, Curley, and Spanier had all been fired. Sandusky was initially charged with "more than 50 charges stemming from accusations that he molested boys for years on Penn State property, in his home and elsewhere."[14] The charges included involuntary sexual intercourse, indecent assault, unlawful contact with a minor, corruption of minors, and endangering the welfare of a minor.

In the most shameful of ironies, the national response to the story has similarly engaged in a covering-up of the violent victimization of children that lies at its core. The young boys who were sexually abused have been relegated to a footnote in a larger and more glamorous story about the rise and sudden fall and eventual death of the legendary Joe Paterno, a larger-than-life athletic icon. Their erasure is also evident in the equally sensational narrative about how the university attempted to hide the horrific details of Sandusky's history of sexual abuse by perpetuating a culture of silence in order to protect the privilege and power of the football and academic elite at Penn State. If any attention was paid at all to distraught and disillusioned youth, it was to focus on the Penn State students who rallied around "Joe-Pa," not on the youth who bore the weight into their adulthood of the egregious crimes of rape, molestation, and abuse. As many critics have pointed out, both dominant media narratives fail to register just how deeply this tragedy descends in terms of what it reveals about our nation's priorities about youth and our increasing unwillingness to shoulder the responsibility—as much moral and intellectual as financial—for their care and development as human beings.

Michael Bérubé rightly asserts that the scandal at Penn State and the ensuing "student riots on behalf of a disgraced football coach" should not be used to condemn the vast majority of teachers, researchers, and students at Penn State, "none of whom had anything to do with this mess."[15] Equally pertinent is his observation that Penn State has a long history of rejecting any viable notion of shared governance and that "decisions, even about academic programs, are made by the central administration, and faculty members are 'consulted' afterward."[16] The American Association of University Professors (AAUP) extended Bérubé's argument, insisting that the lack of faculty governance has to be understood as a consequence of a university system that favors the needs of a sports empire over the educational needs of students, the working conditions of faculty, and health and safety of vulnerable children. As Cary Nelson and Donna Potts point out,

> Recent accounts of the systemic cover-up of allegations of sexual assaults on young boys at Penn State indicate that the unchecked growth of a sports empire held unaccountable to the rest of the university community coincided with the steady erosion of faculty governance. Genuine shared governance, which involves meaningful participation by the faculty in all aspects of an institution, could have resulted in these

alleged crimes being reported to city and state police years ago, and might have spared some of the victims the trauma they endured, and indeed continue to endure, because of the memories that remain, and the legal and judicial processes they still face. The national Council of the American Association of University Professors joins with Penn State faculty member Michael Bérubé in calling on the Penn State administration to begin treating faculty members, and their elected representatives on the Faculty Senate, as equal partners in the institution.[17]

The call for forms of shared governance in which faculty through their elected representatives are treated with respect and exercise power alongside administrators signals an important issue—namely, how many university administrations operate in nontransparent and unaccountable ways that prioritize financial matters over the well-being of students and faculty. At the same time, it is not uncommon for entrepreneurial faculty members to transgress established strategic priorities and circumvent layers of university oversight and adjudication altogether by bringing in earmarked funding for a pet project (through which s/he stands to gain), confident no administrator can refuse cash up front, whatever the Faustian bargain attached to it.

Big money derived from external sources has changed the culture of universities across the United States in other ways as well. For example, in 2010, Penn State made $70,208,584 in total football revenue and $50,427,645 in profits; moreover, it was ranked third among US universities in bringing in football revenue. As part of the huge sports enterprise that is NCAA Division I Football, Penn State and other high-profile "Big Ten" universities not only make big money but also engage in a number of interlocking campus relationships with private-sector corporations. Lucrative deals that generate massive revenue are made through media contracts involving television broadcasts, video games, and Internet programming. Substantial profits flow in from merchandizing football goods, signing advertising contracts, and selling an endless number of commodities from toys to alcoholic beverages and fast food at the stadium, tailgating parties, and sports bars. Yet the flow of capital is not unidirectional. Universities also pay out impressive amounts of money to support such enterprises and to attract star athletes; they hire support staffing from janitorial positions to top physicians in sports medicine and celebrity coaches; they pay to maintain equipment, grounds, stadia, and myriad other associated services. Consider Beaver Stadium—the outdoor college football monument to misplaced academic priorities—which has a seating capacity of 106,572 seats that require cleaning and maintenance. The stadium holds as many people as the entire population of State College, including Penn State students, all of whom require armies of staff to accommodate their needs. In this instance, the circulation of money and power on university campuses mimics its circulation in the corporate world, saturating public spaces and the forms of sociality they encourage with the imperatives of the market. Money from big sports programs also has an enormous influence on shaping agendas *within* the university that play to their advantage, from the neoliberalized, corporatized commitments of an increasingly ideologically incestuous central administration to the allocation of university funds to support the athletic complex and the transfer of scholarship money to athletes rather than academically qualified but financially disadvantaged students. As *Slate* writer J. Bryan Lowder puts it, big sports "wield too much influence over college life. In an institution that is meant to instill the liberal values of critical thinking and an egalitarian sense of equality in its students, having special dining rooms or living quarters for athletes . . . is a bad idea."[18]

In addition to the enormous distraction from academic mission that college sports have come to represent (for the students no less than the administration), one could also argue that these highly profitable and much celebrated sports programs have consolidated a culture of white masculine privilege, gender illiteracy, and sexual violence—violence that the Penn State scandal reveals has extended to both young women and children. We cannot emphasize enough the fact that young men are not biologically predisposed to any of these attitudes or behaviors; they have learned them. Sexism, misogyny, and violence run through US culture like an electric current; big-money sports only add more juice. What should be deeply unsettling and yet remains unspoken in mainstream media analyses is that the youth have also learned these lessons *at the university*, where they have been immersed in a culture that favors entertainment over education—the more physical and destructive the better—competition over collaboration, a worshipful stance toward iconic sports heroes over thoughtful engagement with academic leaders who should inspire by virtue of their intellectual prowess and moral courage, and herd-like adhesion to coach and team over and against one's own capacity for informed judgment and critical analysis. The consolidation of masculine privilege in such instances enshrines patriarchal values and exhibits an astonishing indifference to repeated cases of sexual assaults on college campuses.

Sexual assault is a major problem on college campuses across the United States, as revealed in national statistics demonstrating that "one in five women [was] sexually assaulted while in college, and approximately 81 percent of students experienced some form of sexual harassment during their school years."[19] However, in the years we taught at Penn State, it reached alarming proportions. According to the Center for Women Students on the university's main campus, "At Penn State approximately 100 students sought assistance for sexual assault during the 1996–97 academic year."[20] For those familiar with the behavior often exhibited by victims of sexual violence, the fact that one hundred students came forward in a single year is simply shocking, given the overwhelming reticence most victims feel about reporting attacks. In addition to feeling fear and shame, the reluctance to report an assault is reinforced when the victim believes that it will seldom result in arrest or conviction. Put simply, this means that the extent of cases and many of the consequences of sexual assault, physical abuse, hazing, and violence on college campuses are probably much greater than what is actually known.

The Penn State scandal clearly revealed that women are not the only victims of rising masculinist aggression and sometimes lethal violence, as did a number of stories released in subsequent weeks about sexual abuse at Syracuse University and the death of Robert Champion from hazing by other band members at Florida A&M University. Julian White, the band director, said he had notified the university administration repeatedly about the hazing, but that nothing was done about it. He also claimed that there has been a long history of hazing among college marching bands.[21] With respect to the ritual hazing associated with athletic teams, *New York Times* columnist Joe Nocera argues that at the heart of such violence is the refusal of big sports schools either to acknowledge such behavior or to punish those who engage in it. In the end, Nocera offers the rather anemic proposal that universities should "treat players and coaches the same way everyone else is treated," and in doing so can impart the right lessons.[22] This suggestion may be sincere, but it ignores the larger governmental and institutional forces that make the postsecondary sector so vulnerable and so attractive to sources of external funding.

Perhaps equally alarming is that such banal solutions overlook the dramatic cultural shifts that big-money sports—at the professional no less than the collegiate level—have introduced to both campus life and the mainstream culture, the essence of which can be summed up in the title of a December 2011 opinion column in the *New York Times*: "Are We Not Man Enough?" The thrust (so to speak) of the argument by author Steve Kettmann is that through the influence of sports culture, more and more men have become attracted to steroid use, seeking to feel younger, more powerful, more aggressive, more virile, and more "sexy." In fact, serial steroid abuse scandals in professional baseball in recent years have proven a perverse boon to the "juicing" industry. Kettmann notes:

> Total testosterone prescriptions have skyrocketed, from 1.75 million in 2002 to 4.5 million last year. The demand, said John Hoberman, author of "'Testosterone Dreams," isn't limited to would-be pro athletes; it extends to "police officers, bouncers, biker gangs and the 'anti-aging' industry that provides legal prescriptions to millions of older males."[23]

The illegal, illicit, and dangerous dimensions of steroid use notwithstanding, the shift in cultural norms relating to gender and sexuality raises some troubling questions. What Kettmann pointedly asks of a corporate culture that pushes "juicing" like a new line of soft drinks, we would do well to pose to colleges and universities: "Do we really want to feed a business culture that increasingly elevates cocksure confidence and pushiness above all else, especially if it filters into everyday life? In an era marked by the dangerous decisions of an entire industry full of gung-ho alpha males, shouldn't we be wary of a culture that pushes us even further in that direction?"[24]

To be sure, recent events on a number of college campuses reveal that business culture is not the only culprit in perpetuating the abuses of masculinist power and privilege. Claire Potter, writing in the *Chronicle of Higher Education*, argues that Penn State and universities in general have a vested interest in safeguarding their reputations by covering up acts of sexual violence. For Potter, "Universities substitute private hearings, counseling and mediation for legal proceedings: while women often choose this route, rather than filing felony charges against their assailants, it doesn't always serve their interest to do so. But it always serves the interests of the institution not to have such cases go to court."[25] Given how events have unfolded at the university, Potter's withering charge that Penn State has a greater interest in protecting its brand name than in protecting students—who are reduced to revenue-producing entities rather than seen as young people to whom it has the responsibility intellectually and ethically to shape and inspire—gains considerable force. For Potter, social power at universities dominated by a big sports culture often expresses itself not just in the glory of the game, the reputation of the coaches, or the herd-like devotion to a team, but also in forms of sexual power aimed at abusing female students. Potter wants to move these incidents away from the sports pages and popular media into classrooms where they can be understood within a larger set of economic, social, and political contexts and appropriately challenged.

In writing about Penn State's patriarchal culture and its relationship to big sports programs, Katha Pollitt contributes an insightful analysis about what she calls "the patriarchal aspect of the Penn State scandal." Pollitt writes:

> I know it's predictable and boring, but come on, people! There really is a message here about masculine privilege: the deification of a powerful old man who can do no wrong, an all-male hierarchy protecting itself (hello, pedophile priests), a culture of entitlement and a truly astonishing lack of concern about sexual violence. This last is old news, unfortunately: sexual assaults by athletes are regularly covered up or lightly punished by administrations, even in high school, and society really doesn't care all that much . . . According to *USA Today*, an athlete accused of a sex crime has a very good chance of getting away with it. If Sandusky had abused little girls, let alone teenage or adult women, would he be in trouble today? Or would we say, like the neighbors of an 11-year-old gang-raped in Cleveland, Texas, that she was asking for it?[26]

Pollitt argues that college sports distort academic programs and promote a culture of violence. Her answer to such problems is to close down college sports that make money and simply transform all athletic programs into nonprofit entities, hence removing them from the money, power, and profit-oriented influence that make them a semi-autonomous force on so many college campuses. Sophia McClennen, a professor at Penn State, argues that the fact that all of the people involved in the Penn

State scandal were men not only tarnishes the entire campus but offers no understanding of what alternative models of masculinity might look like, models based on what she calls an "ethical masculinity."[27]

The hardened culture of masculine privilege, big money, and sports at Penn State is reinforced as much through a corporate culture that makes a killing off the entire enterprise as it is through a retrograde culture of illiteracy—defined less in terms of an absence of knowledge about alternatives to normative gender behavior and more in terms of a wilfully embraced ignorance—that is deeply woven into the fabric of campus life. Even and especially in higher education, one cannot escape the visual and visceral triumph of consumer culture, given how campuses have come to look like shopping malls, treat students as customers, confuse education with training, and hawk entertainment and commodification rather than higher learning as the organizing principles of student life. Across universities, the ascendancy of corporate values has resulted in a general decline in student investment in public service, a weakening of social bonds in favor of a survival-of-the-fittest atmosphere, and a pervasive undercutting of the traditional commitments of a liberal arts education: critical and autonomous thinking, a concern for social justice, and a robust sense of community and global citizenship.

As academic labor is linked increasingly to securing financial grants or downsized altogether, students often have little other option than to take courses that have a narrow instrumental purpose, and those who hold powerful administrative positions increasingly spend much of their time raising money from private donors. The notion that the purpose of higher education might be tied to the cultivation of an informed, critical citizenry capable of actively participating and governing in a democratic society has become cheap sloganeering on college advertising copy, losing all credibility in the age of big money, big sports, and corporate influence. Educating students to resist injustice, refuse anti-democratic pressures, or learn how to make authority and power accountable remains at best a receding horizon—in spite of the fact that such values are precisely why universities are pilloried by moneyed Republicans as hotbeds of Marxist radicals.

The displacement of academic mission by a host of external corporate and military forces surely helps to explain the spontaneous outbreak

of rioting by a segment of Penn State students once the university announced that Joe Paterno had been fired as the coach of the storied football team. Rather than holding a vigil for the minors who had been
repeatedly sexually abused, students ran through State College wrecking
cars, flipping a news truck, throwing toilet paper into trees, and destroying public property. J. Bryan Lowder understands this type of behavior
as part of a formative culture of social indifference and illiteracy reinforced by the kind of frat-house insularity produced on college campuses
where sports programs and iconic coaches wield too much influence.
He writes:

> Building monuments to a man whose job is, at the end of the day,
> to teach guys how to move a ball from one place to another, is . . .
> inappropriate. And, worst of all, allowing the idea that anyone is in-
> fallible—be it coach, professor or cleric—to fester and infect a stu-
> dent body to the point that they'd sooner disrupt public order than
> face the truth is downright toxic to the goals of the university. . . .
> Blind, herd-like dedication to a coach or team or school is perni-
> cious. Not only does it encourage the kind of wild, unthinking be-
> havior displayed in the riot, but it also fertilizes the lurid collusion
> and willful ignorance that facilitated these sex crimes in the first
> place. But what to do? As David Haugh asked in the *Chicago Trib-
> une*: "When will [the students] realize, after the buzz wears off and
> sobering reality sinks in, that they were defending the right to cover
> up pedophilia?"[28]

A number of critics have used the Penn State scandal to call attention
to the crisis of moral leadership that characterizes the neoliberal managerial models that now exert a powerful influence over how university administrations function. As democratic culture and values are replaced by
market mentalities and moralities, once laudable commitments to socially
ameliorative reform are replaced by a narrow focus on individual achievement. Collective responsibility and agency have given way to individual
self-interest and the privatization of rights discourse, such that students'
"rights" to freely express sexist or racist views are routinely upheld at the
expense of an entire social group's right to a respectful learning environment free of insult and harassment. The results of such cultural shifts at
institutions like Penn State and Florida A&M have been nothing short
of abhorrent and appalling. As the investment in the public good collapses, leadership cedes to reductive forms of management, concerned

less with big ideas than with appealing to the pragmatic demands of the market, such as raising capital, streamlining resources, and separating learning from any viable understanding of social change. Anything that impedes profit margins and the imperatives of instrumental rationality with its cult of measurements and efficiencies is seen as useless. Within the logic of the new managerialism, there is little concern for matters of justice, fairness, equity, and the general improvement of the human condition insofar as these relate to expanding and deepening the imperatives and ideals of a substantive democracy. Discourses about austerity, budget shortfalls, managing deficits, restructuring, and accountability so popular among college administrators serve largely as a cover "for a recognisably ideological assault on all forms of public provision."[29]

Critics of a now dominant managerial approach to higher education, such as Cathy Davidson, an English professor and former vice-provost at Duke University, point to the recent attacks by campus police on students—highlighting in particular the aggressive pepper-spraying of peacefully demonstrating students at the University of California at Davis in particular—as egregious examples of the failure of university leadership.[30] And so it would appear that too many administrators are incapable of engaging students as students, rather than as consumers or even criminals. Penn State and UC Davis are only two of the latest examples that bespeak an absence of intellectual leadership and moral authority in the postsecondary sector, precisely in that vaunted space essential for the articulation of new ideas and visions that speak to the profound economic, social, and political problems that students confront at this time in history. Goldie Blumenstyk and Jack Stripling argue that ethically challenged leadership at universities such as Penn State suggests broader questions about the moral credibility of postsecondary administrators. They rightfully argue that such scandals send the message that university leaders are more concerned about big money and protecting corporate interests than they are about educating and protecting students.[31] For instance, consider the fate of Graham B. Spanier, who was not only fired as president of Penn State in 2011 but also has been indicted on eight counts, five of which are felonies, that include perjury, obstruction of justice, endangering the welfare of children, and failure to properly report suspected abuse. Nevertheless, Spanier's legal fees are covered by Penn

State and the university, in terminating him "without cause," offered him "$1.2 million in severance pay, $1.2 million in deferred compensation, and $700,000 for a one-year sabbatical that began when he was fired," making him the highest paid "leader of any other major public college" for 2011–2012.[32] It appears that the culture of secrecy has its privileges, at least at Penn State University, even after it was exposed for the corrupt role it played in covering up the horrendous sexual assaults committed against a number of young boys.

One consequence of this failure of leadership is that it continues to feed the negative press that universities have increasingly been saddled with because they are no longer understood to serve the greater good; they are instead seen by many as insular and ineffectual in educating the next generation of critical thinkers and responsible citizens. Not only do they increasingly appear to be the preserve of private and commercial interests, but they have become symbols of bad faith. What is the public to think when university leaders, such as UC Davis's Linda P. Katehi, call in police in riot gear to deal with students setting up tents? Or when university leaders allow billionaires such as the Koch brothers to pledge $1.5 million to Florida State University in exchange for allowing their representatives to "screen and sign off on" faculty hired in the economics department?[33] What happens to the moral high ground and public trust once invested in university leaders when they become complicit with policies that underfund universities and strip students of needed social provisions, while at the same time supporting state budgets that increase prison construction and cut taxes for the rich?

If university presidents cannot defend the university as a public good, but instead, as in the case of Penn State, align themselves with big money, big sports, and the instrumentalist values of finance capital, they will not be able to mobilize the support of the broader public and will have no way to defend themselves against the neoliberal and conservative attempts by state governments to continually defund higher education. In recent years, universities have not thought twice about placing the burden of financial shortfalls on the backs of students—even as that burden grows apace, wrought by austerity measures, or by internal demands for new resources and space to keep up with record growth, or by new competition with international and online educational institutions. All this amounts to a poisonous student tax, one that has the consequence of creating an enormous debt for many students. Penn State has one of the highest tuition rates of any public college—amounting to $14,416 per year. But it is hardly alone in what has become a pitched competition to raise fees. Some public colleges, such as Florida State College, have increased tuition by 49 percent in two years! The lesson here is that abuse of young people comes in many forms, extending from egregious acts of child rape and sexual violence against women to the creation of a generation of students burdened by massive debt and a bleak, if not quite hopeless, jobless future.

The Penn State scandal is indicative of both the ongoing war on youth and the increase in the devaluation of higher education as a democratic public sphere. This is a scandal that has wrought destruction on all levels of schooling and leaves its brutalizing imprint on the social practices and rituals of exchange that shape daily life. Students are no longer seen as harbingers of our dreams. They are no longer treated with the care and concern one would extend to a unique and precious resource; they are no longer the most important symbols of the health and future of a democratic society. Instead, as Jean Comaroff and John Comaroff have insisted, youth have become "creatures of our nightmares, of our social impossibilities and our existential angst."[34] In universities, they are now viewed as revenue streams, potential recruits for the military, or workers to fill proliferating low-wage jobs in the global marketplace. Students are locked into, once again, what has been called "an abyss of failed sociality."[35] They are forced to witness years of a systemic and debilitating disinvestment in their future. They have watched as politicians and state governments have defunded higher education, wasted economic resources on ruinous military adventures, devalued any notion of critical learning in their obsession with high-stakes testing and accountability schemes, and made it impossible for many working- and middle-class students to afford a college education. Instead of entering a world in which they are offered dignity and a good life, young people are aggressively recruited to serve in military death machines, forced to live with their parents because they lack decent employment, and confronted with a future that offers them diminishing resources and even less hope. Surely, they have every right to revolt, not just in London, Montreal, Paris,

Tehran, Toronto, and Damascus but also in Boston, Oakland, and New York City.

All of the aforementioned responses to the scandal at Penn State offer valuable insights into the conditions of its unfolding, and to these we wanted to bring a larger and more historicized conceptual framework. In so doing, we have attempted to connect particularized criticisms with those systemic forces at work nationally and internationally in the transformation of higher education in North America. The Penn State scandal is symptomatic of a much larger set of challenges—and the abuses they almost invariably invite—that are deeply interconnected and mutually informing. On the one hand, Penn State symbolizes the corruption of higher education by big sports, governmental agencies, and corporate power with vested interests and deep pockets. On the other hand, the tragedy can surely be seen as a part of what we have been calling the war on youth. The media emphasis on the fall of Joe Paterno, the indictments and firing of high-ranking university administrators, and the alleged failure of a chain of command, while not incidental to the ongoing abuse, serves ironically to deflect attention from the egregious sexual assault of more than a dozen young boys who have carried this grievous burden into their adulthood. Students, faculty, and administrators also pay a terrible price when a university loses its moral compass and refashions itself in the values, principles, and managerial dictates of a corporate culture.

Neither the media accounts of the rise and fall of a celebrity coach nor what many insiders would like to characterize as a woeful series of administrative miscommunications tell us much about how Penn State is symptomatic of what has happened to a number of universities since at least the mid-1940s, and at a quickened pace since the 1980s. Penn State, like many of its institutional peers, has become a corporate university caught in the grip of the military-industrial complex rather than existing as a semi-autonomous institution driven by an academic mission, public values, and ethical considerations.[36] It is a paradigmatic example of mission drift, one marked by a fundamental shift of the university away from its role as a vital democratic public sphere toward an institutional willingness to subordinate educational values to market values. As Peter Seybold has suggested, the Penn State scandal is indicative of the ongoing corruption of teaching, research, and pedagogy that has taken place in higher education.[37] Beyond the classroom and the lab, evidence of ongoing corporatization abounds: bookstores and food services are franchised; part-time labor replaces full-time faculty; classes are oversold; and online education replaces face-to-face teaching, less as a pedagogical innovation and more as a means to deal with the capacity issues now confronting those universities that pursued financial sustainability through aggressive growth.[38]

The corporate university is descending more and more into what has been called "an output fundamentalism," prioritizing market mechanisms that emphasize productivity and performance measures that make a mockery of quality scholarship and diminish effective teaching—scholarly commitments are increasingly subordinated to bringing in bigger grants to supplement operational budgets negatively impacted by the withdrawal of governmental funding.[39] In the face of such pressures, faculty have experienced unprovoked employer militancy in the name of austerity at universities across the country and the world over in Egypt, Venezuela, Chile, Madagascar, New Zealand, the United Kingdom, and Australia. Higher education no longer makes a claim to those principles or goals grounded in a belief that the health and sustainability of democratic nations depend on the informed judgments, ethical standards, and modes of critical engagement exercised by citizens within the societies they inhabit.

In addition, the student experience has hardly been untouched by these shock waves, which have further undermined the genuinely intellectual, financial, social, and democratic needs of undergraduate and graduate students alike. Young people are increasingly devalued as knowledgeable, competent, and socially responsible, in spite of the fact that their generation will inevitably be the leaders of tomorrow. Put bluntly, many university administrators demonstrate a notable lack of imagination, conceiving of students primarily in market terms and showing few qualms about subjecting young people to forms of education as outmoded as the factory assembly lines they emulate. Campus extracurricular activities unfold in student commons designed in the image of shopping centers and high-end entertainment complexes. Clearly, students are not perceived as worthy of the kinds of financial, intellectual, and cultural investments necessary to enhance their capacities to be critical and informed individual and social agents. Nor are they provided with the knowledge and skills necessary to understand and negotiate the complex political, economic, and social worlds in which they live and the many challenges they face now and will face in the future. Instead of being institutions that foster democracy, public engagement, and civic literacy, universities and colleges now seduce and entertain students as prospective clients, or, worse yet, act as recruitment offices for the armed forces.[40] Put simply, students are being sold on a certain type of collegial experience that often has very little to do with the quality of education they might receive, while university leaders appear content to have faculty provide entertainment and distraction for students in between football games.

Whereas US universities are caught in the iron grip of the "age of austerity," just beyond its so-called ivory towers, citizens are witnessing the mega-prosperity of a rich elite reminiscent of the Gilded Age.[41] Despite their deeply entwined relation with consumer culture, today's youth are well acquainted with austerity, given the disproportionate impact such measures have on their lives, and know very little about prosperity, with the exception of what they see on the screen. The return to an age of greed and corporate monopolies, accompanied by a brutal survival-of-the-fittest ethic, is made obvious by the dreamworlds of consumption circulated by the mass media, and it is also evident in the actions of right-wing politicians who want to initiate policies that take the country back to the late nineteenth century—a time in which the reforms of the New Deal, the Great Society, and the Progressive Era did not exist.

This Gilded Age was a period in which robber barons, big oil, railroad magnates, and others among the superrich spread their corrupting influence throughout the political, economic, and cultural landscapes— without having to deal with irritating social reforms such as Social Security, Medicare, Medicaid, child labor laws, environmental protections, affirmative action, civil rights, union rights, antitrust laws, a progressive income tax, and a host of others. This was a period when money flowed and privilege for the very few shaped practically all aspects of American life, making a mockery out of democracy and imposing massive amounts of human suffering on the vast majority of Americans. Women could not vote and were seen as second-class citizens, Blacks were treated harshly under Jim Crow policies, young people were exploited through brutal labor conditions, education was limited to the moneyed classes, inequality in wealth and income reached extreme disparities, slums festered, and politicians were in the pocket of the rich.

In time, protest movements emerged among students, workers, unions, women, people of color, and others to address these injustices. Labor became a potent force in the first half of the twentieth century. Then Blacks mobilized a formidable civil rights movement, and women's groups organized to address a range of injustices. Students were involved in these as well and advanced the cause of the antiwar movement, thereby infusing new life into the drive for participatory democracy both within and outside of higher education. By the early 1970s, gay, lesbian, and transgender groups were also visibly fighting to gain basic civil rights. These movements produced notable victories in deepening and expanding the promise and possibilities of a substantive democracy. Yet they quickly became the focus of a powerfully organized backlash on the part of conservatives, who organized a right-wing cultural revolution that successfully rolled back many of the progressive gains that had emerged in the decades of struggle that came to define much of the twentieth century.

The attack on higher education has gained considerable momentum since the 1980s and must be understood as part of a much larger assault on all aspects of the welfare state, social provisions, public goods, and democracy itself. Under a regime of neoliberal capitalism with its savage assaults on the public waged through deregulation, privatization, and commodification, all those public spheres that provide the values, social relations, knowledge, and skills to participate meaningfully in the democratic life of the nation are disappearing. And with these, we are losing opportunities to learn how to translate personal troubles to public issues, show respect and care for the rights of others, and recognize those antidemocratic pressures that make a mockery out of freedom and smother the discourses of justice, equality, and social rights. As big money, big sports, and the culture of illiteracy, violence, and corruption they inspire make clear, schooling is no longer about educating students. Rather, it is about exploiting them when not infantilizing them in the name of entertainment. Matters of politics, ethics, and social responsibility are increasingly being replaced with individual self-interest motivated by the imperatives of gaining a competitive edge and instant gratification. What the Penn State scandal reveals is the urgency with which universities must resist all attempts to be harnessed to the commercial demands of big sports, the financial needs of corporations, or the violence of the national security state.

In the aftermath of the Penn State scandal, the university's Board of Trustees commissioned former federal judge and FBI director Louis J. Freeh to investigate how the university handled the Sandusky affair. The Freeh Report makes clear that there was a concerted attempt to cover up the acts of a serial predator, Jerry Sandusky, while willfully disregarding the welfare of the children he abused. In damning fashion, the report stated:

> Our most saddening and sobering finding is the total disregard for the safety and welfare of Sandusky's child victims by the most senior leaders at Penn State. The most powerful men at Penn State failed to take any steps for 14 years to protect the children who Sandusky victimized. Messrs. Spanier, Schultz, Paterno and Curley never demonstrated, through actions or words, any concern for the safety and well-being of Sandusky's victims until after Sandusky's arrest. . . . Taking into account the available witness statements and evidence, it is more reasonable to conclude that, in order to avoid the consequences of bad publicity, the most powerful leaders at Penn State University—Messrs. Spanier, Schultz, Paterno and Curley—repeatedly concealed critical facts relating to Sandusky's child abuse from the authorities, the Board of Trustees, Penn State community, and the public at large. Although concern to treat the child abuser humanely was expressly stated, no such sentiments were ever expressed by them for Sandusky's victims.[42]

Given the reporting that took place as the scandal unfolded, much of this is not news, though the report makes clear the nature and depth of the cover-up and provides some important new details. While the Freeh Report reveals that the cover-up at the top of the Penn State administration "was an active agreement to conceal," it raises further questions about how the justice system works in this country when it comes to prosecuting the rich and powerful, who engage increasingly in a bottomless pit of corruption and moral irresponsibility. At his press conference, Freeh, when asked if criminal charges should be brought against a number of people, including former President Spanier, replied that "it's up to others to decide whether that's criminal." Freeh's reply suggests he was acting cautiously, given that some of the people who hired him might be indicted, but he unknowingly touched on another related and important issue. That is, justice in America works primarily for the rich and powerful and against the poor and marginalized. Freeh's response or equivocation reveals what is well known—the rich and powerful rarely get prosecuted for their crimes or what the *Economist* has called "the rotten heart of finance."[43] Just ask the CEOs who run Barclays, JPMorgan Chase, Citibank, GlaxoSmithKline, and so on.

Soon after the release of the Freeh Report, the NCAA, the governing body of US college sports, announced a series of unprecedented sanctions against Penn State University. These included a record $60 million fine, a reduction in football scholarships, the banning of Penn State from participating in bowl games and any other post-season play for four years, and the nullification of all wins by the Penn State football team from 1998 to 2011. What is unprecedented in this judgment is that the NCAA involved themselves in a case that should have best been resolved as a civil and criminal matter. Not only is the verdict overly harsh, draining money from university academic programs that could benefit disadvantaged students, but it is also hypocritical. As Dave Zirin points out, the NCAA is a "multi-billion dollar entity that builds its money on the idea of turning coaches into deities, turning football programs into too-big-to fail operations, and turning players into basically unpaid campus workers as opposed to student athletes. That's the root of the problem here."[44]

What we have here are echoes of the big banks, corporations, and financial services regulating themselves and "acting without oversight and with the kind of heavy hand that precludes any semblance of democratic oversight."[45] There is no moral high ground to be found in the NCAA's actions, for, as Zirin reminds us, the NCAA has "morphed into this kind of operation where they negotiate $10.8 billion television deals, where they sell the likenesses of players to video games, where they sell the likenesses of players on credit cards for well-heeled boosters. This is what the NCAA has become."[46] It is no wonder that the *Chronicle of Higher Education* published a story, without critical commentary, shamelessly suggesting that faculty and students were the real victims of the Penn State scandal. As Robin Wilson reports in the story, without irony, "Penn State professors and students say they sometimes feel like victims themselves, as they are confronted by outsiders who want to blame them, and the entire university for what Mr. Sandusky did. They wonder how they will ever move on."[47]

One indication of what it would take for Penn State to move on can be gleaned from the decision on the part of the university to pay $59.7 million to twenty-six young men who were victims of sexual abuse. The current university president of Penn State, Rodney Erickson, called the settlement "another step forward in the healing process for those hurt by Mr. Sandusky, and another step forward for Penn State."[48] Settling with the victims of such abuse is no small matter, but if the university truly wants to move forward it must also address with due diligence the elimination of those economic, political, and cultural forces that gave rise to a culture of hypermasculinity and sexual violence—a culture that saturates the larger society and one that Penn State willingly inhabited and celebrated with impunity. Clearly, it will take a great deal more than a much-publicized financial settlement and the punishment of those responsible for the sexual crimes committed against so many young boys for Penn State to come to grips with its sordid history and embrace of a business-oriented sports culture that refused to recognize the damage it did both to its own mission and to the victims of its concentrated bureaucratic power and moral turpitude.

Let's be clear, what is on trial here is not simply those who colluded to protect the reputation of a storied football program and the reputation of Penn State University but a society governed by large corporate entities, radicalized market-driven values, a survival-of-the-fittest ethic, and an unregulated drive for profit-making regardless of the human and social costs. This is an ethic that views many children and young people as disposable, refusing to acknowledge its responsibility to future generations while creating the social, economic, and political conditions in which the pain and suffering of young people simply disappear. As a number of recent banking scandals reveal, big money and the institutions it creates now engage unapologetically in massive criminal behavior and corruption, but the individuals who head these corporations, extending from JPMorgan Chase Bank to Barclays, are rarely prosecuted. The message is clear. Once again, crime pays for the rich and powerful. We can only understand what happened to the young victims at Penn State if we also acknowledge what recently was revealed about the criminal actions against children perpetrated by pharmaceutical giant GlaxoSmith-Kline. In this instance, Glaxo illegally marketed Paxil to children, gave kickbacks to doctors, and made false claims about the drug, even though one major clinical trial found "that teens who took the drug for depression were more likely to attempt suicide than those receiving placebo pills."[49] Penn State and Glaxo are symptomatic of a much larger shift in the culture and the relations of power that shape it.

Rather than representing a society's dreams and hope for the future, young people, especially poor white and minority children, have become a nightmare, an excess, and disposable in the age of casino capitalism and big money. It is crucial that the American public connect the kind of institutional abuse we see from Penn State, GlaxoSmithKline, and Barclays with the values and relations of power that are responsible for a society in which 53 percent of college graduates are jobless, social provisions for young people are being slashed, corporations get tax deductions while state governments eliminate vital public services, and students assume a massive debt because it is easier for the federal government to fund wars and invest in prisons than in public and higher education. Connect these dots and Penn State becomes only one shameful and corrupt marker in a much larger scandal that reveals an ongoing and aggressive war on youth. Everywhere we look, young people are under siege. Twenty percent of young people live in poverty and over 42 percent live in low-income homes. Young people now find themselves in debt, jobless, incarcerated, or unemployed. Stories about young people being denied the right to vote, being abused in juvenile detention centers, taking on jobs that pay the minimum wage or worse, living at home with their parents while unemployed, and facing a bleak future rarely seem to arouse the concerns of the American public or its governing politicians. All the while, the ruling corporate and financial elite use their power to punish those marginalized by class, race, and ethnicity—slashing social benefits, increasing tuition, refusing to abolish punitive bankruptcy laws, denigrating young people as lazy, and refusing to invest in their future.

Against the notion that the neoliberal market should organize and mediate every human activity, including how young people are educated, we need a vision for democratic politics and institutions that guides the creation of a formative culture that teaches students and others that "they are not fated to accept the given regime of educational degradation" and the eclipse of civic and intellectual culture in the academy.[50] What is crucial to recognize is that higher education may be the most viable public sphere left in which democratic principles, modes of knowledge, and values can be taught, defended, and exercised. Surely, public higher education remains one of the most important institutions in which a country's commitment to young people can be made visible and concrete. The scandal at Penn State illuminates a profound crisis in American life, one that demands critical reflection—for those inside and outside the academy—on the urgent challenges facing higher education as part of the larger interconnecting crisis of youth and democracy. It demands that we connect the dots between the degradation of higher education and those larger economic, political, cultural, and social forces that benefit from such an unjust and unethical state of affairs—and which, in the end, young people will pay for with their sense of possibility and their hope for the future.

Learning from the Penn State scandal requires that faculty, parents, artists, cultural workers, and others listen to students who are mobilizing all across the country and around the world as part of a broader effort to reclaim a democratic language and political vision. These insightful and motivated youth are rejecting the narrow prescriptions and heavy burdens that would be foisted upon them, and choosing instead to invent a new understanding of what it means to make substantive democracy possible (see chapter 6). Until we understand how the larger culture of political, institutional, and economic corruption abuses young people, rewards the rich, and destroys democracy, Penn State will remain a sideshow that simply distracts from the real issue of what constitutes child abuse: the scandal of Penn State represents the scandal of America.

CHAPTER FIVE

On the Urgency for Public Intellectuals in the Academy

"The university is a critical institution or it is nothing."
—**Stuart Hall**

I want to begin with the words of the late African American poet, Audre Lorde, a formidable writer, educator, feminist, gay rights activist, and public intellectual, who displayed a relentless courage in addressing the injustices she witnessed all around her. She writes:

> Poetry is not a luxury. It is a vital necessity of our existence. It forms the quality of the light within which we predicate our hopes and dreams toward survival and change, first made into language, then into idea, then into more tangible action. Poetry is the way we help give name to the nameless so it can be thought. The farthest horizons of our hopes and fears are cobbled by our poems, carved from the rock experiences of our daily lives.[1]

And although Lorde refers to poetry here, I think a strong case can be made that the attributes she ascribes to poetry can also be attributed to higher education—a genuine higher education.[2] In this case, an education that includes history, philosophy, all of the arts and humanities, the criticality of the social sciences, the world of discovery made manifest

131

by natural science, and the transformations in health and in law wrought by the professions that are at the heart of what it means to know something about the human condition. Lorde's defense of poetry as a mode of education is especially crucial for those of us who believe that the university is nothing if it is not a public trust and social good: that is, a critical institution infused with the promise of cultivating intellectual insight, the imagination, inquisitiveness, risk-taking, social responsibility, and the struggle for justice. At best, universities should be at the "heart of intense public discourse, passionate learning, and vocal citizen involvement in the issues of the times."[3] It is in the spirit of such an ideal that I first want to address those larger economic, social, and cultural interests that threaten this notion of education, especially higher education.

As I have stated throughout this book, in spite of being discredited by the economic recession of 2008, market fundamentalism or unfettered free-market capitalism has once again become a dominant force for producing a corrupt financial service sector, runaway environmental devastation, egregious amounts of human suffering, and the rise of what has been called the emergence of "finance as a criminalized, rogue industry."[4] The Gilded Age is back with huge profits for the ultra-rich, banks, and other large financial service institutions while at the same time increasing impoverishment and misery for the middle and working classes. The American dream, celebrating economic and social mobility, has been transformed into not just an influential myth but also a poisonous piece of propaganda. One indication of the undoing of the American dream into an American nightmare can be seen in the fact that "the most striking change in American society in the past generation—roughly since Ronald Reagan was elected President—has been the increase in the inequality of income and wealth" and the concentration of wealth into fewer and fewer hands.[5]

I want to revisit the state of inequality in America because any discourse about the purpose of higher education and the responsibility of academics as public intellectuals has to begin with how matters of wealth and power are changing the purpose and meaning of education, teaching, and the conditions under which academics now labor. The current assaults on higher education cannot be removed from the war on youth, unions, students, public servants, and the public good. Moreover, the financial crisis of the last few years has become a cover for advancing the neoliberal revolution and assault on higher education. For example, when University of Texas at Austin president Bill Powers argues for what he calls a "business productivity initiative" to save money, he is not simply responding to a projected budget shortfall. Under the dictates of neoliberal austerity policies, he is changing the nature of education at UT by arguing that the research initiatives will be evaluated and deemed most profitable in terms of their benefits to various industries. Those academic courses and departments that are aligned with and provide potential profits for industry will receive the most funding. As Reihaneh Hajibeigi points out, "this means liberal arts majors and departments will be given minimal funding if the benefits of those studies aren't seen as being profitable to UT."[6]

The figures listed below point to a different kind of crisis, one that puts in peril the most basic and crucial institutions that make a democracy possible along with the formative culture and critical agents that support and protect it. We need to be reminded as part of the pedagogy of public memory that these figures matter, given their role as both flashpoints that signal a rupture from the increasingly lost promises of a democracy to come and a call to conscience in addressing the horrors of the growing antidemocratic tendencies that make clear the presence of an emerging authoritarianism in the United States. We live at a time of immense contradictions, problems, and antagonisms, and such figures offer us a way to both make visible disparities in power relations and to address the necessity of combining moral outrage with ongoing political struggles. If democracy needs a keen sense of the common good and a robust understanding of education as a public good, these statistics signify the death of both—a vanishing point at which the ideas, policies, and institutions that sustain democratic public life and civic education dissolve into the highest reaches of power, avarice, and wealth.

The United States now "has the highest level of inequality of any of the advanced countries."[7] One measure of the upward shift in wealth is evident in Joseph E. Stiglitz's claim that "in the 'recovery' of 2009–2010, the top 1% of US income earners captured 93% of the income growth."[8] The vast inequities and economic injustice at the heart of the mammoth gap in income and wealth become even more evident in a number of revealing statistics. For example, "the average pay for people working in U.S. investment banks is over $375,000 while senior officers at Goldman Sachs averaged $61 million each in compensation for 2007."[9] In addition, the United States beats out every other developed nation in producing extreme income and wealth inequalities for 2012. The top 1 percent now owns "about a third of the American people's total net worth, over 40 percent of America' total financial wealth . . . and half of the nation's total income growth."[10] Andrew Gavin Marshall provides even more granular figures. He writes:

> Looking specifically at the United States, the top 1% own more than 36% of the national wealth and more than the combined wealth of the bottom 95%. Almost all of the wealth gains over the previous decade went to the top 1%. In the mid-1970s, the top 1% earned 8% of all national income; this number rose to 21% by 2010.[11]

In this instance, the absolute acceleration of the gap in income and especially wealth results in the quickening of misery, impoverishment, and hardship for many Americans while furthering what might be called a thin and failed conception of democracy. At the same time, political illiteracy and religious fundamentalism have cornered the market on populist rage, providing support for an escalating political and economic crisis.[12] Pointing to some of the ugly extremes produced by such inequality, Paul Buchheit includes the following: each of the right-wing, union-busting Koch brothers made $3 billion per hour from their investments; the difference in hourly wages between CEOs and minimum-wage workers was "$5,000.00 per hour vs. $7.25 per hour," "The poorest 47% of Americans have no wealth," and "the 400 wealthiest Americans own as much wealth as 80 million families—62% of America."[13]

At the risk of being repetitious, I want to stress a range of statistics that may say little about cause and effect but that do, as Bauman notes, "challenge our all-too-common ethical apathy and moral indifference . . . they also show, and beyond reasonable doubt, that the idea of the pursuit of a good life and happiness being a self-referential business for each individual to pursue and perform on his or her own is an idea that is grossly misconceived."[14] While wealth and income are redistributed to the top 1 percent, the United States fails to provide adequate health and safety for its children and citizens. Both a 2007 UNICEF report and a 2009

OECD study ranked the United States near the bottom of the advanced industrial countries for children's health and safety and twenty-seventh out of thirty for child poverty. Median wealth for Hispanic and Black households has been reduced to almost zero as a result of the recession; young people are increasing unable to attend college because of soaring tuition rates, and those that do attend are increasingly strapped with unmanageable debts and few jobs that will enable them to pay off their loans. More than 50 million Americans lack health care and many will die as a result of state cutbacks in Medicaid programs. The justice system is racially and class bound and increasingly incarcerates large numbers of poor minorities of class and color while refusing to prosecute hundreds of executives responsible for billions of dollars lost due to fraud and corruption.[15]

It is important to note that the violence of unnecessary hardship and suffering produced by neoliberal ideology and values is not restricted to the economic realm. Neoliberal violence also wages war against the modernist legacy of "questioning the givens, in philosophy as well as in politics and art."[16] Ignorance is no longer a liability in neoliberal societies but a political asset endlessly mediated through a capitalist imaginary that thrives on the interrelated registers of consumption, privatization, and depoliticization. Manufactured ignorance is the new reigning mode of dystopian violence, spurred on by a market-driven system that celebrates a passion for consumer goods over a passionate desire for community affairs, the well-being of the other, and the principles of a democratic society.[17] As the late Cornelius Castoriadis brilliantly argues, under neoliberalism, the thoughtless celebration of economic progress becomes the primary legitimating principle to transform "human beings into machines for producing and consuming."[18]

Under such circumstances, to cite C. W. Mills, we are seeing the breakdown of democracy, the disappearance of critical intellectuals, and "the collapse of those public spheres which offer a sense of critical agency and social imagination."[19] In the last few decades, we have seen the forces of market fundamentalism attempt to strip education of its public values, critical content, and civic responsibilities as part of its broader goal of creating new subjects wedded to consumerism, risk-free relationships, and the destruction of the social state. Tied largely to instrumental ideologies and measurable paradigms, many institutions of higher education are now committed almost exclusively to economic goals, such as preparing students for the workforce and transforming faculty into an army of temporary subaltern labor—all done as part of an appeal to rationality, one that eschews matters of inequality, power, and ethical grammars of suffering.[20] Universities have not only strayed from their democratic mission, they also seem immune to the plight of students who have to face a harsh new world of high unemployment, the prospect of downward mobility, debilitating debt, and a future that mimics the failures of the past.

The question of what kind of education is needed for students to be informed and active citizens is rarely asked.[21] In the absence of a democratic vision of schooling, it is not surprising that some colleges and universities are not only increasingly opening their classrooms to the Defense Department and national intelligence agencies but also aligning themselves with those commanding apparatuses that make up the punishing state.[22] In the first instance, one cannot but be puzzled by Yale University's decision to allow the Department of Defense to fund the US Special Operations Command Center of Excellence for Operational Neuroscience—a program designed to "teach special operations personnel the art of 'conversational,' and 'cross cultural intelligence gathering, and pay volunteers from the community's vast immigrant population (mainly poor Hispanics, Moroccans and Iraqis) to serve as test subjects."[23] In other words, Yale would invite "military intelligence to campus to hone their wartime interrogation techniques on the local nonwhite population."[24] In another symptomatic instance of mission drift, Florida Atlantic University in Boca Raton attempted to put together a deal to rename its football stadium after the GEO Group, a private prison corporation "whose record is marred by human rights abuses, by lawsuits, by unnecessary deaths of people in their custody and a whole series of incidents."[25] One Mississippi judge called GEO "an inhuman cesspool."[26] And as Dave Zirin points out, GEO's efforts to spend $6 million "to rename the home of the FAU Owls was an effort to normalize their name: GEO Group, just another corporation you can trust, the Xerox of private prisons."[27] As a result of numerous protests by FAU students, faculty, and outside civil rights groups, the company withdrew its $6 million donation.[28] The "Stop Owlcatraz" campaign exposed not only the often poisonous links between corporations and universities but also the workings of a "deeply racist system of mass incarceration" that should be high on the list of issues faculty and students should be addressing as part of a broader campaign to connect the academy to public life.[29]

The antidemocratic values that drive free-market fundamentalism are embodied in policies now attempting to shape diverse levels of higher education all over the globe. The script has now become overly familiar and increasingly taken for granted, especially in the United States. As I have mentioned throughout this book, shaping the neoliberal framing of public and higher education is a corporate-based ideology that embraces standardizing the curriculum, top-down governing structures, courses that promote entrepreneurial values, and the reduction of all levels of education to job training sites. For example, one university is offering a master's degree to students who commit to starting a high-tech company while another allows career advisers to teach capstone research seminars in the humanities. In one of these classes, the students were asked to "develop a 30-second commercial on their 'personal brand.'"[30]

Central to this neoliberal view of higher education is a market-driven paradigm that wants to eliminate tenure, turn the humanities into a job preparation service, and reduce most faculty to the status of part-time and temporary workers, if not simply a new subordinate class of disempowered educators. The indentured service status of such faculty is put on full display as some colleges have resorted to using "temporary service agencies to do their formal hiring."[31] Faculty in this view are regarded as simply another cheap army of reserve labor, a powerless group that universities are eager to exploit in order to increase the bottom line while disregarding the needs and rights of academic laborers and the quality of education that students deserve.

There is little talk in this view of higher education about shared governance between faculty and administrators, nor of educating students as critical citizens rather than potential employees of Walmart. There are few attempts to affirm faculty as scholars and public intellectuals who have both a measure of autonomy and power. Instead, faculty members are increasingly defined less as intellectuals than as technicians and grant writers. Students fare no better in this debased form of education and are treated either as consumers or as restless children in need of high-energy entertainment—as was made clear in the 2012 Penn State scandal, as mentioned in chapter 4. Nor is there any attempt to legitimate higher education as a fundamental sphere for creating the agents necessary for an aspiring democracy. This neoliberal, corporatized model of higher education exhibits a deep disdain for critical ideals, public spheres, knowledge, and practices that are not directly linked to market values, business culture, the economy, or the production of short-term financial gains. In fact, the commitment to democracy is beleaguered, viewed less as a crucial educational investment than as a distraction that gets in the way of connecting knowledge and pedagogy to the production of material and human capital. Such modes of education do not foster a sense of organized responsibility central to a democracy. Instead, they foster what might be called a sense of organized irresponsibility—a practice that underlies the economic Darwinism and civic corruption at the heart of American politics.

Higher Education and the Crisis of Legitimacy

In the United States, many of the problems in higher education can be linked to low funding, the domination of universities by market mechanisms, the rise of for-profit colleges, the intrusion of the national security state, and the lack of faculty self-governance, all of which not only contradicts the culture and democratic value of higher education but also makes a mockery of the very meaning and mission of the university as a democratic public sphere. Decreased financial support for higher education stands in sharp contrast to increased support for tax benefits for the rich, big banks, the defense budget, and megacorporations. Rather than enlarge the moral imagination and critical capacities of students, too many universities are now wedded to producing would-be hedge fund managers, depoliticized students, and creating modes of education that promote a "technically trained docility."[32] Strapped for money and increasingly defined in the language of corporate culture, many universities are now "pulled or driven principally by vocational, [military], and economic considerations while increasingly removing academic knowledge production from democratic values and projects."[33] While there has never been a golden age when higher education was truly liberal and democratic, the current attack on higher education by religious fundamentalists, corporate power, and the apostles of neoliberal capitalism appears unprecedented in terms of both its scope and intensity. The issue here is not to idealize a past that has been lost but to reclaim elements of a history in which the discourses of critique and possibility offered an alternative vision of what form higher education might take in a substantive democratic society.

Universities are losing their sense of public mission, just as leadership in higher education is being banalized and stripped of any viable democratic vision. College presidents are now called CEOs and move without apology between interlocking corporate and academic boards. With few exceptions, they are praised as fundraisers but rarely acknowledged for the force of their ideas. In this new Gilded Age of money and profit, academic subjects gain stature almost exclusively through their exchange value on the market. It gets worse. In one egregious recent example, BB&T Corporation, a financial holdings company, gave a $1 million gift to Marshall University's business school on the condition that *Atlas Shrugged* by Ayn Rand (Paul Ryan's favorite book) be taught in a course. What are we to make of the integrity of a university when it accepts a monetary gift from a corporation or rich patron demanding as part of the agreement the power to specify what is to be taught in a course or how a curriculum should be shaped? Some corporations and universities now believe that what is taught in a course is not an academic decision but a market consideration.

Questions regarding how education might enable students to develop a keen sense of prophetic justice, utilize critical analytical skills, and cultivate an ethical sensibility through which they learn to respect the rights of others are becoming increasingly irrelevant in a market-driven and militarized university. As the humanities and liberal arts are downsized, privatized, and commodified, higher education finds itself caught in the paradox of claiming to invest in the future of young people while offering them few intellectual, civic, and moral supports.[34]

If the commercialization, commodification, and militarization of the university continue unabated, higher education will become yet another of a number of institutions incapable of fostering critical inquiry, public debate, acts of justice, and public values.[35] But the calculating logic of the corporate university does more than diminish the moral and political vision and practices necessary to sustain a vibrant democracy and an engaged notion of social agency. It also undermines the development of public spaces where critical dialogue, social responsibility, and social justice are pedagogically valued—viewed as fundamental to providing students with the knowledge and skills necessary to address the problems facing the nation and the globe. Such democratic public spheres are especially important at a time when any space that produces "critical thinkers capable of putting existing institutions into question" is under siege by powerful economic and political interests.[36]

Higher education has a responsibility not only to search for the truth regardless of where it may lead but also to educate students to be capable of holding authority and power politically and morally accountable, while at the same time sustaining "the idea and hope of a public culture."[37] Though questions regarding whether the university should serve *strictly* public rather than private interests no longer carry the weight of forceful criticism they did in the past, such questions are still crucial in addressing the purpose of higher education and what it might mean to imagine the university's full participation in public life as the protector and promoter of democratic values. Toni Morrison is instructive in her comment that "if the university does not take seriously and rigorously its role as a guardian of wider civic freedoms, as interrogator of more and more complex ethical problems, as servant and preserver of deeper democratic practices, then some other regime or ménage of regimes will do it for us, in spite of us, and without us."[38]

What needs to be understood is that higher education may be one of the few public spheres left where knowledge, values, and learning offer a glimpse of the promise of education for nurturing public values, critical hope, and a substantive democracy. It may be the case that everyday life is increasingly organized around market principles, but confusing a market-determined society with democracy hollows out the legacy of higher education, whose deepest roots are moral, not commercial. This is a particularly important insight in a society where not only is the free circulation of ideas being replaced by ideas managed by the dominant media, but also where critical ideas are increasingly viewed or dismissed as banal, if not reactionary. Celebrity worship and the commodification of culture now constitute a powerful form of mass illiteracy and increasingly permeate all aspects of the educational force of the wider cultural apparatus. But mass illiteracy does more than depoliticize the public; it also becomes complicit with the suppression of dissent. Intellectuals who engage in dissent and "keep the idea and hope of a public culture alive,"[39] are often dismissed as irrelevant, extremist, elitist, or un-American. We now live in a world in which the politics of dis-imagination dominates, such that any writing or public discourse that bears witness to a critical and alternative sense of the world is dismissed as having nothing to do with the bottom line. Imagine how this quote from the late and great public intellectual James Baldwin would be received today.

> You write in order to change the world knowing perfectly well that you probably can't, but also knowing that [writing] is indispensable to the world. The world changes according to the way people see it, and if you alter even by a millimeter the way people look at reality, then you can change it.[40]

In a dystopian society, utopian thought becomes sterile and even Baldwin's prophetic words are out of place, though more important than ever. In spite of the legacy and existence of public intellectuals that extend from Baldwin and C. Wright Mills to Naomi Klein and Barbara Ehrenreich, we live in a new and more dangerous historical conjuncture. Anti-public intellectuals now dominate the larger cultural landscape, all too willing to flaunt co-option and reap the rewards of venting insults at their assigned opponents while being reduced to the status of paid servants of powerful economic interests. But the problem is not simply with the rise of a right-wing cultural apparatus dedicated to preserving the power and wealth of the rich and corporate elite. As Stuart Hall recently remarked, the state of the Left is also problematic in that, as he puts it, "The left is in trouble. It's not got any ideas, it's not got any independent analysis of its own, and therefore it's got no vision. It just takes the temperature. . . . It has no sense of politics being educative, of politics changing the way people see things."[41]

The issue of politics being educative, of recognizing that matters of pedagogy, subjectivity, and consciousness are at the heart of political and moral concerns should not be lost on either academics or those concerned about not only what might be called writing in public but also the purpose and meaning of higher education itself. Democracy places civic demands upon its citizens, and such demands point to the necessity of an education that is broad-based, critical, and supportive of meaningful civic values, participation in self-governance, and democratic leadership. Only through such a formative and critical educational culture can students learn how to become individual and social agents, rather than merely disengaged spectators, able both to think otherwise and to act upon civic commitments that "necessitate a reordering of basic power arrangements" fundamental to promoting the common good and producing a meaningful democracy.[42] This is not a matter of imposing values on education and in our classrooms. The university and the classroom are already defined through power-laden discourses and a myriad of values that are often part of the hidden structures of educational politics and pedagogy. A more accurate position would be, as Toni Morrison notes, to take up our responsibility "as citizen/scholars in the university to accept the consequences of our own value-redolent roles." She continues: "Like it or not, we are paradigms of our own values, advertisements of our own ethics—especially noticeable when we presume to foster ethics-free, value-lite education."[43]

Dreaming the Impossible

Reclaiming higher education as a democratic public sphere begins with the crucial project of challenging, among other things, those market fundamentalists, religious extremists, and rigid ideologues who harbor a deep disdain for critical thought and healthy skepticism, and who look with displeasure upon any form of education that teaches students to read the word and the world critically. The radical imagination in this discourse is considered dangerous and a dire threat to political authorities. Needless to say, education is not only about issues of work and economics, but also about questions of justice, social freedom, and the capacity for democratic agency, action, and change, as well as the related issues of power, inclusion, and social responsibility.[44] These are educational and political issues, and they should be addressed as part of a broader effort to reenergize the global struggle for social justice and democracy.

Martin Luther King Jr. is instructive here because he recognized clearly that when matters of social responsibility are removed from matters of agency, the content of politics and democracy are deflated. He writes:

> When an individual is no longer a true participant, when he no longer feels a sense of responsibility to his society, the content of democracy is emptied. When culture is degraded and vulgarity enthroned, when the social system does not build security but induces peril, inexorably the individual is impelled to pull away from a soulless society.[45]

If young people are to develop a respect for others, social responsibility, and keen sense of civic engagement, pedagogy must be viewed as the cultural, political, and moral force that provides the knowledge, values, and social relations to make such democratic practices possible. If higher education is to characterize itself as a site of critical thinking, collective work, and public service, educators and students will have to redefine the knowledge, skills, research, and intellectual practices currently favored in the university. Central to such a challenge is the need to position intellectual practice "as part of an intricate web of morality, rigor and responsibility"[46] that enables academics to speak with conviction, use the public sphere to address important social problems, and demonstrate alternative models for bridging the gap between higher education and the broader society. Connective practices are crucial in that it is essential to develop intellectual practices that are collegial rather than competitive, refuse the instrumentality and privileged isolation of the academy, link critical thought to a profound impatience with the status quo, and connect human agency to the idea of social responsibility and the politics of possibility.

Connection also means being openly and deliberately critical and worldly in one's intellectual work. Increasingly, as universities are shaped by a culture of fear in which dissent is equated with treason, the call to be objective and impartial, whatever one's intentions, can easily echo what George Orwell called the official truth or the establishment point of view. Lacking a self-consciously democratic political focus, teachers are often reduced to the role of a technician or functionary engaged in formalistic rituals, unconcerned with the disturbing and urgent problems that confront the larger society or the consequences of one's pedagogical practices and research undertakings. In opposition to this model, with its claims to and conceit of political neutrality, I argue that academics should combine the mutually interdependent roles of critical educator and active citizen. This requires finding ways to connect the practice of classroom teaching with the operation of power in the larger society and to provide the conditions for students to view themselves as critical agents capable of making those who exercise authority and power answerable for their actions. Such an intellectual does not train students solely for jobs but also educates them to question critically the institutions, policies, and values that shape their lives, relationships to others, and connections to the larger world.

I think Stuart Hall is on target here when he insists that educators also have a responsibility to provide students with "critical knowledge that has to be ahead of traditional knowledge: it has to be better than anything that traditional knowledge can produce, because only serious ideas are going to stand up."[47] At the same time, he insists on the need for educators to "actually engage, contest, and learn from the best that is locked up in other traditions," especially those attached to traditional academic paradigms.[48] Students must be made aware of the ideological and structural forces that promote needless human suffering while also recognizing that it takes more than awareness to resolve them. This is the kind of intellectual practice that Zygmunt Bauman calls "taking responsibility for our responsibility,"[49] one that is attentive to the suffering and needs of others. At the very least, such responsibility means rejecting what Irving Howe calls the honored place that capitalism has found for intellectuals who now speak for power rather than for the truth and consider themselves noble guardians of the status quo.[50]

Education cannot be decoupled from what Jacques Derrida calls a democracy to come, that is, a democracy that must always "be open to the possibility of being contested, of contesting itself, of criticizing and indefinitely improving itself."[51] Within this project of possibility and impossibility, education must be understood as a deliberately informed and purposeful political and moral practice, as opposed to one that is either doctrinaire, instrumentalized, or both. Moreover, a critical pedagogy should be engaged at all levels of schooling. Similarly, it must gain part of its momentum in higher education among students who will go back to the schools, churches, synagogues, and workplaces in order to produce new ideas, concepts, and critical ways of understanding the world in which they live. This is a notion of intellectual practice and responsibility that refuses the insular, overly pragmatic, and privileged isolation of the academy. It also affirms a broader vision of learning that links knowledge to the power of self-definition and to the capacities of students to expand the scope of democratic freedoms, particularly those that address the crisis of education, politics, and the social as part and parcel of the crisis of democracy itself.

In order for critical pedagogy, dialogue, and thought to have real effects, they must advocate the message that all citizens, old and young, are equally entitled, if not equally empowered, to shape the society in which they live. This is a message we heard from the brave students fighting tuition hikes and the destruction of civil liberties and social provisions in Quebec and to a lesser degree in the Occupy Wall Street movement. These young people who are protesting against the 1 percent recognize that they have been written out of the discourses of justice, equality, and democracy and are not only resisting how neoliberalism has made them expendable, they are also arguing for a collective future very different from the one on display in the current political and economic systems in which they feel trapped. These brave youth are insisting that the relationship between knowledge and power can be emancipatory, that their histories and experiences matter, and that what they say and do counts in their struggle to unlearn dominating privileges, productively reconstruct their relations with others, and transform, when necessary, the world around them.

If educators are to function as public intellectuals, they need to listen to young people who are producing a new language in order to talk about inequality and power relations, attempting to create alternative democratic public spaces, rethinking the very nature of politics, and asking serious questions about what democracy is and why it no longer exists in the United States. Simply put, educators need to argue for forms of pedagogy that close the gap between the university and everyday life. Their curricula need to be organized around knowledge of those communities, cultures, and traditions that give students a sense of history, identity, place, and possibility. More importantly, they need to join students in engaging in a practice of freedom that points to new and radical forms of pedagogies that have a direct link to building social movements in and out of the colleges and universities.

Although there are still a number of academics such as Noam Chomsky, Angela Davis, John Ralston Saul, Bill McKibben, Germaine Greer, and Cornel West who function as public intellectuals, they are often shut out of the mainstream media or characterized as marginal, unintelligible, and sometimes unpatriotic figures. At the same time, many academics find themselves laboring under horrendous working conditions that either don't allow for them to write in a theoretically rigorous and accessible manner for the public because they do not have time—given the often intensive teaching demands of part-time academics and increasingly of full-time, nontenured academics as well. Or they retreat into a kind of theoreticism in which theory becomes lifeless, detatched from any larger project or the realm of worldly issues. In this instance, the notion of theory as a resource—if not theoretical rigor itself—is reduced to a badge of academic cleverness, shorn of the potential to advance thought within the academy or to reach a larger audience outside their academic disciplines.

Consequently, such intellectuals often exist in hermetic academic bubbles cut off from both the larger public and the important issues that impact society. To no small degree, they have been complicit in the transformation of the university into an adjunct of corporate and military power. Such academics have become incapable of defending higher education as a vital public sphere and unwilling to challenge those spheres of induced mass cultural illiteracy and firewalls of jargon that doom to extinction critically engaged thought, complex ideas, and serious writing for the public. Without their intervention as public intellectuals, the university defaults on its role as a democratic public sphere capable of educating an informed public, a culture of questioning, and the development of a critical formative culture connected to the need, as Cornelius Castoriadis puts it, "to create citizens who are critical thinkers capable of putting existing institutions into question so that democracy again becomes society's movement."[52]

Before his untimely death, Edward Said, himself an exemplary public intellectual, urged his colleagues in the academy to directly confront those social hardships that disfigure contemporary society and pose a serious threat to the promise of democracy. He urged them to assume the role of public intellectuals, wakeful and mindful of their responsibilities to bear testimony to human suffering and the pedagogical possibilities at work in educating students to be autonomous, self-reflective, and socially responsible. Said rejected the notion of a market-driven pedagogy, one that created cheerful robots and legitimated organized recklessness and illegal legalities. In opposition to such a pedagogy, Said argued for what he called a pedagogy of wakefulness and its related concern with a politics of critical engagement. In commenting on Said's public pedagogy of wakefulness, and how it shaped his important consideration of academics as public intellectuals, I begin with a passage that I think offers a key to the ethical and political force of much of his writing. This selection is taken from his memoir, *Out of Place*, which describes the last few months of his mother's life in a New York hospital and the difficult time she had falling to sleep because of the cancer that was ravaging her body. Recalling this traumatic and pivotal life experience, Said's meditation moves between the existential and the insurgent, between private pain and worldly commitment, between the seductions of a "solid self" and the reality of a contradictory, questioning, restless, and at times, uneasy sense of identity. He writes:

> "Help me to sleep, Edward," she once said to me with a piteous trembling in her voice that I can still hear as I write. But then the disease spread into her brain—and for the last six weeks she slept all the time—my own inability to sleep may be her last legacy to me, a counter to her struggle for sleep. For me sleep is something to be gotten over as quickly as possible. I can only go to bed very late, but I am literally up at dawn. Like her I don't possess the secret of long sleep, though unlike her I have reached the point where I do not want it. For me, sleep is death, as is any diminishment in awareness. . . . Sleeplessness for me is a cherished state to be desired at almost any cost; there is nothing for me as invigorating as immediately shedding the shadowy half-consciousness of a night's loss than the early morning, reacquainting myself with or resuming what I might have lost completely a few hours earlier. I occasionally experience myself as a cluster of flowing currents. I prefer this to the idea of a solid self, the identity to which so many attach so much significance. These currents like the themes of one's life, flow along during the waking hours, and at their best, they require no reconciling, no harmonizing. They are "off" and may be out of place, but at least they are always in motion, in time, in place, in the form of all kinds of strange combinations moving about, not necessarily forward, sometimes against each other, contrapuntally

yet without one central theme. A form of freedom, I like to think, even if I am far from being totally convinced that it is. That skepticism too is one of the themes I particularly want to hold on to. With so many dissonances in my life I have learned actually to prefer being not quite right and out of place.[53]

Said posits here an antidote to the seductions of conformity, a disciplinarily induced moral coma, and the lure of corporate money. For Said, it is a sense of being awake, displaced, caught in a combination of diverse circumstances that suggests a pedagogy that is cosmopolitan and imaginative—a public-affirming pedagogy that demands a critical and engaged interaction with the world we live in, mediated by a responsibility for challenging structures of domination and for alleviating human suffering. That is, a pedagogy that writes the public. As an ethical and political practice, a public pedagogy of wakefulness rejects modes of education removed from political or social concerns, divorced from history and matters of injury and injustice. Said's notion of a pedagogy of wakefulness includes "lifting complex ideas into the public space," recognizing human injury inside and outside of the academy, and acting on the assumption that there is more hope in the world when we can use theory to question what is taken for granted and change things.[54] This is a pedagogy in which academics are neither afraid of controversy or the willingness to make connections that are otherwise hidden, nor are they afraid of making clear the connection between private issues and broader elements of society's problems.

For Said, being awake becomes a central metaphor for defining the role of academics as public intellectuals, defending the university as a crucial public sphere, engaging how culture deploys power, and taking seriously the idea of human interdependence while at the same time always living on the border—one foot in and one foot out, an exile and an insider for whom home was always a form of homelessness. As a relentless border-crosser, Said embraced the idea of the "traveler" as an important metaphor for engaged intellectuals. As Stephen Howe, referencing Said, points out, "It was an image which depended not on power, but on motion, on daring to go into different worlds, use different languages, and 'understand a multiplicity of disguises, masks, and rhetorics. Travelers must suspend the claim of customary routine in order to live in new rhythms and rituals . . . the traveler crosses over, traverses territory, and abandons fixed positions all the time.'"[55] And as a border intellectual and traveler, Said embodied the notion of always "being quite not right," evidenced by his principled critique of all forms of certainties and dogmas and his refusal to be silent in the face of human suffering at home and abroad.

Being awake meant refusing the now popular sport of academic-bashing or embracing a crude call for action at the expense of rigorous intellectual and theoretical work. On the contrary, it meant combining rigor and clarity, on the one hand, and civic courage and political commitment, on the other. A pedagogy of wakefulness meant using theory as a resource, recognizing the worldly space of criticism as the democratic underpinning of public-ness, defining critical literacy not merely as a competency but as an act of interpretation linked to the possibility of intervention in the world. It pointed to a kind of border literacy in the plural, in which people learned to read and write from multiple positions of agency; it also was indebted to the recognition forcibly stated by Hannah Arendt that "Without a politically guaranteed public realm, freedom lacks the worldly space to make its appearance."[56]

For those brave academics such as Said, Pierre Bourdieu, Ellen Willis, and others, public intellectuals have a responsibility to unsettle power, trouble consensus, and challenge common sense. The very notion of being an engaged public intellectual is neither foreign to nor a violation of what it means to be an academic scholar but central to its very definition. According to Said, academics have a duty to enter into the public sphere unafraid to take positions and generate controversy, functioning as moral witnesses, raising political awareness, making connections to those elements of power and politics often hidden from public view, and reminding "the audience of the moral questions that may be hidden in the clamor and din of the public debate."[57] At the same time, Said criticized those academics who retreated into a new dogmatism of the disinterested specialist that separates them "not only from the public sphere but from other professionals who don't use the same jargon."[58] This was especially unsettling to him at a time when complex language and critical thought remain under assault in the larger society by all manner of antidemocratic forces. But there is more at stake here than a retreat into convoluted discourses that turn theory into a mechanical act of academic referencing and a deadly obscurantism, there is also the retreat of intellectuals from being able to defend the public values and democratic mission of higher education. Or, as Irving Howe put it, "intellectuals have, by and large, shown a painful lack of militancy in defending the rights which are a precondition of their existence."[59]

The view of higher education as a democratic public sphere committed to producing young people capable and willing to expand and deepen their sense of themselves, to think about the world critically, "to imagine something other than their own well-being," to serve the public good, and to struggle for a substantive democracy has been in a state of acute crisis for the last thirty years.[60] When faculty assume, in this context, their civic responsibility to educate students to think critically, act with conviction, and connect what they learn in classrooms to important social issues in the larger society, they are often denounced for politicizing their classrooms and for violating professional codes of conduct, or, worse, labeled as unpatriotic.[61] In some cases, the risk of connecting what they teach to the imperative to expand the capacities of students to be both critical and socially engaged may cost academics their jobs, especially when they make visible the workings of power, injustice, human misery, and the alterable nature of the social order. What do the liberal arts and humanities amount to if they do not teach the practice of freedom, especially at a time when training is substituted for education? Gayatri Spivak provides a context for this question with her comment: "Can one insist on the importance of training in the humanities in [a] time of legitimized violence?"[62]

In a society that remains troublingly resistant to or incapable of questioning itself, one that celebrates the consumer over the citizen and all too willingly endorses the narrow values and interests of corporate power, the importance of the university as a place of critical learning, dialogue, and social justice advocacy becomes all the more imperative. Moreover, the distinctive role that faculty play in this ongoing pedagogical project of democratization and learning, along with support for the institutional conditions and relations of power that make it possible, must be defended as part of a broader discourse of excellence, equity, and democracy.

Despite the growing public recognition that market fundamentalism has fostered a destructive alignment among the state, corporate capital, and transnational corporations, there is little understanding that such an alignment has been constructed and solidified through a neoliberal disciplinary apparatus and corporate pedagogy produced in part in the halls of higher education and through the educational force of the larger media culture. The economic Darwinism of the last thirty years has done more than throw the financial and credit systems into crisis; it has also waged an attack on all those social institutions that support critical modes of agency, reason, and meaningful dissent. And yet, the financial meltdown most of the world is experiencing is rarely seen as part of an educational crisis in which the institutions of public and higher education have been conscripted into a war on democratic values. Such institutions have played a formidable, if not shameless, role in reproducing market-driven beliefs, social relations, identities, and modes of understanding that legitimate the institutional arrangements of cutthroat capitalism. William Black calls such institutions purveyors of a "criminogenic environment"—one that promotes and legitimates market-driven practices that include fraud, deregulation, and other perverse practices.[63] Black claims that the most extreme pedagogical expression of such an environment can be found in business schools, which he calls "fraud factories" for the elite.[64]

There seems to be an enormous disconnect between the economic conditions that led to the devastating financial meltdown and the current call to action by a generation of young people and adults who have been educated for the last several decades in the knowledge, values, and identities of a market-driven society. Clearly, this generation will not solve this crisis if they do not connect it to the assault on an educational system that has been reduced to a lowly adjunct of corporate interests and the bidding of the warfare state.

Higher education represents one of the most important sites over which the battle for democracy is being waged. It is the site where the promise of a better future emerges out of those visions and pedagogical practices that combine hope, agency, politics, and moral responsibility as part of a broader emancipatory discourse. Academics have a distinct and unique obligation, if not political and ethical responsibility, to make learning relevant to the imperatives of a discipline, scholarly method, or research specialization. If democracy is a way of life that demands a formative culture, educators can play a pivotal role in creating forms of pedagogy and research that enable young people to think critically, exercise judgment, engage in spirited debate, and create those public spaces that constitute "the very essence of political life."[65]

Finally, I want to suggest that while it has become more difficult to imagine a democratic future, we have entered a period in which young people all over the world are protesting against neoliberalism and its pedagogy and politics of disposability. Refusing to remain voiceless and powerless in determining their future, these young people are organizing collectively in order to create the conditions for societies that refuse to use politics as an act of war and markets as the measure of democracy. They are taking seriously the words of the great abolitionist Frederick Douglass, who bravely argued that freedom is an empty abstraction if people fail to act, and "if there is no struggle, there is no progress."[66] Their struggles are not simply aimed at the 1 percent but also at the 99 percent as part of a broader effort to get them to connect the dots, educate themselves, and develop and join social movements that can rewrite the language of democracy and put into place the institutions and formative cultures that make it possible. Stanley Aronowitz is right in arguing that

> The system survives on the eclipse of the radical imagination, the absence of a viable political opposition with roots in the general population, and the conformity of its intellectuals who, to a large extent, are subjugated by their secure berths in the academy. [At the same time,] it would be premature to predict that decades of retreat, defeat and silence can be reversed overnight without a commitment to what may be termed "a long march" though the institutions, the workplaces and the streets of the capitalist metropoles.[67]

The protests that began in 2011 in the United States, Canada, Greece, and Spain make clear that this is not—indeed, *cannot be*—only a short-term project for reform but a political movement that needs to intensify, accompanied by the reclaiming of public spaces, the progressive use of digital technologies, the development of public spheres, the production of new modes of education, and the safeguarding of places where democratic expression, new identities, and collective hope can be nurtured and mobilized. A formative culture must be put in place pedagogically and institutionally in a variety of spheres extending from churches and public and higher education to all those cultural apparatuses engaged in the production and circulation of knowledge, desire, identities, and values.

Clearly, such efforts need to address the language of democratic revolution rather than the seductive incremental adjustments of liberal reform. This suggests calling for a living wage, jobs programs (especially for the young), the democratization of power, economic equality, and a massive shift in funds away from the machinery of war and big banks, as well as building a social movement that not only engages in critique but also makes hope a real possibility by organizing in order to seize power. We need collective narratives that inform collective struggles. In this instance, public intellectuals can play a crucial role in providing theoretical resources and modes of analyses that can help to shape such narratives along with broader social movements and collective struggles. There is no room for failure here because failure would cast us back into the clutches of authoritarianism—which, while different from previous historical periods, shares nonetheless the imperative to proliferate violent social formations and a death dealing blow to the promise of a democracy to come.

Given the urgency of the problems faced by those marginalized by class, race, age, and sexual orientation, I think it is all the more crucial to take seriously the challenge of Derrida's provocation that "We must do and think the impossible. If only the possible happened, nothing more would happen. If I only I did what I can do, I wouldn't do anything."[68] We may live in dark times, as Hannah Arendt reminds us, but history is open and the space of the possible is larger than the one on display. Academics in their role as public intellectuals can play a crucial part in raising critical questions, connecting critical modes of education to social change, and making clear that the banner of critical independence and civic engagement, "ragged and torn though it may be, is still worth fighting for."[69]

CHAPTER SIX

Days of Rage:
The Quebec Student Protest Movement and the New Social Awakening[1]

This isn't a student strike, it's the awakening of society.
—Quebec protest banner

I n many countries throughout the world, young people are speaking out.[2] They are using their voices and bodies to redefine the boundaries of the possible and to protest the crushing currents of neoliberal regimes that ruthlessly assert their power and policies through appeals to destiny, political theology, and the unabashed certainty bred of fundamentalist faith. From Paris, Athens, and London to Montreal and New York City, young people are challenging the current repressive historical conjuncture by rejecting its dominant premises and practices. Many young people are protesting to create a future inclusive of their dreams in which the principles of justice and equality become key elements of a radicalized democratic and social project. Their efforts importantly involve protests against tuition hikes, austerity measures, joblessness, and deep cuts in public spending. Such protests also signal the awakening of a revolutionary ideal in the service of a new society. In the aftermath of the mass mobilizations spurred by Occupy Wall Street in 2011–12 and

155

the Quebec student strike in 2012, a number of student groups across the United States are now working in a less spectacular fashion to develop democratically based student unions that are capable of advocating for sustainable transformations of higher education and society at large. Through such measures, youth have dared to call for a different world and, in doing so, have exhibited great courage in taking up a wager about the future made from the standpoint of an embattled present. To understand the shared concerns of these youthful protesters and the global nature of the forces they are fighting, it is crucial to situate these diverse student protests within a broader analysis of global capital and the changing nature of its assaults on young people.

The Tyranny of Neoliberalism

Unapologetic in its implementation of austerity measures that cause massive amounts of human hardship and suffering, neoliberal capitalism consolidates class power on the backs of young people, workers, and others marginalized by class, race, and ethnicity.[3] And it appears to no longer need the legitimacy garnered through its false claim to democratic ideals such as free speech, individual liberty, or justice—however tepid these appeals have always been. In the absence of alternative social visions to market-driven values and the increasing separation of global corporate power from national politics, neoliberalism has wrested itself free of any regulatory controls while at the same time removing economics from any consideration of social costs, ethics, or social responsibility. Since the economic collapse of 2008–2009, it has become increasingly evident that neoliberalism's only imperatives are profits and growing investments in global power structures unmoored from any form of accountable, democratic governance.

The devastating fallout of neoliberal capitalism's reorganization of society—the destruction of communities and impoverishment of individuals and families—now becomes its most embraced mode of expression as it is championed, ironically, as the only viable route to economic stability. In this widely accepted, yet dystopian world view, collective misfortune is no longer interpreted as a sign of failing governance or of the tawdry willingness of politicians to serve corporate interests, but attributed to the character flaws of individuals and defined chiefly as a matter of personal responsibility. In fact, government-provided social protections are viewed as pathological. Matters of life and death are removed from traditional modes of democratic governance and made subject to the sovereignty of the market. In this new age of biocapital or "bioeconomics," as Eric Cazdyn calls it, "all ideals are at the mercy of a larger economic logic"[4]—one that unapologetically generates policies that "trample over millions of people if necessary."[5] Neoliberalism's defining ideologies, values, and policies harness all institutions, social practices, and modes of thought to the demands of corporations and the needs of the warfare state. They are as narrowly self-serving as they are destructive.

As collective responsibility is privatized, politics loses its social and democratic character, and the formative culture necessary for the production of engaged critical agents is gravely undermined. An utterly reduced form of agency is now embodied in the figure of the isolated automaton, who is driven by self-interest and eschews any responsibility for the other. As Stuart J. Murray points out, neoliberalism's totalizing discourse of privatization, commodification, deregulation, and hyper-individualism "co-opts and eviscerates the language of the common good."[6] The ascendancy of neoliberal ideology also manifests in an ongoing assault on democratic public spheres, public goods, and any viable notion of equality and social justice. As corporate power is consolidated into fewer and fewer hands, ideological and structural reforms are implemented to transfer wealth and income into the clutches of a ruling financial and corporate elite. This concentration of power is all the more alarming since both Canada and the United States have experienced unprecedented growth in wealth concentration and income inequality since the 1970s. In Canada, as Bruce Campbell notes,

> The richest Canadian 1% has almost doubled its share of the national income pie—from 7% to almost 14%—over the last three decades. The average top 100 CEO's compensation was $6.6 million in 2009, 155 times the average worker's wage [while] 61 Canadian billionaires have a combined wealth of $162 billion, twice as much as the bottom 17 million Canadians.[7]

The United States holds the shameful honor of being "perched at the very top of the global premier league of inequality,"[8] with 1 percent of Americans holding 40 percent of all wealth and 24 percent of all income.[9] Fraud and corruption run rampant through the financial sectors of many advanced industrial countries, burning everything in their path.[10] As Charles Ferguson observes, "major U.S. and European banks have been caught assisting corporate malfeasance by Enron and others, laundering money for drug cartels and the Iranian military, aiding tax evasion, hiding the assets of corrupt dictators, colluding in order to fix prices, and committing many forms of financial fraud."[11] In light of the recent scandals exposing the predatory practices and criminal acts of financial institutions such as HSBC, JPMorgan Chase, and the banking giant Barclays, it is clear that the financial sector has devolved into a financial oligarchy and a global criminal enterprise.[12]

A dire consequence of growing inequality is that more and more people are facing joblessness and poverty, while many already feel they have been written out of a future that might offer them a decent and dignified life. What many have learned the hard way in North America and across the globe is that the impacts of inequality cannot be adequately captured with empirical measures based in the GNP or median incomes. Inequality has a lived experience in which there is "a fatal attraction between poverty and vulnerability, corruption and the accumulation of dangers, as well as humiliation and the denial of dignity."[13] Young people, particularly those transitioning to independent adulthood, have certainly felt the brunt of the intensification of neoliberal policies and are increasingly unemployed, deprived of the most basic social provisions, denied access to decent health care and affordable housing, and faced with diminished educational opportunities. Zygmunt Bauman argues that today's youth have become "outcasts and outlaws of a novel kind, cast in a condition of liminal drift, with no way of knowing whether it is transitory or permanent."[14] That is, the generation of youth in the early twenty-first century has no way of grasping if they will ever "be free from the gnawing sense of the transience, indefiniteness, and provisional nature of any settlement."[15] And those young people further marginalized by race and class now inhabit a social landscape in which they are increasingly disparaged as flawed consumers with no adequate role to play and are considered disposable, while forced to inhabit "zones of social abandonment" extending from bad schools to bulging detention centers and prisons.[16]

With so many young people globally facing a present whose future promises only to preserve and expand those spaces that have become sites of "terminal exclusion,"[17] youth in North America and Europe have exhibited a growing recognition that the real marker of their generation is an ever-expanding mode of precarity. Increasingly stripped of their dignity as students and workers, young protesters in both the United States and Canada have recognized that "the current mode of production and reproduction has become a mode of *production for elimination,* a reproduction of populations that are not likely to be productively used or exploited but are always already superfluous."[18] By some estimates, "nearly 75 million young people around the world are out of work, an increase of four million since the economic crisis of 2008."[19] Youth unemployment rates in Europe are staggering, reaching as high as 50 percent in both Spain and Greece and over 35 percent in Ireland. In the United States, 53 percent of recent college graduates are either unemployed or underemployed.[20] Regardless of its diminished promise of social and economic mobility, higher education now subsidizes institutional budgets with exorbitant tuition rate hikes that effectively prevent working-class and many middle-class youth from even getting an education.

The security that once came with access to public and higher education, the prospect of a decent job, and a state that provided social protections against unexpected and horrible misfortunes has vanished. In a world marked by what Bauman calls "liquid modernity," social structures that depend on long-term planning and investment have disappeared, just as social problems have been individualized along with the task of resolving them.[21] The era of "fixed addresses," stable communities, and social stability is over. Youth are now condemned to unskilled or temporary jobs, commodified social bonds, transient living conditions, and personal commitments that carry a short expiration date. Identities are now temporary, shifting endlessly amid a glut of consumer choices fed by celebrity culture and the corporate evisceration of all significant cultural institutions. Matters of social and personal security are left to the embattled devices of each individual, even as the means for providing genuine safety are largely monopolized by the rich and powerful.[22] As Bauman points out, casino capitalism's "order of egoism" and obsession with privatization "shifts the task of fighting against and (hopefully) resolving socially produced problems onto the shoulders of individual men and women, in most cases much too weak for the purpose, depending on their mostly inadequate skills and insufficient resources."[23]

Nowhere is the precarity that defines the current state of young people more obvious than in the consequences they face daily as the social state is being dismantled, individual rights are effaced, political freedoms are criminalized, and collective rights are all but obliterated. Young people are now told that freedom is about doing what you want without any impediments, especially from the government. What they are not told is that individualized notions of freedom neither address nor provide the social, economic, and political conditions necessary to ensure access to a meaningful job, quality education, decent health care, clean air, and a life of dignity in a just society. Individual freedom removes any sense of community, social responsibility, and solidarity from the discourse of freedom. Individual freedom has to take a detour through collective endeavors of freedom in order to become meaningful. Individual freedom without robust communities is simply code for a stripped-down notion of humanity as disconnected, self-interested automatons lacking any sense of moral accountability, social responsibility, or civic courage. Within the vocabulary of neoliberalism, too many young people are removed from the discourses of community and collective freedom, pushed to the margins of society, and forced to inhabit zones of terminal uncertainty, despair, and exclusion.

Increasingly unemployed, pushed into poverty, politically disenfranchised, and subject to the discipline of a growing punishing state,[24] young people across the globe face a bleak future marked by uncertainty, vulnerability, insecurity, and the burden of mounting debt.[25] Instead of being viewed as a crucial social investment, many youth—especially protesting students and minorities of race and class—are now the objects of law and order, caught in an expanding web of surveillance, criminalization, and governing-through-crime modes of social control.[26]

Tuition Hikes in the Age of Mounting Debt

It is precisely against this background of expanding policies of neoliberal austerity, precarity, despair, diminishing expectations, and state violence that young people in Quebec have organized a protest movement that may be one of the most "powerful challenges to neoliberalism on the continent."[27] Thousands of students have raised their voices in unprecedented opposition to the ideology, modes of governance, and policies of the neoliberal state. The initial cause of the protest movement began in response to an increase in tuition fees announced by the Quebec provincial government in March 2011. The tuition hike was "part of the government's effort to advance neoliberalism in Quebec by introducing new fees for public services and raising existing ones."[28] The government's proposal included raising tuition by $325 per year over five years with the increased fees going into effect in September 2012. The hike amounted to a 75 percent increase over five years, rising from $2,319 to $3,793 by 2017. In February 2012, after the government refused to negotiate with organizations representing student interests, the student leaders called for a strike. Tens of thousands of students responded immediately by boycotting their classes. Many of the province's colleges and universities were shut down as a result.

Mainstream media consistently sided with the Quebec government, downplaying the significance of the tuition increases—even as they pertained to those students who could least afford them and for whom it would have the greatest impact. Critics of the strike repeatedly drew the public's attention to the fact that, even with the increase, tuition fees in Quebec would remain among the lowest in Canada: "Average undergraduate tuition in Canada for 2011–12 is $5,366, but ranges widely from province to province. Quebec has the lowest fees, followed closely by Newfoundland and Labrador. Ontario has the highest average tuition, at $6,640 a year."[29] However, it soon became apparent that the students viewed the tuition increase as only one symptom of an ailing and unjust social order about which they could no longer be silent. The students preferred to speak for themselves rather than have others speak abstractly for them and about them, especially when it came to the material conditions of their own educations and their own futures. It is telling, and will remain telling, that government officials and newspaper pundits instantly responded with anxious indignation, as if wholly caught off guard by the simple fact that students can speak—and speak intelligently, passionately, and urgently about the most pressing issues facing themselves and their society. In a reversal of roles familiar to anyone who actually works in a classroom, the student can also teach the teacher. The first lesson to be learned from the striking students was that the protests were about much more than fee structures. Yet, the government seemed unwilling to assimilate this pedagogical insight, and its heavy-handedness touched a nerve in the larger social body of Quebec, activating new forms of dissent and solidarity.

The action that began as a protest against increasing tuition fees soon developed into a popular uprising, with tens of thousands of postsecondary students and their supporters marching nightly in the streets of Quebec cities and in solidarity demonstrations across Canada.[30] It became a student strike of unprecedented proportions, involving more than two hundred thousand students and rallying many additional supporters for a mass demonstration on March 22, 2012. As the strike progressed and expanded its base of support, over a quarter of a million people joined the demonstrations on a number of occasions and an estimated half million marched in Montreal on May 25, 2012. By July 2012, the Quebec student strike had emerged as not only "the longest and largest student strike in the history of North America," but also "the biggest act of civil disobedience in Canadian history."[31] Now a major broad-based opposition movement against neoliberal austerity measures, the Quebec student strike initiated one of the most powerful, collectively organized challenges to neoliberal ideology, policy, and governance that has occurred globally in some time.

The initial phase of the movement focused almost exclusively on higher-educational reform. The issues addressed in the early stage of the protests included a rejection of the province's call for a tuition increase, a sustained critique of the underfunding of postsecondary education, a critical interrogation of the perils facing a generation forced to live on credit and tied to the servitude of debt, and the opening up of a new conversation about the meaning and purpose of education—in particular, the kind of educational system that is free and removed from corporate influences, and whose mission is defined by its commitment to justice, equality, and support for the broader public good.

Students rejected the tuition hike by arguing that the increase would not only force many working-class students to drop out but also prevent economically disadvantaged students from gaining access to higher education altogether. Expanding this critique, many young people spoke of the tuition increase as symbolic of repressive neoliberal austerity measures that forced them to pay more for their education while offering them a diminished future of dismal job prospects when they graduated. Situating the protest against tuition hikes within a broader critique of neoliberal austerity measures, students were then able to address the fee hikes as part of the growing burden of suffocating debt, government-funding priorities that favor the financial and corporate elite, Prime Minister Harper's ruinous transfer of public funds into an expanding military-industrial complex, and the imposition of corporate culture and corporate modes of governance on all aspects of daily life.

By stressing a pervasive crisis of debt as an issue rather than focusing exclusively on tuition, students were able to highlight the darker registers of finance capital that increasingly foreclose any possibility of a better life for this generation and generations to come. Andrew Gavin Marshall has provided a theoretical service in highlighting the broader effects and politics of the debt crisis. He writes:

> Total student debt now stands at about $20 billion in Canada ($15 billion from Federal Government loans programs, and the rest from provincial and commercial bank loans). In Quebec, the average student debt is $15,000, whereas Nova Scotia and Newfoundland have an average student debt of $35,000, British Columbia at nearly $30,000 and Ontario at nearly $27,000. Roughly 70% of new jobs in Canada require a post-secondary education. Half of students in their 20s live at home with their parents, including 73 per cent of those aged 20 to 24 and nearly a third of 25- to 29-year-olds. On average, a four-year degree for a student living at home in Canada costs $55,000, and those costs are expected to increase in coming years at a rate faster than inflation. It has been estimated that in 18 years, a four-year degree for Canadian students will cost $102,000. Defaults on government student loans are at roughly 14%. The Chairman of the Canadian Federation of Students warned in June of 2011 that, "We are on the verge of bankrupting a generation before they even enter the workplace." The notion, therefore, that Quebec students should not struggle against a bankrupt future is a bankrupted argument.[32]

Connecting student opposition to the tuition hike with the broader issue of expanding debt and the fact that "the average debt for [Canadian] university graduates is around $27,000" helped shift the focus of the strike—viewed by some critics as a narcissistic, collective temper tantrum by whiny students—to a much more public and broader set of considerations. In this instance, what was being indicated by the students calling for higher educational reforms, as Randy Boyagoda points out, was "a profound crisis of faith in the socioeconomic frameworks that have structured and advanced societies across North America and Europe since World War II [as well as] a rejection of the premise of the postwar liberal state: that large-scale institutions and elected leaders are capable of creating opportunities for individual citizens to flourish."[33]

Defending a Free and Democratic Postsecondary Education System

The Quebec protesters made clear how rising tuition fees could be connected to the savage dictates of a debt machine that increases the profits of banks and other financial institutions. But they also went further and raised broader questions about what kind of university system would support such measures. In doing so, they have called into question the increasing corporatization of the university with its market-oriented view of governance, its valuing of research in instrumentalized market terms, its substitution of training for broad-based education, and its view of higher education as a commercial entity. Writing about the Quebec strike, Malav Kanuga states,

> For the students there has been a growing sense of urgency and a shared recognition that increased tuition means a heavier student debt burden, hundreds of more hours a year spent working instead of studying, less access for working-class students, and a shift in university culture toward the market, the commodification of education, the financialization of student life, and the privatization of the university.[34]

But the student activists have not simply denounced the university's role in the reproduction of neoliberal values, gated communities for the affluent, and the engines of social and economic inequality. Student protesters have also strongly argued for a wholesale transformation of higher education in terms of both its mission and how it is funded. Moving from "the crisis of negation" to a project of transformation, the protesters have argued for higher education to be not only free and accessible to all students but also dedicated to the role of educating students to take intellectual risks, think imaginatively, and assume the social responsibilities of critically engaged citizens.[35]

The Quebec student protesters are correct in their demand that Canadian society needs a wholesale revision of how educational institutions and democracies in general listen to and treat young people in a world in which their voices, needs, desires, and growing hardships have been excluded from a public space of articulation. The students have passionately rejected the neoliberal view of higher education as an economic investment unapologetically designed to turn students into consumers and the university into a profit-making entity. They have been strongly critical of neoliberal modes of governance that impose a top-down business culture on faculty, demanding that they assume the role of entrepreneurs rather than autonomous and critically engaged teachers and scholars. In addition, they have rejected the restructuring of academic departments into revenue production units and classrooms into training grounds that mimic the business culture of call centers and Walmarts. Presenting an alternative to the neoliberal model, Quebec students have argued for higher education as a democratic public sphere that does more than provide private returns for individuals and institute policies that aim to banish forever the "horrors" of teaching students to question authority. They have demanded the kind of education that takes seriously the impending challenges of a global democracy and will enable them to mediate the world in terms of democratic rather than commercial values.

More and more young people are insisting that the real value of higher education lies in its capacity to offer everyone the opportunity to receive a free, quality education and the prospect of living in an educated society, both of which are crucial for creating genuine social security, critical agents, and the formative culture necessary for a democracy to thrive. In developing their critique, the protesters have resurrected "the ideal of free post-secondary education—recommended in the 1960s by a famous state-commissioned inquiry, but long since snuffed out among the economic elite."[36] They have made clear the political and moral fault lines between those who believe that education is a "commodity purchased by 'consumers' for self-advancement, and those who would protect it as a right funded by the state for the collective good"—and, in doing so, they have "sparked a fundamental debate about the entire society's future."[37]

Funding the Neoliberal State

Clearly there is more at stake in the Quebec protest movement than concerns over tuition hikes and skyrocketing student debt. A disquieting narrative about the future of young people entering adult life has been extended to the troubling reality of a broader social system that increasingly places its political allegiances, social investments, and economic support in the service of rich and powerful financial institutions while eviscerating the social state and the public treasury. As Martin Lukacs insists, one achievement of the Quebec protest movement has been

> to clarify for a broad swath of society that a tuition hike is not a matter of isolated accounting, but the goal of a neoliberal austerity agenda the world over. Forcing students to pay more for education is part of a transfer of wealth from the poor and middle class to the rich—as with privatization and the state's withdrawal from service provision, tax breaks for corporations, and deep cuts to social programs.[38]

The hidden order of politics at the center of neoliberal austerity measures is difficult to miss and helps explain the misplaced priorities of a Quebec government that in 2006–07 provided $437 million for funding private schools—funds that, as Erika Shaker points out, "would pay for a fee freeze at Quebec universities and have money left over for bursaries for low-income students [while] the remainder could be redirected towards public schools."[39] Shaker suggests that this transfer of funds to private schools "demonstrate[s] that when public money is used to facilitate private access, it's the public infrastructure and the people accessing it who pay the price."[40] The defunding of the social state and higher education and the increasing attack on the social contract are also evident in the Canadian state's willingness in the latter half of the 1990s "to reduce by 50% the federal transfers to the provinces for post-secondary education [which has amounted] to a loss of income of $800 million per year for Quebec."[41] Federal funds that could be used for investing in higher education have instead been reallocated to support the conservative government's tough-on-crime agenda and either squandered on prison expansion or diverted into a growing Canadian military budget.

Current tuition fee increases would raise about $200 million from students; yet such fees could be completely eliminated and free education provided to all students if the Canadian government cut back on its bloated military budget. Former Quebec premier Jean Charest and his fellow apostles of neoliberalism had no trouble contributing $4.5 billion in 2011 to the $24.7 billion that "the Canadian government is spending . . . on its military budget, a budget that is proportionally higher today than it was during the Cold War" and places Canada fourteenth in global military spending.[42] Offloading more costs to the provinces, the federal government refuses assistance that could offset rising student tuition fees and pushes ahead with a military budget that is still considering an astronomical expenditure on F-35 fighter jets that will cost as much as $45.8 billion.[43] The asymmetry of the situation would be laughable if it weren't so grotesque: students are vilified as irresponsible for protesting against tuition fee increases while the Department of National Defence spends billions at will and remains mostly unopposed. What isn't laughable is the students' demands for free education. At the core of the demand for free education is a rethinking of education as a right, a public good, rather than an entitlement. As a number of studies have pointed out, when education is understood as a public good, you get an educated society; people have the opportunity to develop analytic skills to be actively engaged agents; moreover, people are healthier, there is less crime, and various conditions are put into place that allow an educated society to work.[44]

Commentators in the national newspapers bleat about the putative naïveté or selfishness of Quebec youth but remain conspicuously mute about the increased militarization of the culture, even as Canada attempts to extricate itself from a disastrous and costly war in Afghanistan. In fact, neoliberal governments in the United States, United Kingdom, and Canada express little to no concern about providing students with quality higher education or supporting investment in universities, libraries, health care, or a job creation program for young people. Increasingly, it appears such social investments are viewed as far less important than siphoning off billions to fund a culture of violence and a permanent war machine. Misplaced priorities that shut down economic, educational, and political opportunities suggest that these countries have become societies that are waging a war on their children, even as government policies increasingly reveal the savagery of a system that considers profits more important than the lives of its citizens.

Confronting the Backlash of Smears, Insults, and Police Violence

The student strike in Quebec emerged in February 2012, when it became clear that then-premier Charest and the Quebec government were not interested in opening up a dialogue with the province's major student unions. Various student groups joined hands and organized a massive strike of forty thousand students on February 21, 2012. As the strike became more cohesive under the leadership of the CLASSÉ—the Coalition large de l'Association pour une Solidarité Syndicale Étudiante, Quebec's largest student association and the most vocal in supporting direct action and rejecting the regime of neoliberal capitalism—the tactics employed by the students became both more disruptive and more effective. The strike in turn alarmed a number of business elites, conservative media pundits, and members of the Charest government.

Not surprisingly, the business community in the province supported both the government's effort to raise tuition and its use of state force to crush the strike. Roger Annis notes that "The Conseil du Patronat du Québec (Employers Council of Quebec) issued the results of a survey of its members on June 1 showing 95 percent support for the government's proposed hike in tuition fees that sparked the student strike last February and 68 percent support for Bill 78"—the latter referring to legislation whose purpose was largely viewed as an attempt to break the student unions, suppress democratic expression, bankrupt individuals, and undermine the unity and solidarity that had been forged among the largest student groups.[45]

A massive progovernment smear campaign emerged against the students, labeling them as "self-seeking brats, whining about modest tuition increases and seeking mayhem for its own sake."[46] Margaret Wente, writing for the *Globe and Mail*, echoed the sentiments of many mainstream journalists and derided the student protesters by referring to them as "kids" who "are on another planet."[47] According to Wente, the students were too immature to understand the nature of their own actions, never mind put forth a serious criticism of both market-based higher education and the wider neoliberal order. She judged their complaints about tuition increases as meaningless since, as she put it to her well-heeled readership, not only do the students have "the lowest tuition fees in North America [but] the total increase would amount to the cost of a daily grande cappuccino."[48] Of course, this would make sense if education were literally about nothing more than consuming a product. Wente has a long history of blaming young people for being narcissistic and invoking clichés of "dangerous" youth. For example, in previous articles, she criticized unemployed young men (code for poor minority youth) for creating what she calls a "huge social problem" because "they refuse to work."[49] Yet Wente has appeared strangely untroubled by the billion-dollar crimes committed by corrupt corporations, thus exhibiting what Alain Badiou calls "zero tolerance" for youthful protesters and "infinite tolerance for the crimes of bankers and government embezzlers which affect the lives of millions."[50]

For Wente, the victims of social inequality are now blameworthy. In this view, the real culprits behind an ailing society are the youth—characterized by their alleged moral turpitude and declining values—instead of a global financial meltdown caused by the willingness of finance capitalism to sacrifice the future of young people for short-term political and economic gains. Accordingly, the issue that the protesters should really be addressing is the necessity to rid higher education of those academic disciplines not directly tied to the market because the only purpose of education, in Wente's instrumentalist world view, is to train people to take their place in the neoliberal order she so fervently defends.

Some critics went further than Wente and called for outright violence to be used against the protesters. Roger Annis claimed that not only were many business leaders in favor of using the police to crush the strike but also many "politicians and editorialists were calling for greater use of police violence and court injunctions to break up student picket lines."[51] Michael Den Tandt, writing in the *National Post*, was quite explicit in calling for the government to crack down on the protesters, going so far as to suggest dishing out medieval forms of punishment such as "caning."[52] Bernard Guay, a member of the Quebec Liberal Party and head of the tax office in the Municipal Affairs Department, published a letter on the website of *Le Soleil* in which, according to Andrew Gavin Marshall, he unapologetically recommended

> using the fascist movements of the 1920s and 1930s as an example in how to deal with "leftists" in giving them "their own medicine." He suggested organizing a political "cabal" to handle the "wasteful and anti-social" situation, which would mobilize students to not only cross picket lines, but to confront and assault students who wear the little red square (the symbol of the student strike).[53]

Imitating fascist thuggery, Guay suggested, would "help society 'overcome the tyranny of Leftist agitators.'"[54] In spite of their differences, these attacks all share what *New York Times* columnist Frank Bruni has called, in a different context, an "emphasis on personal advantage over the public good."[55] One might conclude that they all exhibit a hatred for democracy itself.[56]

While Premier Charest eventually agreed to open up talks with the main student groups, he held fast to student tuition increases, though he later made a paltry offer to lower the rate of increase. It is impossible to determine if the bellicose assault against the protesters in the mainstream media, along with the support of a large portion of Quebec's business community, encouraged the Charest government to resort to repressive measures. However, the Charest government did just that by passing Bill 78 into law on May 18, 2012—and proceeding to implement antiprotest legislation that gave sweeping powers to the police and was designed to suppress peaceful protests and shut down student opposition while violating the most basic rights of free speech, association, and assembly.[57]

Representing the dissent expressed by the students "as a criminal rather than political issue," the emergency legislation was a desperate attempt to portray the protest movement as an act of criminality and students as figures of lawlessness, despite the validity of the issues being raised and the general peacefulness of the student demonstrations.[58] In the service of legitimating an alarmist set of regulations and substituting an emotional discourse for a reasoned and thoughtful attempt at dialogue, Law 12 (formerly Bill 78) proved to be a draconian piece of legislation so extreme that Montreal police expressed reluctance about enforcing certain parts of it.[59]

The most prohibitive and irresponsible measures of Law 12 included giving the police eight hours' notice and a precise itinerary for any demonstration involving more than fifty people; fines running as high as $125,000 for unions and student federations and $35,000 for individuals who violate the law; giving police the power to prosecute a person if he or she offers support or encouragement to protesters at a school; making it illegal for any demonstration to be held within fifty meters of any school campus; giving the government the right to order faculty and staff to show up for work on any designated day; and doubling all fines for repeat offenders. But Law 12 was much more than a gross violation of the rights of students to engage in peaceful assembly and protest austerity measures aimed at curtailing access to postsecondary education. It also provided a green light for police violence, making clear that the state was willing to employ aggressive levels of force against students and others in order to sustain its refusal to address major social and economic problems through peaceful public dialogue and debate.

Broadening the Struggle from an Event to a Social Strike

The government's decision to assume a defensive posture on behalf of rich elites and corporate power backfired and the passage of Bill 78 in May 2012 signified a major turning point for the Quebec protest movement. Rather than creating a climate of fear in order to intimidate students, faculty, and other sympathizers, the law outraged both civil libertarians and ordinary citizens and became a catalyst for attracting a much wider following of nonstudent supporters. Not only did public anger explode in a massive demonstration on May 25, in which an estimated five hundred thousand people marched, it also inaugurated nightly demonstrations in Montreal neighborhoods in which people in the streets and on balconies banged their pots and pans at 8:00 p.m. to protest the law as an act of public support and solidarity for the students.

Inspired by the "pots and pans" movement that developed in Chile in the '70s, the "casseroles" demonstrations in Montreal and other cities functioned as a mode of collective performance and a loud but peaceful way to express public outrage and disgust at the Charest government. In addition, crowds of supporters embraced the red square as a symbol of resistance to a future of debt (being "squarely in the red"), pinning it on their clothing and waving red flags from their balconies, donning a powerful symbolic image of defiance as a way to demonstrate their anger over a generation of young people being trapped in a ruinous system of usurious credit and loans.

As public support shifted in favor of the strikers, what initially emerged as a specific set of concerns over tuition hikes evolved into a broader narrative of complaint and resistance toward a global neoliberal order, further providing an opportunity for students to connect their limited set of grievances to a comprehensive set of social problems. What began as a student protest morphed into a social strike in which the assault on the university could be addressed as part of a wider attack on the social state, the environment, unemployed workers, the land rights of indigenous peoples, and young people across the globe. The changing nature of both the debate and the politics that informed it was evident in the CLASSÉ's three-pronged action plan and the "Manifesto for a Maple Spring."[60]

These documents situated the Quebec movement in a broader historical context of social resistance, illuminating a shared opposition to "the laws of an unjust global economy that is mortgaging the future of all of us [and mortgaging] its youth as nothing more than an exploitable resource."[61] In CLASSÉ's "Share Our Future Manifesto," the call for a social strike was presented passionately through a more capacious political narrative as imaginative as it is daring in its call to forge sustainable communal bonds, treat human beings with dignity, build democratic social relations, and construct a new vision of the future. One gets a glimpse of this daring embrace of a revolutionary ideal in the following section from the manifesto, which is worth repeating in full:

> This burden is one that we all shoulder, each and every one of us, whether we are students or not: this is one lesson our strike has taught us. For we, students, are also renters and employees; we are international students, pushed aside by discriminating public services. We come from many backgrounds, and, until the color of our skin goes as unnoticed as our eye color, we will keep on facing everyday racism, contempt and ignorance. We are women, and if we are feminists it is because we face daily sexism and roadblocks set for us by the patriarchal system; we constantly fight deep-rooted prejudice. We are gay,

straight, bisexual, and proud to be. We have never been a separate level of society. Our strike is not directed against the people. We are the people. Our strike goes beyond the $1625 tuition-fee hike. If, by throwing our educational institutions into the marketplace, our most basic rights are being taken from us, we can say the same for hospitals, Hydro-Québec, our forests, and the soil beneath our feet. We share so much more than public services: we share our living spaces, spaces that were here before we were born. We want them to survive us....This is the meaning of our vision, and the essence of our strike: it is a shared, collective action whose scope lies well beyond student interests. We are daring to call for a different world, one far removed from the blind submission our present commodity-based system requires. Individuals, nature, our public services, these are being seen as commodities: the same tiny elite is busy selling everything that belongs to us. And yet we know that public services are not useless expenditures, nor are they consumer goods.[62]

In Badiou's terms, these documents demonstrate a strategy for changing a temporary event into a political organization capable of mobilizing a united idea in the service of a historical awakening.[63]

In both its ideas and actions, the Quebec protest movement was clearly channelling more than the defanged spirit of revolt that Slavoj Žižek warned might dilute the Occupy Wall Street movement. Not only did the Quebec movement symbolize "the awakening of democratic values," but it also signaled the birth of a revolutionary idea grounded in the reality of burgeoning collective organizations and a "minimal positive program of socio-political change."[64] Debates about rising tuition rates were effectively tied to debates about inequality, economic injustice, racial discrimination, the corporatization of education, the destruction of public spheres, and the expanding number of societies willing to wage war on their youth. At the same time, the transformation of the student movement in Montreal into a social movement did not proceed without challenges.

As the Quebec student movement gained in strength and developed into a broad popular uprising intent on transforming government policy and reconfiguring the lines of political and economic power, state-sanctioned law enforcement resorted to more violence. Thousands of students were arrested, one young person lost an eye, and numerous reports surfaced of excessive force used on peaceful demonstrators. Such violence appeared to replay the horrific attacks by the police on students occupying university campuses in the United States. In both instances, the emerging specter of a police state canceled out the fictive portrayal of young people, manufactured by the conservative media, pundits, and government officials, as insignificant whiners and self-indulgent brats. Quite to the contrary, students were making themselves increasingly visible as the harbingers of a social movement willing and capable of challenging the neoliberal nightmare. And because they had become more visible, they were more vulnerable to state violence.

Another distinctive characteristic of the Quebec movement was that it clearly positioned young people as part of the 99 percent. In doing so, it connected with and went far beyond the limited tactic of mass mobilizations. Protesting students opted instead for a permanent presence and media profile through ongoing demonstrations, democratic assemblies, study groups, media outreach, community engagement, policy interventions, and performance art. Thinking otherwise in order to act beyond the boundaries of the given was a characteristic of the Quebec student movement from its inception. These brave young students not only appropriated the language of the dare by displaying their civic courage but also provided a concrete expression of what can be called "educated hope."

The student protesters consequently gave new meaning to what the philosopher Ernst Bloch once referred to as "something that is missing," and, in so doing, resurrected a claim on a future that does not imitate the present. And while the Quebec resistance movement shared the spirit of direct democracy evident in the Occupy movement, it extended its critique of neoliberalism and its embrace of the principles of participatory democracy beyond the boundaries of the nation-state, singular political issues, and temporary political organizations. It connected its democratic project to other student movements in Chile,[65] England, and the United States as well as to a growing worldwide resistance to global capitalism. And it discerningly provided an overarching discourse in which it could begin to address a number of related political and economic issues responsible for mass suffering and human hardships.

In offering the public a new language through which to challenge neoliberal prerogatives, Quebec youth made clear that the financial and corporate interests at work in the drive to raise tuition and push thousands of students into bankruptcy were also responsible for privatizing public services, raising and creating new user fees for health care, eliminating public sector jobs, closing factories, exploiting natural resources for financial gain, extending the retirement age, curbing the power of trade unions while slashing their benefits, promoting tax cuts that benefit the rich, and criminalizing social problems along with anyone who dares to protest such actions. Moreover, the Quebec student movement raised important questions about the role of the university in society and what relationships will exist in the future between corporate power and all aspects of public and political life.

What was also unique about the Quebec movement was its level of organization—a reflection of how the students prepared for the demonstrations before they actually took place by networking and mobilizing small groups to talk to peers, faculty, staff, union representatives, and workers. In addition, the students made use of existing broad-based and powerful associations through which they could advocate for issues directly related to educational reform, rather than outward-facing advocacy movements such as those organized by US students, one example of which is the antisweatshop movement. By activating student unions around demands rooted in knowledge gained from their own lived experiences and the plight of the university, it became easier for the protesters to retain a distinct identity while reaching outside of the university to create a broad-based movement. Moreover, the students organized around an idea—simply that tuition hikes need to be addressed within the suffering and injustices produced by neoliberal austerity measures— which proved revolutionary in its scope, flexible in its ability to connect to other forms of oppression, and decisive in mobilizing other students and the public at large. The Occupy movement began with a slogan about the 99 percent but it lacked the student unions, organizational skills, and sustainable strategies employed by Quebec youth. Of course, the system of higher education in the United States is more complex, given its mix of public and private universities, but this should not prevent the emergence of massive and shared organizational initiatives to develop student organizations at local, state, and national levels.

In addition, the Quebec students developed what Peter Hallward called a "culture of solidarity and confrontation."[66] This strategy was designed to win over students and public opinion while refusing to compromise with official power. For instance, when the leadership of the more moderate student unions suggested the students accept a government offer that would not have lowered tuition fees, the students refused what they thought was a compromising position taken by the unions. They also rejected as insignificant a government offer "to reduce the proposed tuition hike by $35.00 a year over seven years."[67] At the same time, the ongoing strike and widening boycott confronted daily the oppressive power of the state. In doing so, the students made visible on a continuing basis their concerns and the need to extend the ideological and political parameters of their grievances against the state and neoliberalism in general. Clearly, the Quebec students' organizing strategy could provide some useful lessons for the Occupy movement that might enable it to focus on sustained resistance rather than largely disparate and isolated events.

The Quebec resistance movement developed a series of strategies and tactics that awakened society to an ideal of both what a radical democracy might look like and how crucial free, accessible higher education is to such a struggle. What the organizers recognized was that being faithful to this ideal demanded tactics that focused on more than temporary disruptions, occupations, and slogans. It necessitated a new kind of politics in which people become unified around both a collective sense of justice, freedom, and the hope of building a new society. It did not simply criticize the dominant order but pointed to alternatives designed to overthrow it. By engaging in a social strike, the Quebec protesters reopened history, articulated a call for collective and shared struggles, and made visible those groups who are increasingly ignored or viewed as disposable—"people, who are present in the world but absent from its meaning and decisions about its future."[68]

The Quebec student protests against rising university tuition will continue to face a number of crucial challenges, despite the ousting of Charest and his neoliberal government in the 2012 provincial election by the Parti Quebecois (PQ) and leader Pauline Marois. One of Marois's election campaign promises included a planned summit with student unions regarding the province's higher education policies. The day after the election, Marois announced the party's decision to repeal the student tuition fee hike instituted by the Charest government and a plan to cancel Law 12.[69] Yet, at the promised February 2013 education summit, the new provincial leadership was viewed by many as failing to defend the role of higher education as a crucial democratic public sphere when it announced a 3 percent tuition hike (indexed to the rate of inflation) and sparked a protest demonstration by ten thousand students.[70] In spite of this rebuttal, the party announced that the student tuition protests were over. It has also become evident that police repression in Quebec is still being used to restrict public expressions of dissent, and the criminalization of social protests appears no less restrained since the PQ came to power. On the national level, the Harper government has both cut back crucial research on the environment and censored scientists critical of the government's policies on "climate change, fisheries, and aquaculture [that] affect Canadian ocean biodiversity."[71] The Harper government has also withdrawn public funds from scientists, archivists, statisticians, and librarians who use their research and scholarship to address crucial issues that affect the public good. Ideology now trumps evidence, and science gives way to the brutal demands of neoliberalism.

Increasing tuition costs, student debt, and the growing inaccessibility of postsecondary education along with the corporatization of education remain crucial concerns. And additional pressing matters loom on the horizon for higher education in Canada and other democratic states affected by the global economic crisis. As employment opportunities diminish and the baby boomer generation reaches retirement age, there will be significant battles over whether public funding will go to higher education or other valuable public services. One of the most important questions to ask is whether the students will continue to organize and take a progressive stand on a range of social and economic issues extending from the demand for free education to the rebuilding of the social state. In other words, what role will the students take in developing organizations that will push the PQ to reverse the neoliberal politics and policies that have dominated the province and Canada for far too long while expanding the demands of a radical democratic society? Regardless of how the Quebec movement turns out, the protesters have demonstrated a degree of courage, skill, organization, and solidarity that will not easily fade away. A revolutionary idea has been born and now waits for the conditions through which it can become a more powerful, inspiring political and moral force.

Learning from the Quebec Student Resistance: Student Unionism in the United States

Clearly, more was at stake in Quebec than tuition increases, however important the issue in galvanizing students who would be most impacted by them. As Eric Pineault has pointed out, "Neoliberalism has nothing original to offer outside of austerity" and the redeployment of progressive alternatives by students must include a broader sense of struggle that connects "environment and labour struggles to the student struggle."[72] Student organizations in the United States have been working toward forging such connections, taking their cues from the recent student movements in Quebec and Chile. Rather than wait for the leadership of business unions or rely solely on "spectacular politics" of protest demonstrations, as student Marianne Garneau argues, groups of students have been organizing themselves around a range of issues extending from labor rights to education to social justice.[73]

Graduate students at New York University are working with labor leaders from the United Auto Workers to unionize graduate student teaching assistants, which would set a precedent for private universities in the United States.[74] A group called All in the Red emerged as an activist collective in New York City in the wake of solidarity marches inspired by the Quebec student strike. The group challenges "policies that limit access to higher education and financial entities that profit from the burgeoning student debt crisis."[75] As documented in biweekly updates in the *Nation*, recent student activism has addressed not only tuition hikes, university budget cuts, the imposition of new student fees, and rising student debt, but also cutbacks of ethnic studies programs, labor union and outsourcing struggles within the university, and the funding of universities by corporations and right-wing organizations (for example, New York Students Rising). Students along with faculty supporters are also mobilizing more broadly in favor of election campaign-finance reform (for example, 99Rise), harsh anti-immigrant legislation (for example, Freedom University), and divestiture of shares in fossil fuel companies (a nationwide movement led by Bill McKibben and 350.org).[76]

What becomes clear is that the new student activism encompasses student-focused issues as well as wider social, educational, and workforce issues. In this way, the goals and organizing strategies of the US movement have been inspired by the Quebec students, whom they watched exercise legitimate power in public and political arenas, express solidarity without imposing uniformity, mobilize broader public support, and sit down with politicians and major policy decision-makers. Although organizing is still in its initial stages and must be adapted to US contexts, a number of student voices have drawn lessons from the Quebec movement's use of information campaigns, town hall meetings, mobilization training camps, and joint actions with other universities.[77] Of particular interest has been Quebec student unionism and the federation model of organization deployed to organize the student resistance movement. In the federated model, smaller student groups voted autonomously on issues to address their local contexts but also worked to forge connections with other groups as part of a larger movement.[78]

According to Zachary Bell, this structure allowed for greater student participation across the political spectrum, accountability, and collective action—three critical hallmarks of any genuine democratic process.[79] Across the United States, student groups have been challenging the representation of traditional student governments and business unions. At the University of California, Berkeley, a grassroots activist group called Academic Workers for a Democratic Union ousted its "previously bureaucratic" union leadership and now controls the UC Student-Workers Union UAW Local 2865. It is forming coalitions with other student activist groups to protest the privatization of public education in advance of negotiating a new contract in summer 2013.[80] A common principle vocalized by several of the new student activists (like the more radical Quebec student union, ASSÉ) is the ultimate goal of achieving an egalitarian and free university—as well as the need for students to establish mechanisms for achieving real power within their institutions and the broader society.

One of the major recent examples of US student organizing was the National Student Power Convergence held in Columbus, Ohio, in August 2012. As Kathryn Seidewitz suggests, students attending the massive summit-style meeting expressed a desire to build "power for themselves, within their institutions" in order to demand a greater role in their education and the decision-making structures of the campus.[81] Notably, the students recognize the need for a combination of local campaigns (and the broad-based training and support these require) and horizontal networking at the state level. They are also working to form state-wide and nationwide associations capable of addressing state legislatures thatcontrol education budgets.[82] For instance, a number of student groups have organized to challenge new discriminatory laws against undocumented students, enacted when several state legislatures responded to President Obama's June 2012 Executive Order on "Deferred Action for Childhood Arrivals" by preventing undocumented students from applying for financial aid and requiring them to pay higher out-of-state tuition, or, in the case of Georgia, excluding undocumented youth from attending state universities altogether.[83] As Seidewitz observes, as a result of organizing, undocumented students feel empowered to view themselves as "intellectual workers with rights and agency."[84] Whether emerging student movements in the United States will be able to organize in a sustainable way and continue to engage in ideological and political struggle remains to be seen, but the promise of change now appears on the horizon.

Both the Occupy movement and the Quebec student resistance have ignited a new generation of young people who now face the ongoing challenge of developing a language and a politics that both integrate a meaningful consideration of public life and public values and imagine the possibilities of an insurrectionist democracy not wedded to the dictates of global capitalism.[85] The key challenge for these movements will be to continue to circulate and advance their views in the public sphere through forms of political organization that are as coordinated as they are flexible and open to new ideas. In addition, there is the crucial need to develop sustainable educational institutions and enlarge public spaces in which matters of knowledge, desire, identity, and social responsibility become central to creating a democratic formative culture—understood as the very precondition for the modes of agency and engaged citizenship necessary for any just and inclusive society. This formative culture must make pedagogy central to its understanding of politics and work diligently to provide alternative narratives, stories, subjects, power relations, and values that point to a future when young people and all those others excluded from the savage politics of casino capitalism will create a society in which justice and dignity mutually inform each other.

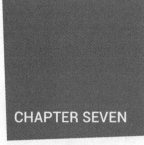

CHAPTER SEVEN

Democracy Unsettled:
From Critical Pedagogy to the War on Youth

**AN INTERVIEW WITH HENRY A. GIROUX
BY MICHAEL A. PETERS**

*I want to conclude with an interview that provides a histor-
ical context for much of the work on critical pedagogy, youth
studies, social justice, cultural politics, and higher education
that I have addressed in this book. For me, this work has not
been easy. As a working-class intellectual, I found myself at
an institution that was largely hostile to my experiences, cultural capital, and the critical scholarship that informed my
work at the university. I believe that such narratives and
struggles need to be made visible in order to articulate the
broader pressures that many academics marginalized by their
backgrounds experience when they push against the grain or
find themselves under assault as part of a hidden curriculum
that has a powerful and invisible order of politics. At the same
time, my own struggle is not meant to reaffirm the often
dystopian nature of the university but to make clear that such*

181

spaces are not without their contradictions and that power is never absolute—social and political change is always possible. Moreover, the interview provides a glimpse into how the interaction between the private and the public have informed my role as a public intellectual in higher education and my attempts to develop an understanding of critical pedagogy as central to the very nature of agency, politics, and democracy itself. Amid the pressures of an institution rife with the legacy of cultural elitism, class structures, racism, and repression, the interview provides an archive and a narrative of critique and possibility, despair and hope, and a glimpse into a particular kind of memory work that illuminates past struggles and the problems of a new historical conjuncture as well as what it means to address them.

Michael Peters: Henry, it is a great pleasure to do this interview with you, as a colleague and friend I have much admired over the years and someone who helped me enormously to develop my work and professional self when I was a young academic. As a young New Zealand academic, I remember reading your work in the 1980s. I was a graduate fresh from a philosophy department, hungry for material that took a critical look at the world. I discovered your early work on postmodern criticism and used the book you wrote with Stanley Aronowitz, *Education Under Siege*, as a text in one of the classes I was teaching. You expressed eloquently many ideas that I was then grappling with and led the way, I suspect, for a generation when you developed as a public intellectual and cultural critic concerned for the fate of young people. In particular, you generously mentored and supported me in publishing my first book, *Education and the Postmodern Condition* (foreword by Lyotard) in your Bergin and Garvey series coedited with Paulo Freire. The experience really kick-started my academic career and, under your auspices, I went on to publish some six books in your series. This was a generous and collegial act for which I am very grateful. I know there must be many other scholars whom you mentored and helped along the way. And this speaks to your role as a public intellectual located increasingly in a networked environment that transforms the concept of intellectual collaboration and enhances the notions of collegiality and the public space of knowledge development.

Let me start this interview by asking you to reflect on your childhood, upbringing, and undergraduate experience. What was it in your background that predisposed you to issues of social justice? Tell us when and under what circumstances you felt outraged at social injustice and became determined to do something about it.

Henry Giroux: I grew up in a working-class neighborhood in the 1950s and '60s that was marked by an ongoing juxtaposition of violence, loyalty, and solidarity. On the one hand, it was a neighborhood where people defined themselves in terms of specific communities, places, and spaces. The notion of the detached individual going it alone and defining his or her existence in mostly individualistic and competitive terms was an anomaly in such a neighborhood. People helped each other in times of need, socialized together, and looked out for each other. At the same time, there was a lot of violence in the neighborhood, often inflicted by the police and other repressive institutions such as the schools. One could not survive in that neighborhood without friends, without recognizing that the protections that offered one a sense of agency and freedom came from the group, not the isolated uncommitted individual so celebrated today. Social justice for me was forged in the bonds of solidarity and the need to recognize both some notion of the common good and the importance of the social.

As a working-class male in a neighborhood where masculinity was a shifting marker of courage, brutality, and identity, the body became the most resourceful tool I had. It was the ultimate source of agency, required in order to survive, ensure respect, and provide a framing mechanism to mediate between oneself and the larger world. Violence in that neighborhood was both personal and institutional. People were poor, many unemployed, and their lives were often lost before they had any chance of maturing. Young people existed in a kind of dead time, waiting to graduate from high school and hoping to get a job, perhaps as a priest, firefighter, or police officer and eventually go on disability. Gender was a dividing line and the violence that permeated our relations with women was rarely ever physical as much as it was ideological and political. Women just didn't matter much outside of very traditional roles. I saw a lot of hardship and love in that neighborhood, and it affected me deeply. On a personal level, my family was very poor, and my father struggled tirelessly to feed us and make sure we had the basic necessities, though he was not always successful. We usually ran out of food by Thursday, one day before my dad got paid. But at least we were not homeless, and we managed to survive less as victims than as a family fighting against larger systemic forces that we were not in a position to control. Such hardships created enormous problems, but they also strengthened our resolve to struggle, embrace the warmth of others, and develop a sense of both humility and outrage in the face of such unnecessary and systemically determined deprivations. But poverty does not just build character, it also produces tensions, injustices, and violence. Surviving was not made for reality TV, it was an effort that put one on guard constantly; it turned time into a deprivation rather than a luxury, and it redefined the parameters of agency, learning, and survival. Justice came quickly in that neighborhood, and it was not always on the side of the angels. Much of my youth until I went to high school was based on getting by, surviving in a world in which my biggest strength was talking fast rather than proving myself as a neighborhood fighter. At six feet and 145 pounds, that wasn't a viable option.

What I lacked at that time was a language to mediate the inequalities, suffering, and modes of solidarity I saw all around me. I got a glimpse of the need for such a discourse when I went to high school, which ironically was named Hope High School. At the time, Hope High School was segregated along class and racial lines. Poor white and Black kids were in what were labeled as the "junk" courses, played sports, and were seen for the most part as both deficit-ridden and delinquent. Most of us entered the school through the back entrance; wealthy white kids came through the front door. It was hard for me to miss the class and racial dimensions of all of this, especially as I was a basketball player and hung out with many of the Black kids on my team. Visiting their neighborhood and playing in gyms on their turf was relatively easy, but they could not come into my neighborhood without suffering the indignities of racial slurs or much worse.

My sense of social justice began at that moment when the lived experience of solidarity and loyalty rubbed up against my own unquestioned racism and sexism, which had a long history in the daily encounters of my youth. Sometimes the contradictions that characterize the "common sense" of racism and sexism were challenged and became unraveled. Treating people as objects or understanding them through established stereotypes was being constantly tested as I moved through high school and met Black men and women who refuted those stereotypes and had the kindness and intelligence to open my eyes through both their own lived experiences and their access to a critical language that I lacked.

Everything changed when I went to college, at least on my second attempt. The first time I left for college, I attended a junior college on a basketball scholarship, but I was not ready for the cultural shift. I felt terribly insecure in that space, did not know how to navigate the cultural capital of middle-class kids, and within a short time dropped out. After working for two years in odd jobs, I got another basketball scholarship to a small school in Maine. This all took place in the sixties—a time in which language, social relations, and culture itself were changing at an accelerated rate. It was hard to miss the changes, ignore the civil rights struggles, and not feel the collective hope that was driving student protests against the Vietnam War and middle-class mores. I got caught up in it very quickly. Knowledge took on a new register for me, just as the changing cultural mores deeply affected my sense of both the present and the future. As a result, knowledge was not just powerful but sexy; language became my weapon of choice. Social justice as a means to live in a better world was the preeminent issue touching the lives of most of the people around me at the time. In college, I read avidly, moving between Marx and James Baldwin, immersing myself in Beat literature and trying to figure out how all of this made sense in terms of my own critical agency and what role I might play in shaping a better world.

Enrolling in a teacher education program was enormously important for me because I quickly realized the ethical and political dimensions of teaching and how important the issue of developing a critical consciousness and formative culture was to any viable democratic society. After graduating, I went to Appalachian State University for an MA in history and became a research assistant for a young and passionate assistant professor named Bob Sandels. Bob was an incredibly sharp leftist intellectual, and he did more than anyone at the time to connect the dots for me around a number of domestic and foreign policy issues in which social and economic justice were central. Once I graduated, I ended up teaching at the high school level for several years and started reading Paulo Freire and Howard Zinn, both of whom eventually became close friends. From that point, I was on fire, and fortunately the fire never went out.

MP: So your working-class credentials have stayed with you. I'm interested in the tensions and contradictions of those born into the working class who become professors. May I hear your reflections on your own experience of education as self-transformation? I suspect the reason that Paulo Freire and Howard Zinn resonated with you was in part because of your background. Perhaps you could also detail the nature of your relationships with these two thinkers.

HG: Being an academic from the working class is, of course, impacted by many registers, extending from ideology and cultural capital to politics. When I first started teaching at Boston University I did not have the knowledge, theoretical tools, or the experience to move into a world largely dominated by middle- and ruling-class cultural capital. I was constantly confronted with faculty and students who assumed a god-given right of privilege and power, especially with regards to their academic credentials, middle-class language skills, and lifelong experience in which people like me were defined through our deficits and largely as outsiders—as imaginary others incapable of narrating ourselves. Or, even worse, our very presence in the academy meant that we had to assimilate mentally to the middle class, or at least act as if we were. This often meant dressing a particular way, speaking in elaborate code, and immersing oneself into the cultural circuits that middle-class people enjoyed.

All of these requisite changes were brought home to me during my second semester. My father had just died of a heart attack, and I had returned to the campus after attending his funeral. My dean at the time was a guy named Bob Dentler, an Ivy League–educated scholar. I ran into him on the street shortly after my father's death and he said to me, "I am sorry to hear about your father. It must have been difficult settling his estate." Estate? My father left a hundred dollars in an envelope taped behind a mirror. That was his estate. I was immediately struck by how out of touch so many academics are with respect to those others who are not replicas of themselves. But as I began to understand how class was mapped onto academia, I was determined not to play the role of the subservient, aspiring-to-be-middle-class professional. I had no intention of letting myself morph into a golf-playing suburbanite living a politically irrelevant academic life. I viewed myself as being on the left, and my politics provided me with the tools to be not only self-reflective but also critical of the cultural capital that dominated the academy and passed itself off as entirely normalized. I had no interest in narrowly defined, almost-choking specializations, stifling forms of professionalism, appeals to positivism, or a politics that largely removed the university from the society.

I was also lucky in that before I became an academic, I lived in Providence, Rhode Island, and took advantage of the many free lectures Brown University offered. Watching the radical lawyer William Kunstler and scholar-activist Stanley Aronowitz in many ways saved my life. Here were two working-class intellectuals whose cultural capital was unmistakable. And they knew much more than most of the Ivy League types who invited them. They were passionate, brilliant, and spoke directly to public issues. Of course, I had a certain familiarity with the discourses of radical education, history, and the civil rights movement, having read Paulo Freire, Howard Zinn, and James Baldwin, but it was the existential grounding of such work that quickened in me a willingness to fight for social justice that changed my life. I had been told all my life that the body should not connect with one's head, that passion was a liability in making an argument or taking a position. These figures uprooted that myth very quickly, and I never let go of my working-class sensibility, even though I had to learn middle-class skills and knowledge in order to be a border-crosser—to cross over into a middle-class institution such as academia without burning the bridges that enabled me to get there.

I also remember having a conversation with Joe Kincheloe, who had a similar background. Joe was always such a pleasure to be around because we shared a cultural capital that defined us both within and outside of the academy as outsiders: we were working class and allegedly deficient, unsanctified by Ivy League degrees and harboring a pedigree that connected the body and mind in a way that was often defined by the overly scrubbed and passionless as lacking civility. Of course, it was this shared space that allowed us not only to reject an easy and unproductive sense of resentment but also to interrogate the strengths of the resources hard-wired into our working-class backgrounds, along with what it meant to develop a more expansive and democratic politics. We got along with many different kinds of people, but we were especially sensitive to poor white and minority kids who shared our background and sometimes found a model in what we represented that changed their lives and prepared them for the long struggle ahead.

The starting point for my politics began with questioning what the middle- and ruling-class types alleged were working-class "deficiencies." It was necessary to flip the script on this type of stereotyping aimed at working-class kids. I began to see that my cultural capital could not be reduced to deficits or lack. In fact, I had learned some time back that while my background was problematic in terms of a range of issues extending from violence to sexism, it also provided me with a deep commitment to solidarity and a humility that recognized that people had different capacities and intellectual strengths. My sense of what constitutes a crisis is generally different from my peers. I never bought the arrogance and I never bought the notion that if one were educated in an Ivy League school that guaranteed superior knowledge and a strong set of skills. In due time, the university seemed, with some exceptions of course, to produce academics who were uptight, conservative politically, and personally arrogant. When accompanied by rigorous modes of reflection and discrimination, these alleged lacks became for me a formidable resource and source of strength for a more viable sense of critical agency and democratic political commitment. Neither Joe nor I ever faltered on this issue, and I think it served us and our working-class students well.

I have often laughed over the seeming incongruity of being a working-class intellectual, and how such a term often rubbed against the grain of many colleagues whose cultural capital seemed to mark them less by what they knew than by how much they had to unlearn. It was often difficult to listen to, experience, and tolerate the pompous self-flattery, the impenetrable discourses, the rigid specializations, the flat affect, and the decidedly antipolitical posturing that characterized so many in the academy. These were academics who were both clever and frivolous, antipolitical, and often indifferent to the growing plight of human suffering. Their academic work was often utterly privatized and unconnected to important social issues and always haughty—and they were quite unaware of the caricatures they had become. For others, intellectual courage had given way to the comfortable space of accommodation, and the notion of the public intellectual had been replaced by the "public relations intellectual," the overheated talking head spewing out sound bites and providing "scholarshit" to various media outlets. I increasingly came to believe that I was in an educational setting where most academics had withdrawn into a world in which the measure of theoretical prowess was determined by the degree to which it escaped from any sense of responsibility, or for that matter any notion of consequential thinking.

Being in the academy for me was a form of soft exile. I have always felt as if I did not belong there, though I was far from alienated over the issue. I simply did my work, published, taught, and used the academy as a site from which to do what I was thought was important educational and democratically inspired political work. I realized early that coming from a working-class background gave me at least a couple of advantages in academia. Because I did not have to unlearn all of the cultural junk that came with middle- and ruling-class ideologies, I had more time to be reflective about my own work, politics, and the role I would play in furthering the discourses of critical agency, education, pedagogy, politics, and hope.

I have felt isolated, but not alone, in the academy. Fortunately, a number of friends, including Joe Kincheloe, Richard Quantz, Paulo Freire, Stanley Aronowitz, Roger Simon, Peter McLaren, and Donaldo Macedo helped me to find solidarity in often dark places. These spaces are no longer as dark for me as they were when I was first teaching at Boston University, and I believe being an outsider in the academy offers both the possibility for developing an opening to consider critical insights forged within a working-class sensibility and the never ending challenge presented by class lines.

MP: Thanks.This is exactly the kind of reflection and autobiographical detail I was hoping would emerge. There is a need for those traditionally excluded from the academy to be able to identify with those who have negotiated the class experience so successfully as you have. I am also interested in your remarks about privilege and the way in which many professors simply take class position for granted. To what extent is the university a class-based institution? One other aspect that you allude to in your experience is the way university administrations are often out of sync with the professoriate. I know that you have been targeted because of your beliefs. I know also that you have theorized the institution and its development under the conditions of neoliberalism. Please share with us your thoughts on the neoliberal and neoconservative attacks on the Left and the rise of the neoliberal university.

HG: Higher education in the United States has the appearance of a meritocracy, but that belies the ways in which wealth and power shape the hierarchical nature of the system. Working-class kids in the United States, if they have aspirations of getting a college diploma, generally do not have the funds to support such an endeavor, particularly given the spiralling tuition rates of the last few decades. And when they do go on to some form of higher education, many of them wind up in community colleges or technical schools. Of course, in the past we had programs like the GI Bill that made access easier, but those days are over. Economic inequality is now hardwired into the central core and structure of the university thanks to neoliberalization, though mass access to higher education has always been a kind of holy grail. So access is largely a class issue, but also a racial issue. The culture of much of higher education has little to do with the histories, experiences, languages, and cultural backgrounds of many working-class and minority kids. Middle- and upper-class cultural capital tends to crush these kids, and the damage is inflicted more heavily when there are no remedial programs available to compensate for the poor education they often receive in underfunded and neglected schools that largely serve to contain and criminalize the behaviors of the disenfranchised. For many working-class youth, time is a burden, not a luxury, and they have to often work while trying to take classes and make the requisite grades. College for these kids is an uphill battle. They often compete with middle-class kids who can spend most of their time studying or attending classes.

In terms of the university itself, the attack on higher education by right-wing ideologues and corporate power has been going on for a long time, but at the current historical conjuncture it has gotten much worse. As a democratic public sphere, it offers students the skills, knowledge, and values to develop the capacity for critique, dialogue, and informed judgment. Increasingly in a market-driven and militarized society, such capacities are viewed as irrelevant, if not dangerous. As public funds are drained from university budgets, the liberal arts downsized, and tuition increases, higher education aligns itself more closely with the culture, values, and incentives of the business world. One consequence is that economic Darwinism is now undermining the civic and intellectual promises that make higher education a public good. Managerial modes of governance, the rise of part-time faculty, and the prevalence of an empirically based audit culture now drives the mission of higher education, which increasingly is about training the elite and low-paid workers for the global workforce. Moreover, the most important value of higher education is now tied to the need for credentials. In the search for adopting market values and cutting costs, classes have ballooned in size, and there is an increased emphasis on rote learning and standardized testing. Disciplines and subjects that do not fall within the purview of mathematical utility and economic rationality are now seen as dispensable. Like most neoliberal models of education, higher education only matters to the extent that it promotes national prosperity and drives economic growth, technical innovation, and market transformation.

In the United States, this neoliberal model can be understood through a number of corporatizing tendencies. Under the rubric of austerity, higher education has for all intents and purposes adopted the organizational structure, values, and culture of medium-sized or big corporations. University presidents now speak in the name of big ideas or inspiring social visions, they now align themselves with business values, and they openly associate themselves with corporate interests. As business culture permeates higher education, all manner of school practices from food services to specific modes of instruction and the hiring of temporary faculty are now outsourced to private contractors. In some universities, new college deans are shifting their focus outside of the campus in order to take on fundraising and establish industry partnerships that were once the job of the university president. Academic leadership now draws less from the reservoir of democratic ideals, struggles, and modes of witnessing than from the corporate playbook of strategic planning and fundraising. This is not meant to wholeheartedly condemn the necessity for fundraising, which can also be productive, as much as it is to insist that it cannot take priority over modes of leadership rooted in more democratic, emancipatory, and noncommodified values.

Neoliberal austerity and disciplinary measures now dominate most major universities. Moreover, as higher education becomes more corporatized it becomes more conservative, more willing to bend to right-wing ideological interests that would have been anathema to higher education just a few decades ago. For instance, the prestigious Washington University in St. Louis gave a doctorate in 2008 to Phyllis Schlafly. This is the same person who opposes "the Equal Rights Amendment, the United Nations, Darwinism . . . blamed the Virginia Tech massacre on the English department [and] advocated banning women from traditionally male occupations like construction, firefighting, and the military."[1] At the same time, one of the most serious threats to higher education is the increasing reliance on part-time faculty—who generally have no power, are paid starvation wages, lack benefits, and have no prestige. Currently more than 70 percent of undergraduate college instruction is in the hands of part-time faculty who are overworked and underpaid. Not only is the quality of instruction, the welfare of students, and the democratic function of the university undermined under such circumstances, but the governance structure of the university is largely in the hands of a corporate-oriented managerial class that has little respect for the liberal arts and has harnessed the future of higher education to a business culture that mimics the culture of the corporate boardroom. This new class of precarious academic labor and growing pool of students who define themselves largely as consumers cancels out the democratic mission of the university and has potentially disastrous consequences for the future of higher education, wherever this model is emulated.

As higher education is increasingly restructured by the interests of corporations and the security state, academic freedom is compromised and faculty live in fear of losing their jobs for being too critical of established authority. The loss of faculty autonomy breeds academic unfreedom and makes the faculty vulnerable to outside right-wing interests who are increasingly monitoring what faculty teach, what they say, and what they publish. For example, Republican Party legislators in Wisconsin have used the courts to gain access to faculty e-mails—a new form of digital terrorism designed to keep academics in their place or in a state of constant fear about what they say or publish. As state spending is slashed to the bone, the university is transformed into a training ground for corporate and military interests, as I have pointed out in *The University in Chains: Confronting the Military-Industrial-Academic Complex.* In addition, the university is transformed into a credentializing factory, one that eschews teaching students the skills necessary for them to be engaged critical citizens and to keep democracies alive. As management principles drive the organization and culture of higher education, research becomes more entrepreneurial, student access is driven by purchasing power, public values are replaced by market values, departmental resources are determined by how close the latter align with corporate interests, and teaching is geared toward producing human capital for the global economy.

If it is viewed as simply a training ground for the corporate order and the national security state, then higher education will default on its promise of a democratic future for young people and its investment in a social state. The antipublic social formation that has emerged with neoliberalism has no interest in fostering the formative cultures and social relationships necessary for young people to imagine themselves as critically engaged and socially responsible citizens. While the difficulty of overcoming these conditions cannot be exaggerated, it is time for educators and concerned citizens to develop a new political language that connects the dots between the wars abroad and the war happening at home—a language that understands the assault on higher education as part of a broader assault on the welfare state, critical thought, and democracy itself. The consequences of such an egregious assault on the university will be the destruction of any vestige of higher education as a public good and democratic public sphere. Clearly, there is more at stake here than the abrogation of workers' bargaining rights and skyrocketing university tuition rates. There are also questions regarding what kind of society we want to become and what is going to have to be done to stop the arrogant and formidable assault on all aspects of democratic life now being waged by the financial elite, corporations, conservatives, reactionary think tanks, authoritarian politicians, and a right-wing media that ignores every principle of honor, decency, and truth. Of course, the point is for intellectuals and others to make it clear that neoliberal and neoconservative forces are transforming the university into an antidemocratic public sphere and to provide a discourse of possibility that challenges this terrible reconfiguration of higher education. Let me mention a few possibilities informed by my own work on the neoliberalization of the university.

First, educators and others need to figure out how to defend more vigorously higher education as a public good. If we can't do that, we're in trouble. Secondly, we need to address what the optimum conditions are for educators, artists, activists, and so on, to perform their work in an autonomous and critical fashion. In other words, we need to think through the conditions that make academic labor fruitful, engaging, and relevant. Third, we need to turn the growing army of temporary workers now swelling the ranks of the academy into full-time, permanent staff. The presence of so many part-time employees is scandalous and both weakens the power of the faculty and exploits them. Fourth, we need to educate students to be critical agents, to learn how to take risks, engage in thoughtful dialogue, and address what it means to be socially responsible. Pedagogy is not about training; it is about educating people to be self-reflective, critical, and self-conscious about their relationship with others and to know something about their relationship with the larger world. Pedagogy in this sense not only provides important thoughtful and intellectual competencies; it also enables people to act effectively upon the societies in which they live.

Pedagogy also takes on a new dimension and impact with the rise of digital technologies and the endlessly multiplying forms of screen culture, each attempting to win over new and larger audiences and more often than not mark them as potential consumers. These new technologies and the proliferating sites in which they are appearing constitute powerful configurations of what C. Wright Mills termed "cultural apparatuses" engaged in modes of popular education. They represent more specifically pervasive forms of public pedagogy that increasingly function to divorce learning from any vestige of critical thought. These powerful forms of public pedagogy need to be addressed, both for how they distort and how they can create important new spaces for emancipatory forms of pedagogy. Not only do we need to understand who controls these cultural apparatuses and how they mobilize new desires, needs, modes of identity, and social relations, we also need to challenge the new media in terms of their power, what they represent and how they present it. Public pedagogy is a site of struggle in which critically engaged intellectuals can address broader audiences and raise in the public domain a number of important social and political issues. The articulation of knowledge to experience, the construction of new modes of agency, the production of critical knowledge, the recovery of critical histories, and the possibility of linking knowledge to social change cannot be limited to influencing students in the classroom. Everyone, but especially those of us working in education, have to extend our roles as public intellectuals to other pedagogical sites, audiences, and institutions. It is politically imperative to organize a whole range of people outside of the academy. For this, as I mentioned above, we need a new political language with broader narratives. I am not against identity politics or single-based issues, but we need to find ways to connect these issues to more encompassing, global narratives about democracy so we can recognize their strengths and limitations in building broad-based social movements. In short, it is imperative that as educators and socially responsible intellectuals, artists, parents, and concerned citizens, we must act for justice and against injustice. And such a call to pursue the truth with a small "t" must be shaped by informed judgments, self-reflection, searing forms of critique, civic courage, and a deep commitment to education as central to the struggle for democracy and social change. Needless to say, we need to find new ways to connect education to the struggle for a democratic future, which is now being undermined in ways that were unimaginable thirty years ago.

MP: Thanks, Henry. I appreciate the way in which your analysis proceeds from a combination of personal experience and critical theory. Your works have sustained us for many decades now and the thrust of your work in terms of critical pedagogy, cultural studies, youth culture, and global studies in communication provides both a powerful theoretical lens and a practical critique of contemporary neoliberal society. I know these interests did not develop chronologically and there are many overlapping characteristics. It would be interesting to hear of the evolution of your thought in terms of these perspectives and what you think is required to be a critical thinker today, in an age of global media.

HG: My interest in critical pedagogy grew out of my experience as a secondary school teacher. I came of age in the 1960s as a teacher and there was a great deal of latitude in what we were allowed to teach then. I taught a couple of seminars in social studies and focused on feminist studies, theories of alienation, and a range of other important social issues. While I had no trouble finding critical content, including progressive films I used to rent from the Quakers (Society of Friends), I did not know how to theorize the various approaches to teaching I tried in the classroom. This all came to a head when an assistant principal confronted me after class once and demanded that I not put the students in a circle while teaching the class. I really could not defend my position theoretically. Fortunately, I was introduced to Paulo Freire's *Pedagogy of the Oppressed*, and from then on my interest in radical pedagogy began to develop. My interest in young people also developed during that time, though I don't believe I had any idea that it would later become a serious object of scholarship and political intervention for me. After graduating from Carnegie-Mellon University in 1977, I became deeply involved with the work being produced around the sociology of education in England, the work of Bowles and Gintis on the political economy of schooling as well as the Marxist ethnographic work developed by Paul Willis at the Birmingham Center for Cultural Studies. All of this scholarship was heavily influenced by various shades of Marxism, and while I learned a great deal from it, I felt that it erred on the side of political economy and did not say enough about either resistance, pedagogy, or the importance of cultural politics. The structural nature of this work was gloomy, overdetermined, and left little room for seizing upon contradictions, developing a theory of power that did not collapse into domination or imagining a language of struggle and hope.

I began to look elsewhere for theoretical models to develop a more comprehensive understanding of schooling and its relationship to larger social, economic, and cultural forces and found it in the work of contemporary critical theorists, especially those of the Frankfurt School. I drew upon critical theory to challenge the then dominant culture of positivism as well as the overemphasis on the political economy of schooling. *Theory and Resistance in Education* was the most well-known outcome of that investigation. And while it is considered a classic in some quarters, I must say that I had a hard time publishing my work in the late 1970s and early 1980s. Work in educational theory and practice in the United States was dominated by Routledge Press, which was inclined to publish mostly scholarship that moved safely within the parameters of Marxism and political economy. I was fortunate at that time to meet Roger Simon, who not only published my work in the prestigious journal *Curriculum Inquiry* but also taught me a great deal about how to theorize matters of pedagogy and schooling. Roger was brilliant, and his work in my estimation far exceeded anything being published on critical education at the time, especially his book *Teaching Against the Grain*. I believe that *Theory and Resistance in Education* would never have been written if it had not been for my ongoing conversations with Roger.

In the 1970s and '80s, I developed a friendship with Donaldo Macedo and Paulo Freire, and we soon started an education series with Bergin and Garvey that later became the Greenwood series. It opened up a new space for publishing a variety of work from theorists dealing with critical pedagogy and educational theory more broadly. Crucial to my own conception of pedagogy is that I saw it as a moral and political practice that was about more than analyzing classrooms and schools. Pedagogy for me was central to proclaiming the power and necessity of ideas, knowledge, and culture as central to any viable definition of politics, and the goal of living in a just world with others. Pedagogy remains a crucial political resource in theorizing the importance of establishing a formative culture conducive to creating subjects and values that can sustain a substantive democracy.

I was also deeply influenced in the 1980s by the cultural studies movement in the United States and England, particularly the work of Larry Grossberg, Meaghan Morris, Paul Gilroy, Paul Willis, Angela McRobbie, Richard Johnson, and Stuart Hall. The early work in cultural studies on education and youth was very important to my own theoretical development. Not only did it emphasize the importance of pedagogy inside of the academy, but Raymond Williams opened up the concept with an exploration of what he called "permanent education" and offered the beginning of a theoretical framework for taking seriously the educational force of the wider culture. At that point, I attempted to revive the centrality of pedagogy for cultural studies, particularly given that many of the theorists who followed Williams seem either to display little interest in it or to assume that it meant teaching cultural studies in schools. Pedagogy in this case had become the present absence in cultural studies, just as youth had become the present absence among left theorizing in general. While there was considerable talk about class, race, and gender, there were very few people writing in the United States about the plight of young people and the transformation from a society of production to a society of consumption, or, as Zygmunt Bauman points out, the move from solid modernity to liquid modernity. Young people, especially minorities of class and color, were under siege in a particularly harsh way at the beginning of the 1980s, and there were very few people addressing what I called the "war on youth." I argued then and continue to insist that since the 1980s we have seen a series of political, economic, and cultural shifts that mark the beginning of a form of economic Darwinism, on the one hand, and the rise of the punishing state, on the other. And one consequence of the merging of these two movements is this war on youth. I have attempted to chart and engage the shifting parameters of the war on youth in a number of books, with the recent and perhaps most definitive being *Youth in a Suspect Society: Democracy or Disposability?*

In the aftermath of Reagan and Thatcher, neoliberalism was becoming normalized all over the globe. This was particularly evident to me by the early 1990s, as neoliberal capitalism became more ruthless, consolidated, and poisonous in its ever-expanding support for a culture of cruelty and a survival-of-the-fittest ethic in which market-driven values and relations acted as the template for judging all aspects of social life. By transforming society into the image of the market, the space and conditions for thinking outside of market values and relations became more difficult, and one particularly grim consequence was the demolition of nonmarket values, public spheres, and forms of community. As democratic social forms diminished, so did social values, the public good, social responsibility, and the very nature of politics. This was a very destructive moment for both the United States and the rest of the world. Just as corporate sovereignty replaced or weakened political sovereignty, the attack on the social state intensified, the power of capital became detached from the traditional politics of the nation state, the punishing state was on the rise, and there emerged a new set of economic and social formations in which social protections were weakened, social problems were increasingly criminalized, and all public spheres were subjected to the forces of privatization and commodification, especially public and higher education.

Under neoliberalism, we have witnessed the rise of an unfettered free-market ideology and economic Darwinism in which market values supplant civic values. Everything is for sale. A hyper-individualism is celebrated. Profit-making is seen as the essence of democracy, and the obligations of citizenship are reduced to the practice of consuming. This is a system in which a dehumanizing mode of consumerism and the unencumbered concentration of capital are matched by the endless disposing not only of goods, but also human beings, many of whom as flawed consumers, immigrants, or low-income whites and poor minorities are considered redundant and disposable. This is also a system in which everything is privatized, with one grave consequence being that the public collapses into the private. It becomes increasingly difficult to translate private concerns into public issues. My work in the last decade has aimed at connecting neoliberal forms of public pedagogy and authoritarian disciplinary practices with the rise of new modes of individualism and what it means to make such forces visible in order to collectively resist them. This project has been deeply influenced by the work of diverse figures such as Pierre Bourdieu, Angela Davis, Edward Said, Zygmunt Bauman, Hannah Arendt, Nancy Fraser, C. Wright Mills, Stanley Aronowitz, and more recently David L. Clark.

Bourdieu's work on neoliberalism and Bauman's work on liquid modernity and the transformation of the public sphere are treasure troves of insight regarding the changing conditions of modernity, the politics of consumerism, and the call for new modes of ethical responsibility. Arendt's work on authoritarianism and its potentially recurring conditions, albeit in new forms, along with Nancy Fraser's brilliant work on feminist public spheres provided me with a new language to think about the institutions and spaces necessary for a formative culture that makes democratic modes of agency and subjectivity possible. Said's and Bourdieu's work on the responsibility of academics as public intellectuals had a profound effect on my scholarship. Similarly, C. Wright Mills deeply influenced me on the importance of connecting private issues to public considerations, the centrality of cultural apparatuses in the transformation of political culture, and the role public intellectuals might play as agents of change.

Stanley Aronowitz may be one of the most brilliant public intellectuals in North America. His broad understanding of various domains of knowledge and his ability to bring vastly different issues together and to engage them in relation to a larger totality is a model for how to do scholarship that is public, rigorous, and dialectical. Finally, I would be remiss to not underscore the more recent influence of my colleague David L. Clark. His erudition—which never fails to astound me—has been instrumental in fine-tuning my knowledge of critical theory, Derrida, and a range of other theoretical traditions that he engages and writes about in ways that are as insightful as they are poetic. David's sense of solidarity and commitment is remarkable in an academy that increasingly seems addicted to the insularities of careerism, cronyism, and the need to comfort students—now viewed as customers with rights rather than obligations—rather than prepare them intellectually for a world that needs to be engaged, not merely enjoyed.

To be an intellectual in the current historical juncture is not only to rethink the profound changes wrought by the rise and power of the new media and the ways in which it has transformed the very concept of the social, communal, and political but to redefine what it means to be a public intellectual capable of working across a number of disciplines and speaking to a variety of audiences. The old model of the intellectual writing and speaking in a narrow and obtuse theoretical language seems unproductive at this particular point in history. Theory needs to be rigorous *and* accessible, and it needs to address not merely the outer limits of disciplinary scholarship but also important social problems. Equally important, it needs to include and engage people who are not versed in the specialized disciplinary vocabularies of the academy. Theory is neither a metaphor for scholasticism and formalism nor is it politically irrelevant. Nor can it be dismissed as something distinctly American or French, or a thing exotic or foreign. Theory is essential and inescapable and cannot be so neatly abstracted from the responsibilities of political criticism, but how we do it and for what reason is a more problematic and troubling issue. What does it mean to *use* theory rather than simply apply it as many graduate students and professors tend to do?

Theory is the enemy of "common sense," and hence hated by many of our newly minted anti-intellectual authoritarian populists who ran against Obama in the 2012 elections. Of course, there is another important question regarding when theory becomes toxic, an immunity against immunity, turning in on itself, functioning, to use Derrida's term, as kind of autoimmunity. Given the bankruptcy of the current anti-intellectual politics of the "self-evident," theory is all we have left and functions as a kind of toolbox to be used to break the consensus of common sense, develop better forms of knowledge, and promote more just social relations. Theory is an indispensable resource in the task of thinking through and developing new modes of agency, power, and action in the service of connecting knowledge and power, meaning and social relevance, and private troubles and public issues. Clearly, self-reflection, mastering broad bodies of knowledge, and engaging with new technologies as a way to reach broader audiences all matter—just as it is only through theory that we can recover what survives of the defeated, the repressed, the marginalized, and those ideas relegated as obsolete, un-American, and indigestible. But there is also something more fundamental at work in this project. The global Left doesn't need to abandon theory; it needs to find a new language in order to move away from the kinds of fractured politics that have dominated Western societies since the 1980s.

In a similar manner, the politics of identity has to guard against becoming exclusionary and needs to be rethought of as part of a much broader set of connections and projects. In the 1980s, I believe that a group of highly influential feminist theorists in education did a great deal of damage politically and ethically to the understanding of both critical pedagogy and radical education as a practice of transformation and freedom. Rather than build upon and critically engage the complex traditions out of which this work developed, interrogating both its strengths and weaknesses, treating it as a developing and ongoing theoretical discourse and practice, they falsely labeled critical pedagogy as the enemy of empowerment. Operating out of comforting absolutes on the model of us versus them, this rhetoric of simplistic oppositions furthered a manipulative discourse and a climate for political opportunism. A crude type of essentialism and reductionism structured this work. Rather than engage a complex tradition of work, it simply demonized it, reducing it to one side of a binarism in which all doubt, mediation, complexity, and nuance disappeared.

What made this intervention even worse was that it was followed by an endless stream of endorsements by supine white male academics who cited this work to prove their own faux feminist credentials. This was truly as ideologically disingenuous as it was politically reactionary, or even worse, dangerous. Unaware of its own refusal to engage in nuanced and thoughtful analytic and deconstructive work, this type of feminist educational theory put forth its own mechanical and positivist calculations as if such work offered political guarantees, buttressed by the absolutism and vitriol in which it was sometimes delivered. This was symptomatic of what a particular version of identity politics can become when it is driven by moralism, a politics of purity, a logic of certainty, and a disregard for critical and scholarly exchange. There is more at work here than simply hubris and a denial of the complexity of the work under review; there is also a claim to moral and political clarity that actually produces its opposite. Fortunately, some of this work was offset by a smaller number of feminist scholars working in critical pedagogy who rejected this type of friend/enemy distinction. This was particularly evident at the time in the brilliant work by Linda Brodkey, bell hooks, Deborah Britzman, Sharon Todd, Chandra Mohanty, Sharon Crowley, Lynn Worsham, and later by Robin Truth Goodman and Susan Searls Giroux.

Rather than fire missiles at each other, public intellectuals need to address how we can effectively understand our differences as part of a broader and more powerful movement for engaging in critical exchanges, pushing the frontiers of transformative knowledge, extending democratic struggles, and addressing the massive suffering and hardships, particularly for young people, now being caused by various fundamentalist and authoritarian institutions, policies, and practices. As my partner, Susan Searls Giroux, has stated with characteristic precision, "As a consequence of our devastatingly misguided priorities and our negligence we have, in short, produced smart bombs and explosive children."

We need to make connections, build broad social movements, make pedagogy central to politics, and dismantle the reactionary forms of neoliberalism, racism, and media culture that have become normalized. We need to take up and develop more relational theories concerned with broader totalities and the ways in which the forces of difference, identity, local politics, cultural pedagogy, and other social formations interact in ways that speak to new and more threatening forms of global politics. Power is now free floating; it has no allegiances except to the accumulation of capital and is not only much more destructive but also more difficult to contain. Any viable notion of politics has to be relational and connected; it has to think within and beyond the boundaries of nation-states, invent new vocabularies, invest in more broad-based groups beyond simply workers, address the plight of young people, and resurrect the power of the social state and democracy as a radical mode of governance and politics. This suggests taking matters of specificity and context seriously, while at the same time changing the level of magnification to a more global view.

One of the most important considerations necessary for a new vision of politics is incorporating economic rights and social protections into the political sphere. Political and personal rights become dysfunctional without social rights. As Zygmunt Bauman reminds us, freedom of choice and the exercise of political and personal rights become a cruel joke in a society that does not provide social rights—that is, some form of collectively endorsed protections that provide the time and space for the poor and disenfranchised to participate in the political sphere and help shape modes of governance. In order to exercise any real sense of civic agency, people need protections from those misfortunes and hardships that are not of their own doing. At the same time, a movement for democracy must challenge the erosion of social bonds, the crumbling of communal cohesion, and the withering of social responsibility that have taken place under a neoliberal apparatus that promotes deregulation, privatization, and individualization. We also need to think in terms of what it means to create the formative cultures necessary to fight racism, celebrity culture, the culture and institutions of casino capitalism, the assault on the environment, and the growing inequality in wealth and income that is destroying every vestige of democratic politics in the world. We need a language that takes both history and the current dangerous authoritarian period seriously, one that recognizes, as Bauman points out, that shared humanity is the lifeboat. Too many people on the left are acting as if they are living in the nineteenth century and are completely out of touch with the new technologies, modes of domination, and emerging social formations that are taking shape all over the world.

A viable politics in the present has to take seriously the premise that knowledge must be meaningful in order to be critical, in order to be transformative. This is about more than reclaiming the virtues of dialogue, exchange, and translation. It is about recovering a politics and inventing a language that can create democratic public spheres in which new subjects and identities can be produced that are capable of recognizing and addressing the plight of the other and struggling collectively to expand and deepen the ongoing struggle for justice, freedom, and democratization. The global Left needs to be thorough, accessible, and rigorous in our critiques, especially amid the political and cultural illiteracy produced by neoliberalism's cultural apparatuses. But we also need a language of hope, one that is realistic rather than romantic about the challenges the planet is facing and yet electrified by a realization that things can be different, that possibilities can not only be imagined but engaged, fought for, and realized in collective struggles.

Opposing the forces of domination is important, but it does not go far enough. We must move beyond a language of pointless denunciations and offer instead a language that moves forward with the knowledge, skills, and social relations necessary for the creation of new modes of agency, social movements, and democratic economic and social policies. We need to open up the realm of human possibility, recognize that history is open, that justice is never complete, and that democracy can never be fully settled. I fervently believe in the need for both critique and hope, and have faith that the Left can develop the public spheres that make such possibilities possible, whether they be schools, classrooms, workshops, newspapers, online journals, community colleges, or other spaces where knowledge, power, ethics, and justice merge to create new subjectivities, new modes of civic courage, and new hope for the future.

NOTES

Introduction: Neoliberalism's War on Democracy

1. These themes are taken up extensively in David Harvey, *A Brief History of Neoliberalism* (New York: Oxford University Press, 2005), David Harvey, *The Enigma of Capitalism* (New York: Oxford University Press, 2010), and Colin Crouch, *The Strange Non-Death of Neoliberalism* (Cambridge: Polity, 2011).

2. This quote is from Andrew Reszitnyk, "Beyond Difference and Becoming: Towards a Non-Differential Practice of Critique," a paper presented as part of his 2013 doctoral comprehensive exam. For other sources on neoliberalism, see Manfred B. Steger and Ravi K. Roy, *Neoliberalism: A Very Short Introduction* (New York: Oxford University Press, 2010); Juliet B. Schor, *Plenitude: The New Economics of True Wealth* (New York: Penguin Press, 2010); Henry A. Giroux, *Against the Terror of Neoliberalism* (Boulder, CO: Paradigm, 2008); Harvey, *Brief History of Neoliberalism*; and John Comaroff and Jean Comaroff, eds., *Millennial Capitalism and the Culture of Neoliberalism* (Durham, NC: Duke University Press, 2001). On the moral limits and failings of neoliberalism, see Michael J. Sandel, *What Money Can't Buy* (New York: Farrar, Straus and Giroux, 2012). And for positing a case for neoliberalism as a criminal enterprise, see Jeff Madrick, *Age of Greed: The Triumph of Finance and the Decline of America, 1970 to the Present* (New York: Vintage, 2011); Charles Ferguson, *Predator Nation: Corporate Criminals, Political Corruption, and the Hijacking of America* (New York: Crown Business, 2012); Henry A. Giroux, *Zombie Politics in the Age of*

Casino Capitalism (New York: Peter Lang, 2010).

3. João Biehl, *Vita: Life in a Zone of Social Abandonment* (Berkeley and Los Angeles: University of California Press, 2005). These zones are also brilliantly analyzed in Chris Hedges and Joe Sacco, *Days of Destruction, Days of Revolt* (New York: Knopf, 2012).

4. For instance, see Henry A. Giroux, *Youth in a Suspect Society* (New York: Routledge, 2010) and Annette Fuentes, *Lockdown High* (New York: Verso, 2013).

5. Zygmunt Bauman, "Does 'Democracy' Still Mean Anything? (And in Case It Does, What Is It?)" *Truthout*, January 21, 2011, http://truth-out.org/index.php?option=com_k2&view=item&id=73:does-democracy-still-mean-anything-and-in-case-it-does-what-is-it.

6. Lauren Berlant cited in Michael Dawson, *Blacks In and Out of the Left* (Cambridge, MA: Harvard University Press, 2013), 181–182.

7. George Lakoff and Glenn W. G. Smith, "Romney, Ryan and the Devil's Budget," *Reader Supported News*, August 22, 2012, http://blogs.berkeley.edu/2012/08/23/romney-ryan-and-the-devils-budget-will-america-keep-its-soul/.

8. Robert Reich, "Mitt Romney and the New Gilded Age," *Reader Supported News*, June 30, 2012, http://robertreich.org/post/26229451132.

9. David Theo Goldberg, "The Taxing Terms of the GOP Plan Invite Class Carnage," *Truthout*, September 20, 2012, http://truth-out.org/news/item/11630-the-taxing-terms-of-the-gop-plan-invite-class-carnage.

10. Paul Krugman, "Galt, Gold, and God," *New York Times*, August 23, 2012.

11. Ibid.

12. Marian Wright Edelman,"Ending Child Poverty: Child Poverty in America: 2011," Children's Defense Fund, http://www.childrensdefense.org/child-research-data-publications/data/2011-child-poverty-in-america.pdf.

13. Marian Wright Edelman, "Ryanomics Assault on Poor and Hungry Children," *Huffington Post*, September 14, 2012, http://www.huffingtonpost.com/marian-wright-edelman/ryanomics-assault-on-poor_b_1885851.html.

14. Richard D. Wolff, "The Truth about Profits and Austerity," *MR Zine*, March 31, 2013, http://mrzine.monthlyreview.org/2013/wolff310313.html. Wolff develops this position in Richard D. Wolff, *Democracy at Work: A Cure for Capitalism* (Chicago: Haymarket Books, 2012).

15. Igor Volsky, "Pick Your Poison," *Progress Report*, March 4, 2013, http://thinkprogress.org/progress-report/pick-your-poison/?mobile=nc.

16. ThinkProgress War Room, "Sequester: "A Fancy Word for a Dumb Idea," *Think Progress*, March 1, 2013, http://thinkprogress.org/progress-report/?mobile=nc.

17. Reich, "Mitt Romney and the New Gilded Age"; Ferguson, *Predator Nation*; Daisy Grewal, "How Wealth Reduces Compassion: As Riches Grow, Empathy for Others Seems to Decline," *Scientific American*, April 10, 2012, http://www.scientificamerican.com/article.cfmid=how-wealth-reduces-compassion.

18. Bauman, "Does 'Democracy' Still Mean Anything?"

19. Lewis H. Lapham, "Feast of Fools: How American Democracy Became the Property of a Commercial Oligarchy," *Truthout*, September 20, 2012, http://truth-out.org/opinion/item/11656-feast-of-fools-how-american-democracy

-became-the-property-of-a-commercial-oligarchy.

20. Ibid.
21. Zygmunt Bauman, *This Is Not a Diary* (Cambridge: Polity Press, 2012), 102.
22. Lapham, "Feast of Fools."
23. Eric Lichtblau, "Economic Downturn Took a Detour at Capitol Hill," *New York Times*, December 26, 2011, http://www.nytimes.com/2011/12/27/us/politics/economic-slide-took-a-detour-at-capitol-hill.html?pagewanted=all.
24. Peter Grier, "So Much Money, So Few Lobbyists in D.C.: How Does the Math Work?" *DC Decoder*, February 24, 2012, http://www.csmonitor.com/USA/DC-Decoder/Decoder-Wire/2012/0224/So-much-money-so-few-lobbyists-in-D.C.-How-does-that-math-work.
25. Bill Moyers and Bernard Weisberger, "Money in Politics: Where Is the Outrage?" *Huffington Post*, August 30, 2012, http://www.huffingtonpost.com/bill-moyers/money-in-politics_b_1840173.html.
26. Erika Eichelberger, "See How Citigroup Wrote a Bill So It Could Get a Bailout," *Mother Jones*, May 24, 2013, http://www.motherjones.com/politics/2013/05/citigroup-hr-992-wall-street-swaps-regulatory-improvement act.
27. The inhumanity of such modes of punishment are captured brilliantly in Lorna A. Rhodes, *Total Confinement: Madness and Reason in the Maximum Security Prison* (Berkeley and Los Angeles: University of California Press, 2004).
28. It is difficult to access this study because Citigroup does its best to make it disappear from the Internet. See the discussion of it by Noam Chomsky in "Plutonomy and the Precariat: On the History of the U.S. Economy in Decline," *Truthdig*, May 8, 2012, http://www.truthdig.com/report/item/plutonomy_and_the_precariat_the_history_of_the_us_economy_in_decline_201205/.
29. Chrystia Freeland, *Plutocrats: The Rise of the New Global Super-Rich and the Fall of Everyone Else* (New York: Penguin, 2012).
30. See Olivia Ward's interview with Chrystia Freeland. Olivia Ward, "The Rise of the Super-rich: Is the Economy Just Going Through a Bad Patch?" *Truthout*, April 1, 2013, http://truth-out.org/news/item/15452-the-rise-of-the-super-rich-is-the-economy-just-going-through-a-bad-patch.
31. Salvatore Babones, "To End the Jobs Recession, Invest an Extra $20 Billion in Public Education," *Truthout*, August 21, 2012, http://truth-out.org/opinion/item/11031-to-end-the-jobs-recession-invest-an-extra-$20-billion-in-public-education.
32. John Atcheson, "The Real Welfare Problem: Government Giveaways to the Corporate 1%," *Common Dreams*, September 3, 2012, http://www.commondreams.org/view/2012/09/03-7.
33. John Cavanagh, "Seven Ways to End the Deficit (Without Throwing Grandma Under the Bus)," *Yes! Magazine*, September 7, 2012, http://www.yesmagazine.org/new-economy/seven-ways-to-end-the-deficit-without-throwing-grandma-under-the-bus.
34. Ibid.
35. Joseph Stiglitz, "Politics Is at the Root of the Problem," *European Magazine*, April 23, 2012, http://theeuropean-magazine.com/633-stiglitz-joseph/634-austerity-and-a-new-recession.

36. Lynn Parramore, "Exclusive Interview: Joseph Stiglitz Sees Terrifying Future for America If We Don't Reverse Inequality," *AlterNet,* June 24, 2012, http://www.alternet.org/economy/155918/exclusive_interview%3A_joseph_stiglitz_sees_terrifying_future_for_america_if_we_don%27t_reverse_inequality.

37. Editorial, "America's Detainee Problem," *Los Angeles Times,* September 23, 2012, http://articles.latimes.com/2012/sep/23/opinion/la-ed-detention-20120923.

38. Glenn Greenwald, "Unlike Afghan Leaders, Obama Fights for Power of Indefinite Military Detention," *Guardian,* September 18, 2012, www.guardian.co.uk/commentisfree/2012/sep/18/obama-appeals-ndaa-detention-law. See also Glenn Greenwald, "Federal Court Enjoins NDAA," *Salon,* May 16, 2012, www.salon.com/2012/05/16/federal_court_enjoins_ndaa/. See also Henry A. Giroux, *Hearts of Darkness: Torturing Children in the War on Terror* (Boulder, CO: Paradigm, 2010).

39. Charlie Savage, "Judge Rules against Law on Indefinite Detention," *New York Times,* September 12, 2012, www.nytimes.com/2012/09/13/us/judge-blocks-controversial-indefinite-detention-law.html?_r=0.

40. Karen J. Greenberg, "Ever More and Ever Less," *TomDispatch,* March 18, 2012, www.tomdispatch.com/archive/175517/.

41. Catherine Poe, "Federal Judge Emails Racist Joke about President Obama," *Washington Times,* March 1, 2012, http://communities.washingtontimes.com/neighborhood/ad-lib/2012/mar/1/federal-judge-emails-racist-joke-about-president-o/.

42. Amanda Turkel and Sam Stein, "Mitt Romney, on *60 Minutes,* Cities Emergency Room as Health Care Option for Uninsured," *Huffington Post,* September 23, 2012, www.huffingtonpost.com/2012/09/23/mitt-romney-60-minutes-health-care_n_1908129.html?.

43. Editorial, "Why Romney Is Slipping," *New York Times,* September 25, 2012.

44. Brennan Keller, "Medical Expenses: Top Cause of Bankruptcy in the United States," *GiveForward,* October 13, 2011, www.giveforward.com/blog/medical-expenses-top-cause-of-bankruptcy-in-the-united-states.

45. Stanley Aronowitz, *Against Schooling: For an Education That Matters* (Boulder, CO: Paradigm Publishers, 2008), xviii.

46. Reuters, "Goldman Sachs CEO Lloyd Blankfein Says Banks Do 'God's Work,'" *Daily News,* November 9, 2009, http://articles.nydailynews.com/2009-11-09/news/17938614_1_year-end-bonuses-goldman-sachs-lloyd-blankfein.

47. Paul Krugman, "Defining Prosperity Down," *New York Times,* August 1, 2010.

48. Zygmunt Bauman is the most important theorist writing about the politics of disposability. Among his many books, see *Wasted Lives* (London: Polity Press, 2004).

49. Bauman, *Wasted Lives,* 5.

50. Robert Reich, "The Rebirth of Social Darwinism," *Robert Reich's Blog,* November 30, 2011, http://robertreich.org/post/13567144944.

51. Tony Judt, *Ill Fares the Land* (New York: Penguin, 2010).

52. This argument has been made against academics for quite some time, though it has either been forgotten or conveniently ignored by many faculty. See, for example, various essays in C. Wright Mills, "The Powerless People: The Role of

the Intellectual in Society" in C. Wright Mills, *The Politics of Truth: Selected Writings of C. Wright Mills* (Oxford: Oxford University Press, 2008), 13–24; Edward Said, *Humanism and Democratic Criticism* (New York: Columbia University Press, 2004); and Henry A. Giroux and Susan Searls Giroux, *Take Back Higher Education* (New York: Palgrave, 2004).

53. On the university's relationship with the national security state, see David Price, "How the CIA Is Welcoming Itself Back Onto American University Campuses: Silent Coup," *CounterPunch*, April 9–11, 2010, www.counterpunch.org/price04092010.html. See also Nick Turse, *How the Military Invades Our Everyday Lives* (New York: Metropolitan Books, 2008); and Henry A. Giroux, *The University in Chains: Confronting the Military-Industrial-Academic Complex* (Boulder, CO: Paradigm Publishers, 2007).

54. Robert McChesney, *The Problem of the Media* (New York: Monthly Review Press, 2004). See the interesting table by Ashley Lutz, "These Six Corporations Control 90% of the Media in America," *Business Insider*, June 14, 2012, www.businessinsider.com/these-6-corporations-control-90-of-the-media-in-america-2012-6.

55. See, for instance, Chris Mooney, *The Republican War on Science* (New York: Basic Books, 2005).

56. Frank Rich, "Could She Reach the Top in 2012? You Betcha," *New York Times*, November 20, 2010.

57. Cornelius Castoriadis, "Democracy as Procedure and Democracy as Regime," *Constellations* 4, no. 1 (1997): 5.

58. Toni Morrison, "How Can Values Be Taught in This University," *Michigan Quarterly Review* (Spring 2001): 278.

59. Stephen Holden, "Perils of the Corporate Ladder: It Hurts When You Fall," *New York Times*, December 10, 2010.

60. Hart Research Associates, *American Academics: Survey of Part Time and Adjunct Higher Education Faculty* (Washington, DC: AFT, 2011);Steve Street, Maria Maisto, Esther Merves, and Gary Rhoades, *Who Is Professor "Staff" and How Can This Person Teach So Many Classes?* (Los Angeles: Center for the Future of Higher Education, 2012).

61. Andrew Martin and Andrew W. Lehren, "A Generation Hobbled by the Soaring Cost of College," *New York Times*, May 12, 2012.

62. Paul Buchheit, "Five Ugly Extremes of Inequality in America—the Contrasts Will Drop Your Chin to the Floor," *AlterNet*, March 24, 2013, www.alternet.org/economy/five-ugly-extremes-inequality-america-contrasts-will-drop-your-chin-floor.

63. For an excellent defense of critical thinking not merely as a skill, but as a crucial foundation for any democratic society, see Robert Jensen, *Arguing for Our Lives* (San Francisco: City Lights Books, 2013).

64. Cited in Richard J. Bernstein, *The Abuse of Evil: The Corruption of Politics and Religion since 9/11* (London: Polity Press, 2005), 7–8.

65. Paul Buchheit, "Now We Know Our ABCs and Charter Schools Get an F," *CommonDreams*, September 24, 2012, https://www.commondreams.org/view/2012/09/24-0.

66. See Giroux, *The University in Chains*.

67. See, for instance, Robert B. Reich, "Slashed Funding for Public Universities Is Pushing the Middle Class Toward Extinction," *AlterNet*, March 5, 2012, www .alternet.org/education/154410/slashed_funding_for_public_universities_is _pushing_the_middle_class_toward_extinction. For a brilliant argument regarding the political and economic reasons behind the defunding and attack on higher education, see Christopher Newfield, *Unmaking the Public University: The Forty-Year Assault on the Middle Class* (Cambridge, MA: Harvard University Press, 2008).

68. Les Leopold, "Crazy Country: 6 Reasons America Spends More on Prisons Than on Higher Education," *AlterNet*, August 27, 2012, www.alternet.org/ education/crazy-country-6-reasons-america-spends-more-prisons-higher -education?paging=off. On this issue, see also the classic work by Angela Y. Davis, *Are Prisons Obsolete?* (New York: Open Media, 2003) and Michelle Alexander, *The New Jim Crow: Mass Incarceration in the Age of Colorblindness* (New York: New Press, 2012).

69. Leopold, "Crazy Country."

70. Zygmunt Bauman, *The Individualized Society* (London: Polity, 2001), 4.

71. See, for instance, Rebecca Solnit, "Rain on Our Parade: A Letter to the Dismal Left," *TomDispatch*, September 27, 2012, www.tomdispatch.com/blog/175598/ tomgram%3A_rebecca_solnit,_we_could_be_heroes/. *TomDispatch* refers to this article as a call for hope over despair. It should be labeled as a call for accommodation over the need for a radical democratic politics. For an alternative to this politics of accommodation, see the work of Stanley Aronowitz, Chris Hedges, Henry Giroux, Noam Chomsky, and others.

72. This term comes from Daniel Bensaïd. See Sebastian Budgen, "The Red Hussar: Daniel Bensaïd, 1946–2010," *International Socialism* 127 (June 25, 2010), http://www.isj.org.uk/?id=661.

73. Castoriadis, "Democracy as Procedure," 5.

74. Archon Fung, "The Constructive Responsibility of Intellectuals," *Boston Review*, September 9, 2011, www.bostonreview.net/BR36.5/archon_fung_noam _chomsky_responsibility_of_intellectuals.php.

75. Heather Gautney, "Why Do Political Elites All Hate Democracy?" *LA Progressive*, September 19, 2012, www.laprogressive.com/hate-democracy.

76. Stuart Hall and Les Back, "In Conversation: At Home and Not at Home," *Cultural Studies* 23, no. 4 (July 2009), 681.

77. Guy Standing, *The Precariat: The New Dangerous Class* (New York: Bloomsbury, 2011), 20.

Chapter One: Dystopian Education in a Neoliberal Society

1. Some important sources include: Henry A. Giroux, *Education and the Crisis of Public Values* (Boulder, CO: Paradigm Publishers, 2012); Kenneth J. Saltman, *The Failure of Corporate School Reform* (Boulder, CO: Paradigm Publishers,

2012); Diane Ravitch, *The Death and Life of the Great American School System: How Testing and Choice Are Undermining Education* (New York: Basic Books, 2011); Gaston Alonso, Noel S. Anderson, Celina Su, and Jeanne Theoharis, *Our Schools Suck: Students Talk Back to a Segregated Nation on the Failures of Urban Education* (New York: NYU Press, 2009).

2. Graeme Turner, *What's Become of Cultural Studies* (New York: Sage, 2011), 183.

3. See, for example, Madrick, *Age of Greed: The Triumph of Finance and the Decline of America*; Ferguson, *Predator Nation*; Giroux, *Zombie Politics in the Age of Casino Capitalism*.

4. David Theo Goldberg, "The Taxing Terms of the GOP Plan Invite Class Carnage," *Truthout*, September 20, 2012, http://truth-out.org/news/item/11630 -the-taxing-terms-of-the-gop-plan-invite-class-carnage.

5. Jolle Fanghanel, *Being an Academic* (New York: Routledge, 2012), 15.

6. See, for example, Gaye Tuchman, *Wannabe U: Inside the Corporate University* (Chicago: University of Chicago Press, 2009); Martha C. Nussbaum, *Not for Profit: Why Democracy Needs the Humanities*, (Princeton, NJ: Princeton University Press, 2010); Michael Bailey and Des Freedman, eds., *The Assault on Universities: A Manifesto for Resistance* (London: Pluto Press, 2011); Henry A. Giroux, *Twilight of the Social: Resurgent Politics in the Age of Disposability* (Boulder, CO: Paradigm Publishing, 2012).

7. On the religious Right, see Chris Hedges, *American Fascists: The Christian Right and the War on America* (New York: Free Press, 2008) and Clyde Wilcox and Carin Robinson, *Onward Christian Soldiers? The Religious Right in American Politics* (Boulder, CO: Westview Press, 2010).

8. I have taken up the attack on higher education in a number of books. See, for example, Giroux and Searls Giroux, *Take Back Higher Education* and *The University in Chains* (Boulder, CO: Paradigm, 2009).

9. David Theo Goldberg, "The University We Are For," *Huffington Post*, November 28, 2011, http://www.huffingtonpost.com/david-theo-goldberg/university -california-protests_b_1106234.html.

10. Marc Bousquet, *How the University Works: Higher Education and the Low-Wage Nation* (New York: NYU Press, 2008).

11. For a sustained analysis of how inequality undermines democracy and public services, see Richard Wilkinson and Kate Pickett, *The Spirit Level: Why Equality Is Better for Everyone* (New York: Penguin, 2010).

12. John Atcheson, "The Real Welfare Problem: Government Giveaways to the Corporate 1%," *Common Dreams*, September 3, 2012, www.commondreams.org/ view/2012/09/03-7.

13. See Joseph E. Stiglitz, *The Price of Inequality* (New York: W. W. Norton, 2012) and Michael Sandel, *What Money Can't Buy* (New York: FSG Publishing, 2012).

14. Goldberg, "The Taxing Terms of the GOP Plan."

15. Sandel, *What Money Can't Buy*.

16. Les Leopold, "Hey Dad, Why Does This Country Protect Billionaires, and Not Teachers?" *AlterNet*, May 5, 2010, www.alternet.org/module/printversion/146738.

17. David Glenn, "Public Higher Education Is 'Eroding from All Sides,' Warns Po-

litical Scientists," *Chronicle of Higher Education*, September 2, 2010, http://chronicle.com/article/Public-Higher-Education-Is/124292/.

18. Noam Chomsky, "Public Education Under Massive Corporate Assault—What's Next? *AlterNet*, August 5, 2011, www.alternet.org/story/151921/chomsky%3A _public_education_under_massive_corporate_assault_%E2%80%94_what's_next.

19. Peter Seybold, "The Struggle Against the Corporate Takeover of the University," *Socialism and Democracy* 22, no. 1 (March 2008): 1–2.

20. Nancy Hass, "Scholarly Investments," *New York Times*, December 6, 2009.

21. Diane Ravitch, "Two Visions for Chicago's Schools," *Common Dreams*, September 14, 2012, www.commondreams.org/view/2012/09/14-3?print.

22. See Christopher Robbins, *Expelling Hope: The Assault on Youth and the Militarization of Schooling* (Albany: SUNY Press, 2008); Giroux, *Youth in a Suspect Society*; Fuentes, *Lockdown High*; Sadhbh Walshe, "US Education Orientation for Minorities: The School-to-Prison Pipeline," *Guardian*, August 31, 2012, www.guardian.co.uk/commentisfree/2012/aug/31/us-education-orientation -minorities. See also the ACLU report *Locating the School-to-Prison Pipeline*, www.aclu.org/racial-justice/school-prison-pipeline.

23. I have taken this issue up in Henry A. Giroux (co-authored with Susan Searls Giroux), "Scandalous Politics: Penn State and the Return of the Repressed in Higher Education," *JAC* 32, no. 1–2.

24. Charles M. Blow, "Plantations, Prisons and Profits," *New York Times*, May 25, 2012, www.nytimes.com/2012/05/26/opinion/blow-plantations-prisons-and -profits.html. For a detailed analysis of the racist prison-industrial complex, see Angela Y. Davis, *Abolition Democracy: Beyond Empire, Prisons, and Torture* (Seven Stories Press, 2005); Michelle Brown, *The Culture of Punishment: Prison, Society and Spectacle* (New York: NYU Press, 2009); Alexander, *The New Jim Crow*.

25. Amanda Terkel, "Arizona Expands Its Discrimination: Teachers with Heavy Accents Can't Teach English, Ethnic Studies Are Banned," *ThinkProgress*, April 30, 2010, http://thinkprogress.org/politics/2010/04/30/94567/arizona-teachers/.

26. Miriam Jordan, "Arizona Grades Teachers on Fluency," *Wall Street Journal*, April 30, 2010, http://online.wsj.com/article/SB100014240527487035725 04575213883276427528.html.

27. Zygmunt Bauman, *Society under Siege* (Malden, MA: Blackwell, 2002), 170.

28. Salvatore Babones, "To End the Jobs Recession, Invest an Extra $20 Billion in Public Education," *Truthout*, August 21, 2012, http://truth-out.org/ opinion/item/11031-to-end-the-jobs-recession-invest-an-extra-$20-billion-in -public-education.

29. FT's Lex blog, "U.S. Defense Spending: What's the Real Figure?," *Globe and Mail*, May 28, 2012, www.theglobeandmail.com/report-on-business/international -business/us-defence-spending-whats-the-real-figure/article4217831/.

30. Daniel Trotta, "Cost of War $3.7 Trillion and Counting, 258,000 Dead," Reuters, June 28, 2011, http://uk.reuters.com/article/2011/06/29/uk-usa-war -idUKTRE75S76R20110629.

31. Dominic Tierney, "The F-35: A Weapon That Costs More Than Australia," *Atlantic*, November 11, 2011, www.theatlantic.com/national/archive/

2011/03/the-f-35-a-weapon-that-costs-more-than-australia/72454/.

32. Babones, "To End the Jobs Recession."
33. Cited in Zygmunt Bauman, *Liquid Life* (Cambridge: Polity Press, 2005), 138.
34. Bill Readings *The University in Ruins* (Cambridge, MA: Harvard University Press,) 11, 18.
35. Zygmunt Bauman, *In Search of Politics* (Stanford, CA: Stanford University Press, 1999), 170.
36. Bauman, *Society under Siege*, 70.
37. Lynn Worsham and Gary A. Olson, "Rethinking Political Community: Chantal Mouffe's Liberal Socialism," *Journal of Composition Theory* 19, no. 2 (1999): 178.
38. Cavanagh, "Seven Ways to End the Deficit."
39. Ibid.
40. Noam Chomsky, "Paths Taken, Tasks Ahead," *Profession* (2000): 34.
41. Pierre Bourdieu, "For a Scholarship of Commitment," *Profession* (2000): 44.
42. Jacques Derrida, "Intellectual Courage: An Interview," trans. Peter Krapp, *Culture Machine* 2 (2000): 9.
43. A Conversation between Lani Guinier and Anna Deavere Smith, "Rethinking Power, Rethinking Theater," *Theater* 31, no. 3 (Winter 2002): 34–35.

Chapter Two: At the Limits of Neoliberal Higher Education

1. This theme is taken up powerfully by a number of theorists. See C. Wright Mills, *The Sociological Imagination* (New York: Oxford University Press, 2000); Richard Sennett, *The Fall of Public Man* (New York: Norton, 1974); Zygmunt Bauman, *In Search of Politics* (Stanford, CA: Stanford University Press, 1999); and Henry A. Giroux, *Public Spaces, Private Lives* (Lanham, MD: Rowman and Littlefield, 2001).
2. Stuart Hall interviewed by James Hay, "Interview with Stuart Hall," *Communication and Critical/Cultural Studies* 10, no. 1 (2013): 11.
3. Vivian Yee, "Grouping Students by Ability Regains Favor in Classroom," *New York Times*, June 10, 2013, www.nytimes.com/2013/06/10/education/grouping -students-by-ability-regains-favor-with-educators.html?pagewanted=all&_r=0.
4. Craig Calhoun, "Information Technology and the International Public Sphere," in *Shaping the Network Society: The New Role of Society in Cyberspace*, ed. Douglas Schuler and Peter Day (Cambridge, MA: MIT Press, 2004), 241.
5. Michael D. Yates, "Occupy Wall Street and the Significance of Political Slogans," *Counterpunch*, February 27, 2013, www.counterpunch.org/2013/02/27/ occupy-wall-street-and-the-significance-of-political-slogans/.
6. Zaid Jilani, Faiz Shakir, Benjamin Armbruster, George Zornick, Alex Seitz-Wald, and Tanya Somanader, "Rewarding Corporations While Punishing Workers," *Progress Report*, March 18, 2011, http://pr.thinkprogress.org/2011/03 /pr20110318/index.html.

7. Jeffrey Sachs, "America's Deepening Moral Crisis," *Guardian*, October 4, 2010, www.guardian.co.uk/commentisfree/belief/2010/oct/04/americas-deepening -moral-crisis.

8. Classic examples of this can be found in the work of Milton Friedman and the fictional accounts of Ayn Rand. It is a position endlessly reproduced in conservative foundations and institutes such as the American Enterprise Institute, Heritage Foundation, Hudson Institute, Manhattan Institute for Policy Research, and the Hoover Institute. One particularly influential book that shaped social policy along these lines is Charles Murray, *Losing Ground* (New York: Basic, 1994).

9. Jacques Rancière, *Hatred of Democracy* (London: Verso 2006).

10. Ellen Schrecker, *The Lost Soul of Higher Education* (New York: The New Press, 2010), 3.

11. A number of important critiques of the Browne Report and the conservative-liberal attack on higher education include: Simon Head, "The Grim Threat to British Universities," *New York Review of Books*, January 13, 2011, www.nybooks .com/articles/archives/2011/jan/13/grim-threat-british-universities/; Anthony T. Grafton, "Britain: The Disgrace of the Universities," *New York Review of Books*, March 10, 2010, 32; Nick Couldry, "Fighting for the Life of the English University in 2010," unpublished manuscript; Stefan Collini, "Browne's Gamble," *London Review of Books* 32, no. 21 (November 4, 2010) 23–25; Stanley Fish, "The Value of Higher Education Made Literal," *New York Times*, December 13, 2010, http://opinionator.blogs.nytimes.com/2010/12/13/the-value-of-higher-education -made-literal/; Aisha Labi, "British Universities and Businesses Are Forming Stronger Research Ties," *Chronicle of Higher Education*, October 4, 2010, http://chronicle.com/article/British-Universities-and/124814; and Terry Eagleton, "The Death of Universities," *Guardian*, December 17, 2010, www.guardian .co.uk/commentisfree/2010/dec/17/death-universities-malaise-tuition-fee.

12. Michael Collins, "Universities Need Reform—but the Market Is Not the Answer," *OpenDemocracy.net*, November 23, 2010, www.opendemocracy.net/ ourkingdom/michael-collins/universities-need-reform-but-market-is-not-answer.

13. Luke Johnson, "Marco Rubio on Climate Change: 'The Government Can't Change the Weather,'" *Huffington Post*, February 13, 2013, www.huffingtonpost .com/2013/02/13/marco-rubio-climate-change_n_2679810.html.

14. Ibid.

15. Collini, "Browne's Gamble."

16. Head, "The Grim Threat to British Universities."

17. Stanley Aronowitz, "Introduction," *Against Schooling: For an Education That Matters* (Boulder, CO: Paradigm, 2008), xv.

18. Kathryn Masterson, "Off Campus Is Now the Place to Be for Deans," *Chronicle of Higher Education*, March 6, 2011, http://chronicle.com/article/For-Deans -Off-Campus-Is-Now/126607/.

19. Jason Del Gandio, "Neoliberalism and the Academic-Industrial Complex," *Truthout*, August 12, 2010, www.truth-out.org/neoliberalism-and-academic -industrial-complex62189.

20. Scott Jaschik, "New Tactic to Kill Faculty Unions," *Inside Higher Ed*, March 3,

2011, www.insidehighered.com/news/2011/03/03/ohio_bill_would_kill_faculty
_unions_in_unexpected_way.

21. The Coalition on the Academic Workforce, *A Portrait of Part-Time Faculty Members: A Summary of Findings on Part-Time Faculty Respondents to the Coalition on the Academic Workforce Survey of Contingent Faculty Members* (Washington, DC: CAW, June 2012), www.academicworkforce.org/CAW_portrait_2012.pdf.

22. Schrecker, *The Lost Soul of Higher Education*, 206–215.

23. Evan McMorris-Santoro, "Conservative Think Tank Seeks Michigan Profs' Emails About Wisconsin Union Battle . . . and Maddow," *Talking Points Memo*, March 29, 2010; Paul Krugman, "American Thought Police," *New York Times*, March 27, 2011, A27.

24. I take up these attacks in great detail in *The University in Chains*.

25. Stanley Aronowitz, "The Knowledge Factory," *Indypendent*, March 16, 2011, www.indypendent.org/2011/03/17/the-knowledge-factory/.

26. John Pilger, "The Revolt in Egypt Is Coming Home," *Truthout*, February 10, 2011, www.truth-out.org/the-revolt-egypt-is-coming-home67624.

27. Courtney E. Martin, *Do It Anyway: A New Generation of Activists* (Boston: Beacon Press, 2010).

28. Courtney E. Martin, "Why Class Matters in Campus Activism," *American Prospect*, December 6, 2010, www.prospect.org/cs/articles?article=why_class
_matters_in_campus_activism.

29. Cited in ibid.

30. Mark Edelman Boren, *Student Resistance: A History of the Unruly Subject* (New York: Routledge, 2001), 227.

31. Simeon Talley, "Why Aren't Students in the U.S. Protesting Tuition, Too?" *Campus Progress*, December 23, 2010, http://www.campusprogress.org/articles/why
_arent_students_in_the_u.s._protesting_tuition_too.

32. Susan Searls Giroux, *Between Race and Reason: Violence, Intellectual Responsibility, and the University to Come* (Stanford: Stanford University Press, 2010), 79.

33. Edelman Boren, *Student Resistance*, 228.

34. Robert Reich, "The Attack on American Education," *Reader Supported News*, December 23, 2010, www.readersupportednews.org/opinion2/299-190/4366
-the-attack-on-american-education.

35. Ibid.

36. There are many books and articles that take up this issue. One of the most incisive commentators is Jeffrey Williams, "Student Debt and the Spirit of Indenture," *Dissent* (Fall 2008), www.dissentmagazine.org/article/?article=1303.

37. David Mascriota, "The Rich Get Richer and the Young Go into Deep Debt," *BuzzFlash*, December 6, 2010, http://blog.buzzflash.com/node/12045.

38. Head, "The Grim Threat to British Universities."

39. Jean-Luc Nancy, *The Truth of Democracy*, trans. Pascale-Anne Brault and Michael Naas (New York: Fordham University Press, 2010), 9.

40. Tom Engelhardt, "An American World War: What to Watch for in 2010," *Truthout*, January 3, 2010, www.truth-out.org/topstories/10410vh4. See also Andrew Bacevich, *The New American Militarism* (New York: Oxford University

218 Henry Giroux

Press, 2005); and Chalmers Johnson, *Nemesis: The Last Days of the American Empire* (New York: Metropolitan Books, 2006).

41. Eric Gorski, "45% of Students Don't Learn Much in College," *Huffington Post*, January 21, 2011, www.huffingtonpost.com/2011/01/18/45-of-students-don't -learn_n_810224.html. The study is taken from Richard Arum and Josipa Roksa, *Academically Adrift: Limited Learning on College Campuses* (Chicago: University of Chicago Press, 2011).

42. Surely there is a certain irony in the fact that the work of Gene Sharp, a little-known American theorist in nonviolent action, is inspiring young people all over the world to resist authoritarian governments. Yet his work is almost completely ignored by young people in the United States. See, for instance, Sheryl Gay Stolberg, "Shy U.S. Intellectual Created Playbook Used in Revolution," *New York Times*, February 16, 2011, A1. See, in particular, Gene Sharp, *From Dictatorship to Democracy* (London: Serpent's Tail, 2012).

43. Sheldon S. Wolin, *Democracy Incorporated: Managed Democracy and the Specter of Inverted Totalitarianism* (Princeton, NJ: Princeton University Press, 2008), 259–260.

44. Zygmunt Bauman, *Does Ethics Have a Chance in a World of Consumers?* (Cambridge MA: Harvard University Press, 2008), 159.

45. Ibid., 235. I have also taken up this theme in great detail in *Youth in a Suspect Society*.

46. Zygmunt Bauman, *The Individualized Society* (London: Polity, 2001), 55.

47. Alex Honneth, *Pathologies of Reason* (New York: Columbia University Press, 2009), 188.

48. John Comaroff and Jean Comaroff, "Reflections on Youth from the Past to the Postcolony," in *Frontiers of Capital: Ethnographic Reflections on the New Economy*, ed. Melissa S. Fisher and Greg Downey (Durham, NC: Duke University Press, 2006), 268.

49. Ibid.

50. Cited in Pascale-Anne Brault and Michael Naas, "Translator's Note," in Nancy, *The Truth of Democracy*, xii.

Chapter Three: Intellectual Violence in the Age of Gated Intellectuals

1. This issue has been taken up in detail in Schrecker, *The Lost Soul of Higher Education*, and Edward J. Carvalho and David Downing, eds., *Academic Freedom in the Post-9/11 Era* (New York: Palgrave, 2011).

2. Theodor Adorno, *Authoritarian Personality* (New York: Harper & Row, 1950).

3. Lutz Koepnick, "Aesthetic Politics Today—Walter Benjamin and Post-Fordist Culture," *Critical Theory—Current State and Future Prospects*, ed. Peter Uwe Hohendahl and Jaimey Fisher (New York: Berghahn Books: 2002), 96.

4. Mumia Abu-Jamal, "The U.S. Is Fast Becoming One of the Biggest Open-Air

Prisons on Earth," *Democracy Now!*, February 1, 2013, www.democracynow.org/2013/2/1/mumia_abu_jamal_the_united_states.

5. Michel Foucault, *Society Must Be Defended: Lectures at the College de France 1975–1976*, (New York: Picador, 2003), 47.
6. Ibid., 256.
7. Ibid., 56.
8. On this see, in particular, Bauman, *Society under Siege*.
9. Brad Evans and Mark Duffield, "Biospheric Security: How the Merger Between Development, Security & the Environment [Desenex] Is Retrenching Fortress Europe," in *A Threat Against Europe? Security, Migration and Integration*, eds. Peter Burgess and Serge Gutwirth (VUB Press: Brussels, 2011).
10. This critique of instrumental reason was a central feature of the Frankfurt School and is most notable in the work of Herbert Marcuse. See also Zygmunt Bauman's brilliant critique in *Modernity and the Holocaust* (Ithaca, NY: Cornell University Press, 2010), reprint edition.
11. See, for example, World Bank and Carter Centre, *From Civil War to Civil Society*, (Washington, DC: World Bank and Carter Centre, 1997).
12. Cited in Matt Phillips, "Goldman Sachs' Blankfein on Banking: 'Doing God's Work,'" *Marketbeat* (blog), *Wall Street Journal*, November 9, 2009, http://blogs.wsj.com/marketbeat/2009/11/09/goldman-sachs-blankfein-on-banking-doing-gods-work/.
13. C. Wright Mills, *The Politics of Truth: Selected Writings of C. Wright Mills* (New York: Oxford University Press, 2008), 200.
14. Aronowitz, *Against Schooling*, xii. See also http://archive.truthout.org/the-disappearing-intellectual-age-economic-darwinism61287 - 13.
15. Kate Zernike, "Making College 'Relevant,'" *New York Times*, January 3, 2010.
16. While this critique has been made by many critics, it has also been made recently by the president of Harvard University. See Drew Gilpin Faust, "The University's Crisis of Purpose," *New York Times*, September 6, 2009.
17. Harvey cited in Stephen Pender, "An Interview with David Harvey," *Studies in Social Justice* 1, no. 1 (Winter 2007): 14.
18. See, in particular, Giorgio Agamben, *Homo Sacer: Sovereign Power and Bare Life* (Stanford, CA: Stanford University Press, 1995); and Giorgio Agamben, *State of Exception* (Chicago: University of Chicago Press, 2005).
19. This term is first developed in Henry A. Giroux, *Twilight of the Social* (Boulder, CO: Paradigm, 2012).
20. David Theo Goldberg, *The Threat of Race: Reflections on Racial Neoliberalism* (Malden, MA: Wiley-Blackwell, 2009), 338-339.
21. Zygmunt Bauman, "Has the Future a Left?" *The Review of Education/Pedagogy/Cultural Studies* (2007): 2. Henry Giroux takes up the issue of gated intellectuals in greater detail in Henry A. Giroux, *The Education Deficit and the War on Youth* (New York: Monthly Review Press, 2013).
22. Judith Butler, *Frames of War: When Is Life Grievable?* (London: Verso, 2009), 3,4.
23. Ibid., 4.

24. Henry Giroux, "Counter-Memory & the Politics of Loss," *Truthout*, September 13, 2011, www.truth-out.org/counter-memory-and-politics-loss-after-911/1315595429.
25. Marjorie Cohn, ed., *The United States and Torture: Interrogation, Incarceration, and Abuse* (New York: NYU Press, 2011); Medea Benjamin, *Drone Warfare* (London: Verso Press, 2013); Nick Turse and Tom Englehardt, *Terminator Planet: The First History of Drone Warfare, 2001–2050* (New York: Dispatch Press, 2012).
26. Roger Simon, "A Shock of Thought," *Memory Studies* (February 21, 2011).
27. See Michael Hardt and Antonio Negri, *Declaration* (New York: Argo Navis Author Services, 2012).
28. Simon Critchley, "September 11 and the Cycle of Revenge," *The Stone* (blog), *New York Times*, September 8, 2011, http://opinionator.blogs.nytimes.com/2011/09/08/the-cycle-of-revenge/.
29. Jacques Derrida, *On Cosmopolitanism and Forgiveness* (New York: Routledge, 2005), 32.
30. Ibid., 37.
31. Brad Evans, *Liberal Terror* (Cambridge: Polity Press, 2013).
32. Leo Lowenthal, "Atomization of Man," *False Prophets: Studies in Authoritarianism* (New Brunswick, NJ: Transaction Books, 1987), 181–82.
33. Walter Benjamin, "Critique of Violence," in *Reflections: Essays, Aphorisms, Autobiographical Writings*, ed. Peter Demetz (Schocken Books: New York, 1986), 277–300.
34. Stanley Aronowitz, "Introduction," in Paulo Freire, *Pedagogy of Freedom* (Boulder, CO: Rowman and Littlefield, 1998), 7.
35. Michel Foucault, "Preface," in Gilles Deleuze and Felix Guattari, *Anti-Oedipus: Capitalism and Schizophrenia* (London: Continuum, 2003), xv.
36. Gilles Deleuze, *Desert Islands and Other Texts, 1953–1974*, ed. David Lapoujade, trans. Michael Taormina (New York: Semiotext[e], 2004), 139–40.
37. Stuart Hall, "Epilogue: Through the Prism of an Intellectual Life," in *Culture, Politics, Race, and Diaspora: The Thought of Stuart Hall*, ed. Brian Meeks (Miami: Ian Rundle Publishers, 2007), 289–90.
38. See also Giroux and Searls Giroux, *Take Back Higher Education*.
39. Jacques Rancière, *On the Shores of Politics* (London: Verso Press, 1995), 3.
40. Edward Said, *Humanism and Democratic Criticism* (New York: Columbia University Press, 2004), 50.
41. C. Wright Mills, "Culture and Politics: The Fourth Epoch," in *The Politics of Truth: Selected Writings of C. Wright Mills* (New York: Oxford University Press, 2008), 199.
42. Editors, "A Conversation with David Harvey," *Logos: A Journal of Modern Society & Culture* 5, no. 1 (2006).

Chapter Four: Universities Gone Wild

1. Elizabeth Stone, "Student Private Loan Debt Tops 1 Trillion?" *Examiner*, April 16, 2012, www.examiner.com/article/student-private-loan-debt-tops-1-trillion-dollars.

2. Stanley Aronowitz, *The Knowledge Factory: Dismantling Corporate Education and Creating True Higher Learning* (Boston: Beacon Press, 2001). See also Giroux, *The University in Chains.*

3. Anya Kamenetz, *Generation Debt* (New York: Riverhead, 2006); Alan Collinge, *The Student Loan Scam: The Most Oppressive Debt in U.S. History and How We Can Fight Back* (Boston: Beacon Press, 2009).

4. Larry Wilmore, "Newt Gingrich's Poverty Code," *The Daily Show with Jon Stewart* (video), December 13, 2011.

5. Russell Goldman, "Looking to 2012, Gingrich Strikes an Old Chord and Assails the Unemployed," *ABC News.com*, December 22, 2010, http://abcnews.go.com/Politics/2012-gingrich-strikes-chord-assails-unemployed/story?id=12453191.

6. See, for instance, Ferguson, *Predator Nation*; John Bellamy Foster and Robert W. McChesney, *The Endless Crisis: How Monopoly-Finance Capital Produces Stagnation and Upheaval from the USA to China* (New York: Monthly Review Press, 2012).

7. Clark Kerr, "Shock Wave II: An Introduction to the Twenty-First Century," in *The Future of the City of Intellect: The Changing American University*, ed. Steven Brint (Stanford, CA: Stanford University Press, 2002), 1–19.

8. Paul Krugman, "Depression and Democracy," *New York Times*, December 12, 2011.

9. See the Centre County Grand Jury Indictment against Gerald A. Sandusky, www.freep.com/assets/freep/pdf/C4181508116.PDF, 3.

10. Tim Rohan, "Sandusky Gets 30 to 60 Years for Sexual Abuse," *New York Times*, October 9, 2012, www.nytimes.com/2012/10/10/sports/ncaafootball/penn-state-sandusky-is-sentenced-in-sex-abuse-case.html.

11. Krugman, "Depression and Democracy."

12. Associated Press, "Casey Says He Received Death Threats," *ABC Sports*, December 13, 2002, http://espn.go.com/abcsports/bcs/s/2001/0516/1200265.html.

13. Brentin Mock, "The Other Penn State Cover-Up: Death Threats Against Black Students," *Huffington Post*, November 16, 2011, www.huffingtonpost.com/2011/11/16/penn-state-racism_n_1098237.html.

14. "Jerry Sandusky Arrested on New Charges of Child Sex Abuse: The Former Penn State Assistant Football Coach Faces More than 50 Child Sex Abuse Charges," *Los Angeles Times*, December 7, 2011, www.latimes.com/sports/la-sp-newswire-20111208,0,265641,print.story. See also "Penn State Charges: News on the Cases against Sandusky, Curley and Schultz," *StateCollege.com*, December 20, 2011, www.statecollege.com/news/penn-state-charges-sandusky-curley-schultz/.

15. Michael Bérubé. "At Penn State, a Bitter Reckoning," *New York Times*, November 17, 2011.

16. Ibid.

17. Cary Nelson and Donna Potts, "The Dangers of a Sports Empire," *AAUP Newsroom*, November 2011, www.aaup.org/AAUP/newsroom/2011PRs/psu.htm.

18. J. Bryan Lowder, "The Danger of Joe Paterno's 'Father-Figure' Mystique," *Slate*, November 10, 2011, www.slate.com/blogs/xx_factor/2011/11/10/the_danger

_of_joe_paterno_s_father_figure_mystique.html.

19. Katherine Greenier, "From Fear to Safety: Confronting Sexual Assault and Harassment on Campuses," *RH Reality Check*, November 21, 2011, www.rhrealitycheck.org/article/2011/11/18/schools-must-protect-students-from-sexual-violence.

20. Penn State Division of Student Affairs, "Know the Facts—Rape and Sexual Assault," Penn State Center for Women Students, December 20, 2011, http://studentaffairs.psu.edu/womenscenter/awareness/rapeandassault.shtml.

21. Brent Kallest, "Fired College Band Head Warned of Hazing," *Time*, November 28, 2011, www.time.com/time/nation/article/0,8599,2100507,00.html.

22. Joe Nocera, "It's Not Just Penn State," *New York Times*, December 2, 2011.

23. Steve Kettmann, "Are We Not Man Enough?" *New York Times*, December 17, 2011.

24. Ibid.

25. Claire Potter, "The Penn State Scandal: Connect the Dots Between Child Abuse and the Sexual Assault of Women on Campus," *Chronicle of Higher Education*, November 10, 2011, http://chronicle.com/blognetwork/tenuredradical/2011/11/1401/.

26. Katha Pollitt, "Penn State's Patriarchal Pastimes," *The Nation*, November 16, 2011, www.thenation.com/article/164655/penn-states-patriarchal-pastimes.

27. Sophia A. McClennen,"Is There a Way to Be Good Again? How to Be a Man after the Penn State Pedophilia Scandal," *Truthout*, November 28, 2011, www.truth-out.org/there-way-be-good-again-how-be-man-after-penn-state-pedophilia-scandal/1322491679.

28. J. Bryan Lowder, "The Danger of Joe Paterno's 'Father-Figure' Mystique," *Slate*, November 10, 2011, www.slate.com/blogs/xx_factor/2011/11/10/the_danger_of_joe_paterno_s_father_figure_mystique.html.

29. Stefan Collini, "Browne's Gamble," *London Review of Books* 32, no. 21 (November 4, 2010).

30. Kathy N. Davidson, "A Plea to College Presidents: Exercise Your Moral Leadership," *Chronicle of Higher Education*, November 21, 2011, http://chronicle.com/article/A-Plea-to-College-Presidents-/129863/.

31. Goldie Blumenstyk and Jack Stripling, "Leaders'Choices Put Colleges in Uneasy Spot,"*Chronicle of Higher Education*, November 27, 2011, http://chronicle.com/article/Questionable-Decisions-Cast/129901/.

32. Jack Stripling, "Farewell Payout to Spanier Made Him Priciest President," *Chronicle of Higher Education*, May 17, 2013.

33. Juan Cole, "The Koch Brothers and the End of State Universities," *Informed Comment*, May 13, 2011, www.juancole.com/2011/05/the-koch-brothers-and-the-end-of-state-universities.html.

34. Jean Comaroff and John Comaroff, "Reflections of Youth: From the Past to the Postcolony," in *Frontiers of Capital: Ethnographic Reflections on the New Economy,* ed. Melissa S. Fisher and Greg Downey (Durham, NC: Duke University Press, 2006), 268.

35. Alex Honneth, *Pathologies of Reason,*(New York: Columbia University Press, 2009), 188.

36. Giroux, *The University in Chains.*

37. Peter Seybold, "The Struggle against Corporate Takeover of the University," *Socialism and Democracy* 22, no. 1 (March 2008): 1–11.

38. Steven Higgs, "The Corporatization of the American University," *CounterPunch*, November 21, 2011, www.counterpunch.org/2011/11/21/the-corporatization -of-the-american-university/. See also Seybold, "The Struggle against Corporate Takeover of the University."

39. Sydney University Academics, "Sydney University Academics Speak Out," *New Matilda*, December 5, 2011, http://newmatilda.com/2011/12/05/sydney -university-academics-speak-out.

40. Nick Turse, *The Complex: How the Military Invades Our Everyday Lives* (New York: Metropolitan Books, 2008). See also David H. Price, *Weaponizing Anthropology*, (Oakland, CA: AK Press, 2011).

41. Henry Giroux, *Against the Terror of Neoliberalism* (Boulder, CO: Paradigm, 2008).

42. Remarks of Louis Freeh in Conjunction with Announcement of Publication of Report Regarding the Pennsylvania State University. Community Voices, July 12, 2012, http://communityvoices.sites.post-gazette.com/index.php/news/154 -ipso-facto-pr/33663-remarks-of-louis-freeh-in-conjunction-with-announcement -of-publication-.

43. Editorial, "The Rotten Heart of Finance," Economist, July 7, 2012, www.econ-omist.com/node/21558281.

44. Quoted in Amy Goodman, "Penn State Students Bear Brunt of NCAA Sanctions for Sandusky Cover-Up as Trustees Emerge Unscathed," *Democracy Now!*, July 24, 2012, www.democracynow.org/2012/7/24/penn_state_students_bear _brunt_of.

45. Quoted in ibid.

46. Ibid.

47. Robin Wilson, "As Students Return, Penn State Begins the Year Under a Cloud," *Chronicle of Higher Education*, September 3, 2012, http://chronicle.com/ article/Penn-State-Begins-Academic/134062/.

48. Joe Drape, "Penn State to Pay Nearly $60 Million to 26 Abuse Victims," *New York Times*, October 28, 2013, www.nytimes.com/2013/10/29/sports/ncaafootball/ penn-state-to-pay-59-7-million-to-26-sandusky-victims.html?hp.

49. Alexandra Sifferlin, "Breaking Down GlaxoSmithKline's Billion-Dollar Wrong-doing," *Time*, July 5, 2012, http://healthland.time.com/2012/07/05/breaking -down-glaxosmithklines-billion-dollar-wrongdoing/.

50. Aronowitz, *Against Schooling*, xviii.

Chapter Five: On the Urgency
for Public Intellectuals in the Academy

1. Audre Lorde, "Poetry is not a Luxury," *Sister Outsider: Essays and Speeches* (Freedom, CA: The Crossing Press, 1984), 38.

2. I have taken this idea of linking Lorde's notion of poetry to education from Martha Nell Smith, "The Humanities Are a Manifesto for the Twenty-First Century," *Liberal Education* (Winter 2011): 48–55.

3. Debra Leigh Scott, "How the American University Was Killed, in Five Easy Steps," The Homeless Adjunct Blog, August 12, 2012, http://junctrebellion.wordpress.com/2012/08/12/how-the-american-university-was-killed-in-five-easy-steps/.

4. Ferguson, *Predator Nation*, 21.

5. Nicholas Lemann, "Evening the Odds: Is There a Politics of Inequality?" *New Yorker*, April 23, 2012, www.newyorker.com/arts/critics/atlarge/2012/04/23/120423crat_atlarge_lemann.

6. Reihaneh Hajibeigi, "Resisting Corporate Education: Is 'Business Productivity' Coming to the University of Texas?" *Nation of Change*, June 13, 2013, www.nationofchange.org/resisting-corporate-education-business-productivity-coming-university-texas-1371133921.

7. Joseph E. Stiglitz, "The Price of Inequality," *Project Syndicate*, June 5, 2012, www.project-syndicate.org/commentary/the-price-of-inequality.

8. Ibid.

9. Ferguson, *Predator Nation*, 8

10. Ibid.

11. Andrew Gavin Marshall, "The Shocking Amount of Wealth and Power Held by 0.001% of the World Population," *AlterNet*, June 12, 2013, www.alternet.org/economy/global-power-elite-exposed?akid=10567.40823.Q_uvw_&rd=1&src=newsletter854356&t=3.

12. Alex Honneth, *Pathologies of Reason* (New York: Columbia University Press, 2009), 188.

13. Buchheit, "Five Ugly Extremes."

14. Zygmunt Bauman, *Collatoral Damage: Social Inequalities in a Global Age* (Cambridge, UK: Polity Press, 2011), 39.

15. I have taken these figures from Paul Buchheit, "Five Facts That Put America to Shame," *Common Dreams*, May 14, 2012, www.commondreams.org/view/2012/05/14-0.

16. Cornelius Castoriadis, *A Society Adrift: Interviews & Debates 1974–1997*, trans. Helen Arnold (New York: Fordham University Press, 2010), 7.

17. The genealogy from anti-intellectualism in American life to the embrace of illiteracy as a virtue is analyzed in the following books: Richard Hofstadter, *Anti-Intellectualism in American Life* (New York: Vintage, 1966); Susan Jacoby, *The Age of American Unreason* (New York: Pantheon, 2008); Charles P. Piece, *Idiot America: How Stupidity Became a Virtue in the Land of the Free* (New York: Anchor Books, 2009).

18. Castoriadis, *A Society Adrift*, 8.

19. Mills, *The Politics of Truth*, 200.

20. Frank B. Wilderson III, "Introduction: Unspeakable Ethics," in *Red, White, & Black* (London, UK: Duke University Press, 2012), 2.

21. Stanley Aronowitz, "Against Schooling: Education and Social Class," in *Against*

Schooling (Boulder, CO: Paradigm, 2008), xii.

22. See most recently Kelly V. Vlahos, "Boots on Campus," *AntiWar.com*, February 26, 2013, http://original.antiwar.com/vlahos/2013/02/25/boots-on-campus/; and David H. Price, *Weaponizing Anthropology* (Oakland, CA: AK Press, 2011).

23. Kelley B. Vlahos, "Boots on Campus: Yale Flap Highlights Militarization of Academia," *Truthout*, February 27, 2013, http://truth-out.org/news/item/ 14837-boots-on-campus-yale-flap-highlights-militarization-of-academia.

24. Ibid.

25. Greg Bishop, "A Company that Runs Prisons Will Have Its Name on a Stadium," *New York Times*, February 19, 2013, www.nytimes.com/2013/02/ 20/sports/ncaafootball/a-company-that-runs-prisons-will-have-its-name-on-a -stadium.html?_r=0.

26. Dave Zirin, "Victory! The Stopping of Owlcatraz," *Common Dreams*, April 3, 2013, www.commondreams.org/view/2013/04/03.

27. Ibid.

28. Scott Travis, "GEO Withdraws Gift, Naming Rights for FAU Stadium," *South Florida Sun Sentinel*, April 1, 2013, www.sun-sentinel.com/news/palm-beach/ fl-fau-geo-stadium-20130401,0,6857150.story.

29. Zirin, "Victory! The Stopping of Owlcatraz."

30. Zernike, "Making College 'Relevant.'"

31. Scott Jaschik, "Making Adjuncts Temps—Literally," *Inside Higher Education*, August 9, 2010, www.insidehighered.com/news/2010/08/09/adjuncts.

32. Martha C. Nussbaum, *Not for Profit: Why Democracy Needs the Humanities* (Princeton, NJ: Princeton University Press, 2010), 142.

33. Greig de Peuter, "Universities, Intellectuals, and Multitudes: An Interview with Stuart Hall," in *Utopian Pedagogy: Radical Experiments against Neoliberal Globalization*, eds. Mark Cote, Richard J. F. Day, and Greig de Peuter (Toronto: University of Toronto Press, 2007), 111.

34. Nussbaum, *Not for Profit*.

35. On the militarization of higher education, see Giroux, *The University in Chains*. See also Philip Zwerling, ed., *The CIA on Campus: Essays on Academic Freedom and the National Security State* (Jefferson, NC: McFarland and Company, 2011); David H. Price, *Weaponizing Anthropology* (Petrolia, CA: CounterPunch, 2011).

36. Castoriadis, "Democracy as Procedure and Democracy as Regime," 5.

37. George Scialabba, *What Are Intellectuals Good For?* (Boston: Pressed Wafer, 2009) 4.

38. Toni Morrison, "How Can Values Be Taught in This University,"*Michigan Quarterly Review* (Spring 2001): 278.

39. Scialabba, *What Are Intellectuals Good For?*

40. James Baldwin interview by Mel Watkins, *New York Times Book Review*, September 23, 1979, 3.

41. Zoe Williams, "The Saturday Interview: Stuart Hall," *Guardian*, February 11, 2012, www.guardian.co.uk/theguardian/2012/feb/11/saturday-interview -stuart-hall.

42. Sheldon S. Wolin, *Democracy, Inc.: Managed Democracy and the Specter of In-

verted Totalitarianism (Princeton, NJ: Princeton University Press, 2008), 43.

43. Morrison, "How Can Values Be Taught in This University," 276.

44. On this issue, see the brilliant essay by Susan Searls Giroux, "On the Civic Function of Intellectuals Today," in *Education as Civic Engagement: Toward a More Democratic Society,* eds. Gary Olson and Lynn Worsham (Boulder, CO: Paradigm Publishers, 2012), ix–xvii.

45. Martin Luther King, Jr., "The Trumpet of Conscience," in *The Essential Writings and Speeches of Martin Luther King, Jr.*, ed. James M. Washington (New York: Harper Collins, 1991), 644.

46. Arundhati Roy, *Power Politics* (Cambridge, MA: South End Press, 2001), 6.

47. de Peuter, "Universities, Intellectuals, and Multitudes," 113–14.

48. Ibid., 117.

49. Cited in Madeline Bunting, "Passion and Pessimism," *Guardian*, April 5, 2003, http:/books.guardian.co.uk/print/0,3858,4640858,00.html.

50. Irving Howe, "This Age of Conformity," *Selected Writings 1950–1990* (New York: Harcourt Brace Jovanovich, 1990), 27.

51. Giovanna Borriadori, ed., "Autoimmunity: Real and Symbolic Suicides—a Dialogue with Jacques Derrida," in *Philosophy in a Time of Terror: Dialogues with Jurgen Habermas and Jacques Derrida* (Chicago: University of Chicago Press, 2004), 121.

52. Cornelius Castoriadis, "Democracy as Procedure and Democracy as Regime," *Constellations* 4, no. 1 (1997): 10.

53. Edward Said, *Out of Place: A Memoir* (New York: Vintage, 2000), 294–99.

54. Said, *Out of Place,* 7.

55. Stephen Howe, "Edward Said: The Traveller and the Exile," *Open Democracy*, October 2, 2003, www.opendemocracy.net/articles/ViewPopUpArticle.jsp?id =10&articleId=1561.

56. Hannah Arendt, *Between Past and Future: Eight Exercises in Political Thought* (New York: Penguin, 1977), 149.

57. Edward Said, "On Defiance and Taking Positions," *Reflections on Exile and Other Essays* (Cambridge, MA: Harvard University Press, 2001), 504.

58. Edward Said, *Humanism and Democratic Criticism* (New York: Columbia University Press, 2004), 70.

59. Howe, "This Age of Conformity," 36.

60. See, especially, Christopher Newfield, *Unmaking the Public University: The Forty-Year Assault on the Middle Class* (Cambridge, MA: Harvard University Press, 2008).

61. See Henry A. Giroux, "Academic Unfreedom in America: Rethinking the University as a Democratic Public Sphere," in Edward J. Carvalho, ed., "Academic Freedom and Intellectual Activism in the Post-9/11 University," special issue of *Works and Days* 51–54 (2008–2009): 45–72. This may be the best collection yet published on intellectual activism and academic freedom.

62. Gayatri Chakravorty Spivak, "Changing Reflexes: Interview with Gayatri Chakravorty Spivak," *Works and Days* 28, no. 55/56 (2010): 8.

63. Bill Moyers, "Interview with William K. Black," *Bill Moyers Journal*, April 23,

2010, www.pbs.org/moyers/journal/04232010/transcript4.html.

64. Ibid.

65. See, especially, Hannah Arendt, *The Origins of Totalitarianism*, third edition, revised (New York: Harcourt Brace Jovanovich, 1968); and John Dewey, *Liberalism and Social Action* (New York: Prometheus Press, 1999/1935).

66. See Frederick Douglass, "West India Emancipation," speech delivered at Canandaigua, New York, August 4, 1857, in *The Life and Writings of Frederick Douglass*, vol. 2, ed. Philip S. Foner (New York: International, 1950), 437.

67. Aronowitz, "The Winter of Our Discontent," 68.

68. Jacques Derrida, "No One Is Innocent: A Discussion with Jacques About Philosophy in the Face of Terror," The Information Technology, War and Peace Project, www.watsoninstitute.org/infopeace/911/derrida_innocence.html.

69. Howe, "The Age of Conformity," 49.

Chapter Six: Days of Rage

1. I want to thank Grace Pollock, Maya Sabados, Danielle Martak, and David L. Clark for their excellent editing suggestions for this chapter.

2. For some excellent sources on the emergence of new social movements in 2011 and afterward, see Paul Mason, *Why It's Kicking Off Everywhere: The New Global Revolutions* (London: Verso, 2012); Manuel Castells, *Networks of Outrage and Hope: Social Movements in the Internet Age* (London: Polity Press, 2012); and Henry A. Giroux, *Youth in Revolt* (Boulder, CO: Paradigm, 2013).

3. David Harvey, "Is This Really the End of Neoliberalism?" *CounterPunch*, March 13–15, 2009, www.counterpunch.org/2009/03/13/is-this-really-the-end-of -neoliberalism/print.

4. Eric Cazdyn, "Bioeconomics, Culture, and Politics after Globalization," in *Cultural Autonomy: Frictions and Connections*, ed. Petra Rethmann, Imre Szeman, and William D. Coleman (Vancouver: UBC Press, 2010), 64.

5. Alain Badiou, *The Rebirth of History*, trans. Gregory Elliott (London: Verso, 2012), 12.

6. Stuart J. Murray, "The Voice of the We Yet to Come," *Canadian Journal of Communication* 37, no. 3 (2012): 495–97.

7. Bruce Campbell, "Rising Inequality, Declining Democracy," *Canadian Centre for Policy Alternatives*, December 12, 2011, www.policyalternatives.ca/publications/ commentary/rising-inequality-declining-democracy.

8. Zygmunt Bauman, *This Is Not a Diary* (Cambridge: Polity Press, 2012), 103.

9. Joseph Stiglitz, *The Price of Inequality: How Today's Divided Society Endangers Our Future* (New York: W. W. Norton, 2012).

10. Some recent and important literature on this issue includes Ferguson, *Predator Nation*; Jacob Hacker and Paul Pierson, *Winner-Take-All Politics: How Washington Made the Rich Richer—and Turned Its Back on the Middle Class* (New York: Simon & Schuster, 2011); David Harvey, *The Enigma of Capital and the Crises of Capitalism* (New York: Oxford University Press, 2011); Paul Krugman,

8. Zygmunt Bauman, *This Is Not a Diary* (Cambridge: Polity Press, 2012), 103.

9. Joseph Stiglitz, *The Price of Inequality: How Today's Divided Society Endangers Our Future* (New York: W. W. Norton, 2012).

10. Some recent and important literature on this issue includes Ferguson, *Predator Nation*; Jacob Hacker and Paul Pierson, *Winner-Take-All Politics: How Washington Made the Rich Richer—and Turned Its Back on the Middle Class* (New York: Simon & Schuster, 2011); David Harvey, *The Enigma of Capital and the Crises of Capitalism* (New York: Oxford University Press, 2011); Paul Krugman, *End This Depression Now!* (New York: W. W. Norton, 2012); Madrick, *Age of Greed*; Stiglitz, *The Price of Inequality*; and Richard D. Wolff and David Barsamian, *Occupy the Economy: Challenging Capitalism* (San Francisco: City Lights Open Media, 2012).

11. Ferguson, *Predator Nation*, 2.

12. Ibid.

13. Zygmunt Bauman, *Living on Borrowed Time: Conversations with Citlali Rovirosa-Madrazo* (Cambridge: Polity, 2010), 68.

14. Bauman, *Wasted Lives,* 76.

15. Ibid.

16. I have borrowed the term "zones of social abandonment" from João Biehl, *Vita: Life in a Zone of Social Abandonment* (Los Angeles and Berkeley: University of California Press, 2005); see also Giroux, *Disposable Youth* and Alexander, *The New Jim Crow.*

17. Biehl, *Vita*, 14.

18. Etienne Balibar, *We, the People of Europe? Reflections on Transnational Citizenship* (Princeton, NJ: Princeton University Press, 2004), 128.

19. Editorial, "Global Youth Jobless Rates Still High," *Hamilton Spectator*, May 23, 2012, A17.

20. Jordan Weissmann, "53% of Recent College Grads Are Jobless or Underemployed–How?" *Atlantic*, April 23, 2012, www.theatlantic.com/business/archive/2012/04/53-of-recent-college-grads-are-jobless-or-underemployed -how/256237/.

21. Bauman, *Liquid Modernity*.

22. See Zygmunt Bauman, *Collateral Damage: Social Inequalities in a Global Age* (Cambridge: Polity, 2011); Stiglitz, *The Price of Inequality*; Lynn Parramore, "Exclusive Interview: Joseph Stiglitz Sees Terrifying Future for America If We Don't Reverse Inequality," *AlterNet*, June 24, 2012, www.alternet.org/economy/155918/exclusive_interview%3A_joseph_stiglitz_sees_terrifying_future_for _america_if_we_don%27t_reverse_inequality; Buchheit, "Five Facts That Put America to Shame"; and Peter Elderman, *So Rich, So Poor: Why It's So Hard to End Poverty in America* (New York: New Press, 2012).

23. Bauman, *Living on Borrowed Time*, 39–40.

24. See the brilliant work of Angela Davis on the prison-industrial complex and the emerging punishing state in the United States, especially *Are Prisons Obsolete?*

25. Report by National Association of Consumer Bankruptcy Attorneys (NACBA), *The Student Loan "Debt Bomb": America's Next Mortgage-Style Economic Crisis,*

February 7, 2012, http://nacba.org/Portals/0/Documents/Student%20Loan %20Debt/020712%20NACBA%20student%20loan%20debt%20report.pdf; Andy Kroll, "Shut Out: How the Cost of Higher Education Is Dividing Our Country," *Truthout*, April 2, 2012, http://archive.truthout.org/040209T; and Collin Harris, "The Student Debt Bubble: Interview with Alan Nasser," *ZSpace*, December 18, 2011, www.zcommunications.org/the-student-debt-bubble -interview-with-alan-nasser-by-collin-harris.

26. Jonathan Simon, *Governing Through Crime: How the War on Crime Transformed American Democracy and Created a Culture of Fear* (New York: Oxford University Press, 2007). See also Giroux, *Youth in a Suspect Society.*

27. Martin Lukacs, "Quebec Student Protests Mark 'Maple Spring' in Canada," *Guardian*, May 2, 2012, www.guardian.co.uk/commentisfree/cifamerica/ 2012/may/02/quebec-student-protest-canada.

28. David Camfield, "Quebec's "Red Square" Movement: The Story So Far," *Socialist Project*, no. 680, August 13, 2012, www.socialistproject.ca/bullet/680.php. Since the "Quiet Revolution" of the 1960s, Quebec has been developing its own distinct political culture. A full understanding of the conditions of possibility that have produced this distinct contemporary student movement would require its contextualization within this history. This is beyond the scope of this chapter.

29. Mark Cardwell, "Quebec Students Begin Strike Action," *University Affairs*, February 21, 2012, www.universityaffairs.ca/quebec-students-begin-strike-action.aspx.

30. Lukacs, "Quebec Student Protests Mark 'Maple Spring.'"

31. Peter Hallward, "The Threat of Quebec's Good Example," *Socialist Project*, no. 647, June 6, 2012, www.socialistproject.ca/bullet/647.php.

32. Andrew Gavin Marshall, "10 Things You Should Know About the Quebec Student Movement," *CounterPunch*, May 23, 2012, www.counterpunch.org/ 2012/05/23/10-things-you-should-know-about-the-quebec-student-movement/. For a brilliant commentary on the history of debt and its effect on the economy, see David Graeber, *Debt: The First 5,000 Years* (Brooklyn, NY: Melville House Publishing, 2011).

33. Randy Boyagoda, "For Student Protesters in Quebec, It's About More Than Tuition," *Chronicle of Higher Education*, June 3, 2012, http://chronicle.com/article/ For-Student-Protesters-Its/132089/.

34. Malav Kanuga, "The Quebec Student Strike Celebrates 100th Day," *In These Times*, May 23, 2012, http://inthesetimes.com/uprising/entry/13252/the _quebec_student_strike_celebrates_its_100th_day/.

35. Alain Badiou cited in John Van Houdt, "The Crisis of Negation: An Interview with Alain Badiou," *Continent* 1, no. 4 (2011): 234.

36. Lukacs, "Quebec Student Protests Mark 'Maple Spring.'"

37. Ibid.

38. Ibid.

39. Erika Shaker, "Don't Kid Yourself: We All Pay for the Defunding of Higher Education," *Common Dreams*, May 12, 2012, www.commondreams.org/view/2012/ 05/12-3.

40. Ibid.

41. Pierre Graveline, "The Strange Disappearance of the Canadian State from the Debate on the Student Strike," *Canadian Dimension*, June 17, 2012, http://canadiandimension.com/articles/4770/.
42. Ibid.
43. CBC News, "Fighter Jet Plan 'Reset' as F-35 Costs Soar," *CBC News*, December 12, 2012, www.cbc.ca/news/canada/story/2012/12/12/pol-f-35-kpmg-report-release.html.
44. For an interesting commentary on this issue, see Shaker, "Don't Kid Yourself." See also W. Craig Riddell, "The Social Benefits of Education: New Evidence on an Old Question," paper prepared for the conference "Taking Public Universities Seriously," University of Toronto, December 3-4, 2004, www.utoronto.ca/president/04conference/downloads/Riddell.pdf.
45. Roger Annis, "Update on Quebec Student Strike: Summer of Protest Ahead," *rabble.ca*, June 4, 2012, http://rabble.ca/blogs/bloggers/campus-notes/2012/06/update-quebec-student-strike-summer-protest-ahead.
46. J. F. Conway, "Quebec: Making War on Our Children," *Socialist Project*, e-Bulletin no. 651, June 10, 2012, www.socialistproject.ca/bullet/651.php.
47. Margaret Wente, "Quebec's University Students Are in for a Shock," *Globe and Mail*, May 1, 2012, http://www.theglobeandmail.com/commentary/quebecs-university-students-are-in-for-a-shock/article4104304/.
48. Ibid.
49. Margaret Wente, "Young Men Without Work," *Globe and Mail*, November 11, 2011, www.theglobeandmail.com/commentary/young-men-without-work/article4183419/.
50. Badiou, *The Rebirth of History*, 18–19.
51. Roger Annis, "Quebec Students Mobilize Against Draconian Law Aimed at Breaking Four-Month Strike," *Socialist Project*, e-Bulletin no. 637, May 19, 2012, www.socialistproject.ca/bullet/637.php. Also see Annis, "Update on Quebec Student Strike."
52. Michael Den Tandt, "It's Time for Tough Treatment of Quebec Student Strikers," *National Post*, May 12, 2012, http://fullcomment.nationalpost.com/2012/05/11/michael-den-tandt-its-time-for-tough-treatment-of-quebec-student-strikers/.
53. For an account of the Bernard Guay letter, see Marshall, "10 Things You Should Know About the Quebec Student Movement." The original letter is no longer posted on Le Soleil's website, but can be downloaded here: http://jhroy.ca/Article-Bernard-Guay.pdf.
54. Ibid.
55. Frank Bruni, "Individualism in Overdrive," *New York Times*, July 17, 2012.
56. Jacques Rancière, *Hatred of Democracy* (London: Verso, 2006).
57. For a critique and summary of the bill, see Annis, "Quebec Students Mobilize"; Common Dreams Staff, "'Biggest Act of Civil Disobedience in Canadian History,'" *Common Dreams*, May 23, 2012, www.commondreams.org/headline/2012/05/23-5; Linda Gyulai, "Bill 78 Contravenes Charter, Lawyer Says," *Montreal Gazette*, May 23, 2012, www.montrealgazette.com/business/Bill+contravenes+charter+lawyer+says/6662877/story.html; Laurence Bherer and Pascale Dufour,

"Our Not-So-Friendly Northern Neighbor," *New York Times*, May 23, 2012, A31; and Ian Austen, "Emergency Law Broadens Canada's Sympathy for Quebec Protests," *New York Times*, June 5, 2012, A4.

58. Hallward, "The Threat of Quebec's Good Example."
59. CBC News, "Montreal Police Cagey about Enforcing Bill 78," *CBC News*, August 11, 2012, www.cbc.ca/news/canada/montreal/story/2012/08/11/montreal-police-bill-78-12-enforcement.html.
60. See "Manifesto for a Maple Spring," *rabble.ca*, April 26, 2012, http://rabble.ca/news/2012/04/quebecs-spring-manifesto-printemps-%C3%A9rable. See also "The CLASSE Manifesto: Share Our Future," *rabble.ca*, July 12, 2012, http://rabble.ca/taxonomy/term/20878.
61. "Manifesto for a Maple Spring."
62. "The CLASSE Manifesto: Share Our Future."
63. Badiou, *The Rebirth of History*.
64. Slavoj Žižek, "Occupy Wall Street: What Is to Be Done Next?" *Guardian*, April 24, 2012, www.guardian.co.uk/commentisfree/cifamerica/2012/apr/24/occupy-wall-street-what-is-to-be-done-next.
65. Students in Chile followed a similar path politically and also have taken to the streets over the neoliberalization of higher education. Students have occupied schools and taken to the streets en masse to protest Chile's president, Sebastián Piñera, who has "defined education as a consumer good." In opposition to Piñera's business-oriented model of education as a consumer product, the students have fiercely argued "that education is a basic right." The government has held firm and the student protests "have been marked by severe brutality, including shooting the students in the face with paintballs and indiscriminately beating them with truncheons [and] during the removal of students from the prestigious Carmela Carvajal school police dragged girls out by their hair." All of these student- and youth-led movements view education as a basic right and central to any viable notion of educational reform and as crucial to the struggle for democracy itself. Jonathan Franklin, "The 18-Year-Old Voice of Chile's Nationwide Student Uprising Moisés Paredes Speaks for a Movement Which Has Defied Police Brutality to Put Education Reform High on the Election Agenda," *Guardian*, June 28, 2013, www.theguardian.com/world/2013/jun/28/chile-student-uprising-election.
66. Hallward, "The Threat of Quebec's Good Example."
67. Sarah Jaffe, "Red Squares Everywhere: Will Quebec's Maple Spring Come South?" *In These Times*, July 9, 2012, www.inthesetimes.com/article/13470/red_squares_everywhere.
68. Badiou, *The Rebirth of History*, 56.
69. Canadian Press, "It's Official: Quebec's Tuition Hikes Are History," *Macleans.ca*, September 20, 2012, http://oncampus.macleans.ca/education/2012/09/20/its-official-quebec-tuition-hikes-are-history/.
70. CBC News, "Quebec Education Summit Ends without Consensus," *CBC News*, February, 2013, www.cbc.ca/news/canada/montreal/story/2013/02/26/montreal-quebec-education-summit-student-fee-protest.html.

71. Jeffrey Hutchings, "Harper Government's Muzzling of Scientists a Mark of Shame for Canada," *Toronto Star*, March 15, 2013, www.thestar.com/opinion/commentary/2013/03/15/harper_governments_muzzling_of_scientists_a_mark_of_shame_for_canada.html.

72. Eric Pineault, "Message from Quebec's Student Movement: Austerity Can Be Fought," *rabble.ca*, May 4, 2012, http://rabble.ca/blogs/bloggers/progressive-economics-forum/2012/05/message-qu%C3%A9becs-student-movement-austerity-can-be.

73. *Class War University*, "Could Students in the US Pull Off a Strike Like in Montreal? An Interview with Marianne Garneau," August 21, 2012, http://classwaru.org/2012/08/31/could-students-in-the-us-pull-off-a-strike-like-in-montreal/. Garneau contrasts the potential of an emerging democratic movement with the traditional representation of student interests by student associations that rely on university administrations to collect and hand them their dues. On business unionism in the context of public education in the United States, see Lois Weiner, *The Future of Our Schools: Teacher Unions and Social Justice* (Chicago: Haymarket, 2012). Weiner argues that teacher unions should not only challenge neoliberal reforms and the corporate assault on public education but also work with other organizations as part of a larger social movement rooted in matters of equity and social justice.

74. Scott Jaschik, "Students or Employees?" *Inside Higher Ed*, July 24, 2012, www.insidehighered.com/news/2012/07/24/organized-labor-and-higher-education-line-opposite-sides-grad-union-issue. NYU, other private universities, and the American Council on Education insist that graduate students are students who are assessed based on academic standards, rather than employees assessed on labor standards, and therefore are not entitled to collective bargaining. Similarly, Brown University argued against reversing a landmark decision in 2004 that prohibited the unionization of graduate students. A brief in favor of student unionization submitted by the largest federation of labor organizations in the United States, the AFL-CIO, was backed by the American Association of University Professors, the American Federation of Teachers, and the National Education Association. On the same issue, see also Peter Schmidt, "College Leaders and Labor Organizers Spar over Possible Graduate Student Unionization," *Chronicle of Higher Education*, July 24, 2012, http://chronicle.com/article/College-LeadersLabor/133119/.

75. Ibid.

76. See, for example, "Dispatches from the US Student Movement: March 1," *Nation*, March 1, 2013, www.thenation.com/blog/173144/dispatches-us-student-movement-march-1.

77. Zachary A. Bell, "Why Don't American Students Strike?" *Nation*, August 12, 2012, http://www.thenation.com/blog/169378/why-dont-american-students-strike.

78. See, for example, Jasper Conner, *Towards a New Student Unionism*, www.lizardelement.com/unionism/unionisminsidewebread.pdf. See also Biola Jeje and Isabelle Nastasia, "Student Activism, Reborn," *Salon*, May 21, 2012, www.salon.com/2012/05/21/student_activism_reborn/.

79. Bell, "Why Don't American Students Strike?" See also Isabelle Nastasia and Biola Jeje, "New York Students Speak on International Protests and Student Power in the U.S.," *Student Voice*, August 18, 2012, www.stuvoice.org/2012/08/18/two-student-organizers-speak-on-internationac-protests-and-student-power-in-the-u-s/.

80. "Dispatches from the US Student Movement," *Nation*, January 18, 2013, www.thenation.com/blog/172303/dispatches-us-student-movement.

81. Kathryn Seidewitz, "What Comes First—Student Issues or Student Power?" *Waging Nonviolence*, February 13, 2013, http://wagingnonviolence.org/feature/what-comes-first-student-issues-or-student-power-2-2/.

82. Kathryn Seidewitz, "Where Is the U.S. Student Movement? Ohio Wants to Know," *Waging Nonviolence*, December 17, 2012, http://wagingnonviolence.org/feature/where-is-the-student-movement-ohio-wants-to-know/.

83. "Dispatches from the US Student Movement," *Nation*, January 18, 2013.

84. Seidewitz, "Where Is the U.S. Student Movement?"

85. Chris Hedges, "Northern Light," *TruthDig*, June 3, 2012, www.truthdig.com/report/item/northern_light_20120603.

Chapter Seven: Democracy Unsettled

1. Katha Pollitt, "Backlash Spectacular," *Nation*, May 26, 2008, www.thenation.com/article/backlash-spectacular.

US House of Representatives, 3, 7
US Senate, 3, 7
Utah, 60

W

Walker, Scott, 66
Wall Street (film), 13
Washington University, 192
Watson Institute for International
     Studies, 25–26, 41
Weiner, Lois, 232n73
Weisberger, Bernard, 7–8
Wente, Margaret, 168–69
White, Julian, 113
Williams, Jeffrey, 67
Williams, Raymond, 198
Willis, Paul, 196, 198
Wilmore, Larry, 105
Wilson, Robin, 126–27
Wisconsin, 14, 60, 66, 69, 193
Wolf, LaKeisha, 109
Wolin, Sheldon, 70–71
World Bank, 1, 85

Y

Yale University, 136
Young Americans for Freedom, 64–65
*Youth in a Suspect Society: Democracy or
     Disposability?* (Giroux), 198

Z

Zapatistas, 92
Zinn, Howard, 186, 187
Zirin, David, 126, 136

About the Author

Henry A. Giroux currently holds the Global TV Network Chair Professorship at McMaster University in the English and Cultural Studies Department and a Distinguished Visiting Professorship at Ryerson University. His most recent books include *Youth in Revolt: Reclaiming a Democratic Future* (Paradigm, 2013) and *America's Educational Deficit and the War on Youth* (Monthly Review Press, 2013).

MATH - MAGIC

Book 5

Textbook in Mathematics for Class V

राष्ट्रीय शैक्षिक अनुसंधान और प्रशिक्षण परिषद्
NATIONAL COUNCIL OF EDUCATIONAL RESEARCH AND TRAINING

First Edition
March 2008 Phalguna 1929

Reprinted
January 2009 Magha 1930
January 2010 Magha 1931
January 2011 Magha 1932
December 2011 Agrahayana 1933
December 2012 Agrahayana 1934
December 2013 Agrahayana 1935
December 2014 Agrahayana 1936

PD 285T IJ

₹ 50.00

Printed on 80 GSM paper with NCERT watermark

Published at the Publication Division by the Secretary, National Council of Educational Research and Training, Sri Aurobindo Marg, New Delhi 110 016 and printed at Pushpak Press Private Limited, 203-204, DSIDC Sheds, Okhla Industrial Area, Phase-I, New Delhi 110 020

ISBN 978-81-7450-828-7

OFFICES OF THE PUBLICATION DIVISION, NCERT

NCERT Campus
Sri Aurobindo Marg
New Delhi 110 016   Phone : 011-26562708

108, 100 Feet Road
Hosdakere Halli Extension
Banashankari III Stage
Bangalore 560 085   Phone : 080-26725740

Navjivan Trust Building
P.O.Navjivan
Ahmedabad 380 014   Phone : 079-27541446

CWC Campus
Opp. Dhankal Bus Stop
Panihati
Kolkata 700 114   Phone : 033-25530454

CWC Complex
Maligaon
Guwahati 781 021   Phone : 0361-2674869

Publication Team

Head, Publication Division	:	*N. K. Gupta*
Chief Production Officer	:	*Kalyan Banerjee*
Chief Editor	:	*Shveta Uppal*
Chief Business Manager	:	*Gautam Ganguly*
Editor	:	*Bijnan Sutar*
Production Assistant	:	*Deepak Jaiswal*

FOREWORD

The National Curriculum Framework (NCF), 2005, recommends that children's life at school must be linked to their life outside the school. This principle marks a departure from the legacy of bookish learning which continues to shape our system and causes a gap between the school, home and community. The syllabi and textbooks developed on the basis of NCF signify an attempt to implement this basic idea. They also attempt to discourage rote learning and the maintenance of sharp boundaries between different subject areas. We hope these measures will take us significantly further in the direction of a child-centred system of education outlined in the National Policy on Education (1986).

The success of this effort depends on the steps that school principals and teachers will take to encourage children to reflect on their own learning and to pursue imaginative activities and questions. We must recognise that given space, time and freedom, children generate new knowledge by engaging with the information passed on to them by adults. Treating the prescribed textbook as the sole basis of examination is one of the key reasons why other resources and sites of learning are ignored. Inculcating creativity and initiative is possible if we perceive and treat children as participants in learning, not as receivers of a fixed body of knowledge.

These aims imply considerable change in school routines and mode of functioning. Flexibility in the daily time-table is as necessary as rigour in implementing the annual calendar so that the required number of teaching days are actually devoted to teaching. The methods used for teaching and evaluation will also determine how effective this textbook proves for making children's life at school a happy experience, rather than a source of stress or boredom. Syllabus designers have tried to address the problem of curricular burden by restructuring and reorienting knowledge at different stages with greater consideration for child psychology and the time available for teaching. The textbook attempts to enhance this endeavour by giving higher priority and space to opportunities for contemplation and wondering, discussion in small groups, and activities requiring hands-on experience.

National Council of Educational Research and Training (NCERT) appreciates the hard work done by the Textbook Development Committee responsible for this book. We wish to thank the Chairperson of the Advisory Committee, Professor Anita Rampal and the Chief Advisor for this book, Professor Amitabha Mukherjee for guiding the work of this committee. Several teachers contributed to the development of this textbook; we are grateful to their principals for making this possible. We are indebted to the institutions and organisations which have generously permitted us to draw upon their resources, material and personnel. We are especially grateful to the members of the National Monitoring Committee, appointed by the Department of Secondary and Higher Education, Ministry of Human Resource Development under the Chairpersonship of Professor Mrinal Miri and Professor G.P. Deshpande, for their valuable time and contribution. As an organisation committed to the systemic reform and continuous improvement in the quality of its products, NCERT welcomes comments and suggestions which will enable us to undertake further revision and refinement.

Director
National Council of Educational
Research and Training

New Delhi
30 November 2007

TEXTBOOK DEVELOPMENT COMMITEE

CHAIRPERSON, ADVISORY COMMITTEE FOR TEXTBOOKS AT THE PRIMARY LEVEL

Anita Rampal, *Professor*, Department of Education, Delhi University, Delhi

CHIEF ADVISOR

Amitabha Mukherjee, *Director*, Centre for Science Education and Communication (CSEC), Delhi University, Delhi

MEMBERS

Anita Rampal, *Professor*, Department of Education, Delhi University, Delhi

Asmita Varma, *Primary Teacher*, Navyug School, Lodhi Road, New Delhi

Bhavna, *Lecturer*, DEE, Gargi College, New Delhi

Dharam Parkash, *Professor*, DESM, NCERT, New Delhi

Hema Batra, *Primary Teacher*, CRPF Public School, Rohini, Delhi

Jyoti Sethi, *Primary Teacher*, Sarvodaya Kanya Vidyalaya, Ashok Vihar, Phase II, Delhi

Kanika Sharma, *Primary Teacher*, Kulachi Hansraj Model School, Ashok Vihar, Delhi

Prakasan V.K., *Lecturer*, DIET, Malappuram, Tirur, Kerala

Preeti Chadha Sadh, *Primary Teacher*, Basic School, CIE, Delhi University, Delhi

Suneeta Mishra, *Primary Teacher*, N.P. Primary School, Sarojini Nagar, New Delhi

MEMBER–COORDINATOR

Inder Kumar Bansal, *Professor*, DEE, NCERT, New Delhi

ILLUSTRATIONS AND DESIGN TEAM

Srivi Kalyan, New Delhi

Nancy Raj, Chennai

Anita Varma, Bangkok

Taposhi Ghoshal, New Delhi

Sougata Guha, The Srijan, Delhi

Cover Design: Srivi Kalyan

Layout and design support
Anita Rampal, Sadiq Saeed

ACKNOWLEDGEMENTS

National Council of Educational Research and Training (NCERT) thanks the following persons and institutions for their contribution towards this textbook. Special thanks are due to the Centre for Science Education and Communication (CSEC), Delhi University, for providing academic support and hosting all the textbook development workshops. The teams were fully supported by the staff, who put in tremendous effort through long working hours even on holidays.

The Council gratefully acknowledges the contributions of Sadiq Saeed *(DTP Operator)*, Inderjeet Jairath *(Proof Reader)* and Shakamber Dutt *(Computer Station Incharge)* in shaping this book.

The Council also acknowledges the support of Mr. Venugopal and the International Collective in Support of Fishworkers (ICSF), Chennai, in providing detailed information and photographs about boats and fishworkers. The stories of the farmers in Vidarbha are adapted from reports by P. Sainath and Jaideep Hardikar. The support offered by K.K. Vashishtha, *Head*, Department of Elementary Education, NCERT is also gratefully acknowledged. The Council acknowledges the support of Eklavya, Bhopal for the children's drawings and some mathematical puzzles.

For the photographs the Council gratefully acknowledges the contribution of the following:

Chapter 1 — MPEDA, (Marine Products Exports Development Authority) Kerala, ICSF (International Collective in Support of Fishworkers), Chennai, and Prakasan V.K.

Chapter 2 — R.C. Das, CIET

Chapter 8 — Raghu Rai and Delhi Tourism Development Corporation, Karnail Singh, Bhavna

Chapter 9 — Anita Rampal, Bhavna, Preeti Chadha Sadh

Chapter 10 — Nan Moore, Tad Arensmeier

Chapter 11 — Bhavna, Hema Batra

Chapter 14 — Bhavna, Kalyani Raghunathan

MATH-MAGIC

What is inside this book?

The Fish Tale

Deep under the sea
See the lovely coloured fish
Swimming peacefully

This special poem in three lines is called a Haiku. Such poems about nature are popular in Japan. Here is another Haiku—

The lake, calm, smooth, still
A fish jumps up and returns
Ripples shake the lake

Do you know any poems about fish?

No

Here are some drawings made by children.

When you think of fishes what shapes come to your mind?

✳ Try to use a square and a triangle to draw a fish.

Navyata Class I

Maya Class IV

Look for fish designs around you — on cloth, in paintings, on mats, etc.

'Meen' means a fish and 'Meenakshi' is a girl whose eyes look like a fish. Can you think of someone who has such eyes?

✳ Draw a face with 'fish eyes'.

Fishes can have very different sizes. The smallest fish is about 1 cm long. How long is the biggest fish you can imagine? 5000 cm

✳ How many times longer is your big fish than the smallest fish?
4999 more cm

The biggest fish is the **whale shark**. It is actually not a whale but

is a big, big fish. Whales are different from fish. Whales breathe like we do, through their noses. But fish have no noses and they take in water, not air. Whales give birth to babies, but fish lay eggs. The whale shark fish looks big and dangerous, but is quite harmless. It does not attack humans.

One whale shark was as long as 18 m. Just think how long that is – almost 12 children of your size standing one on top of the other! And guess what it weighed? Well, much, much more than what 12 of you together weigh! Its weight was about 16000 kg!

✳ About how many kilograms do you weigh? ___35___

✳ So 12 children like you put together will weigh about __420__ kg.

✳ About how much more does the whale shark weigh than 12 children like you put together? _15580_

The Fish Tail

To see the difference between whales and fish look carefully at their tails. Can you see that the fish tail stands flat along its body, but the tail of the whale almost looks like two legs. Can you spot the fish in the picture?

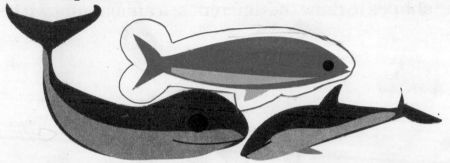

"Schools" of Fish!

Fish like to swim together in the sea in big groups called "schools" of fish. In their school they feel safe from the bigger fish. (Do you feel safe in your school?) Yes

This is a thematic chapter which presents to children the world of fish and fish workers through an integrated approach. Mathematical concepts, such as shapes, estimation, sense of large numbers, simple operations, speed, loans, etc. are woven into real-life contexts to allow a creative revision of some ideas learnt earlier.

To scare away the bigger fish, some small fish drink up a lot of water, swell up and look big!

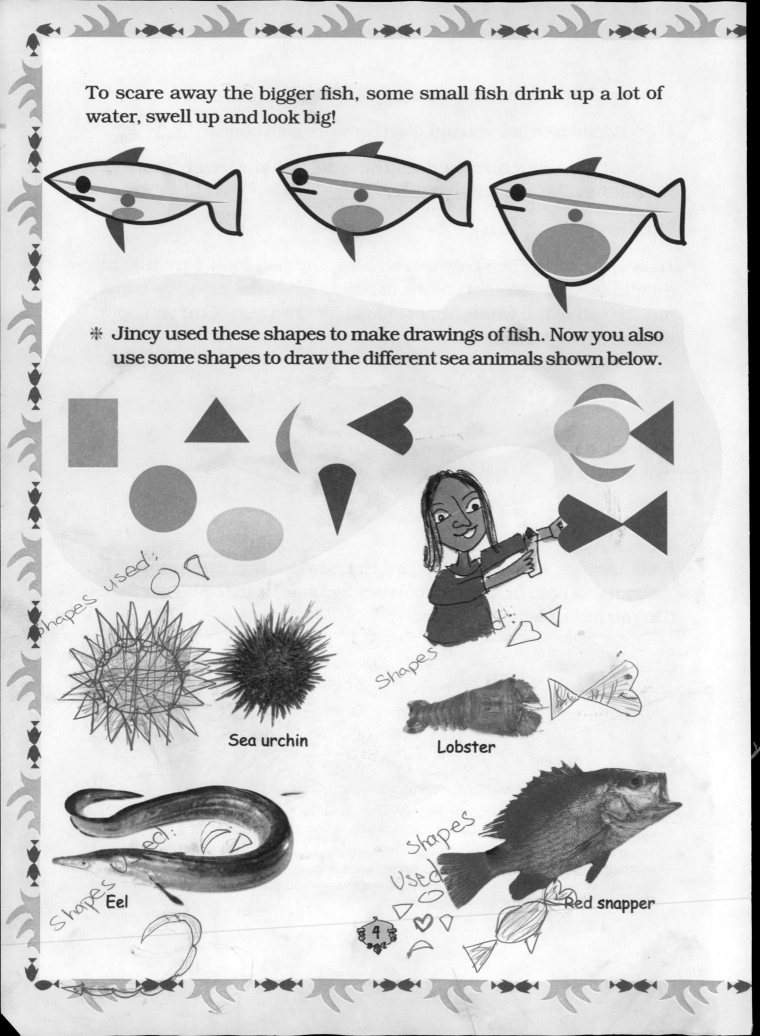

✳ Jincy used these shapes to make drawings of fish. Now you also use some shapes to draw the different sea animals shown below.

Shapes used:

Sea urchin

Lobster

Shapes used:

Eel

Shapes used:

shapes used

Red snapper

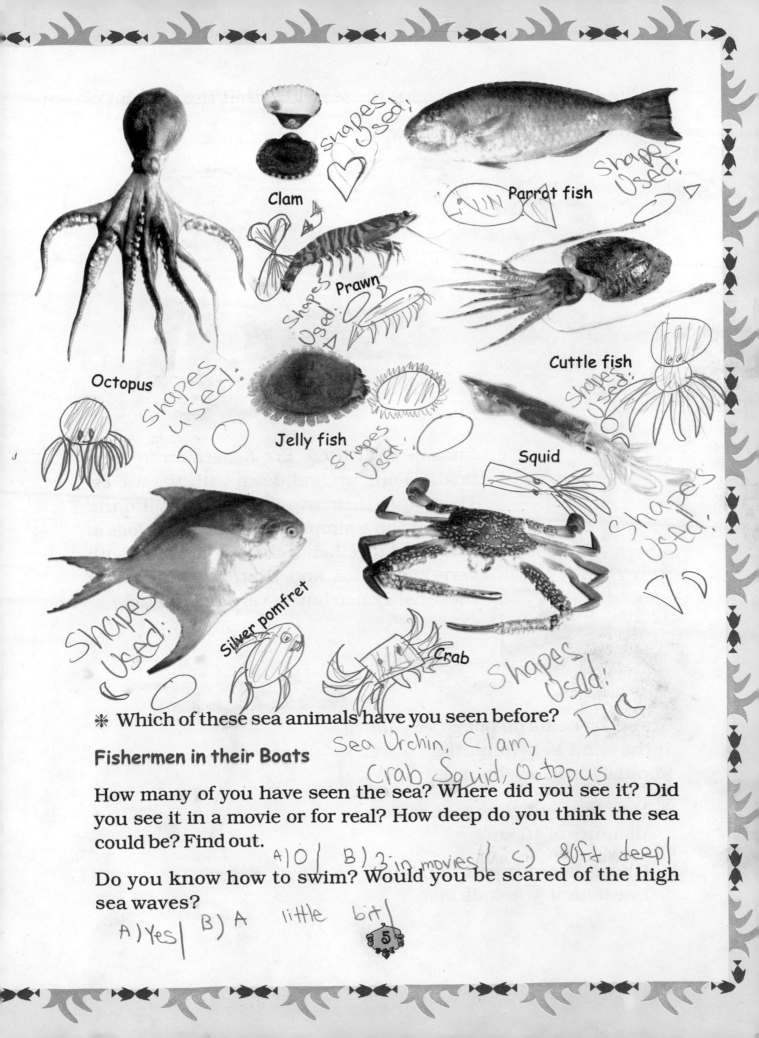

Clam

shapes used: (handwritten)

Parrot fish

shapes used: (handwritten)

Prawn

Octopus

shapes used: (handwritten)

Cuttle fish

shapes used: (handwritten)

Jelly fish

shapes used: (handwritten)

Squid

shapes used: (handwritten)

Silver pomfret

Shapes used: (handwritten)

Crab

shapes used: (handwritten)

✳ Which of these sea animals have you seen before?

Sea Urchin, Clam, Crab Squid, Octopus (handwritten)

Fishermen in their Boats

How many of you have seen the sea? Where did you see it? Did you see it in a movie or for real? How deep do you think the sea could be? Find out.

A) 0 B) 3 in movies C) 80ft deep (handwritten)

Do you know how to swim? Would you be scared of the high sea waves?

A) Yes B) A little bit (handwritten)

✳ Close your eyes and imagine the sea with waves rising high.

✳ How high do you think the waves can go? __1 m__

Imagine that there are fishermen in their boats, going up and down with the waves. They start their trip when it is still dark. Some go on a simple boat made from logs of wood tied together. If the sea is rough, with very high tides and a strong wind, then these fishermen have a very difficult time.

Log boat

These log boats do not go very far. If the wind is helpful, they travel about 4 km in one hour.

✳ How long will they take to go a distance of 10 km? *If the wind is helpful about 2 ½ hours.*

✳ Guess how far you can go in one hour if you walk fast.

2 mls

Log boat

Fishermen can feel the wind and look at the sun to find out which way to go. Many of us would get lost and not be able to find our way on the sea where you only see water, water, and nothing else!

Find out

Look at the sun and find out the direction from where it rises.

East

❋ From where you are, what interesting thing do you see to your east?

a T.V.

❋ Name two things that are lying to your west.

What a Catch!

a lightbulb
a suitcase

Out on the sea, fishermen look for a place where they hope to find a good catch of fish. There they spread their nets. They will have to wait for many hours for the fish to come into their nets.

What a long sword-fish!

❋ Look at the different types of boats.

Some boats have motors and go further into the sea. Since they go far out they can catch more fish. These boats travel faster, at the speed of about 20 km in one hour.

Oar boat

❋ How far would the motor boats go in three and a half hours? *70 km*

❋ How much time will they take to go 85 km?

4h 30min.

Motor boat

Motor boat

Long tail boat

Big machine boat (trawler)

But the fishermen are now very worried. There are some very big machine boats (trawlers) in the business. They go far out and put their big nets deep in the sea. This way they collect a whole lot of fish, leaving very few near the sea shore. They also stay out on the sea for many days.

These big machine boats also catch the small baby fish, which have yet to grow up. Fishermen in the smaller boats always let the baby fish pass through their nets to go back into the sea. They choose a net size in such a way that only the grown up fish are caught.

For hundreds of years fishermen have cared for the sea and its fishes, and fished only a little to eat and sell. They say that if trawlers catch thousands of kilograms of fish everyday, there will be no fish left in the sea!

✳ Write a news report about the dangers faced by the fishes in our rivers and seas.

Which Boat Gets How Much?

In one trip the log boat brings about 20 kg of fish. But other types of boats bring a bigger catch as given in the table. The table also shows the speed of each type of boat, which is how far each boat goes in one hour. Look at the table and calculate —

a) About how much fish in all will each type of boat bring in seven trips?

51940 fish in all.

b) About how far can a motor boat go in six hours?

120 km

c) If a long tail boat has to travel 60 km how long will it take?

5 hours

Type of boat	Catch of fish in one trip (in kg)	Speed of the boat (how far it goes in one hour)
Log boat	20 –140	4 km per hour
Long tail boat	600– 4200	12 km per hour
Motor boat	800 –5600	20 km per hour
Machine boat	6000 – 42000	22 km per hour

Some Big, Big Numbers!

In the Class IV Math-Magic you heard of the number **'lakh'** which is equal to a hundred thousand. You had read that there are about one lakh brick kilns in our country, where bricks are made.

✳ What other things have you heard of in lakhs?

✳ Write the number one thousand. Now write one hundred thousand. So how many zeroes are there in the number one lakh? Easy, isn't it?

✳ There are about two lakh boats in our country. Half of them are without a motor. What is the number of boats with a motor? Write it.

✳ About one fourth of the boats with a motor are big machine boats. How many thousand machine boats are there? Come on, try to do it without writing down.

We might wonder about the number of people whose lives are related to fish. In all there are about one hundred lakh fishworkers — who catch fish, clean and sell them, make and repair nets and boats, etc. We also have a name for this big number — **'one hundred lakh'** is called a **crore**.

✳ Where have you heard of a crore? What was the number used for?

✳ Try writing the number one crore. Don't get lost in all the zeroes!

The Fish Market

Have you been to a fish market? If you have then you might know why a very noisy place is sometimes called a 'fish market'!

This fish market is busy today.

Many boats have brought a good catch. The fisherwomen are shouting out their prices to the buyers.

Mini — "Come here! Come here! Take sardines at Rs 40 a kg".

Gracy — "Never so cheap! Get sword-fish for Rs 60 a kg".

Floramma sells prawns for Rs 150 a kg.

Karuthamma sells squid for Rs 50 a kg.

Look, Fazila can hardly carry this big kingfish! She says, "This fish weighs 8 kg. I will sell the whole for Rs 1200".

Practice Time

1) At what price per kg did Fazila sell the kingfish?

2) Floramma has sold 10 kg prawns today. How much money did she get for that?

3) Gracy sold 6 kg sword fish. Mini has earned as much money as Gracy. How many kg of sardines did Mini sell?

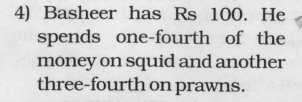

4) Basheer has Rs 100. He spends one-fourth of the money on squid and another three-fourth on prawns.

   a. How many kilograms of squid did he buy?

   b. How many kilograms of prawns did he buy?

Try saying this fast!

Here is a tongue twister. Repeat it fast!

She sells sea shells on the sea-shore.
She is sure that the shells that she sells
will be there no more.

Women's 'Meenkar Bank'

The meeting of the Meenkar Bank has just begun. Fazila is the president. Twenty fisherwomen have made their own bank. Each saves Rs 25 every month and puts it in the bank.

❋ How much money does the group collect each month?

❋ How much money will be collected in ten years?

Practice time

Gracy needs money to buy a net. Jhansi and her sister want to buy a log boat. So they take a loan from their bank. They will return it with interest.

a) Gracy took a loan of Rs 4000 to buy a net. She paid back Rs 345 every month for one year. How much money did she pay back to the Bank?

12

b) Jhansi and her sister took a loan of Rs 21,000 to buy a log boat. They paid back a total of Rs 23,520 in one year. How much did they pay back every month?

Earlier women did not go on the boat to fish. But now Jhansi and some others are going on the boats during the day. Things are changing now and their Bank helps them. They have also got a special bus to take their baskets full of fish.

Why Don't We Start a New Fish-drying Factory?

The women of Meenkar Bank also want to start a factory to dry fish. The Panchayat has given them some land for that. Over the years they have saved Rs 74,000. They find out how much they will need for the factory.

Fazila writes the things they need to buy to begin. See the table for the cost of each item and the number of items they want to buy. Find the total cost.

Item	Price of each	Number of items	Cost
Bore well for fresh water	Rs 3000	1	
Bamboo rack for fish drying	Rs 2000	20	
Cement tank	Rs 1000	4	
Tray and knife	Rs 300	20	
Bucket	Rs 75	20	

Total cost to set up the factory = _____

When fresh fish is dried it becomes 1/3 its weight.

In one month they plan to dry 6000 kg of fresh fish.

How much dried fish will they get in a month? _____

Floramma — Let us first calculate for 6 kg of fresh fish.

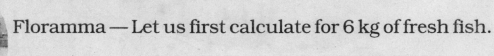

We buy fresh fish for	Rs 15 per kg
We sell dried fish for	Rs 70 per kg

We dry 6 kg fresh fish to get _____ kg dried fish

For 6 kg fresh fish we have to pay   6 × ___ = Rs 90

We will sell 2 kg dried fish and get   2 × ___ = Rs ___

So if we dry 6 kg fresh fish we will earn ___ – 90 = Rs ___

But if we dry 6000 kg we can earn Rs ___ × 1000 in one month!

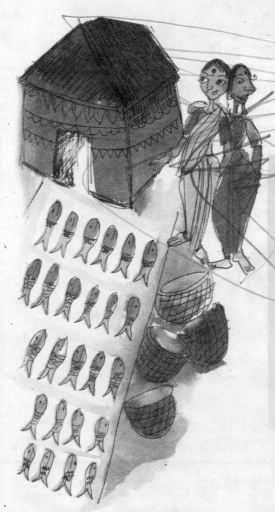

They are all very happy with this plan. The group can make profits and each woman can get a salary for the work she does.

Jhansi — I found that for 6000 kg fish we would need 1500 kg salt every month! Its price is Rs 2 per kg.

Monthly costs:

a) Salt $1500 \times 2 =$ Rs _____

b) Packing and bus charges = Rs 3000

So the total monthly cost of drying and selling the fish   = Rs _____

Fazila — That sounds very good! Our calculations tell us that every month our Bank will earn Rs 44,000!

✳ Check to see if you also get the same answer.

Find out

Songs sung by fishermen are beautiful. Find out about the words and tunes of such songs.

② Shapes and Angles

Rohini and Mohini are twin sisters. They love doing the same things. One day when they were making shapes with matchsticks, Shaila gave them a challenge.

Rohini will make a shape. Mohini has to make the same without looking at it, but she can ask questions.

Oh! That is so simple.

Rohini made this shape.

Mohini — Is it a closed shape or an open shape?

Rohini — It is a closed shape.

Mohini — How many sides are there?

Rohini — It has 6 sides.

Mohini made this.

Now you give the answers.

Is it a closed shape? __Yes__. Does it have 6 sides? __Yes__.

But it is not the same as the one made by Rohini. So Mohini tried again.

This is what she made.

Is it a closed shape with 6 sides? _____Yes_____

Is it the same as the one made by Rohini? _____No_____

Is there some way to say in what way these shapes are different?

✳ Mohini tried again but got different shapes. Guess and make two more shapes Mohini could have made.

Mohini is now tired of trying and asks Shaila what to do.

If you ask for the angles that the matchsticks make at the corners, you can do it.

Oh! So let us look for the angles.

✳ Look at the angles marked in these shapes. Can you see the difference?

Rohini

Mohini

See, how the matchsticks make a small angle, a big angle, and a bigger angle.

Wow! When the angle changes the shape changes so much.

It is important to encourage children to think about the way in which shapes can differ even when the number of sides is the same. This will help them to get a sense of how angles determine the shape of a polygon.

17

Practice Time

1) Look at the shape and answer.

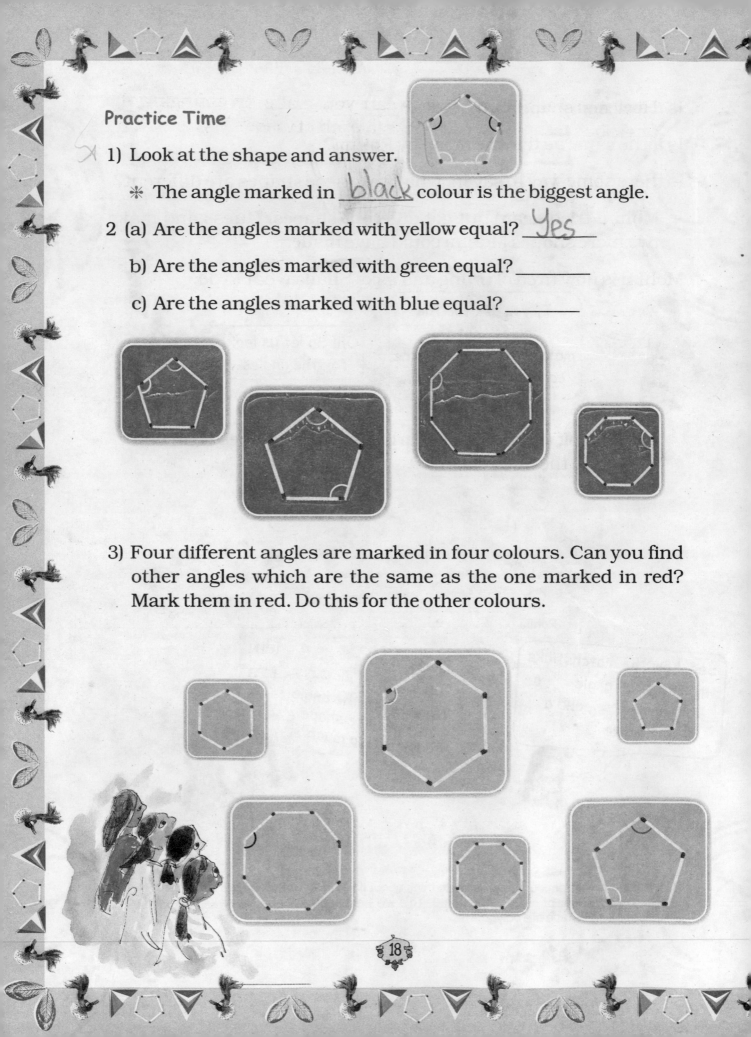

 ✳ The angle marked in ___black___ colour is the biggest angle.

2 (a) Are the angles marked with yellow equal? ___Yes___

   b) Are the angles marked with green equal? _____

   c) Are the angles marked with blue equal? _____

3) Four different angles are marked in four colours. Can you find other angles which are the same as the one marked in red? Mark them in red. Do this for the other colours.

4) How many different shapes can you make by changing the angle between the matchsticks in each of these? Try.

a)

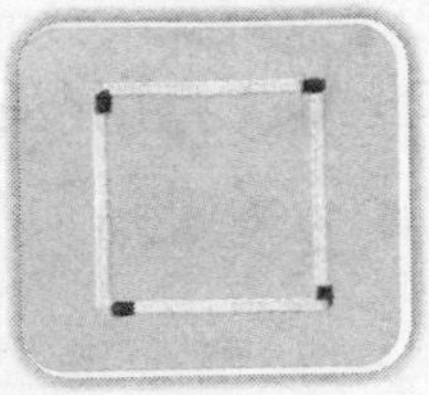

4 matchsticks

b)

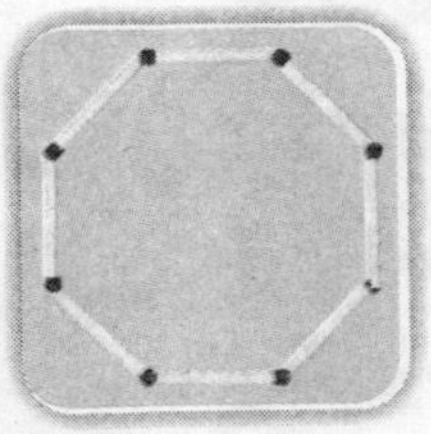

8 matchsticks

c)

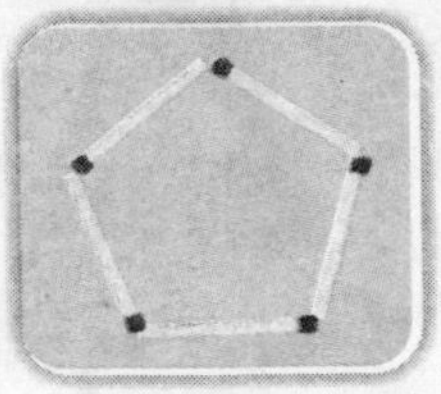

5 matchsticks

d)

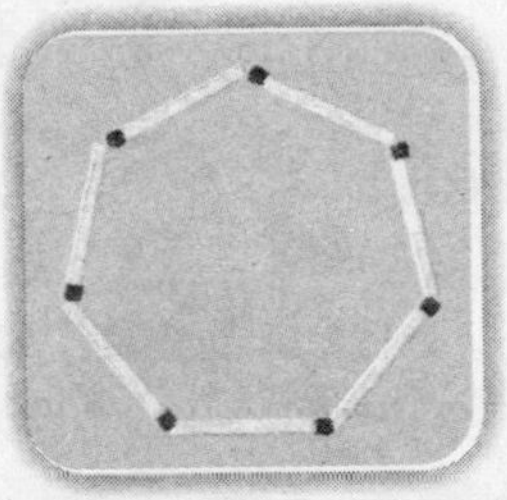

7 matchsticks

e)

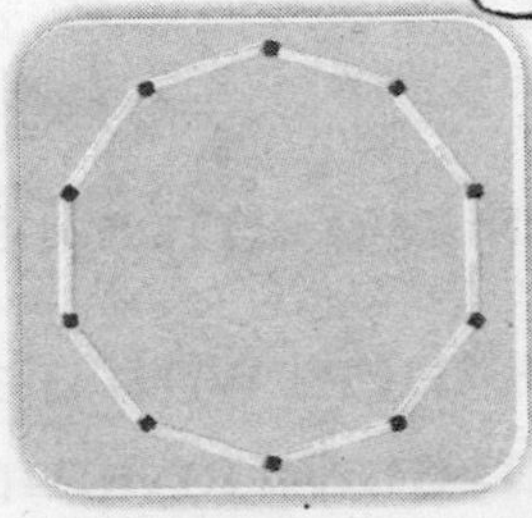

10 matchsticks

Matchstick Puzzles

1) Make 8 triangles using 6 matchsticks. Try!

2) Take 8 matchsticks and make a fish like this. Now pick up any 3 matchsticks and put them in such a way that the fish now starts swimming in the opposite direction. Did it?

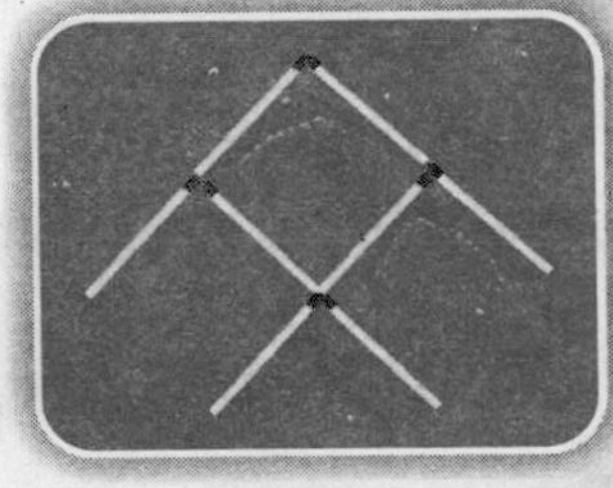

3) Using 10 matchsticks make this shape. Pick up 5 matchsticks and put them in such a way that you get the shape of a house.

If you have not been able to solve these then look for the answers on page 29.

Angle Tester

How do we make equal angles?

Let us make an angle tester.

You also have an angle tester in your geometry box. It is called a divider.

✳ Cut two strips from a cardboard sheet.

✳ Fix them with a drawing pin or ⬭ such that both the strips can move around easily.

Rohini and Mohini went all around with the angle tester to look for different angles in their class.

Rohini tested the angle of the Maths book and the pencil box.

Look at the tester. It has opened like the letter L.

This is a right angle. We write it as L.

20

＊ Go around with your tester and draw here those things in which the tester opens like the letter L. Are you sure they are all right angles?

Practice time

1) Look at the angles in the pictures and fill the table.

Angle	Right angle	More than a right angle	Less than a right angle
			✓
	✓		
	✓		
		✓	
		✓	

2) Sukhman made this picture with so many angles.

Use colour pencils to mark.

✳ right angles with black colour.

✳ angles which are more than a right angle with green.

✳ angles which are less than a right angle with blue.

3) Draw anything of your choice around the angle shown. Also
write what kind of angle it is. The first one is done.

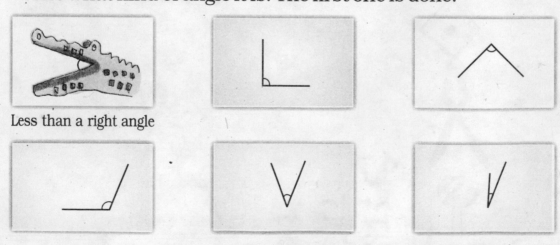

Less than a right angle

Activity

a) Take a square sheet of paper.

b) Fold it in half.

c) Fold it once more and press it.

d) Open the last fold so that the sheet is folded in half.

e) Take one corner and fold it to meet the dotted line.

On the paper you will find lines making a right angle, an angle less than a right angle and an angle more than a right angle.

Look for each of the angles and mark them with different colours.

Activity — Angles with your body

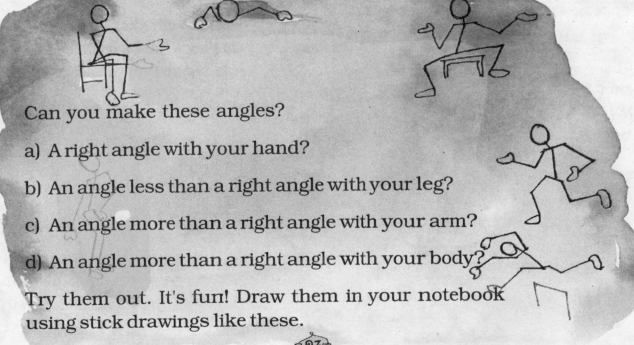

Can you make these angles?

a) A right angle with your hand?

b) An angle less than a right angle with your leg?

c) An angle more than a right angle with your arm?

d) An angle more than a right angle with your body?

Try them out. It's fun! Draw them in your notebook using stick drawings like these.

Angle Garden

My angle dance shows the way!

When I see flowers for making honey, I want to tell other bees. To show them the way I start dancing. My dance shows the angle between the sun and the flower.

Activity

Collect some leaves from the garden. Colour each leaf and print it. Look at the angles on the leaves. Which of them are more/less than a right angle?

Hey! Look at that bird. Its beak has an angle less than a right angle.

I am a woodpecker. My beak is sharp because it has to cut the wood.

❊ Look for the birds which have beaks with small angles.

❊ In the picture mark angles between the two branches. Which two branches have the biggest angle?

Angles in Names

You know, there are angles in the letters of our names too.

In my name there are 11 right angles. There are also 10 angles less than a right angle.

❊ Write 3 names using straight lines and count the angles.

Name	Number of right angles	Number of angles more than a right angle	Number of angles less than a right angle

Activity

a) Put 10 Math-Magic books on top of each other. Keep one book slanting to make a slide.

b) Now do this with six books.

❊ Roll a ball from the top. From which slide does the ball roll down faster?

❊ Which slide has the smaller angle?

25

These are two slides in a park.

✳ Which slide has a larger angle?

✳ Which slide do you think is safer for the little boy? Why?

Changing Shapes

✳ Things you need — used (or new) matchsticks. Piece of rubber tube used in cycle valves.

i) Clean the black end of the matchsticks.

ii) Cut small pieces of the tube (about 1 cm long).

iii) Push two matchsticks into each end of a tube piece.

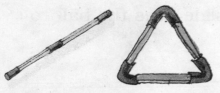

iv) Add more matchsticks to form a triangle.

Now make these 4, 5, 6 sided shapes by using tube pieces and matchsticks.

a)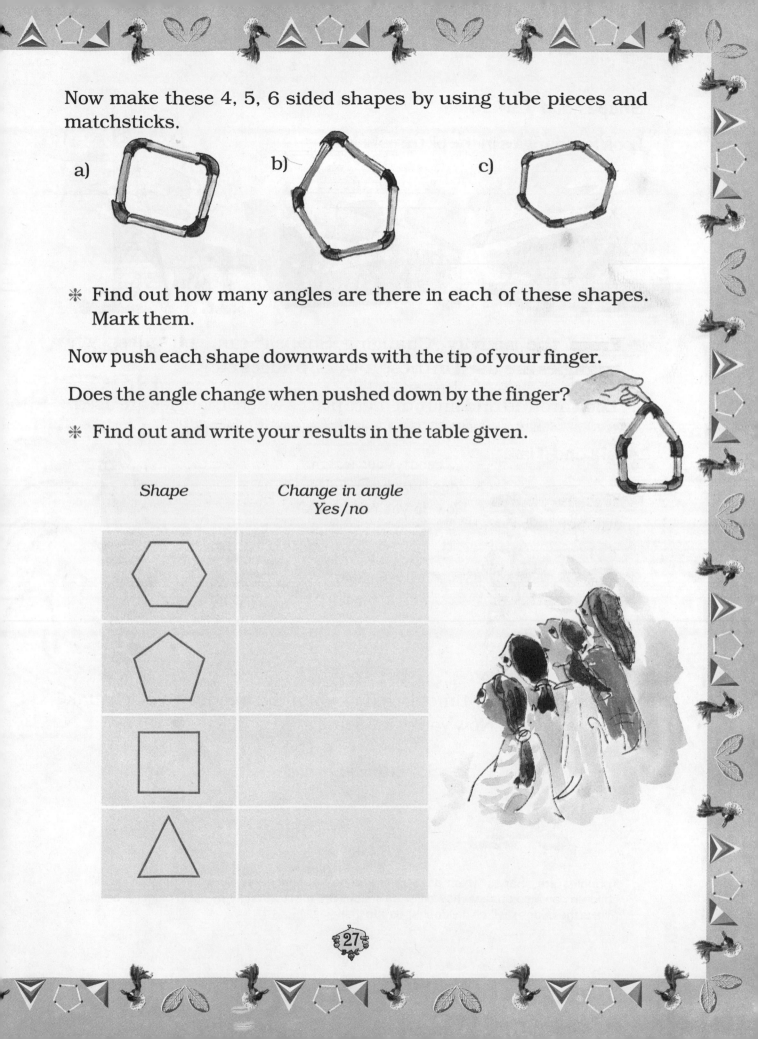

b)

c)

✳ Find out how many angles are there in each of these shapes. Mark them.

Now push each shape downwards with the tip of your finger.

Does the angle change when pushed down by the finger?

✳ Find out and write your results in the table given.

Shape	Change in angle Yes/no

Shapes and Towers

Look for triangles in the pictures below.

✳ From the activity 'Changing Shapes' can you guess why triangles are used in these towers, bridges etc?

✳ Look around and find out more places where triangles are used.

Angle and Time

Zeenat, your watch does not have digits. How do you read time?

I just see the angles. See, when the hands make a right angle, I know it is 9 o'clock.

✳ There are many times in a day when the hands of a clock make a right angle. Now you draw some more.

Triangles are shapes which are strong and do not change easily when pressed. In fact, children can also observe how different shapes are made stronger by using diagonal beams (like in the bridge) which divide shapes into triangles.

✳ Write what kind of angle is made by the hands at these times.
Also write the time.

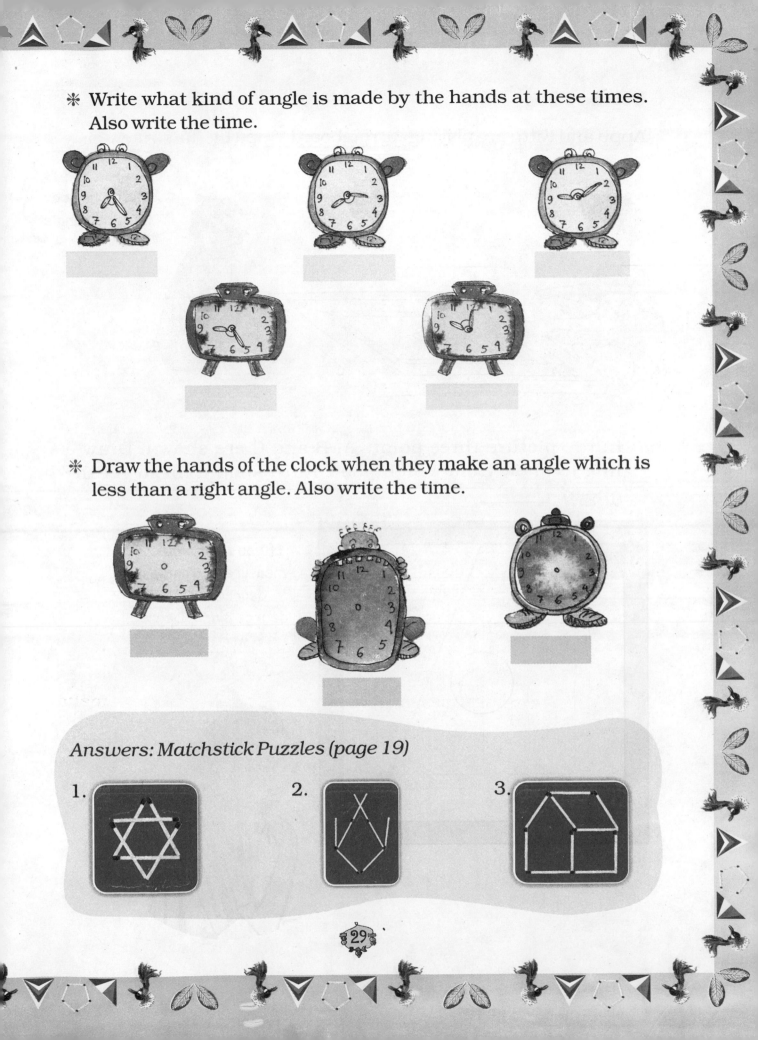

✳ Draw the hands of the clock when they make an angle which is
less than a right angle. Also write the time.

Answers: Matchstick Puzzles (page 19)

1.

2.

3.

Degree Clock

Appu and Kittu are playing carromboard. Appu hit the striker.

Hm Hm........ It comes back at the same angle.

✳ In the picture three points A, B and C are shown. Draw a line to show from which point Kittu should hit to get the queen. _____

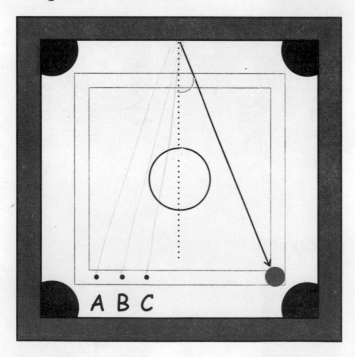

A B C

If you want, you can measure the angle in degrees using a degree clock. Degree is written as °.

Activity: Making a degree clock

1. Cut a circle out of paper.

2. Fold it into half.

3. Fold it once again into a quarter.

4. Fold it once more.

5. Open the paper. You will see lines like this.

6. Now mark 0°, 45°, 90° and 180° as shown.

7. Paste it on an old card.

8. From the centre draw one hand.

9. Make a red hand with a thick paper and fix it to the centre with a drawing pin, so that it is free to move.

Your degree clock is ready.

✳ Use your degree clock to measure the right angle of your pencil box. _____ is the measure of the right angle.

✳ Can you guess how many degrees is the angle which is —

● $\frac{1}{2}$ of a right angle _____

● $\frac{1}{3}$ of a right angle _____

● 2 times of a right angle _____

> 90° is called right angle.

✳ Measure the angle from where Kittu should hit the striker on page 30.

Angles in a Paper Aeroplane

1. Take a square sheet of paper.

2. Fold it in half and open it. ....

3. Fold the corners to the centre. Your paper looks like this.

    P
    Q

4. Fold the green triangle such that P touches Q.

    Q

5. Fold the top two corners of this rectangle along the dotted lines.

6. Your paper will look like this. There is a small triangle in the picture which has to be folded up.

7. Turn it over and fold it in half along the dotted line.

8. Now, to make a wing fold the yellow edge over the red edge.

9. Turn it and do the same on the other side as well.

Your plane is ready to fly. How well does it fly?

❋ Find the angles of 45° and 90° when you open your plane.

In the aeroplane there are folds of 45º, 90º and other angles. The cut-outs of 30º and 60º are on the last page of the book. Children can be encouraged to measure various angles around them.

Angles with Yoga

Rahmat is doing Yoga. These are the pictures of different 'Asanas' he does everyday.

✳ Measure as many angles as you can made by different parts of the body while doing 'Asanas'.

The D Game

You can play the 'D' game with your friends. You draw an angle. Your friend will guess the measure of that angle. Then you use your 'D' to measure it. The difference between the measured angle and the guess will be your friend's score. The one with the lowest score will be the winner.

Come on, play!

Draw Angle	Guess	Measure	Score

You can find this 'D' in your geometry box. Measure the angle on my head fan.

Take this opportunity to introduce the 'D' (protractor). Children will need some help to read the measure of the angle, but they need to do so only approximately.

33

How Many Squares?

* Measure the side of the red square on the dotted sheet. Draw here as many rectangles as possible using 12 such squares.

* How many rectangles could you make? _____

Here's one!

Each rectangle is made out of 12 equal squares, so all have the same area, but the length of the boundary will be different.

Length of the boundary is called **perimeter**.

* Which of these rectangles has the longest perimeter?

* Which of these rectangles has the smallest perimeter?

Children are not expected to learn the definition of the term 'area', but develop a sense of the concept through suitable examples. Give them many opportunities in the classroom to compare things in terms of area and guess which is bigger. Things like stamps, leaves, footprints, walls of the classroom etc. can be compared.

Measure Stamps

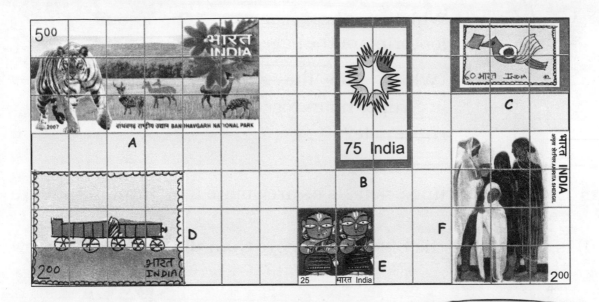

Look at these interesting stamps.

a) How many squares of one centimetre side does stamp A cover? _____

   And stamp B? _____

> Stamp D covers 12 squares. Each square is of side 1 cm. So the area of stamp D is 12 square cm.

b) Which stamp has the biggest area?

   How many squares of side 1 cm does this stamp cover?

   How much is the area of the biggest stamp? _____ square cm.

c) Which two stamps have the same area? _____

   How much is the area of each of these stamps? ____ square cm.

d) The area of the smallest stamp is _____ square cm.

   The difference between the area of the smallest and the biggest stamp is _____ square cm.

Collect some old stamps. Place them on the square grid and find their area and perimeter.

Guess

a) Which has the bigger area — one of your footprints or the page of this book?

b) Which has the smaller area—two five-rupee notes together or a hundred-rupee note?

c) Look at a 10 rupee-note. Is its area more than hundred square cm?

d) Is the area of the blue shape more than the area of the yellow shape? Why?

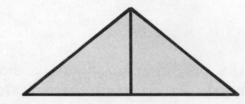

e) Is the perimeter of the yellow shape more than the perimeter of the blue shape? Why?

How Big is My Hand?

Trace your hand on the squared sheet on the next page.

How will you decide whose hand is bigger — your hand or your friend's hand?

What is the area of your hand? _____ square cm.

What is the area of your friend's hand? _____ square cm.

My footprint is longer!

But my footprint is wider. So whose foot is bigger?

My Footprints

✳ Whose footprint is larger — yours or your friend's?

✳ How will you decide? Discuss.

✳ Is the area of both your footprints the same?

My skin has many many folds. So I have a big area! This way the air all over me keeps me cool.

Baby Rhino

What is the area of my footprint?

What is the area of my footprint?

✳ Guess which animal's footprint will have the same area as yours. Discuss.

✳ Here are some footprints of animals — in actual sizes. Guess the area of their footprints.

Hen

Dog

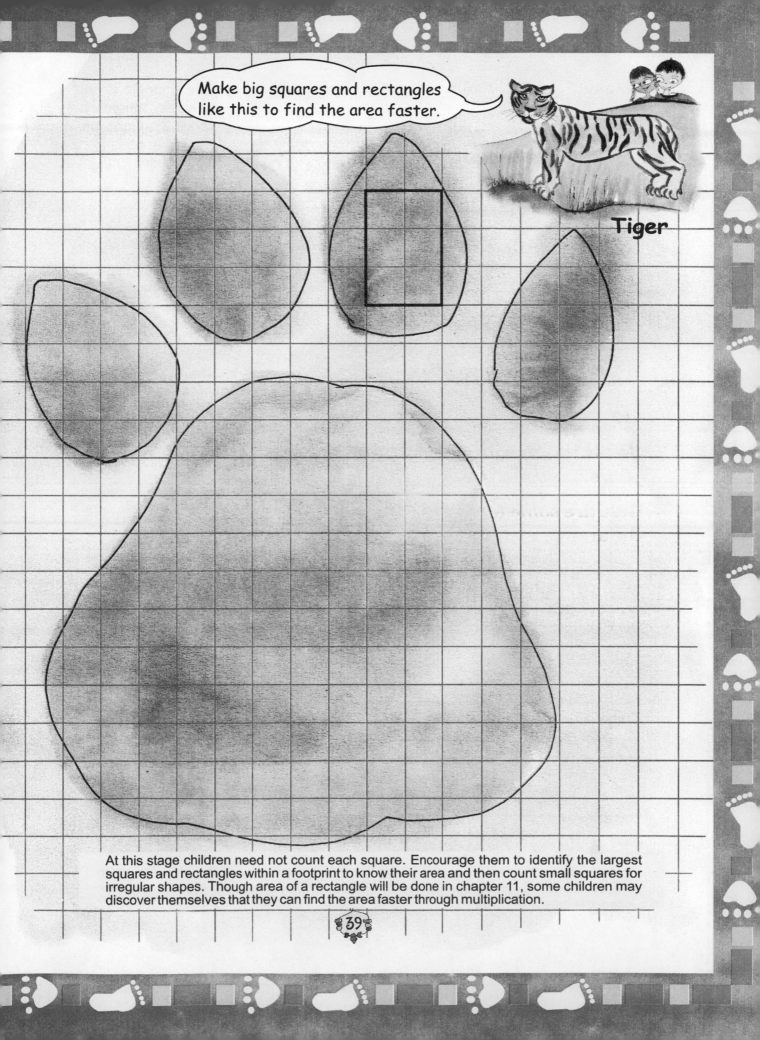

Make big squares and rectangles like this to find the area faster.

Tiger

At this stage children need not count each square. Encourage them to identify the largest squares and rectangles within a footprint to know their area and then count small squares for irregular shapes. Though area of a rectangle will be done in chapter 11, some children may discover themselves that they can find the area faster through multiplication.

How Many Squares in Me?

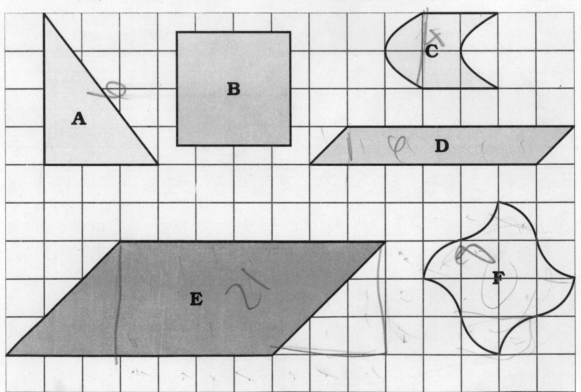

* **Write the area (in square cm) of the shapes below.**

In this exercise children are expected to notice the geometrical symmetry of the shapes to find out their area. Encourage children to evolve their own strategies. Rounding off is not needed in these examples.

Try Triangles

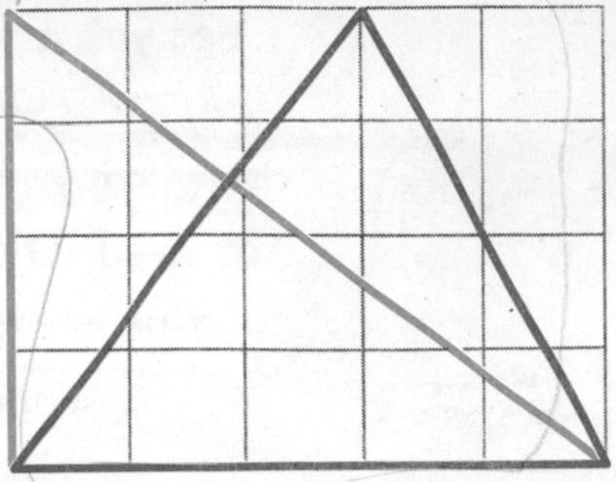

Both the big triangles in this rectangle have the same area.

Sameena

But these look very different.

Sadiq

The blue triangle is half of the big rectangle. Area of the big rectangle is 20 square cm. So the area of the blue triangle is _____10_____ square cm.

And what about the red triangle?

Ah, in it there are two halves of two different rectangles!

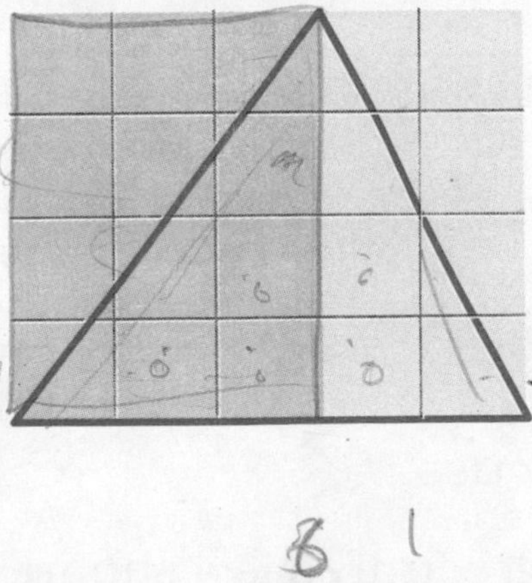

Now you find the area of the two rectangles Sadiq is talking about. What is the area of the red triangle? Explain.

41

Yes you are right. And you know what!! You can draw many more triangles of area 10 square cm in this rectangle. Try drawing them.

Help Sadiq in finding some more such triangles. Draw at least 5 more.

Complete the Shape

Suruchi drew two sides of a shape. She asked Asif to complete the shape with two more sides, so that its area is 10 square cm.

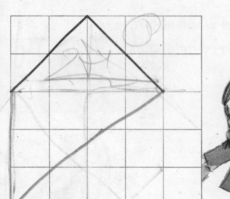

He completed the shape like this.

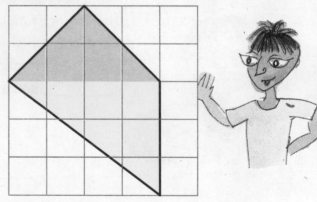

How did you do this?

Oh that's easy! If you look at the green area it is 4 square cm. Below it is the yellow area of 6 square cm. So the area of my shape is 10 square cm!

✳ Is he correct? Discuss.

✳ Explain how the green area is 4 square cm and the yellow area is 6 square cm.

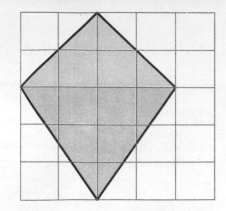

Oh, I thought of doing it differently! If you draw like this, the area is still 10 square cm.

✳ Is Suruchi correct? How much is the blue area? Explain.

✳ Can you think of some other ways of completing the shape?

Every time guests come home, I ask them to do this. But why do they run away!

✳ Try some other ways yourself.

✳ Now ask your friends at home to solve these.

Practice time

1) This is one of the sides of a shape. Complete the shape so that its area is 4 square cm.

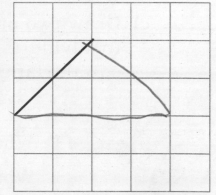

2) Two sides of a shape are drawn here. Complete the shape by drawing two more sides so that its area is less than 2 square cm.

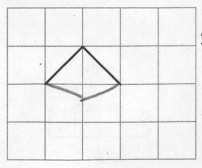

Children can be encouraged to make shapes with either straight edges or curved edges to cover the given area. This exercise can be extended by asking children to draw on squared paper as many shapes as they can of a given area and making guesses for the largest or the smallest perimeter. They can also be asked to check their guesses by measuring the dimensions of the shapes. In case of curved edges, thread can be used for measuring the perimeter.

3) Here is a rectangle of area 20 square cm.

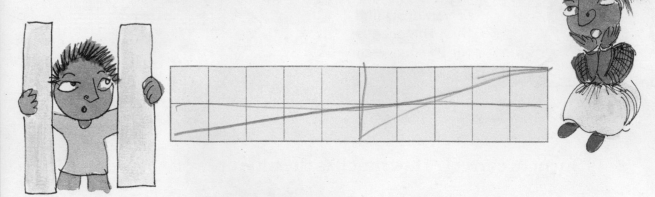

a) Draw one straight line in this rectangle to divide it into two equal triangles. What is the area of each of the triangles?

b) Draw one straight line in this rectangle to divide it into two equal rectangles. What is the area of each of the smaller rectangles?

c) Draw two straight lines in this rectangle to divide it into one rectangle and two equal triangles.

✳ What is the area of the rectangle?

✳ What is the area of each of the triangles?

Puzzles with Five Squares

Measure the side of a small square on the squared paper on page 45. Make as many shapes as possible using 5 such squares. Three are drawn for you.

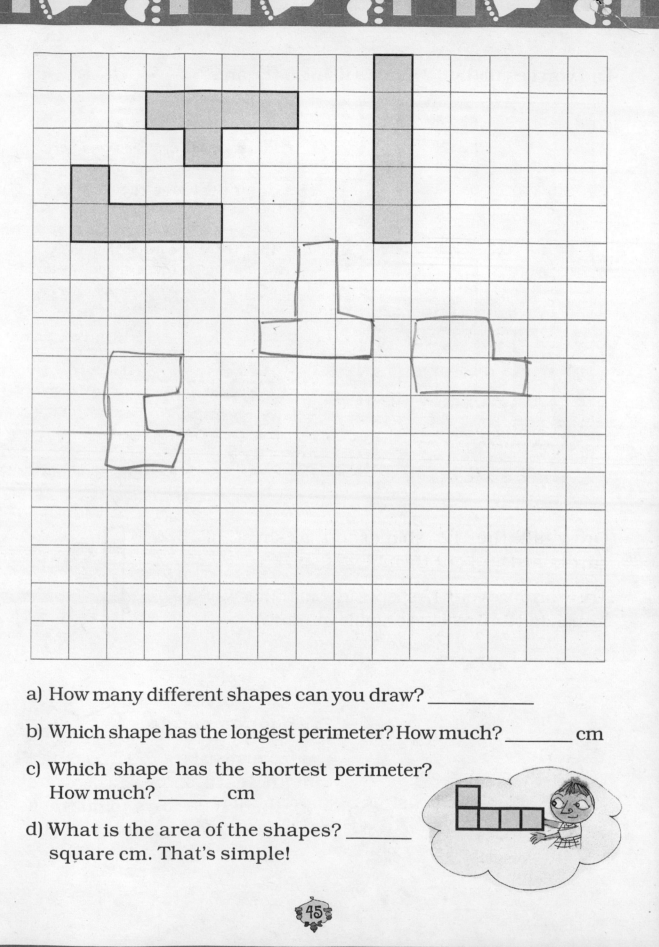

a) How many different shapes can you draw? _____

b) Which shape has the longest perimeter? How much? _____ cm

c) Which shape has the shortest perimeter? How much? _____ cm

d) What is the area of the shapes? _____ square cm. That's simple!

Did you get all the 12 shapes using 5 squares?

All 12 shapes are arranged here to make a rectangle.

This is a 10 X 6 rectangle as there are 10 rows and 6 columns.

You will be surprised to know that there are more than 2000 ways in which these shapes make a 10 X 6 rectangle.

Draw all the 12 shapes on a sheet of cardboard and cut them.

Try to arrange your 12 shapes in some other way to make a 10×6 rectangle. Could you do it?

Try another puzzle

You have to make a 5×12 rectangle with these 12 shapes. There are more than 1000 ways to do it. If you can find even one, that's great!

Game Time

Here is a chessboard. Play this game with your partner, with one set of 12 shapes.

The first player picks one shape from the set and puts it on the board covering any five squares.

The other player picks another shape and puts it on the board, but it must not overlap the first shape.

Keep taking turns until one of you can't go any further.

Whoever puts the last piece wins!

Make Your Own Tile

Remember the floor patterns in Math-Magic Book 4 (pages 117-119). You had to choose the correct tile which could be repeated to make a pattern so that there were no gaps left.

Encourage children to try to do these 'pentomino' puzzles at home. Such exercises can be designed for shapes with 6 squares (hexominoes) in which case there will be 35 different shapes possible.

Ziri went to a shop and was surprised to see the different designs of tiles on the floor. Aren't these beautiful!

❋ Can you find the tile which is repeated to make each of these floor patterns? Circle a tile in each pattern.

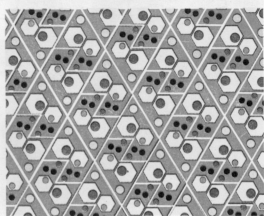

After looking at the patterns Ziri wanted to make her own yellow tile. You too make a tile this way.

Step 1: Take a piece of cardboard or thick paper. Draw a square of side 3 cm on it.

Step 2: Draw a triangle on any one of the sides of this square.

Step 3: Draw another triangle of the same size on another side of the square. But this time draw it inside the square.

Step 4: Cut this shape from the cardboard. Your tile is ready!

What is it's area?

Make a pattern using your tile. Trace the shape to repeat it on a page, but remember there must be no gaps between them.

Ziri made a pattern using her yellow tiles.(You know the area of her tile.)

Answer these —

✳ How many tiles has she used?

✳ What is the area of the floor pattern Ziri has made here?

Practice time

Ziri tried to make some other tiles. She started with a square of 2 cm side and made shapes like these.

Look at these carefully and find out:

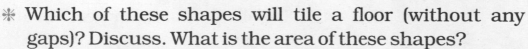

✳ Which of these shapes will tile a floor (without any gaps)? Discuss. What is the area of these shapes?

✳ Make designs in your copy by tiling those shapes.

✳ Now you create your own new tiles out of a square. Can you do the same with a triangle? Try doing it.

In Class III and IV basic shapes like squares, rectangles, hexagons, triangles, circles etc were used to examine which of those can tile and which do not tile to make floor patterns. Children must now be able to modify basic shapes to create different tiling shapes. In the exercise above they may create new shapes out of a square that do not tile even though their area remains the same as that of the square from which they are made.

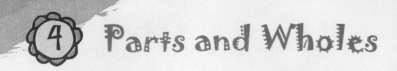

Our Flag

You must have seen the flag of our country. Do you know how to draw the flag?

> Draw a rectangle of length 8 cm and width 6 cm. Divide it into three equal parts and complete the flag.

The top one-third of our flag is saffron (or orange). What is the colour of the middle one-third of the flag? Where will you draw the Ashoka chakra?

How much of the flag will you colour green?

Is the white colour now less than $\frac{1}{3}$ of the flag? Why?

Now look at this flag. How much of it is black? _____

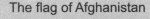

The flag of Afghanistan

The green part of the flag can be written as _____

Is red less than one-third of the flag? Why?

This is the flag of Myanmar, our neighbour.

Is blue more than one-fourth of the flag or less ?

Guess how much of the flag is red. Is it more than $\frac{1}{2}$? Is it more than three-fourths?

Because of the blue chakra in the white part of the Indian flag, the white colour is a little less than 1/3. There can be some discussion on this point.

Find out

Collect as many flags as you can.

How many flags have three colours? Are all the coloured parts equal in these flags?

This is the flag of the Math Club in a school in Kerala. What part of the flag is coloured red? What part is green?

See this black ⬛ logo. Draw it.

Is there a Math Club in your school? If not, ask your teacher how to set it up. Design a flag for your Math Club. Draw it here.

Have you used the red colour? What part of the flag did you colour red?

What were the other colours you chose?

Math Club can be set up in the school in which interesting activities can be taken up like making puzzles, shapes with tangrams, maps of buildings, looking for different geometrical shapes and angles in the environment, calculating area and perimeter of a school ground, etc.

Magic Top

Let us make a magic top.

Take a cardboard piece.

Draw a circle of radius 3 cm and cut it out.

Divide the circle into 8 equal parts. Now each part is $\frac{1}{8}$ of the circle.

Colour $\frac{2}{8}$ red, $\frac{1}{8}$ orange, $\frac{1}{8}$ yellow etc. as shown here. Push a matchstick through the centre of the circle .

Your magic top is ready. Spin it fast!

What do you see? Can you see all the colours? Write what you see in your notebook.

Practice time

A) Chocolate bar

Manju had a chocolate. She gave one-fourth of it to Raji, one-third to Sugatha and one-sixth to Sheela. She ate the remaining part. How many pieces of chocolate did each get? Write here.

Sheela

Raji

Sugatha

Manju

What part of the chocolate did Manju eat?

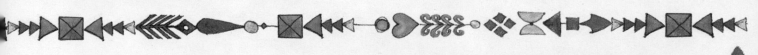

B) Colour the hats

Colour $\frac{1}{3}$ of the hats red.

Colour three-fifth hats blue.

How many hats did you colour red?

How many hats did you colour blue?

What part of the hats are not coloured?

C) Equal parts of a triangle

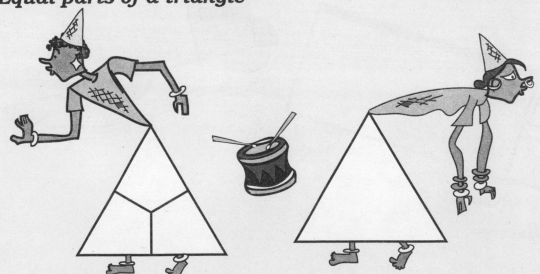

The white triangle is divided into three equal parts. Fill each one-third part with a different colour. Can you show that these parts are equal? Think how.

Now try to make three equal parts of this triangle in a different way. Colour each one-third with a different colour.

D) Six parts of a rectangle

Rani has divided a green rectangle into six equal parts like this.

✳ Now you divide each of these rectangles into six equal parts. Use a different way for each of the three rectangles.

Discuss

✳ How will you check that each part is really one-sixth of that rectangle?

✳ The green rectangle is bigger than the blue one. Can we say that $\frac{1}{6}$ of the green rectangle is bigger than $\frac{1}{6}$ of the blue rectangle?

Greedy Gatekeepers

Remember Birbal, the clever minister of King Akbar? (Math-Magic Class IV, page 14) Do you know how he became a minister?

Birbal was then a young boy living in a village. He was very clever and could write poetry.

He thought he would try his luck in the King's court. So he took some of his poems and set off for the city.

I am a poet

When he reached the outer gate of the palace, he was stopped by the gatekeeper. "Hey! Stop there! Where are you going?", shouted the gatekeeper.

"I am a poet. I want to see King Akbar and show my poems to him", replied the poet.

"Oh, you are a poet! The king is kind, he will surely give you a prize. I will let you in if you give me $\frac{1}{10}$ of your prize".

Young Birbal agreed since he had no other way.

When he went in, the gatekeeper calculated "If he gets 100 gold

coins I will get _____ gold coins".

The poet came to a second gatekeeper.

This gatekeeper also said, "I will let you in if you give me **two-fifth** of your prize". The poet agreed.

The gatekeeper happily calculated, "The poet will get at least 100 gold coins so I will get _____ gold coins!"

The poet reached the last gate. The gatekeeper said, "I will allow you to see the king only if you give me **half** of the prize that you get". The poet had no other way. He agreed and went inside.

The gatekeeper thought, "Today is a great day. If he gets 100 gold coins I will get _____ gold coins. But if he gets 1000 coins — wow! I will get _____".

The king was very happy with the poems and said, "Your work is very good. You can ask anything as your prize".

"My Lord, I want 100 slaps". "What! 100 slaps? _____". The king was shocked —

✳ What happened after that? Complete the story. What part of the prize did the poet get?

Patterns in Parts

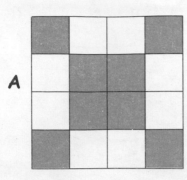

A

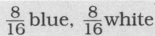
$\frac{8}{16}$ blue, $\frac{8}{16}$ white

1) Make different patterns by colouring some squares in the grids B, C, D. What part of the grid did you colour? What part of the grid remained white? Write.

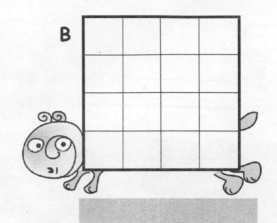

B

C

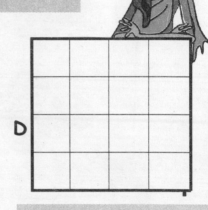

D

2) Look at grid A again. Is the grid coloured —

   a) $\frac{1}{2}$ blue, $\frac{1}{2}$ white?   b) $\frac{2}{4}$ blue, $\frac{2}{4}$ white?

   c) $\frac{3}{8}$ blue, $\frac{5}{8}$ white?   d) $\frac{4}{8}$ blue, $\frac{4}{8}$ white?

Mark (×) on the wrong answer.

3) Draw grids of 16 squares and make patterns with

   a) $\frac{2}{8}$ red, $\frac{1}{2}$ yellow, $\frac{1}{4}$ green

   b) $\frac{3}{16}$ blue, $\frac{5}{16}$ red, $\frac{1}{2}$ yellow

Ramu's Vegetable Field

Ramu's vegetable field has 9 equal parts. What vegetables does he grow?

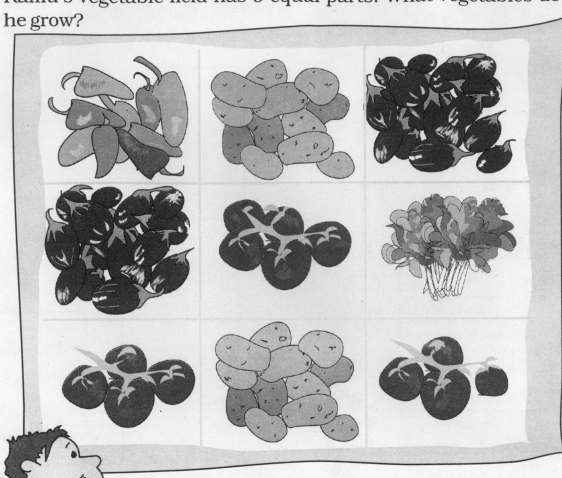

1) Which vegetable grows in the biggest part of his field? What part?

2) On what part of the field does he grow potatoes?

3) What part of the field is used to grow spinach? What part is used for brinjals?

4) Now you write some questions by looking at this picture.

* Ramu wanted to give these vegetables to his friends. He gave Aboobacker one-fifth of these tomatoes and $\frac{1}{3}$ of the potatoes. Srija got $\frac{2}{5}$ of the tomatoes and $\frac{3}{6}$ of the potatoes. Nancy got the rest of these vegetables. Circle Aboobacker's share in blue. Circle Srija's share in yellow.

* How many potatoes and tomatoes did Nancy get?

Game: Who Colours the Circle First?

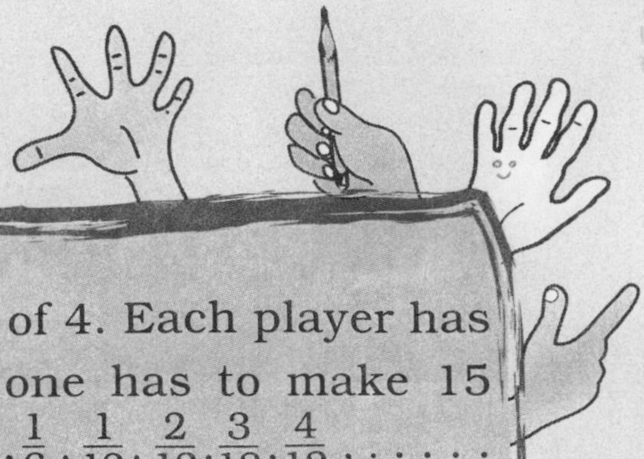

This game is to be played in groups of 4. Each player has to make a circle as shown. Each one has to make 15 tokens on slips of paper. Write $\frac{1}{2}, \frac{1}{3}, \frac{1}{4}, \frac{1}{6}, \frac{1}{12}, \frac{2}{12}, \frac{3}{12}, \frac{4}{12} \cdots \frac{11}{12}$ to make your tokens.

Shuffle the tokens and make a pile in the middle of the group. Now you are ready to start the game.

The first player takes a token from the pile, colours that part of the picture, and puts the token under the pile. The next player does the same, and so on. The winner is the one who first colours the circle completely.

* Who won the game?

* What are the winner's tokens?

* Write the tokens you got.

* What part of the circle did you colour?

The Card Puzzle

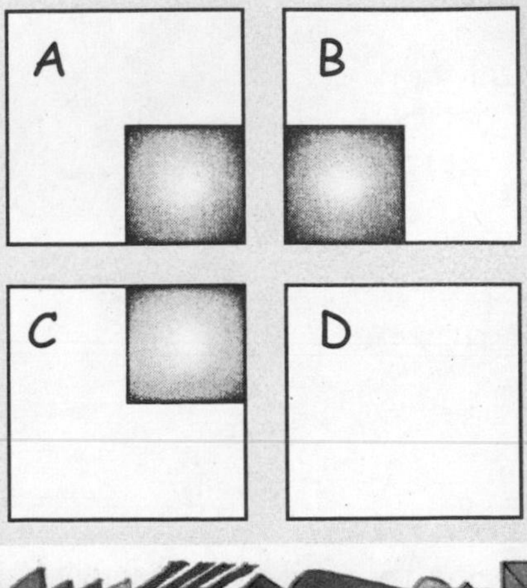

Look carefully at the picture and get ready to answer four questions. Ready?

A B C D

60

1) *Divide the white area in square A into two equal parts.*

   Got the answer? Was that easy?

   Now do the second question.

2) *Divide the white area in square B into three equal parts!*

   That too is easy, isn't it?

   Now see the third question.

3) *Divide the white area in square C into four equal parts!!*

   Is it a bit difficult? Don't worry, take your time.

   Only if you have given up, look for the answer.

   Here comes the last question .

4) *Divide the white area in square D into seven equal parts!!!!*

   The world record for this is 7 scconds. But you can take minutes!

   Tired of thinking? Look for the answer on page 68.

   So was that difficult??

Guess and Check

A) What part of each shape is coloured?

First guess the answer, then check.

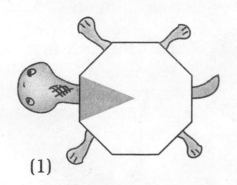

(1)

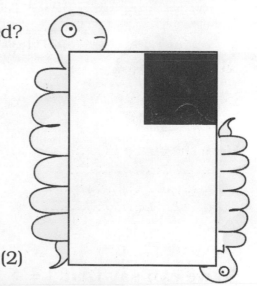

(2)

The colouring circle game and many more such activities should be done in class. The follow-up discussions for all these activities will play a major role in developing children's conceptual understanding about fractions.

(3)    (4)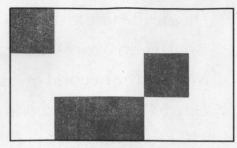

B) Do you remember this picture? Look at the small triangle. What part of the square is it? How will you find this out?

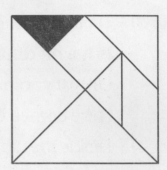

Divide the big triangles and other shapes into small triangles (like the red one). How many small triangles are there altogether?

Coloured Parts

Complete these

1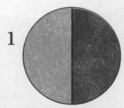

This circle is divided into two equal parts. Out of _____ equal parts one part is coloured blue.

2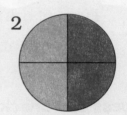

Here the circle is divided into _____ equal parts. Out of _____ equal parts, _____ parts are coloured blue.

3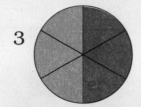

Here the circle is ....
....
....
....

4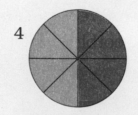

Here the circle is ....
....
....
....

So we can say that $\frac{1}{2} = \frac{2}{....} = \frac{...}{6} = \frac{...}{8}$

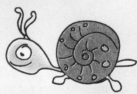

Cutting the Halwa

Ramesh bought a piece of halwa for his children Ammu and Anu.

He divided it equally for them.

✳ Each will get _____ part of halwa.

"This piece is too big. We can't eat it", they said.

So he divided the pieces into half again. Now how many pieces will Ammu get? _____

✳ What part of the halwa is it? _____

"Make it even smaller, Dad" they asked.

So he again cut the halwa into smaller pieces.

"Ok, thank you, Dad."

* Now how many pieces will each get?

* What part of the halwa is each piece now?

* If Ramesh had cut the halwa into 6 equal parts how many pieces would each have got? Look at your answers for questions 1 to 4 and write —

$$\frac{1}{2} = \underline{\quad} = \underline{\quad} = \underline{\quad} = \underline{\quad}$$

Parts of the Strip

Look at the picture. Write what part of the strip is each green piece. Write the part for a piece of each colour.

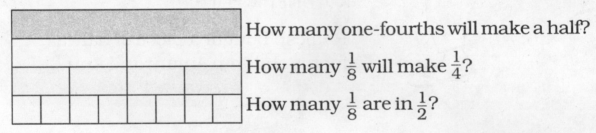

How many one-fourths will make a half?

How many $\frac{1}{8}$ will make $\frac{1}{4}$?

How many $\frac{1}{8}$ are in $\frac{1}{2}$?

Now ask your friends some questions on the same picture.

Patterns

Look at this square.

What part is coloured blue?

What part is green?

Puzzle: Is it Equal?

Ammini says half of half and one-third of three-quarters are equal. Do you agree? How will you show this?

The use of concrete things (such as matchsticks, bottle caps etc.) will help children make sense of equivalent fractions such as $\frac{1}{2} = \frac{2}{4} = \frac{3}{6} = \frac{4}{8} = \frac{5}{10}$. Children must make their own fraction strips using papers of different sizes. Encourage them to compare the strips by colouring them into different fractions.

From a Part to the Whole

1) This show $\frac{1}{5}$ petals of a flower. Complete the flower by drawing the other petals.

2) The picture shows one-third of the blades of a fan. Complete the picture by drawing the other blades.

3) Half of the blades of another fan are shown here. Complete the picture by drawing the other half. How many blades have you drawn?

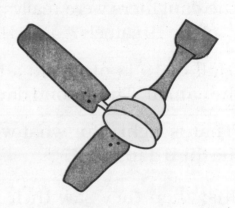

Rupees and Paise

How many 50 will make one rupee?

Is 50 paise half of one rupee?

How many 25 will make one rupee?

25 paise is _____ part of one rupee

20 paise is _____ part of one rupee

How many 10 paise will make one rupee?

So 10 paise is _____ part of one rupee.

An Old Woman's Will

Once there lived an old woman. She lived with her three daughters. She was quite rich and had 19 camels. One day she fell ill. The daughters called the doctor. The doctor tried his best but could not save the woman. After her death, the daughters read what she had written in her will.

> My eldest daughter will get $\frac{1}{2}$ of my camels
> My second daughter will get $\frac{1}{4}$ of my camels
> My third daughter will get $\frac{1}{5}$ of my camels

The daughters were really puzzled. "How can I get $\frac{1}{2}$ of the 19 camels?" asked the eldest daughter.

"Half of 19 is nine and a half. But we can't cut the camel!" The second daughter said.

"That is right. But what will we do now?" asked the third daughter".

Just then they saw their aunt coming. The daughters told her their problem.

"Show me the will. I have an idea. You take my camel. So you have 20 camels. Now can you divide them as your mother wanted?" the aunt said.

"You want half of the camels, don't you? Take 10 camels" she said to the eldest daughter.

"Take your share", the aunt told the second daughter. She took one-fourth of the camels and got _____ camels.

"You can take one-fifth of the camels", the aunt told the third daughter. She got _____ camels. The daughters were very happy and counted their camels 10+ _____ + _____ =19.

"The one remaining is mine", said the aunt and took her camel away!

✳ How did this happen? Discuss.

Arun's Time Table

Sleeping: One third of a day

Use different colours to show

Playing: One eighth of a day

Studying: $\frac{1}{4}$ of a day

How many hours does Arun take for

Sleeping? ☐ hours

Studying? ☐ hours

Playing? ☐ hours

What part of the day does he use for other activities?

Arun sleeps at 10 pm and wakes up at 6 am. He plays from 7 to 8 am and again from 4 to 6 pm.

One day is 24 hours. Then how will I find out one third of a day?

School Magazine

A school has decided to bring out a magazine every quarter of the year. How many magazines will they have in a year? If they want to print it at the end of each quarter of a year, which are the months for printing? Mark the number for those months.

1	2	3	4	5	6	7	8	9	10	11	12

Sleeping Beauty!

Have you heard of Kumbhakarna, the brother of Ravana? He is famous for sleeping for half a year.

Most people sleep about 8 hours a day. Then what part of a day is it? _____

So what part of a year do they sleep? A person 60 years old must have slept _____ years!!!

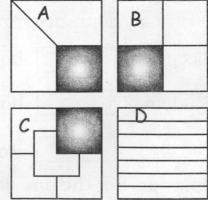

Answer: Card Puzzle (page 61)

Did you get stuck on square D? Actually that was the easiest!!

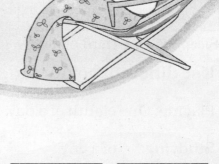

Children should be encouraged to think of what part of a day they spend in different activities. They should be sensitive about those children who have to spend a large part of the day working or helping at home. They should also be encouraged to think about parts of a year.

Price in RS (Per KG)

Item	Price in RS (Per KG)
Tomato	12
Potato	10
Onion	16
Carrot	18
Gourd	8

Keerti's Shopping List

Look at the yellow price list.

a) How much does 2 kg of tomato cost?

b) How much does $\frac{1}{2}$ kg of tomato cost?

c) Kiran wants $2\frac{1}{2}$ kg of tomato. How much will it cost?

d) How much does $3\frac{1}{2}$ kg potato cost?

e) What is the price of $1\frac{1}{4}$ kg of carrot?

f) He bought a gourd of weight $4\frac{3}{4}$ kg and it costs _____

g) Look at the shopping list in Keerti's hand. How much will she have to pay to buy all of these?

h) Make a bill of your own for vegetables you want to buy. Find the total money you will have to pay.

Potato 2 1/4 kg
Carrot 3 3/4 kg
Gourd 1 ½ kg

Item	Price in Rs (per kg)	Amount
	Total	

Children should be encouraged to bring samples of real price lists and bills to discuss in the classroom.

Practice time

1) Raheem's journey

Raheem has to travel $1\frac{1}{4}$ km to reach school. What distance does he travel to go to school and come back home?

2) What coins?

Latha bought a pencil and a pen for seven and a half rupees. She gave Rs 10/–. The shopkeeper gave back the money in half and quarter rupees. What are the coins she got?

3) At the railway station

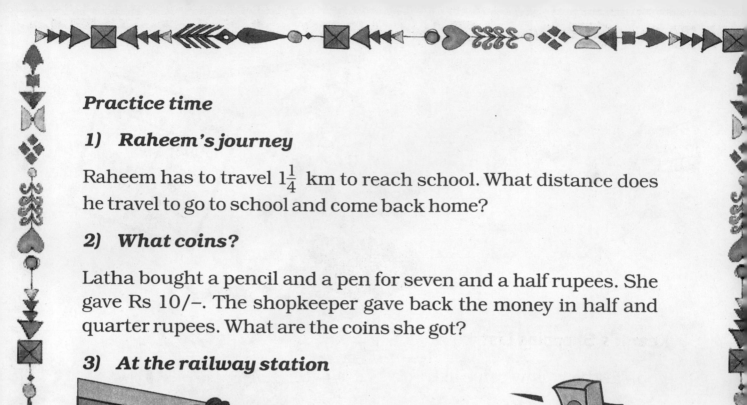

Your attention please. Mangalore Express coming from Mangalore and going to Thiruvananthapuram is now running late by half an hour.

Oh the train is late today. The right time is a quarter to 7.

a) What time is the train expected to come today?

b) Nazia gets off at a station after $2\frac{1}{2}$ hours from this station. What time will she get off?

c) Shaji will take 5 hours to reach Ernakulam by this train. At what time will he reach there?

⑤ Does it Look the Same?

Let's Make Patterns From a Drop of Colour

Pattern A

Pattern B

I have made these patterns from a drop of colour! You can make them too.

Make your pattern

Take a sheet of paper

Fold it into half

Open the fold and put a drop of colour on the middle line

Fold it twice and press it to spread the colour

Open it and see a beautiful pattern

Can you cut this pattern in such a way that you get two similar mirror halves? In how many ways can you do it?

Look at this pattern.

The dotted line divides the shape into two halves. But if you fold it along the dotted line, the left half does not cover the right half completely. So the two halves are not mirror halves.

Now look at another shape.

If you fold it along the dotted line, one half will cover the other similar half completely. So the two here are mirror halves.

Now imagine the same for these pictures.

On the next page, children need to understand that even though the shape is symmetric, the colour scheme of the figure can make it asymmetric (e.g. in shapes 10 and 12). Encourage children to look for asymmetry based on the shape as well as the colour scheme.

Which shapes are divided into two mirror halves by the dotted line?

Mirror Games

1. Here is a picture of a dog. You can place a mirror on the dotted line. Then the part of the dog to the right of the line will be hidden behind the mirror. What you will see is like (a).

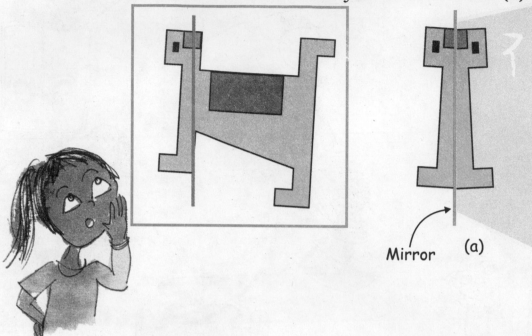

Mirror   (a)

Look at the figure in the white box. On which of the dotted lines will you keep the mirror so that you get shape (b)? Also tell which part of the picture will be hidden when we keep the mirror on the dotted line.

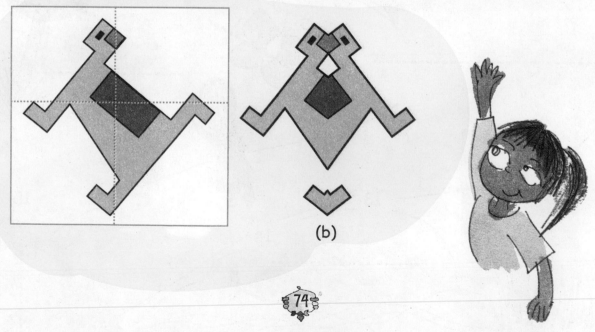

(b)

Now make a line on the white box to show where you will keep the mirror to get the picture next to it.

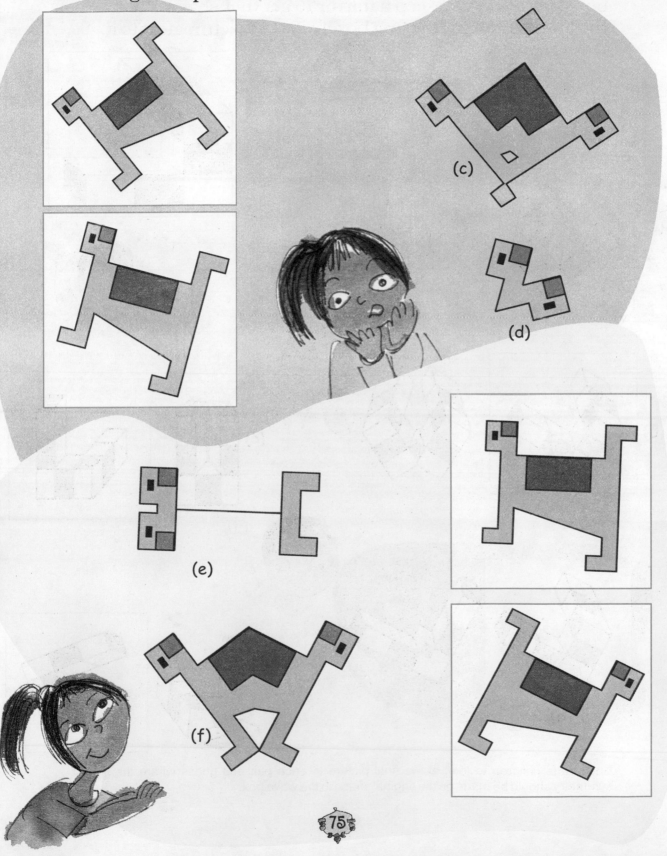

(c)

(d)

(e)

(f)

2. Venky has made a red and white shape. Make a line on the white box where you will keep a mirror to get that shape. Look at how the line is drawn in the first box to get the picture next to it.

(a)

(b)

(c)

(d)

(e)

Encourage children to look at the final picture in each pair and guess where the line of symmetry should be made on the original shape in the white box.

Half a Turn

Once there was a king. He was upset because thieves kept stealing costly jewels from his locker. Here is what the locker looked like:

The locker could be opened by giving its handle half a turn. Another half turn and the locker would be locked again.

The king would often leave the locker open thinking it was locked. Can you guess the reason?

Open

Locked

One day his clever daughter gave him an idea which he liked very much. Now he never got confused.

Can you guess what the idea was?

The king's daughter asked the king to put a dot on one of the yellow blades.

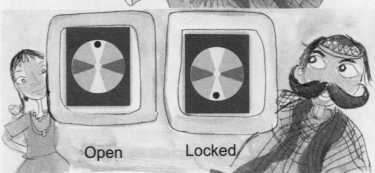

Open   Locked

The king had many such lockers with different handles. Check if, on giving them half a turn, he can get confused with these too.

What will you do to solve the problem for each of these?

Same after ½ turn?

Guess which of the shapes below would look the same after half a turn.

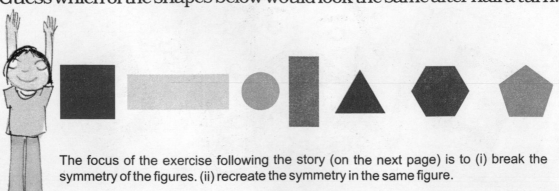

The focus of the exercise following the story (on the next page) is to (i) break the symmetry of the figures. (ii) recreate the symmetry in the same figure.

Do you find it difficult to tell? If yes, then there is a way to check your guess. Here's how you can do it.

Take any of the shapes. Trace its outline on a sheet of paper. Now keep the shape on its outline and give it a half turn. See if the shape fits its outline.

Practice time

1) Find out which letters in the English alphabet look the same after half a turn.

2) Which of these English words reads the same on half a turn?

   ZOOM, MOW, SWIMS, SIS, NOON

3) Give half a turn to the numbers from 0 to 9. Find which of them still looks the same.

4) Think of all 2, 3 and 4 digit numbers which look the same on half a turn.

Example

2 digit numbers   11, _____, _____

3 digit numbers   101, 111, _____, _____, _____,
                  _____, _____, _____

4 digit numbers   1001, 1111, _____, _____, _____,
                  _____, _____

5) Which among the following pictures will look the same on half a turn?

Activity Time

Have you ever seen a windmill? What is it used for?

Let us make a toy windmill.

1. Take a sheet of paper.

2. Fold it as shown in the picture.

3. Cut out the blue part of the paper. Your sheet of paper will now look like a square.

4. Fold it along the red lines and then open the fold. Draw a circle on the sheet as shown in the picture.

5. Cut along the red lines till you reach the circle. The paper will look like this.

6. Take a pin and make holes on the four corners as shown in the picture.

7. Now fold the corners such that all the holes lie one on top of the other.

8. Pass the pin through the holes and fix it in the stick.

Your windmill is ready. Run with it and see how fast it moves.

✳ Does your windmill look the same on $\frac{1}{4}$ of a turn?

✳ Does it look the same on half a turn? Discuss.

One-fourth Turn

Does the fan look the same on $\frac{1}{4}$ turn?

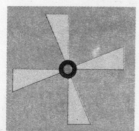

Before turning it

After $\frac{1}{4}$ turn

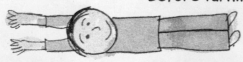

Will this fan also look the same after $\frac{1}{4}$ turn? Draw in the yellow box.

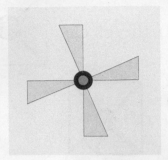

Before turning it   After $\frac{1}{4}$ turn

Practice time

A) ✳ Among the following shapes, find out which ones would look the same after $\frac{1}{4}$ turn. Put a (✓).

✳ Put a (✗) on the shapes that will not look the same after half a turn.

B) Try and change the shapes in such a way that the new shape remains the same on giving it half a turn.

C) Draw what the following shapes would look like on $\frac{1}{4}$ turn and half a turn.

On $\frac{1}{4}$ turn   *On half turn*

a)

b)

c)

d)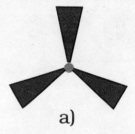

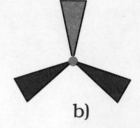

Which of the above shapes do not look the same on $\frac{1}{4}$ turn? Which shapes do not look the same on $\frac{1}{2}$ a turn?

✴ Which fan will look the same on a $\frac{1}{3}$ turn?

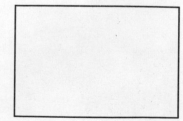

a)   b)

✴ Draw this shape after $\frac{1}{3}$ turn.

Shape after $\frac{1}{3}$ turn

One-sixth Turn

Can you see that this shape looks the same on $\frac{1}{6}$ turn?

Practice Time

1. Look at the following shapes. Draw how they will look on $\frac{1}{3}$ and $\frac{1}{6}$ turn.

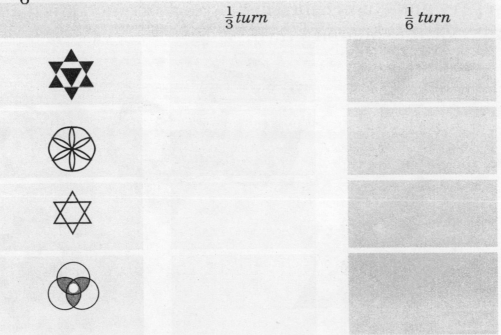

	$\frac{1}{3}$ turn	$\frac{1}{6}$ turn
(star of David, filled)		
(six-petal flower in circle)		
(star of David, outline)		
(three overlapping circles)		

Encourage children to look at the figure and see what kind of a symmetry there is. If they need they can draw six lines to see how to rotate a figure through $\frac{1}{6}$ turn. They should also be able to see that a figure which looks the same on $\frac{1}{6}$ turn will also look the same on $\frac{1}{3}$ turn (which is the same as two $\frac{1}{6}$ turns).

2. Look at the following shapes —

a) Find out which of these figures look the same on $\frac{1}{3}$ turn. Mark them with (✓).

b) Which are the ones that will not look the same after $\frac{1}{3}$ turn? Mark them with (✗).

c) Try and change the shapes below in such a way that they look the same on $\frac{1}{3}$ turn.

3. Draw some shapes which will look the same after $\frac{1}{3}$ turn.

4. Draw some shapes which will look the same after $\frac{1}{6}$ turn.

6 Be My Multiple, I'll be Your Factor

The Mouse and the Cat

The hungry cat is trying to catch Kunjan the mouse. Kunjan is now on the 14th step and it can jump 2 steps at a time. The cat is on the third step. She can jump 3 steps at a time. If the mouse reaches 28 it can hide in the hole. Find out whether the mouse can get away safely!

a) The steps on which the mouse jumps —

   _____

b) The steps on which the cat jumps —

   _____

c) The steps on which both the cat and the mouse jump —

d) Can the mouse get away?

Find out

If the cat starts from the 5th step and jumps five steps at a time and the mouse starts from the 8th step and jumps four steps at a time, can the mouse get away?

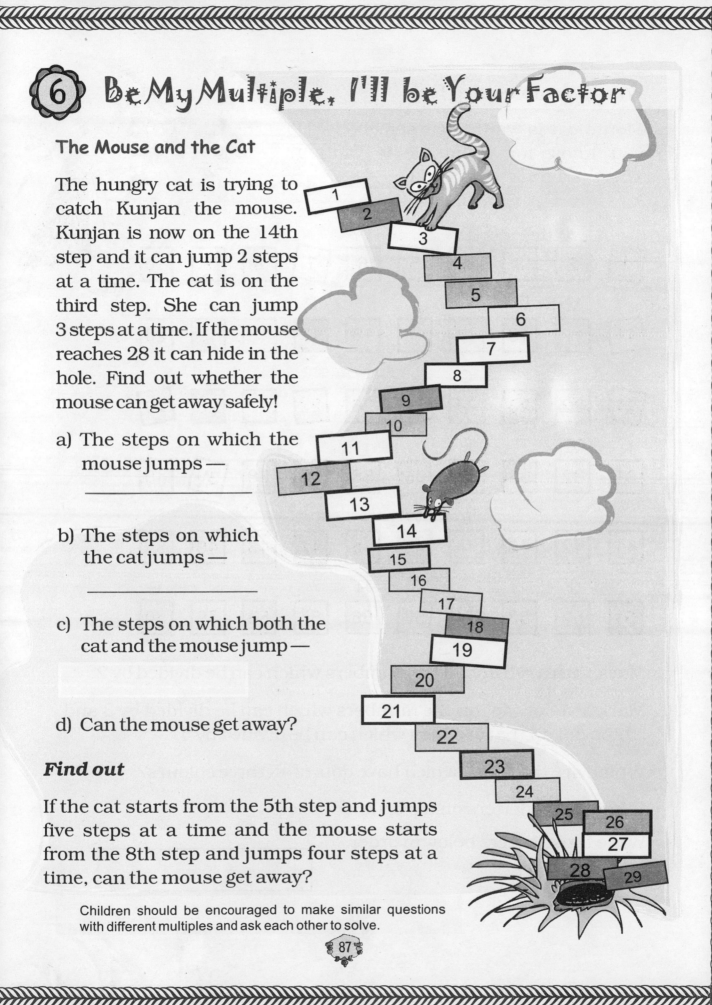

Children should be encouraged to make similar questions with different multiples and ask each other to solve.

87

Who is Monto waiting for?

Monto cat is waiting for somebody. Do you know for whom he is waiting? There is a trick to find out.

Mark with a red dot all the numbers which can be divided by 2.

Mark a yellow dot on the numbers which can be divided by 3 and a blue dot on the numbers which can be divided by 4.

Which are the boxes which have dots of all three colours?

What are the letters on top of those boxes?

Write those letters below in order.

Meow Game

To play this game, everyone stands in a circle. One player calls out 'one'. The next player says 'two' and so on. A player who has to call out 3 or a number which can be divided by 3 has to say 'Meow' instead of the number. One who forgets to say 'Meow' is out of the game. The last player left is the winner.

Which numbers did you replace with 'Meow'?

3, 6, 9..............................

We say these numbers are the **multiples** of 3.

Play the game by changing the number to 4.

Now, which numbers did you replace with 'Meow'?

These numbers are the multiples of 4.

✳ Write any ten multiples of 5.

Make children play this game several times with multiples of different numbers.

Dice Game

Throw two dice together. What are the numbers that turn up on the faces of the dice? Make a two-digit number using them. If it is a multiple of any of the numbers written next to the circles, you can write it in that circle. Then it is your friend's turn. The one who can write more numbers in 10 rounds is the winner.

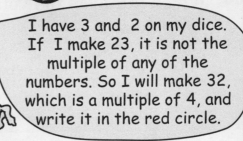

I have 3 and 2 on my dice. If I make 23, it is not the multiple of any of the numbers. So I will make 32, which is a multiple of 4, and write it in the red circle.

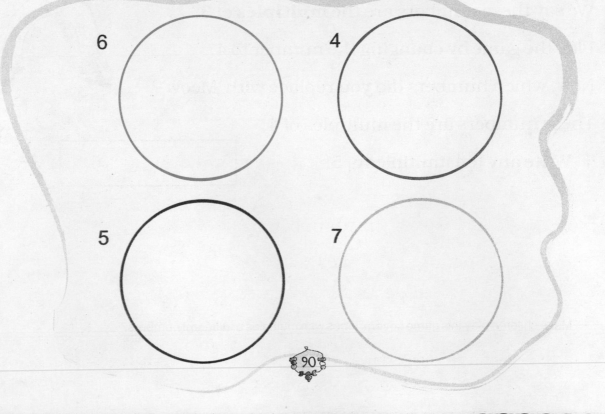

6

4

5

7

Common Multiples

Think of a number. If it is a multiple of 3 write it in the red circle. If it is a multiple of 5 write it in the blue circle.

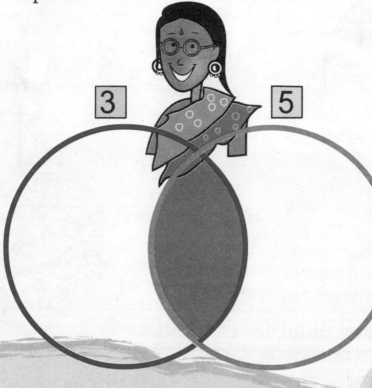

Where do I write 15? It is a multiple of both 3 and 5.

Some numbers are multiples of both 3 and 5.

So we can say that they are **common** to both 3 and 5.

Think! If you write the multiples common to 3 and 5 in the purple part, then will they still be in both the red and the blue circles?

✳ Which is the smallest among these **common multiples**? _____

Repeat the game using the numbers 2 and 7.

✳ Write the common multiples of 2 and 7.

Repeat the game by putting the multiples of 4, 6 and 5 in the circles.

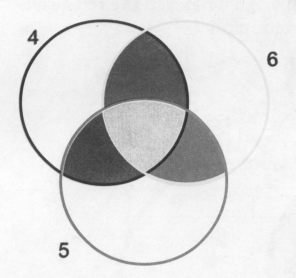

✳ What common multiples of 5 and 6 did you write in the green part?

✳ What common multiples of 4 and 6 are written in the orange part?

✳ In which coloured part did you write the common multiples of 4, 6 and 5?

✳ What is the smallest common multiple of 4, 6 and 5? _____

Puzzle

Tamarind seeds

Sunita took some tamarind (*imli*) seeds. She made groups of five with them, and found that one seed was left over. She tried making groups of six and groups of four. Each time one seed was left over. What is the smallest number of seeds that Sunita had?

Encourage children to try out themselves such activities using seeds, pebbles etc.

More tamarind seeds

Ammini is arranging 12 tamarind seeds in the form of different rectangles. Try to make more rectangles like this using 12 tamarind seeds. How many different rectangles can you make?

If there are 15 tamarind seeds how many rectangles can you make?

Colouring the Grid

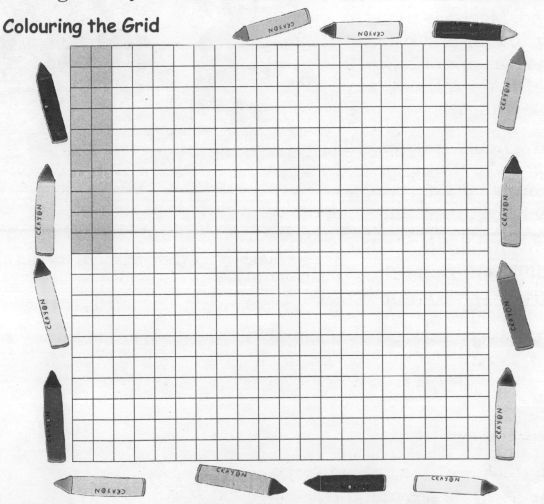

In the grid here, a rectangle made of 20 boxes is drawn.

The width of this rectangle is 2 boxes.

✳ What is its length?

✳ Colour a rectangle made of 20 boxes in some other way.

93

✳ What is the length and width of the rectangle you coloured?

✳ In how many ways can you colour a rectangle of 20 boxes? Colour them all in the grid, and write the length and width of each rectangle you have coloured.

Bangles

There are 18 bangles on the rod. Meena is trying to group them. She can put them in groups of 2, 3, 6, 9 and 18 — without any bangle being left.

✳ How many groups will she have if she makes groups of 1 bangle each? ____

Now complete the table, for different numbers of bangles. For each number see what different groups can be made.

Number of bangles	Different groups we can make
18	1, 2, 3, 6, 9, 18
24	1, 2, ...
5	
9	
7	
2	
10	
1	
20	
13	
21	

Fill the Chart

Complete the multiplication chart given here.

X	1	2	3	4	5	6	7	8	9	10	11	12
1												**12**
2						**12**						
3				**12**			21					
4			**12**							40		
5				20								
6		**12**										
7												
8									72			
9												
10												
11						66						
12	**12**											

Look at the green boxes in the chart. These show how we can get 12 by multiplying different numbers.

12 = 4 × 3, so 12 is a multiple of both 4 and 3. 12 is also a multiple of 6 and 2, as well as 12 and 1. We say 1, 2, 3, 4, 6, 12 are **factors** of 12.

12
4 × 3
6 × 2
1 × 12

✳ What are the factors of 10? _____

   Can you do this from the chart?

10
5 × 2
— — —

✳ What are the factors of 36 ? _____

✳ Find out all the factors of 36 from the multiplication chart.

✳ What is the biggest number for which you can find the factors from this chart?

✳ What can you do for numbers bigger than that?

Common factors

Write the factors of 25 in the red circle and the factors of 35 in the blue circle.

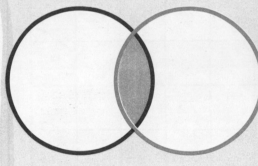

Which are the factors you have written in the common part (purple) of both circles? These are **common factors** of 25 and 35.

Now write the factors of 40 in the red circle and 60 in the blue circle.

What are the factors written in the common (purple) part of the circle? Which is the biggest common factor of 40 and 60?

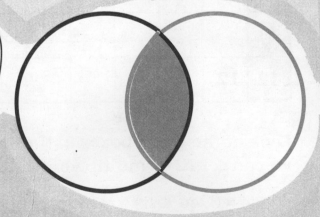

Factor Tree

Look at the factor tree. Now can you make another tree like this?

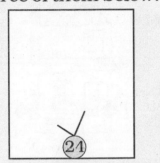

❋ In how many ways can you draw a factor tree for 24? Draw three of them below.

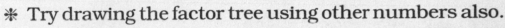

❋ Try drawing the factor tree using other numbers also.

Tiling Problems

1) There is a garden in Anu's house. In the middle of the garden there is a path. They decided to tile the path using tiles of length 2 feet, 3 feet and 5 feet.

The mason tiled the first row with 2 feet tiles, the second row with 3 feet tiles and the third row with 5 feet tiles. The mason has not cut any of the tiles. Then what is the shortest length of the path?

2) Manoj has made a new house. He wants to lay tiles on the floor. The size of the room is 9 feet × 12 feet. In the market, there are three kinds of square tiles: 1 foot × 1 foot, 2 feet × 2 feet and 3 feet × 3 feet. Which size of tile should he buy for his room, so that he can lay it without cutting?

3)

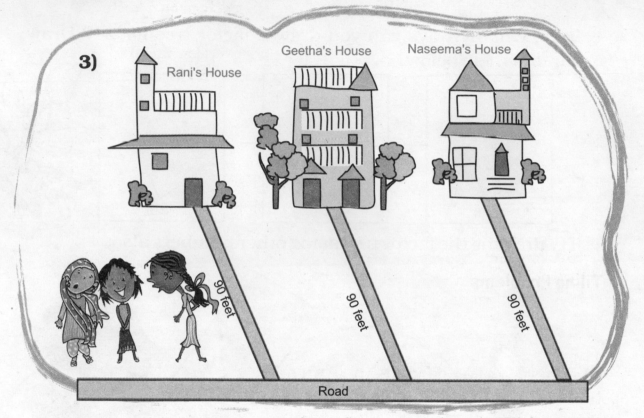

Rani, Geetha and Naseema live near each other. The distance from their houses to the road is 90 feet. They decided to tile the path to the road. They all bought tiles of different designs and length. Rani bought the shortest tile, Geetha bought the middle sized one and Naseema bought the longest one. If they could tile the path without cutting any of the tiles, what is the size of the tiles each has bought? Suggest 3 different solutions. Explain how you get this answer.

It will be useful to have a discussion about a 'foot' and how we use it often to talk about our own heights. Children can use their cm scale to get idea about how long a foot is.

Isha, your skirt is beautiful!

My mother made this pattern

I have seen the same block making a different pattern on a kurta.

How was it different?

In your skirt, the **rule** of the pattern is: one up, one down. Then this is repeated.

But in my brother's kurta, it is once up, then takes a $\frac{1}{4}$ turn every time. The **rule** is to repeat it with a $\frac{1}{4}$ clockwise turn.

Now you use these two rules to make patterns with this block.

Also make your own rule.

In Math-Magic Class IV (page 107- 108) , children have seen how one motif is used in 3 different ways and in Class III (page 145), the same sequence of motifs is repeated. Discuss how the motif here turns clockwise.

Turns and Patterns

Look at this block . We make three different rules to turn it clockwise and see the patterns.

Rule 1: Repeat it with a one-fourth turn.

Rule 2: Repeat it with a half turn.

Rule 3: Repeat it with a three-fourth turn.

Practice time

1) What should come next?

a)

b)

N Z N

Encourage children to think of other alternatives. Answers obtained by anticlockwise turns should also be accepted and discussed.

c)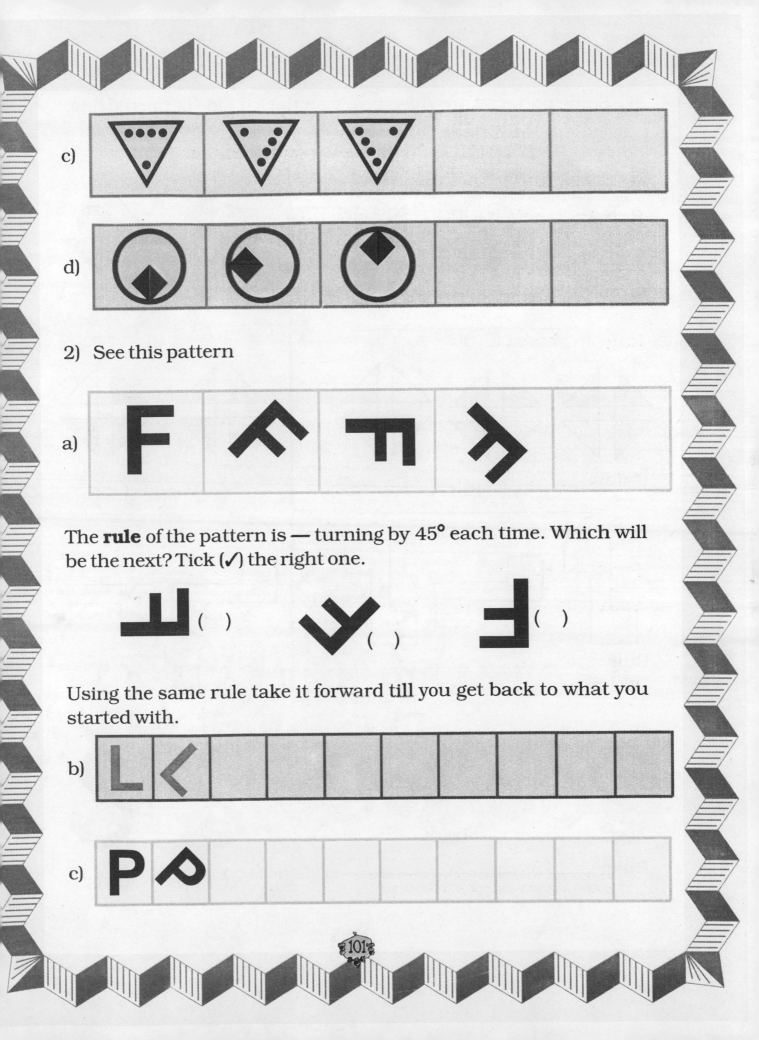

d)

2) See this pattern

a)

The **rule** of the pattern is — turning by 45° each time. Which will be the next? Tick (✓) the right one.

( )   ( )   ( )

Using the same rule take it forward till you get back to what you started with.

b)

c)

3) Some patterns are given below on the left side of the red line. For each pattern, write the rule. Then choose what comes next from the right side of the line and tick (✔) it.

a)

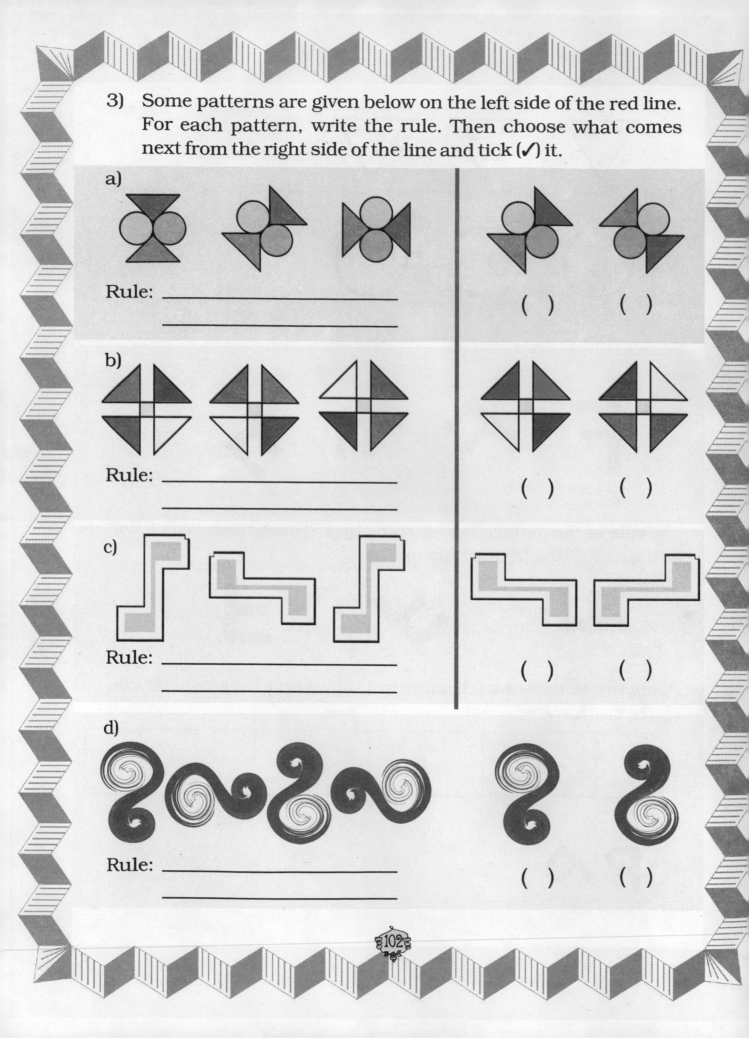

Rule: _____

_____

( )   ( )

b)

Rule: _____

_____

( )   ( )

c)

Rule: _____

_____

( )   ( )

d)

Rule: _____

_____

( )   ( )

Look for a Pattern

Mark that picture which is breaking the rule. Also correct it.

a)

b)

c)

d)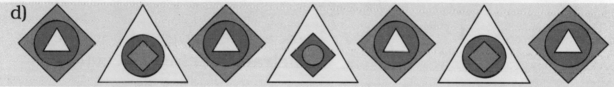

Magic Squares

Do you remember magic triangles? Come now, let's make some magic squares.

✳ Fill this square using all the numbers from 46 to 54.

Rule: The total of each line is 150.

		49
46		
	52	47

	25	

✳ Fill this square using all the numbers from 21 to 29.

Rule: The total of each side is 75.

You can see Math-Magic Class IV (page 11) for similar magic patterns.

Magic Hexagons

Look at the patterns of numbers in hexagons.

Each side has 2 circles and 1 box.

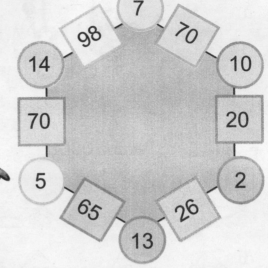

You get the number in each box by multiplying the numbers in the circles next to it.

$5 \times 13 = 65$

$\bigcirc \times \bigcirc = 70$

Look at the number 65 in the box. Which are the circles next to it?

Can you see how the rule works?

✳ Use the same rule to fill the hexagons below.

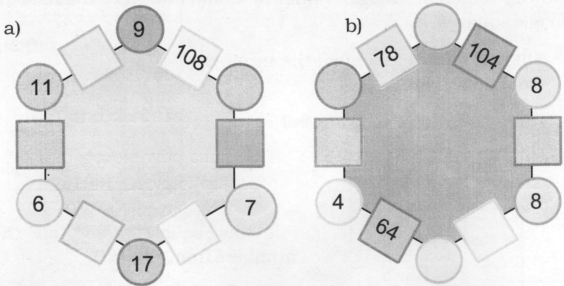

a)

b)

Now you also make your own magic hexagons.

You can discuss that a hexagon is a six-sided closed figure, but this is not to be evaluated.

Numbers and Numbers

$$24 + 19 + 37 = 37 + 24 + 19$$

$$215 + 120 + 600 = 600 + 215 + 120$$

✳ Are they equal?

✳ Fill in the blank spaces in the same way.

a) $14 + \underline{\quad} + \underline{\quad} = 34 + 14 + 20$

b) $\underline{\quad} + 42 + \underline{\quad} = 65 + \underline{\quad} + 80$

c) $200 + 300 + \underline{\quad} = \underline{\quad} + 400 + \underline{\quad}$

d) $\underline{\quad} + \underline{\quad} + \underline{\quad} = \underline{\quad} + \underline{\quad} + \underline{\quad}$

✳ Now, look at this — $48 \times 13 = 13 \times 48$

Check if it is true or not.

Left Right — Same to Same

121

Can you see something special about 121?

What, it's just a number!

See it is the same forward as well as backward.

Oh, yes! It is 1,2,1 from right to left also!

Discuss with students that changing the order of numbers does not make any difference to the sum.

105

Come, let's see how to get such numbers.

Take a number, say   43

Now turn it back to front   34

Then add them together   77

77 is one such special number. There are many such numbers.

You have **reversed** the number by writing it back to front.

Take another number   48

Now turn it back to front   84

Then add them together   132

Is this a special number?   No!   Why not?

OK, carry on with the number   132

Again turn it back to front   231

Then add the two together   363

Ah! 363 is a special number.

So we see that to get special numbers we sometimes need more steps.

✳ Now you try and change these numbers into special numbers —

     a)   28   b)   132   c)   273

Now let's use words in a special way.

N O   L E M O N S   N O   M E L O N

S T E P   N O T   O N   P E T S

Did you notice that it reads the same from both sides — right to left and left to right?

Now try and use words in a special way.

Special words/numbers which read the same both ways are called palindromes. Help children to read them from both the ends.

Calendar Magic

Look at the calendar below.

Let us mark a 3 × 3 box (9 dates) on the calendar and see some magic.

s	m	t	w	th	f	s
1	2	3	4	5	6	7
8	9	10	11	12	13	14
15	16	17	18	19	20	21
22	23	24	25	26	27	28
29	30	31				

I can quickly find the total of these numbers in the box.

Won't that take some time?

The total is 99.

Take the smallest number	3
Add 8 to it	+8
=	11
Multiply it by 9	×9
Total	99

Hey! Just take the middle number and multiply it by 9. See you can get the answer even faster.

Now you choose any 3 × 3 box from a calendar and find the total in the same way. Play this game with your family.

You can see Math-Magic Class III (page 105 -106) for other calendar tricks.

Some more Number Patterns

✳ Take any number. Now multiply it by 2, 3, 4 .... at every step. Also add 3 to it at each step. Look at the difference in the answer. Is it the same at every step?

12	×	2	+	3	=	27
12	×	3	+	3	=	39
12	×	4	+	3	=	51
12	×	5	+	3	=	63
12	×		+	3	=	
	×	7	+	3	=	
	×		+	3	=	
	×		+		=	

Now try doing it with some other number and also take a different number to add at each step .

✳ Look at the numbers below. Look for the pattern. Can you take it forward?

$$(9 - 1) \div 8 = 1$$

$$(98 - 2) \div 8 = 12$$

$$(987 - 3) \div 8 = 123$$

$$(9876 - 4) \div 8 = \underline{\quad}$$

$$(98765 - 5) \div 8 = \underline{\quad}$$

$$(\underline{\qquad} - \underline{\quad}) \div 8 = \underline{\quad}$$

$$(\underline{\qquad} - \underline{\quad}) \div 8 = \underline{\quad}$$

Encourage children to read aloud the numbers on the left hand side, even if they can not read them correctly. Some of the numbers are large. To help children read them, recall the concept of 1 lakh or 100 thousand.

Smart Adding

What if someone gives you to add ten numbers together?

Oh! I can find it quickly.

Smart! How can you do that?

I can get the sum without adding.

$$1 + 2 + 3 + 4 + 5 + 6 + 7 + 8 + 9 + 10 = 55$$

$$11 + 12 + \_ + \_ + \_ + \_ + \_ + \_ + \_ + 20 = 155$$

$$21 + \_ + \_ + \_ + \_ + \_ + \_ + \_ + 30 = \_$$

$$31 + \_ + \_ + \_ + \_ + \_ + \_ + \_ + 40 = \_$$

$$41 + \_ + \_ + \_ + \_ + \_ + \_ + \_ + 50 = \_$$

$$51 + \_ + \_ + \_ + \_ + \_ + \_ + \_ + 60 = 555$$

$$61 + \_ + \_ + \_ + \_ + \_ + \_ + \_ + 70 = \_$$

✳ Did you notice some pattern in the answers?

Fun with Odd Numbers

Take the first two odd numbers. Now add them, see what you get.

Now, at every step, add the next odd number.

$$1 + 3 = 4 = 2 \times 2$$

$$1 + 3 + 5 = 9 = 3 \times 3$$

$$1 + 3 + 5 + 7 = 16 = 4 \times 4$$

$$1 + 3 + 5 + 7 + 9 = \_ = \_ \times \_$$

$$1 + 3 + 5 + 7 + 9 + 11 = \_ = \_ \times \_$$

$$1 + 3 + 5 + 7 + 9 + 11 + 13 = \_ = \_ \times \_$$

How far can you go on?

When we add the first n odd numbers, we will get the sum as n × n . Children should be left free to add the numbers.

Secret Numbers

Banno and Binod were playing a guessing game by writing clues about a secret number. Each tried to guess the other's secret number from the clues.

Can you guess their secret numbers?

❋ It is larger than half of 100

❋ It is more than 6 tens and less than 7 tens

❋ The tens digit is one more than the ones digit

❋ Together the digits have a sum of 11

What is my secret number?
❋ _____

🧢 It is smaller than half of 100

🧢 It is more than 4 tens and less than 5 tens

🧢 The tens digit is two more than the ones digit

🧢 Together the digits have a sum of 6

What is my secret number?
🧢 _____

❋ Write a set of clues for a secret number of your own. Then give it to a friend to guess your secret number.

Number Surprises

a) Ask your friend — Write down your age. Add 5 to it. Multiply the sum by 2. Subtract 10 from it. Next divide it by 2. What do you get?

Is your friend surprised?

b)

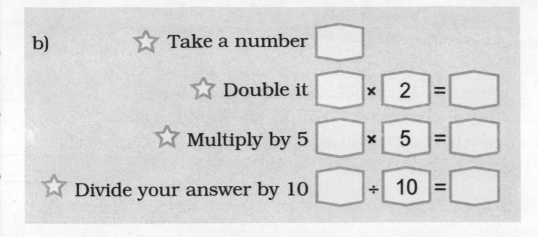

⭐ Take a number ⬡

⭐ Double it ⬡ × [2] = ⬡

⭐ Multiply by 5 ⬡ × [5] = ⬡

⭐ Divide your answer by 10 ⬡ ÷ [10] = ⬡

c)

⭐ Take a number ▭

⭐ Double it ▭ × [2] = ▭

⭐ Again double it ▭ × [2] = ▭

⭐ Add the number you took first to the answer ▭ + ▭ = ▭

⭐ Now again double it ▭ × [2] = ▭

⭐ Divide by 10 ▭ ÷ [10] = ▭

d) Look at this pattern of numbers and take it forward.

$$1 \quad = \quad 1 \times 1$$

$$121 \quad = \quad 11 \times 11$$

$$12321 \quad = \quad 111 \times 111$$

$$1234321 = \quad ?$$

✳ Now make your own number surprises.

Mapping Your Way

Ashi is going to India Gate to see the Republic Day Parade with the other children of her school. As the children settle down, they hear something about India Gate on the loudspeaker. "To the right of the President is the India Gate. This was built in memory of the Indian soldiers who died in the First World War."

There are lots of people sitting on both sides of Rajpath, the main road along which the parade passes. Children are talking about the buildings they can see around them.

Here is a photograph taken from a helicopter. You can see Rajpath — the road which joins India Gate to Rashtrapati Bhawan. Mark where on Rajpath will Aditi be.

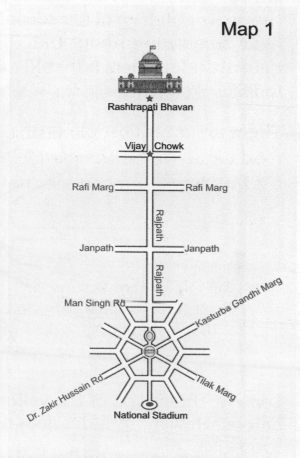

Map 1

Match the map and the photo

1) Have you seen a map of a city? Look at Map 1. Match it with the photo and find out where India Gate is. Draw it on the map.

2) Some roads are shown in this part of the map. Look for them in the photo.

3) Name roads that you will cross on your way from Rashtrapati Bhawan to India Gate.

4) Look for the National Stadium in Map 1. Can you see it in the photo?

The Central Hexagon

If we 'zoom in' to look more closely at one part of the map, it looks like this.

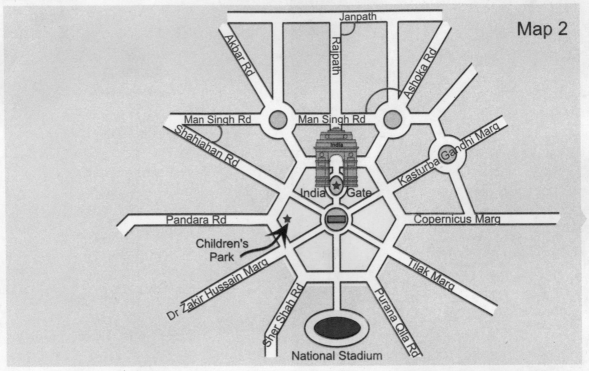

Map 2

Look at the shape of the yellow area. Have you seen this shape before? How many sides does it have?

This place is called the Central Hexagon.

Find out from the map

1) If you are walking on Rajpath then after India Gate on which side would Children's Park be?

2) Which of these roads make the biggest angle between them?

   a) Man Singh Road and Shahjahan Road

   b) Ashoka Road and Man Singh Road (the angle away from India Gate)

   c) Janpath and Rajpath

3) Which of the above pairs of roads cut at right angles?

Waiting for the Parade

While waiting for the parade, Kancha and some of his friends wonder where this parade ends. Kancha is carrying a newspaper in which the route of the parade is written —

Vijay Chowk — Rajpath — India Gate — Tilak Marg — B.S. Zafar Marg — Subhash Marg — Red Fort.

The children look at this map to see the parade route.

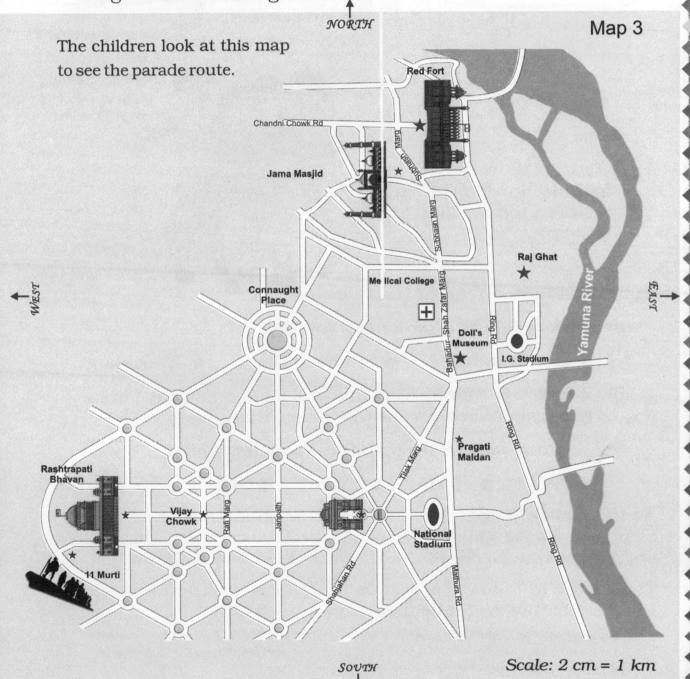

Map 3

Scale: 2 cm = 1 km

Hey! See, that is India Gate and this is Rashtrapati Bhawan.

And the long road between these is Rajpath.

Let's guess how many kilometres long Rajpath is.

My mother told me it is 2 km from Vijay Chowk to India Gate.

On this map, it is about 4 cm. So 4 cm on the map is the same as 2 km on the ground.

You are right! See, it is written at the bottom of this map. *Scale: 2 cm = 1 km*

Mark the route

1) Trace the route of the parade in Map 3 and mark India Gate and Rajpath.

2) Look at the map carefully and find out:

a) Which of these is the longest road?

● B.S. Zafar Marg   ● Subhash Marg   ● Tilak Marg

b) If Rubia is coming from Jama Masjid to join the parade, guess about how far she will have to walk.

c) The total route of the parade is about how long?

● 3 km   ● 16 km   ● 25 km   ● 8 km

As the parade passes by, they see some children coming on an elephant. These children have got bravery awards. They also enjoy the colourful dances and aerobics by school children.

They want to follow the parade to Red Fort. Gappu has seen Red Fort before and tells them about his trip.

Children should understand the need for a scale. We need to discuss that when we show a big area on paper, we have to reduce it by a fixed ratio everywhere, so that the relative distances and positions remain the same.

Trip to Red Fort

"When we reached Red Fort, there was a long queue for tickets. The main entrance is called **Lahori Gate**. After entering it, we turned left into a long corridor with little shops on both sides. This is called **Meena Bazar**. I bought some lovely bangles from there for my sister".

Meena Bazar

Lahori Gate

EAST

Map 4

Yamuna River

Ring Road

Moti Masjid
Hammam
Aram Gah
Rang Mahal
Moti Mahal

Diwan-e-Khaas

NORTH

Diwan-e-Aam

Red Fort

Naqqar Khana

SOUTH

Meena Bazar

Lahori Gate

Subhash Marg

WEST

Scale: 1 cm = 100 m

117

Naqqar Khana — where drums were beaten to shout out the king's messages

"You can go straight through **Naqqar Khana** and reach **Diwan-e-Aam**. This is where the king used to meet the common people.

Walking straight from **Diwan-e-Aam**, we saw **Rang Mahal**. It is a beautiful building! There were three more buildings on our left side. Look for these on the map.

We walked left from Rang Mahal. **Diwan-e-Khaas** was where the king used to meet his ministers and other important (khaas) people."

From the right – Rang Mahal, Aaram Gah and Diwan-e-Khas

Inside Rang Mahal

Inside Diwan-e-Khaas

Find out from Map 4

a) Which of these is nearer to river Yamuna? — the Diwan-e-Aam or the Diwan-e-Khaas?

b) Between which two buildings is Aaram Gah?

c) Which buildings do you pass while going from Rang Mahal to the Hammam?

d) Which building on this map is farthest from Meena Bazar?

e) About how far is Lahori Gate from Diwan-e-Khaas?

Make It Bigger, Make It Smaller.

Here are some pictures drawn on a 1 cm square grid. Try making the same pictures on a 2 cm grid and also on a $\frac{1}{2}$ cm grid. One picture is already done.

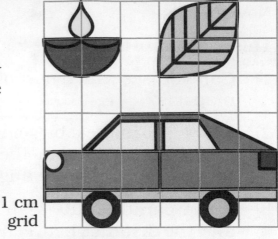

1 cm grid

$\frac{1}{2}$ cm grid

2 cm grid

The side of the square was made two times bigger. Does its area also become two times bigger?

Enlarging or reducing of pictures and maps can be done on the classroom floor, the mud ground etc. This should be related to the use of scale in maps, which keeps the shape the same.

Now try this —

This is a part of the parade-route Map 3.

1 cm grid

1) Can you see which part of the route-map it is?

2) Now try to make it bigger in this 2 cm grid. Remember that the 'shape' of the map should not change.

3) If the parade route map is smaller, and the distance between India Gate and Vijay Chowk becomes 2 cm, what would be its scale?

- 1 cm on map = 1 km on ground
- $\frac{1}{2}$ cm on map = 1 km on ground
- 2 cm on map = 1 km on ground

2 cm grid

Dancers from Different States

The children saw many floats (*jhankis*) and dancers in the parade.

Dancers from Karnataka were the best.

All these people have to travel so much to come to Delhi!

I liked the Tripura dance. From Tripura and Sikkim they have to travel far, but Haryana and Uttarakhand are closer to Delhi.

Look at the map of India below and find the states these children are talking about. Answer the questions:

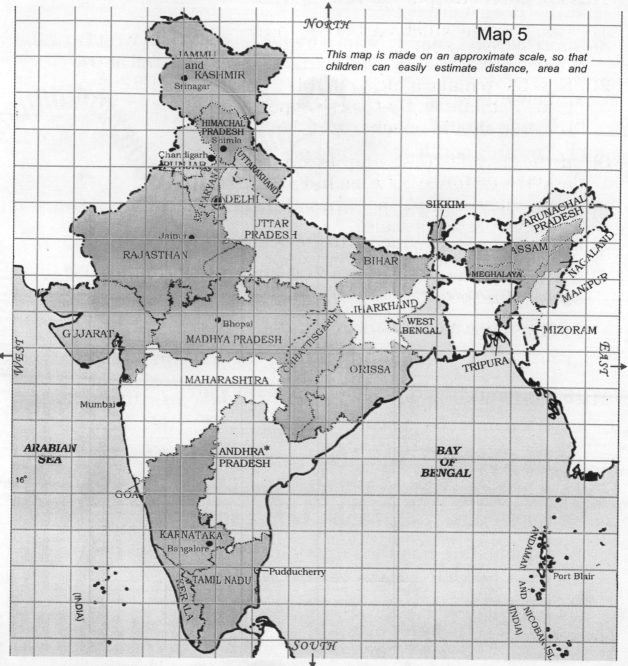

Map 5

This map is made on an approximate scale, so that children can easily estimate distance, area and

* A new (29th) state Telangana has been made in June 2014.

1) The Karnataka team starts from Bangalore and moves in the north direction. Which states does it cross to reach Delhi?

As the children are being introduced to directions for the first time, many activities need to be done to use terms like 'towards north', 'southwards', 'in the east direction', 'to the west of Madhya Pradesh' etc. One can draw maps on the floor and get children themselves to stand on the map and say things like 'Venkat is to the south of Shanti', 'Maharashtra is to the east of Gujarat' etc.

2) Jammu and Kashmir is to the **north** of Delhi so the team from there travels towards **south** to reach Delhi. Which states does it cross?

3) Nonu lives in Gujarat. Nonu's friend Javed lives in West Bengal. Nonu wants to visit his friend. In which direction will he travel?

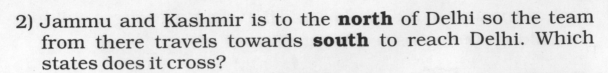

a) Towards west
b) Towards east
c) Towards south
d) Towards north

4) Is there any state which is to the north of Jammu and Kashmir?

5) Is there any state which is to the west of Gujarat?

6) If **1 cm on the map shows 200 km on the ground,** use this scale to find out:

A) About how far is Delhi from Jaipur?

a) 50 km   b) 500 km   c) 250 km

B) Estimate, how far is Jaipur from Bhopal?

On the map = _____ cm.

On the ground = _____ km.

7) Look at the map and tell:

a) Which state is surrounded by four other states?

b) Which state has the largest area? If its name is not in the map, find it from your teacher or parents.

Explain how you got your answer.

c) Which state is about 8 times bigger in area than Sikkim?

● Uttar Pradesh
● Tripura
● Maharashtra
● Himachal Pradesh

d) About how many times of Punjab is the area of Rajasthan?

122

The Sea

Bala is standing on the sea-coast and looking at the vast sea. The sea looks endless .

Have you seen the sea? In the picture where is the sea? Now look for the sea in the map of India. What colour is used to show the sea?

✳ Mark those states which have the sea on one side.

✳ Name one state which does not have the sea on any side.

Find out

Look for different maps. Compare the different scales used in a local area map, a map of India and a world map etc.

Lines between the States

Sabu is confused about the lines shown between the states.

I travelled from Delhi to Haryana, but I never saw any lines on the ground. How do we see them on the map?

No, there are no lines painted on the ground! The map shows us where one state ends and the next begins.

O yes! We paid the toll-tax at the border. I saw a big board saying — Welcome to Haryana.

Distances between Towns

These are five towns. Find out:

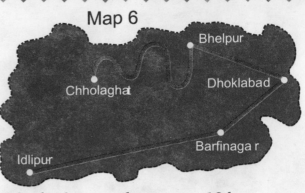

Map 6

Scale: 1 cm on the paper = 10 km

1) How many cm away is Idlipur from Barfinagar on the map?

2) How many kilometres will you have to travel if you go from Idlipur to Barfinagar?

3) There is a place called Thukpagram midway between Idlipur and Barfinagar. Mark it with a 'T'.

4) A town called Jalebipur is 35 kms away from both Chholaghat and Dhoklabad. Where do you think it can be? Mark 'J' for it.

5) Measure the length of the route between Bhelpur and Chholaghat. (You can use a thread)

Ashi's School

Ashi's school looks like this from the top.

Use the squares to find out:

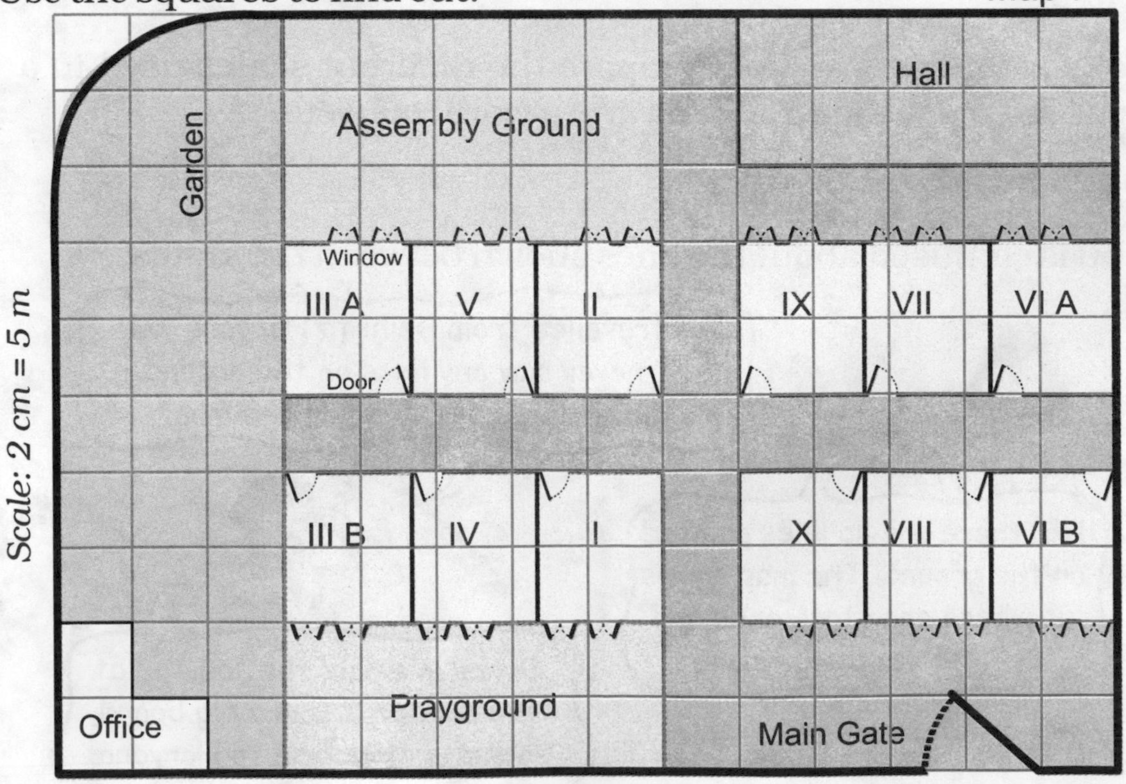

Map 7

Scale: 2 cm = 5 m

Garden

Assembly Ground

Hall

Window

III A   V   II   IX   VII   VI A

Door

III B   IV   I   X   VIII   VI B

Office

Playground

Main Gate

124

1) How many times bigger is the area of the Assembly ground than that of the office?

2) How much is the length and width of each classroom?

   a) length 5 m, width 4 m   b) length 2 m, width 1 m

   c) length 12 m, width 10 m   d) length 5 m, width 5 m

3) All the classrooms in Ashi's school look like this.

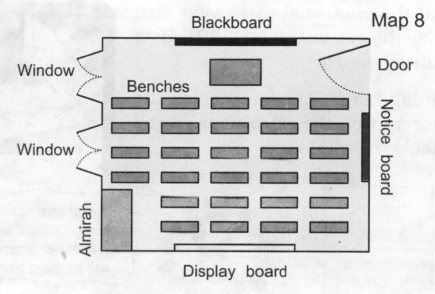

Map 8

Blackboard

Window

Door

Benches

Window

Notice board

Almirah

Display board

Look carefully and answer.

a) Which of these is exactly opposite to the blackboard?

   ✳ Almirah, windows, notice board, display board

b) Now look at the school-map again. Guess and mark where would these be:

   ✳ Blackboard in III A and VII

   ✳ Almirah in IV and X

   ✳ Notice board in V and VI B

   ✳ Last seat of middle-row in II

   ✳ Display board in I.

c) Can a child sitting in III A see the playground?

Boxes and Sketches

Sweet Box

Ramya went to buy sweets. The shopkeeper took a paper cut-out and quickly made a lovely pink box for the sweets!

✳ Look at the photo and make your own box. Use the cut-out on page 201. How fast can you fold it?

After coming home Ramya unfolded the box. She removed the extra flaps so the cut-out looked like this.

This shape makes a box. Let me see what other shapes will make a box.

✳ She made four more shapes. Each is to be folded along the dotted lines. You have to find out which of these can be made into a box.

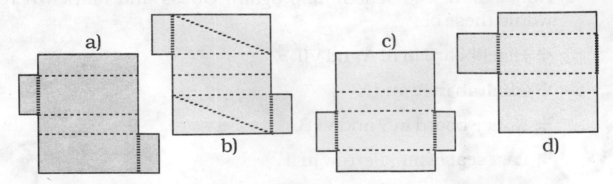

a)

b)

c)

d)

This chapter focuses on visualisation of 3-dimensional shapes and how they can be represented on paper (in 2 dimensions). The representation used here are nets (like the ones above), layout plans for a house, and perspective drawings.

Shapes that Fold into a Cube

A. Buddha wants to make a paper cube using a squared sheet. He knows that all the faces of a cube are squares.

How many faces does the cube have? _____

He draws two different shapes.

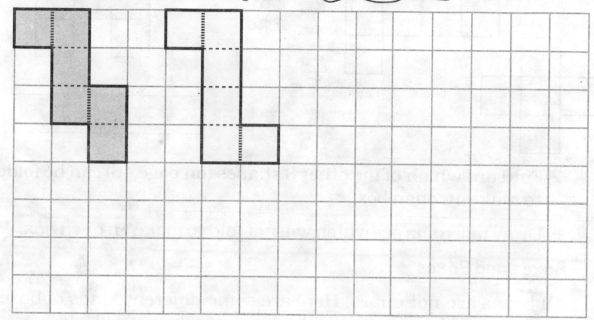

✱ Will both these shapes fold into a cube?

✱ Draw at least one more shape which can fold into a cube.

✱ What will be the area of each face of the cube?

✱ Draw one shape which will not fold into a cube.

✱ Look around and discuss which things around you look like a cube. List a few.

Shapes for an Open Box

Remember the puzzles with five squares in chapter 3? You saw 12 different shapes made with five squares (page 46).

If you cut those shapes and fold them, some of those will fold into an open box (box without a top).

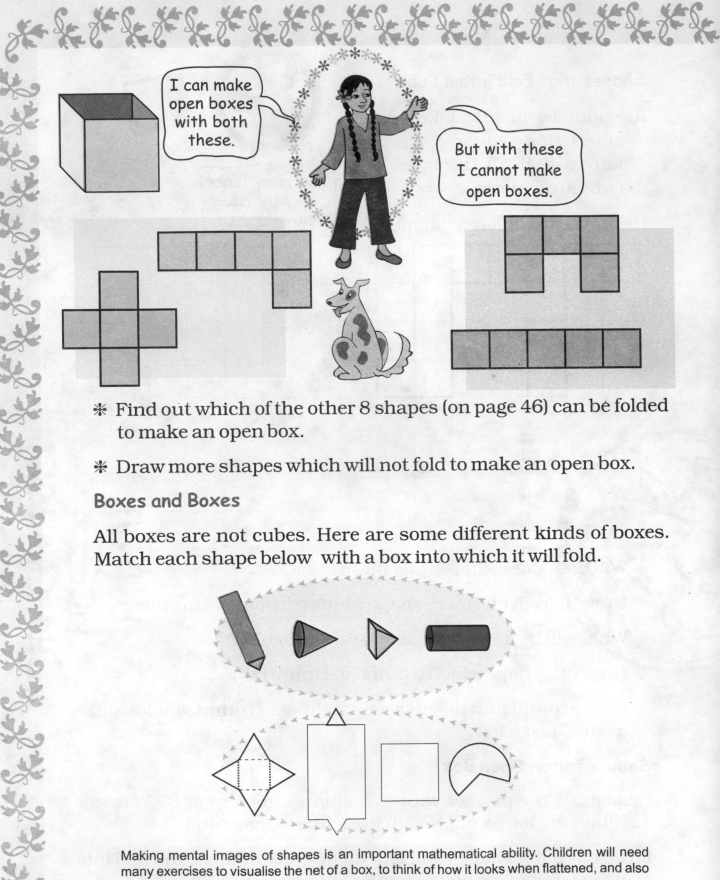

* Find out which of the other 8 shapes (on page 46) can be folded to make an open box.

* Draw more shapes which will not fold to make an open box.

Boxes and Boxes

All boxes are not cubes. Here are some different kinds of boxes. Match each shape below with a box into which it will fold.

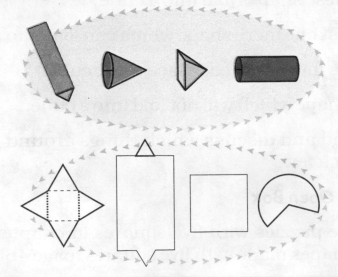

Making mental images of shapes is an important mathematical ability. Children will need many exercises to visualise the net of a box, to think of how it looks when flattened, and also to check which nets (like those on page 126) do not make a box.

Floor Maps

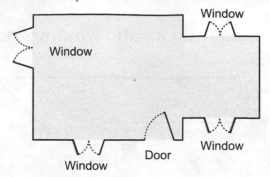

Window

Window

Window

Door

Window

For making a house a floor map is first made. Have you ever seen a floor map? Here is a floor map of Vibha's house. It shows where the windows and the doors are in the house.

✳ Which is the front side of her house? How many windows are there on the front side?

From the floor map we cannot make out what her house really looks like or how high the windows are. So we look for a special way of drawing the house which is deep — to show the length, width and height.

Here are four **deep drawings** of houses.

✳ Which one is Vibha's house?

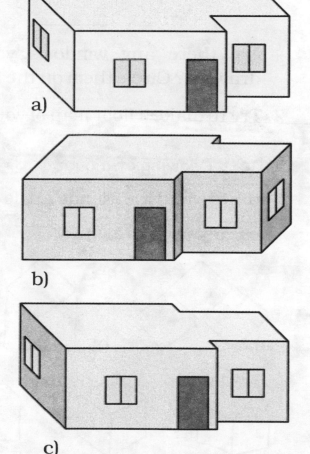

a)

b)

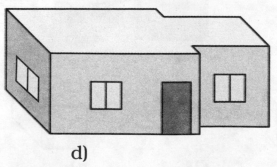

d)

c)

✳ Why do the other three deep drawings not match the floor map? Discuss.

A 3-dimensional perspective drawing has been called a 'deep drawing' so that children get a sense of the need to represent depth. They should be able to see the difference between deep drawings and layout plans.

Practice time

1. Look at this floor map of a house. Make doors and windows on the deep drawing of this house.

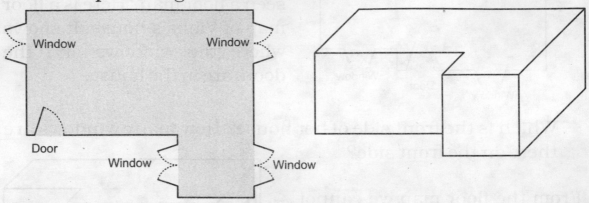

* Are there any windows you couldn't show on the deep drawing? Circle them on the floor map.

2. Try to make a floor map of your own house.

A Deep Drawing of a Cube

Soumitro and his friends made deep drawings of a cube.

These are their drawings.

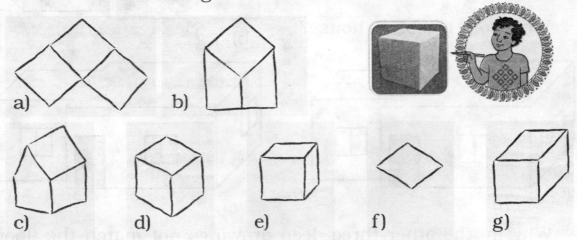

* Which of the drawings look correct to you? Discuss.

* Can you add some lines to make drawing f) into a deep drawing of the cube?

Puzzle

This cut-out is folded to make a cube.

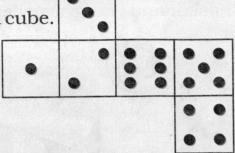

Which of these are the correct deep drawings of that cube?

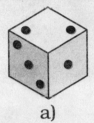 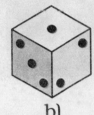  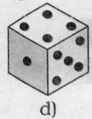 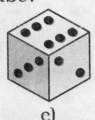

a)   b)   c)   d)   c)

A Simple Way to Draw a Cube

Chanda wants to make a deep drawing of this cube.

She draws the cube like this.

> I drew two squares like this to show the front face and the back face.

> I joined the corners of the squares like this to make the deep drawing of the box.

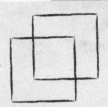  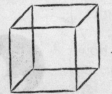

✳ In the same way make a deep drawing of a box which looks like this.

The 2D representation of 3D objects is a matter of convention and is learnt by children through experience. Here the conventional way of drawing the cube is given.

Matchbox Play

Navin, Bhaskar and Pratigya made this bridge using matchboxes.

Navin and Pratigya made drawings of the bridge.

The bridge looks like this to me from where I am standing.

The bridge looks like this to me. My drawing shows how high our bridge is and how wide it is.

From your drawing I can make out how long and how high the bridge is. But I cannot make out how wide it is.

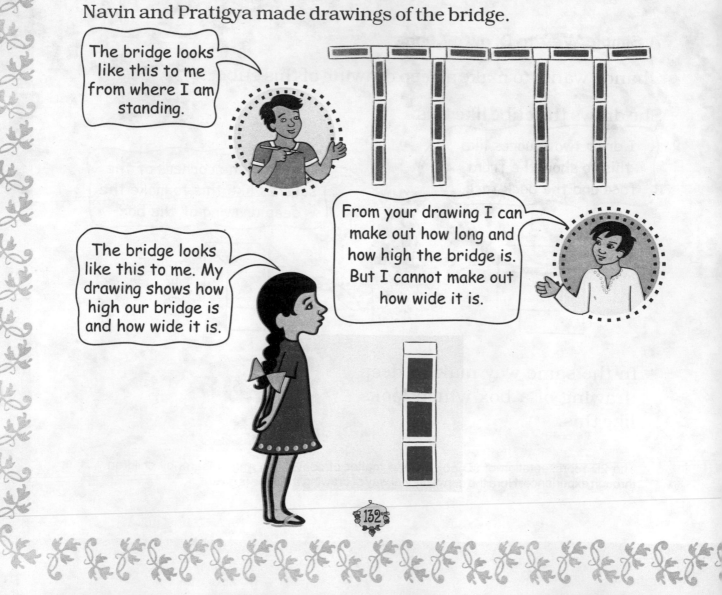

✳ If you look at the bridge from the top, how will it look? Choose the right drawing below:

a)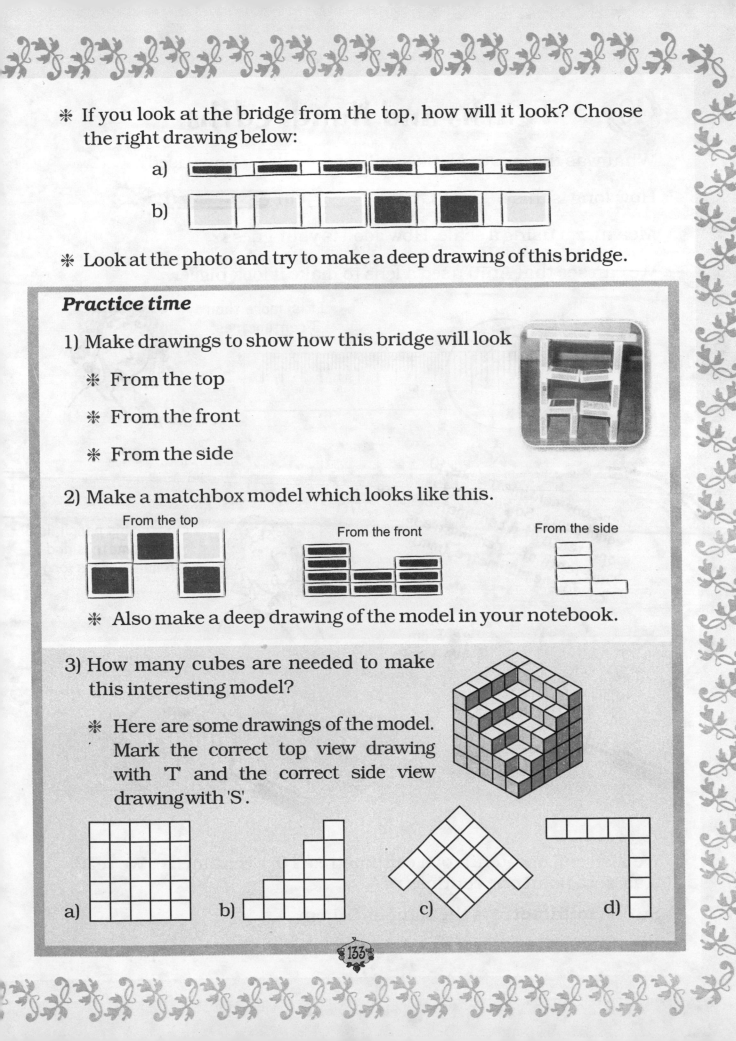

b)

✳ Look at the photo and try to make a deep drawing of this bridge.

Practice time

1) Make drawings to show how this bridge will look

   ✳ From the top

   ✳ From the front

   ✳ From the side

2) Make a matchbox model which looks like this.

   From the top   From the front   From the side

   ✳ Also make a deep drawing of the model in your notebook.

3) How many cubes are needed to make this interesting model?

   ✳ Here are some drawings of the model. Mark the correct top view drawing with 'T' and the correct side view drawing with 'S'.

   a)   b)   c)   d)

10 Tenths and Hundredths

What was the length of the smallest pencil you have used?

How long is this pencil ? Guess _____ cm

Measure it using a scale. How good is your guess?

We can see that Anju used a lens to make it look bigger.

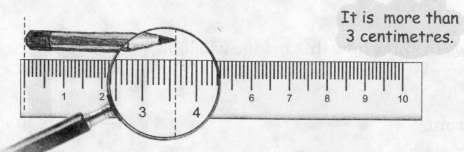

It is more than 3 centimetres.

Here one centimetre has 10 equal parts. So each part is one-tenth of a centimetre. One-tenth of a centimetre is called one **millimetre (mm)**.

Oh, so this pencil is 3 centimetres and 6 millimetres long.

See I am 3 mm long!

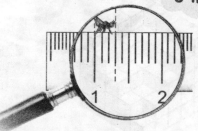

But I am longer! Seven-tenth of a centimetre or _____ millimetres

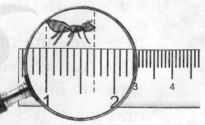

We also call one-tenth of a centimetre as 0.1 centimetre. We read it as 'zero point one centimetre'.

So one **millimetre** is the same as 0.1 cm.

✷ What is the length of this pencil? _____ mm.
What is its length in centimetres?

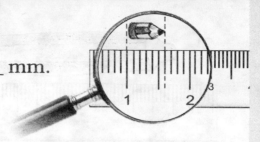

Frogs

Have you seen frogs? Where? How many different types of frogs have you seen? Are all the frogs of the same length? Here are two interesting examples.

Gold Frogs

This kind of frog is among the smallest in the world. Its length is only 0.9 cm!

Guess how many such frogs can sit on your little finger!

Bull Frog

But this is among the biggest frogs. It is as long as 30.5 cm!

What does 0.9 cm mean? It is the same as ____ millimetres. We can also say this is nine-tenths of a cm. Right?

So 30.5 cm is the same as ____ cm and ____ millimetre.

About how many of the big frogs will fit on the 1m scale? _____

If they sit in a straight line about how many of the small frogs will cover 1m? _____

Practice time

1) Length of the nail — 2 cm and ___ mm or 2. ___ cm.

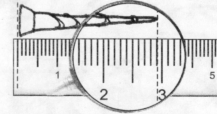

135

2)

The length of this lady's finger *(bhindi)* is _____ cm and _____ mm. We can also write it as _____ cm.

3) Using the scale on this page find the difference in length between candle 1 and candle 3.

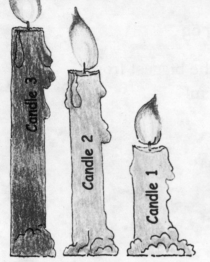

Length of	Length in cm and mm	Length in cm
Candle 1		
Flame 1		
Candle 2		
Flame 2		
Candle 3		
Flame 3		

Guess and Colour

First colour the rods as shown, without measuring! Then check.

Rods of length less than 1 cm   **Red**

Rods of length between 1 cm and 2 cm   **Blue**

Rods of length between 2 cm and 3 cm   **Green**

Rods of length between 3 cm and 4 cm   **Orange**

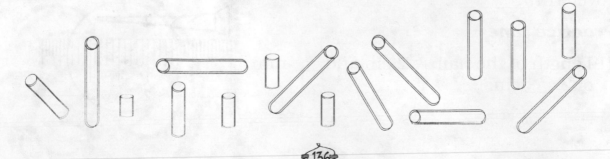

Guess, Draw and Measure

Guess the lengths to draw these things. Ask your friend to draw the same. After you make the drawing use a scale to measure the length. Whose drawing showed a better guess?

Guess its length and draw	Measure of your drawing	Measure of your friend's drawing
An ant of length less than 1 cm		
Pencil of length about 7 cm		
A glass 11 cm high with water up to 5 cm		
A bangle of perimeter 20 cm		
A curly hair of length 16 cm		

Our Eyes Get Confused?

Which line is longer? A or B ? Measure each line and write how long it is in centimetres. How good is your guess?

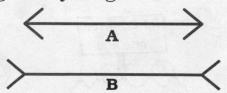

Which line is longer? C or D ? Measure each line.

How good is your guess?

137

Whose Tail is the Longest?

Guess whose tail is the longest. Now measure the tails. How good is your guess?

The Longest Rupee Notes?

What is the length of a 100 rupee note? Guess. Now measure it using a scale.

Now guess the length and width of many other things. Measure and find the difference between your measure and your guess.

Size of	Your guess in cm		Your measure in cm	
	length	width	length	width
100 Rupee note				
10 Rupee note				
20 Rupee note				
5 Rupee note				
Post card				
Math-Magic book				

At the market

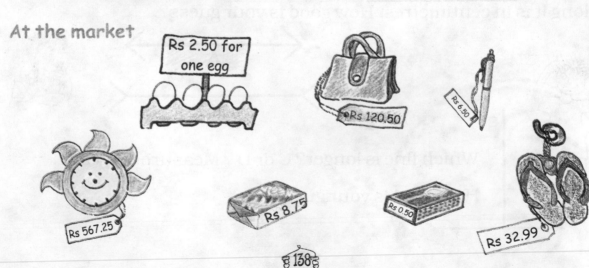

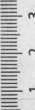

1) How many paise does a matchbox cost? _____

2) How many matchboxes can be got for Rs 2.50? _____

3) How many rupees does the soap cost? _____

4) Arun wanted to buy a soap. He has a five-rupee coin, 2 one-rupee coins and 4 half-rupee coins. Write in rupees what money he will get back.

5a) An egg costs two and a half rupees. How much will one and a half dozen cost?

  b) How many pens can Kannan buy? How much money is left?

6) The price of two pens is Rs _____. Can she buy two pens?

139

Practice time — Match these

Match each yellow box with one green and one pink box.

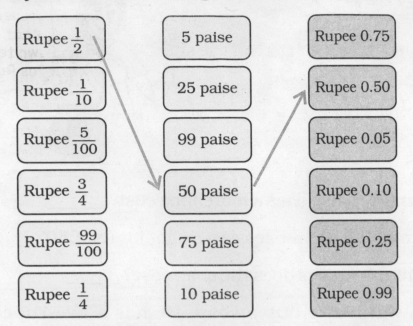

Rupee $\frac{1}{2}$	5 paise	Rupee 0.75
Rupee $\frac{1}{10}$	25 paise	Rupee 0.50
Rupee $\frac{5}{100}$	99 paise	Rupee 0.05
Rupee $\frac{3}{4}$	50 paise	Rupee 0.10
Rupee $\frac{99}{100}$	75 paise	Rupee 0.25
Rupee $\frac{1}{4}$	10 paise	Rupee 0.99

Colourful Design

What part of this sheet is coloured blue? ___/10

What part of the sheet is green? _____

Which colour covers 0.2 of the sheet?

Oh, the blue strip is 0.1 of the sheet.

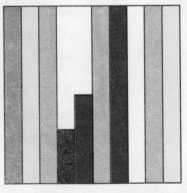

Now look at the second sheet. Each strip is divided into 10 equal boxes. How many boxes are there in all?

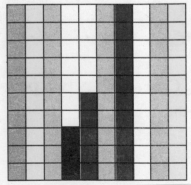

Is each box 1/100 part of the sheet?

How many blue boxes are there? _____

Is blue equal to 10/100 of the sheet? We saw that blue is also equal to 1/10 of the sheet. We wrote it as 0.1 of the sheet.

Can we say 10/100 = 1/10 = 0.10 = 0.1?

Think: Can we write ten paise as 0.1 of a rupee?

How many boxes are red? What part of the sheet is this? 15/____

Can we also write it as 0.15 of the sheet ?

(Hint: *remember we wrote 99 paise as 0.99 rupee!)*

Now 3/100 of the sheet is black. We can say 0.____ sheet is black.

How many white boxes are there in the sheet?

What part of the second sheet is white? ____

> Don't get confused!
> 0.10 is the same as 0.1
> Remember, this ⬤50 is
> Rupee 0.50 and also
> Rupee 0.5

✳ Make your designs.

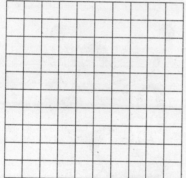

Make a nice design by colouring 0.45 part of this square red.

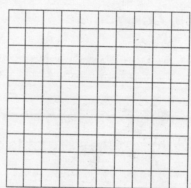

Use four colours. Each colour should cover 0.05 of this square.

Sports Day

The school at Malappuram has its sports day.

The first five children in the Long Jump are:

Teena	3.50 m
Meena	4.05 m
Rehana	4.50 m
Anu	3.05 m
Amina	3.35 m

> Teena jumped 3.50m which is 3 m and 50 cm.

> But how far did Anu jump? ____ m and ____ cm.

Who is the winner in the long jump? _____

141

Write the names of the I, II and III winners on this stand.

Do you remember that 1 metre = 100 centimetres?

So one centimetre is 1/100 of a metre.

We also write 1 cm as _____ m

Write in Metres

3 metre 45 centimetre   [   ]   metres

99 centimetre   [   ]   metres

1 metre and 5 centimetre   [   ]   metres

How Big Can You Get

A)

After breathing out 1.52 m

On taking a deep breath 1.82 m

Difference in size [   ]

Do this for yourself and find the difference.

B)

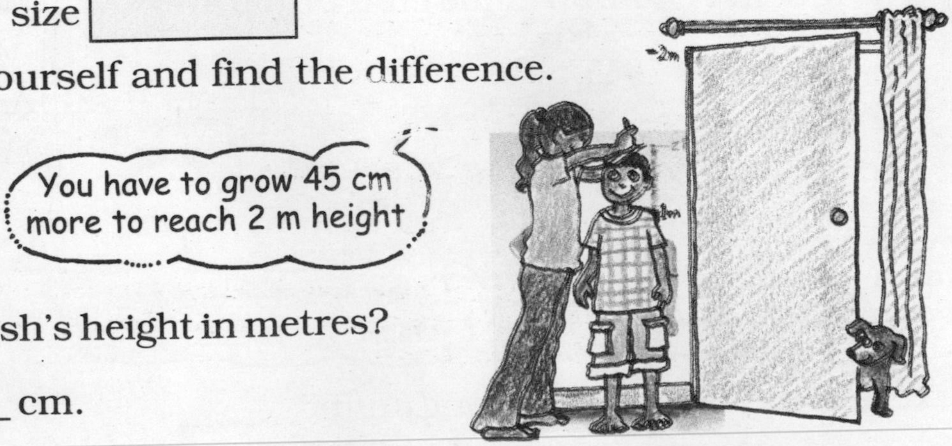

You have to grow 45 cm more to reach 2 m height

What is Dinesh's height in metres?

_____ m _____ cm.

142

Practice time

1) Money from different countries

Have you seen any notes or coins used in any other country?

Shivam Bank has a chart to show us how many Indian rupees we can get when we change the money of different countries.

Country	Money	Changed into Indian Rupees
Korea	Won	0.04
Sri Lanka	Rupee (SL)	0.37
Nepal	Rupee	0.63
Hong Kong	Dollar (HK)	5.10
South Africa	Rand	5.18
China	Yuan	5.50
U.A.E.	Dirham	10.80
U.S.A.	Dollar	39.70
Germany	Euro	58.30
England	Pound	77.76

(This is the rate on 15-2-2008)

A) The money of which country will cost the most in Indian Rupees?

B) Mithun's uncle in America had sent him 10 USA dollars as a gift. Mithun used 350 rupees for a school trip. How much money was left with him?

Children are not expected to carry out long multiplication involving decimals. Instead, encourage them to think in terms of currency. For example, 75 paise × 2 can be thought of as two 50 paisa coins and two 25 paisa coins.

143

C) Majeed's father is working in U.A.E. He gets 1000 Dirham as salary. Arun's father who is working in Sri Lanka gets 2000 Sri Lankan Rupees. Who gets more Indian rupees as salary?

D) Leena's aunty brought a present for her from China. It cost 30 Yuan. Find what it costs in Indian rupees.

E) Astha wants some Hong Kong Dollars and Won.

1) How many Won can she change for Rs 4? For Rs 400?

2) How many Hong Kong Dollars can she change for Rs 508?

2) Kiran went shopping with Rs 200. Look at the bill. The shopkeeper forgot to put the point correctly in the prices. Put the point in the correct place and find out the total amount of the bill.

Item	Quantity	Price (Rupees)
Soap	1	1250
Green gram	1 kg	5025
Tea	250 gm	2725
Coconut Oil	1 Litre	6000
Total		_____

3) **Which city is cool?**

I live in Himachal. There the temperature in winter is 2° Celsius. Sometimes water in pipes freezes into ice.

But in Rajasthan where I live the temperature reaches 48° Celsius. Here it is very hot. One has to walk kilometres to get water.

Children can be encouraged to look at temperatures (in degree Celsius or °C) of different cities in the newspaper and on TV. Without using the terms 'maximum' and 'minimum' this exercise will give them an idea that temperatures can be measured at two different times of the day. Only simple subtractions using decimals have been used here. They will also get familiar with the names of different capital cities and can do similar exercises for the capital cities of other countries.

The temperature in each city was noted at 3 pm on 16 January 2008.

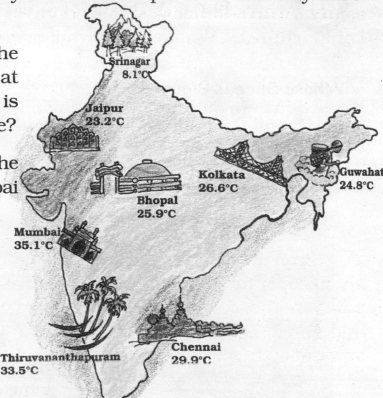

1) Which place had the highest temperature at 3 pm? Which place is the coolest at that time?

2) How much higher is the temperature in Mumbai from that in Srinagar?

Srinagar 8.1°C

Jaipur 23.2°C

Kolkata 26.6°C

Guwahati 24.8°C

Bhopal 25.9°C

Mumbai 35.1°C

Thiruvananthapuram 33.5°C

Chennai 29.9°C

3) How many degrees will the temperature need to rise for it to reach 40° C in Thiruvananthapuram?

4) How much lower is the temperature of Kolkata from that in Chennai?

5) The temperature in these cities was also noted at 3 am on the same day. Look at the table and answer the questions.

a) Which place had the lowest temperature at 3 am? Imagine yourself to be there and describe how it would feel.

City	Temperature at 3 am
Chennai	21.1
Mumbai	19.0
Th'puram	21.6
Kolkata	13.1
Bhopal	9.8
Srinagar	1.3
Guwahati	12.8
Jaipur	10.2

b) What is the difference between the temperatures at 3 pm and 3 am in Chennai? In Bhopal?

145

11

Whose Slice is Bigger?

Parth and Gini bought *aam paapad* (dried mango slice) from a shop.

Their pieces looked like these.

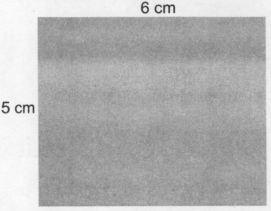

6 cm

5 cm

Piece A

Both could not make out whose piece was bigger.

✳ Suggest some ways to find out whose piece is bigger. Discuss.

A friend of Parth and Gini showed one way, using small squares.

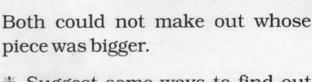

11 cm

3 cm

Piece B

The length of piece A is 6 cm.

So 6 squares of side 1 cm can be arranged along its length.

The width of piece A is 5 cm.

So 5 squares can be arranged along its width.

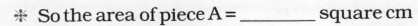

✳ Altogether how many squares can be arranged on it? _____

✳ So the area of piece A = _____ square cm

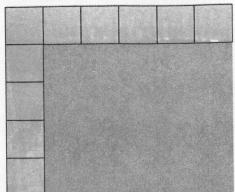

Piece A

It's silly to count them all! Just multiply!

✳ In the same way find the area of piece B.

✳ Who had the bigger piece? How much bigger?

Cover with Stamps

This stamp has an area of 4 square cm. Guess how many such stamps will cover this big rectangle.

Encourage children to first discuss different strategies for comparing the area of things by using different tokens, stamps, etc. In Class IV they have compared irregular shapes by counting squares. In the case of rectangles they can measure the sides to see how many squares of 1 cm side will fit in the whole shape.

Check your guess

a) Measure the yellow rectangle. It is _____ cm long.

b) How many stamps can be placed along its length? _____

c) How wide is the rectangle? _____ cm

d) How many stamps can be placed along its width? _____

e) How many stamps are needed to cover the rectangle? _____

f) How close was your earlier guess? Discuss.

g) What is the area of the rectangle? _____ square cm

h) What is the perimeter of the rectangle? _____ cm

Practice time

a) Arbaz plans to tile his kitchen floor with green square tiles. Each side of the tile is 10 cm. His kitchen is 220 cm in length and 180 cm wide. How many tiles will he need?

b) The fencing of a square garden is 20 m in length. How long is one side of the garden?

c) A thin wire 20 centimetres long is formed into a rectangle. If the width of this rectangle is 4 centimetres, what is its length?

This 'Guess and check' activity can be done in the class by making use of other things present. For example: how many postcards can be placed on the top of the mathematics book, how many charts will cover the classroom walls, etc? Children can be asked to check their guesses by tiling things wherever possible. Once they are able to make close guesses, this work can be further extended by asking them to guess the area in terms of square cm.

d) A square carrom board has a perimeter of 320 cm. How much is its area?

e) How many tiles like the triangle given here will fit in the white design?

This triangle is half of the cm square

Area of design = _____ square cm

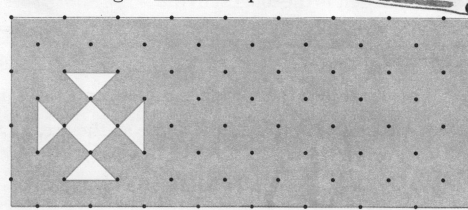

＊ Make your own designs of area 4 and 6 square cm.

f) Sanya, Aarushi, Manav and Kabir made greeting cards. Complete the table for their cards:

Whose card	Length	Width	Perimeter	Area
Sanya	10 cm	8 cm		
Manav	11 cm		44 cm	
Aarushi		8cm		80 square cm
Kabir			40 cm	100 square cm

My Belt is Longest!

Take a thick paper sheet of length 14 cm and width 9 cm. You can also use an old postcard.

＊ What is its area? What is its perimeter?

＊ Now cut strips of equal sizes out of it.

Using tape join the strips, end to end, to make a belt.

✳ How long is your belt?_____

✳ What is its perimeter _____

✳ Whose belt is the longest in the class?_____

Discuss

✳ Why did some of your friends get longer belts than others?

✳ Is the area of your belt the same as the area of the postcard? Why or why not?

✳ What will you do to get a longer belt next time?

This belt is for the elephant.

Look! I can pass through a postcard. I made a loop without cutting the strips.

Puzzle: Pass through a Postcard

Can you think of how to cut a postcard so that you can pass through it? (See photo.) If you have tried hard enough and still not got it... look for the answer somewhere ahead.

The aim of the belt activity is to understand that things with the same area can take different forms and also have very different perimeters. While measuring sides, lengths in mm can be rounded off for this activity.

People People Everywhere

A) You can play this game in a ground.

Make two squares of one square metre each.

Divide your class in two teams. Ready to play!

With four Math-Magic books in a line you can get the length of around one metre 9 cm.

Try these in your teams —

✳ How many of you can sit in one square metre? _____

✳ How many of you can stand in it? _____

✳ Which team could make more children stand in their square? How many? _____

✳ Which team could make more children sit in their square? How many?

B) Measure the length of the floor of your classroom in metres. Also measure the width.

✳ What is the area of the floor of your classroom in square metres? _____

✳ How many children are there in your class? _____

✳ So how many children can sit in one square metre? _____

✳ If you want to move around easily then how many children do you think should be there in one square metre? _____

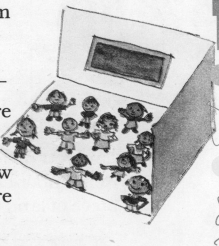

Can you imagine how big a square of side 1 km is! It has an area of _____ square km. Guess how many people can live on that.

In West Bengal there are about 900 people living in a square km.

But in Arunachal Pradesh it feels very lonely! There are less than 15 people living in a square km!

Share the Land

Nasreena is a farmer who wants to divide her land equally among her three children — Chumki, Jhumri and Imran. She wants to divide the land so that each piece of land has one tree. Her land looks like this.

✳ Can you divide the land equally? Show how you will divide it. Remember each person has to get a tree. Colour each person's piece of land differently.

Children are not expected to do conversion of sq m into sq km or vice-versa. The aim of exercise B is to develop a sense of how big or small the units of sq m and sq km are.

* If each square on this page is equal to 1 square metre of land, how much land will each of her children get? _____ square m

Chumki, Jhumri and Imran need wire to make a fence.

* Who will need the longest wire for fencing? _____

* How much wire in all will the three need? _____

Practice time

A. Look at the table. If you were to write the area of each of these which column would you choose? Make a (✔).

	Square cm	Square metre	Square km
Handkerchief	✔		
Sari			
Page of your book			
School land			
Total land of a city			
Door of your classroom			
Chair seat			
Blackboard			
Indian flag			
Land over which a river flows			

B. Draw a square of 9 square cm. Write A on it.

Draw another square with double the side. Write B on it.

Answer these —

1. The perimeter of square A is _____ cm.

2. The side of square B is _____ cm.

3. The area of square B is _____ square cm.

4. The area of square B is _____ times the area of square A.

5. The perimeter of square B is _____ cm.

6. The perimeter of square B is _____ times the perimeter of square A.

Answer — Pass Through a Postcard (page 150)

1.
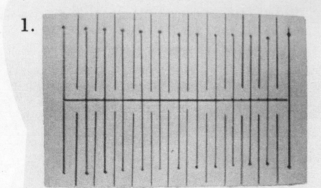
Make lines on a postcard like this.

2.
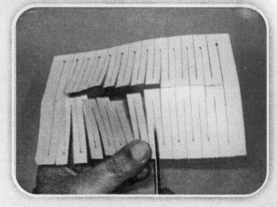
Cut the postcard only on the lines.

3.
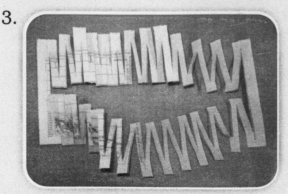

So, can you pass through it!

✳ You know the area of the loop, don't you? It is _____.

Thread Play

Take a 15 cm long thread. Make different shapes by joining its ends on this sheet.

A) Which shape has the biggest area? How much? _____

    What is the perimeter of this shape? _____

B) Which shape has the smallest area? How much? _____

    What is the perimeter of this shape? _____

Also make a triangle, a square, a rectangle and a circle. Find which shape has biggest area and which has the smallest.

Save the Birds

There are two beautiful lakes near a village. People come for boating and picnics in both the lakes. The village Panchayat is worried that with the noise of the boats the birds will stop coming. The Panchayat wants motor boats in only one lake. The other lake will be saved for the birds to make their nests.

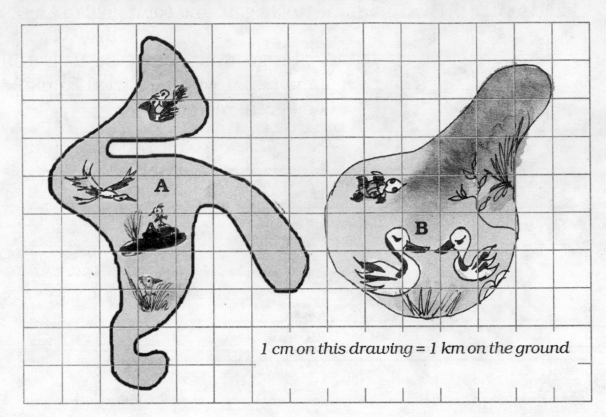

1 cm on this drawing = 1 km on the ground

a) How many cm is the length of the boundary of lake A in the drawing? _____ (use thread to find out)

b) What is the length of the boundary of lake B in the drawing?

c) How many kilometres long is the actual boundary of lake A ?

d) How many kilometres long is the actual boundary of lake B?

e) A longer boundary around the lake will help more birds to lay their eggs. So which lake should be kept for birds? Which lake should be used for boats?

f) Find the area of lake B on the drawing in square cm. What is its actual area in square km?

King's Story

The King was very happy with carpenters Cheggu and Anar. They had made a very big and beautiful bed for him. So as gifts the king wanted to give some land to Cheggu, and some gold to Anar.

Cheggu, take as much land as what comes within 100 meters of wire.

Cheggu was happy. He took 100 metres of wire and tried to make different rectangles.

He made a 10 m × 40 m rectangle. Its area was 400 square metres.

So he next made a 30 m × 20 m rectangle.

✳ What is its area? Is it more than the first rectangle?

✳ What other rectangles can he make with 100 metres of wire? Discuss which of these rectangles will have the biggest area.

Ah! I want this piece of land. It covers an area of 800 square metres.

Cheggu's wife asked him to make a circle with the wire. She knew it had an area of 800 square metres.

✳ Why did Cheggu not choose a rectangle? Explain.

Ok. Cheggu has taken 800 square metres of land. Anar! Now I will give you as much gold wire which can make a boundary for land with area 800 square metres.

So Anar also tried many different ways to make a boundary for 800 square metres of land.

✳ He made rectangles A, B and C of different sizes. Find out the length of the boundary of each. How much gold wire will he get for these rectangles?

A **40 m × 20 m**

Gold wire for A = _____ metres

B **80 m × 10 m**

Gold wire for B = _____ metres

C **800 m × 1 m**

Gold wire for C = _____ metres

But then Anar made an even longer rectangle.... See how long!

D **8000 m × 0.1 m**

So he will get _____ metres of gold wire!!

Gosh! How can I give so much gold?

Now do you understand why the king fainted!!!

Can you make a rectangle with a still longer boundary? I made a rectangle 1 cm wide and 80000 m long. Imagine how long that boundary will be!!! With that much gold wire I can become the king!

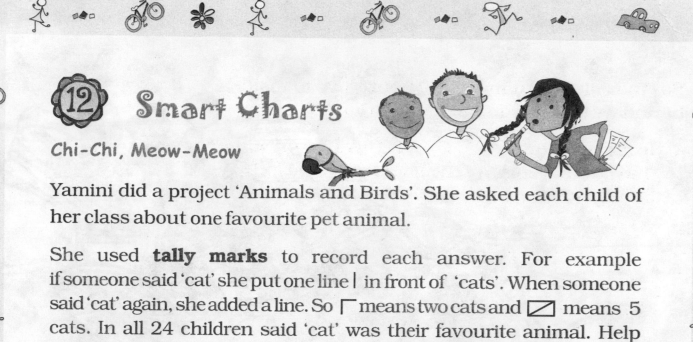

12 Smart Charts

Chi-Chi, Meow-Meow

Yamini did a project 'Animals and Birds'. She asked each child of her class about one favourite pet animal.

She used **tally marks** to record each answer. For example if someone said 'cat' she put one line | in front of 'cats'. When someone said 'cat' again, she added a line. So Γ means two cats and ⊠ means 5 cats. In all 24 children said 'cat' was their favourite animal. Help Yamini complete the table.

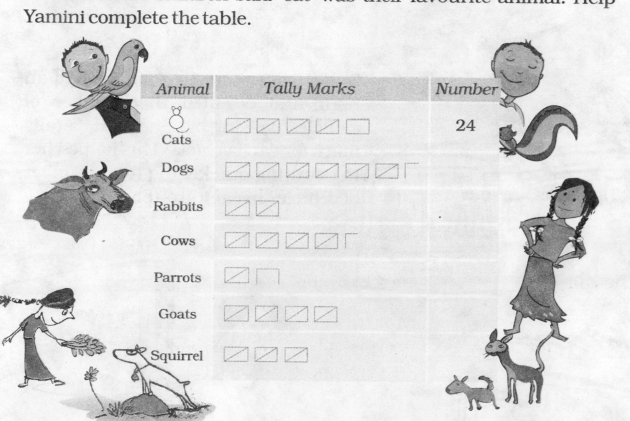

Animal	Tally Marks	Number
Cats	⊠ ⊠ ⊠ ⊠ ☐	24
Dogs	⊠ ⊠ ⊠ ⊠ ⊠ ⊠ Γ	
Rabbits	⊠ ⊠	
Cows	⊠ ⊠ ⊠ ⊠ Γ	
Parrots	⊠ ☐	
Goats	⊠ ⊠ ⊠ ⊠	
Squirrel	⊠ ⊠ ⊠	

♣ Look at the tally marks and write the number for each animal in the table. How many children in all did Yamini talk to?

♣ Which is the most favourite pet animal in this table?

♣ Which pet will you like to have? What will you name it? Which other animals can be kept at home? Discuss.

Making Tally Marks on the Road

Sumita stood on the road for half an hour and counted the number of vehicles passing by. She made a tally mark for each vehicle. This helped her in counting quickly the total number of vehicles in each group.

	Tally Marks	Number
Cycle	⊠ ⊠ ⊠ ⊠ ⊠ ▢	
Car	⊠ ⊠ ⌐	
Auto rickshaw	⊠ ⊠ ⊠ ⌐	
Bus	⊠ ⊠ ⊠	
Cycle rickshaw	⊠ ⊠ ⊠ ⊠ ▢	
Truck	⊠		

❖ Write the number of each vehicle in the table.

❖ How many vehicles in all did Sumita see on the road in half an hour?

❖ Auto rickshaws are thrice the number of trucks — true/false?

❖ Make tally marks for 7 more buses, and 2 more trucks.

Try yourself

❖ Take a round in your colony. Find out how many types of trees you can see there. Do you know their names? You can make drawings. Use tally marks to note the number of different trees.

Children should be encouraged to use tally marks to simultaneously record data of a variety of things with larger numbers.

Helping Hands

In the EVS period, the teacher asked children whether they help their parents at home. There were different answers. Children named the work in which they help their parents the most. The teacher collected their answers and made a table.

Help most in house work	Number of children
Going to the market	47
Washing utensils	15
Washing clothes	3
Making, serving food	25
Cleaning the house	10
Total children who said they help their parents	

Now you can fill the chapati chart to show the numbers given in the table.

1) Look and find out

Children who help in making or serving food are

Cleaning the house 10

> a) One-third of the total children
>
> b) Half of the total children
>
> c) One-fourth of the total children

2) Practice time: After school

Ask 10 of your friends about what they like to do most after school.

What they like to do after school	Number of children
Watching TV	
Playing football	
Reading story books	

Ad Mad!!

Ragini loves to watch cartoons on television. One day she thought of counting the number of ads during the breaks. She found that in each break there were 14 advertisements. In 10 of those ads there were children as actors.

❖ Why do you think that children are used in so many ads?

❖ Use tally marks to count the number of ads during a short break in a programme.

Were there ads during the news programme?

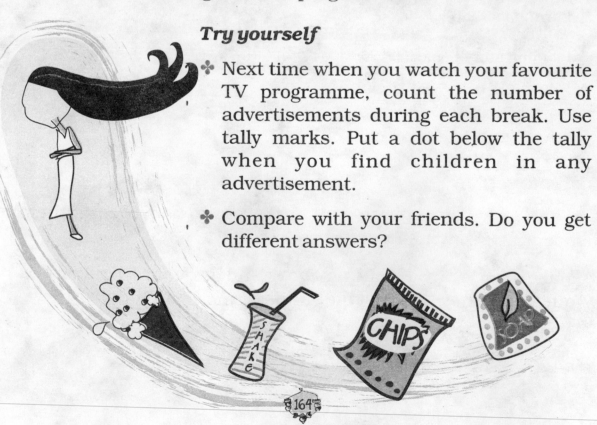

Try yourself

❖ Next time when you watch your favourite TV programme, count the number of advertisements during each break. Use tally marks. Put a dot below the tally when you find children in any advertisement.

❖ Compare with your friends. Do you get different answers?

Hot and Cold

Have you seen the weather report on TV or in a newspaper? These are two bar charts. These show the highest temperature (in degrees Celsius) in four cities, on two different days. The cities are Delhi, Shimla, Bangalore and Jaisalmer.

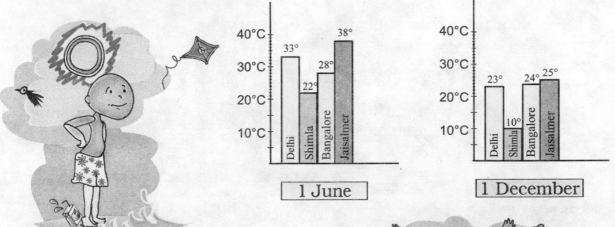

1 June   1 December

Find out from the bar chart —

♣ Which city is the hottest on 1 June?

♣ Which city is the coldest on 1 December?

♣ Which city shows little change in temperature on the two days — 1 June and 1 December.

Try yourself

On any one day, choose any three cities and record their temperature from the TV or newspaper.

♣ Make a bar chart in your notebook and ask your friends a few questions about it. See if they understand your chart!

Encourage children to look at the map of India to locate different cities. They can try to relate the temperature variations in a city to get an idea of the climate there.

Rabbits in Australia

Earlier there were no rabbits in Australia. Rabbits were brought to Australia around the year 1780. At that time there were no animals in Australia which ate rabbits. So the rabbits began to multiply at a very fast rate. Imagine what they did to the crops!

The table shows how rabbits grew every year.

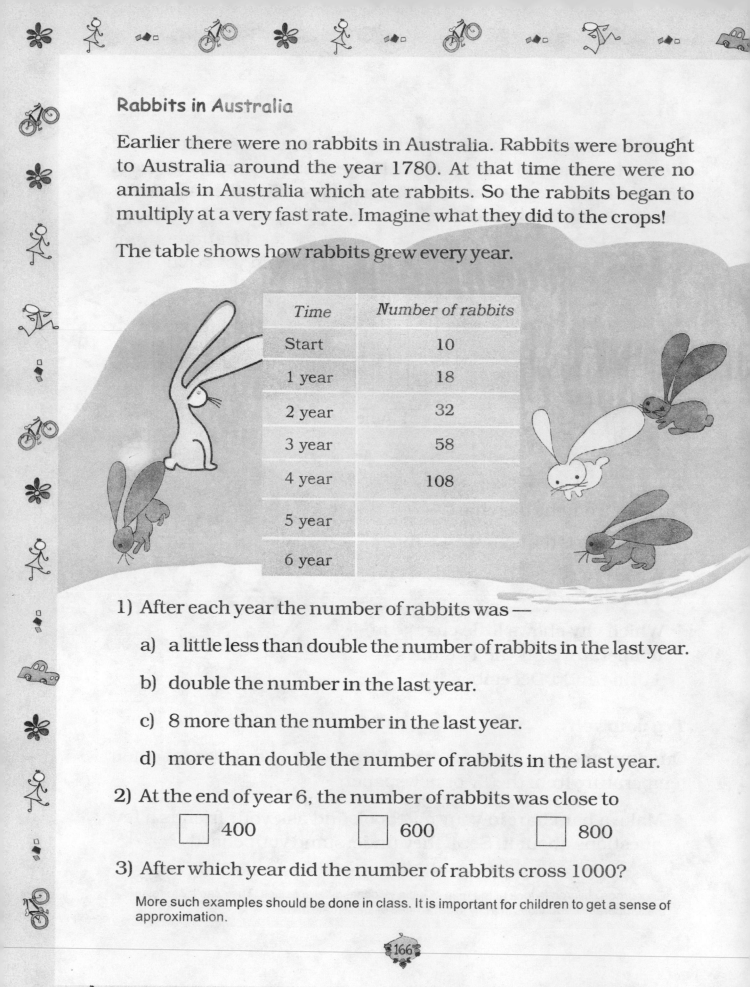

Time	Number of rabbits
Start	10
1 year	18
2 year	32
3 year	58
4 year	108
5 year	
6 year	

1) After each year the number of rabbits was —

   a) a little less than double the number of rabbits in the last year.

   b) double the number in the last year.

   c) 8 more than the number in the last year.

   d) more than double the number of rabbits in the last year.

2) At the end of year 6, the number of rabbits was close to

    ☐ 400   ☐ 600   ☐ 800

3) After which year did the number of rabbits cross 1000?

More such examples should be done in class. It is important for children to get a sense of approximation.

Family Tree

Madhav went to a wedding along with his parents. He met many relatives there. But he didn't know everyone. He met his mother's grandfather, but found that her grandmother is not alive. He also found that her *Dadi's* mother (grandmother's mother) is still alive, and is more than a hundred years old.

Madhav got confused. He couldn't imagine his mother's grandmother's mother! So, Madhav's mother made a family tree for him —

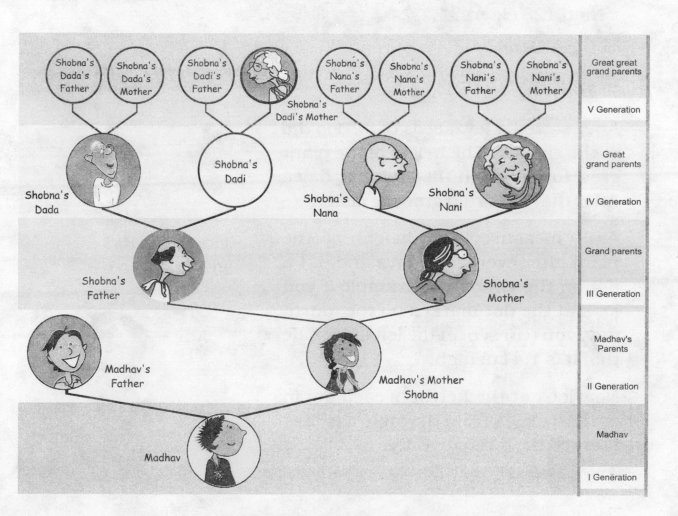

Shobna's Dada's Father | Shobna's Dada's Mother | Shobna's Dadi's Father | Shobna's Dadi's Mother | Shobna's Nana's Father | Shobna's Nana's Mother | Shobna's Nani's Father | Shobna's Nani's Mother — **Great great grand parents** — V Generation

Shobna's Dada | Shobna's Dadi | Shobna's Nana | Shobna's Nani — **Great grand parents** — IV Generation

Shobna's Father | Shobna's Mother — **Grand parents** — III Generation

Madhav's Father | Madhav's Mother Shobna — **Madhav's Parents** — II Generation

Madhav — **Madhav** — I Generation

Madhav's mother helped him understand her family with the help of this drawing. You can also find out about your older generations using such a family tree.

Answer these questions:

1) How many grand parents in all does Shobna have?

2) How many great, great grand parents in all does Madhav have?

3) How many elders will be in the VII generation of his family?

4) If he takes his family tree forward in which generation will he find 128 elders?

Growth Chart of a Plant

Amit sowed a few seeds of *moong dal* in the ground. The height of the plant grew to 1.4 cm in the first four days. After that it started growing faster.

Amit measured the height of the plant after every four days and put a dot on the chart. For example if you look at the dot marked on the fourth day, you can see on the left side scale that it is 1.4 cm high.

Now look at the height of each dot in cm and check from the table if he has marked the dots correctly.

Day	Length of the plant (in cm)
0	0
4	1.4
8	5.3
12	9.5
16	10.2
20	10.9

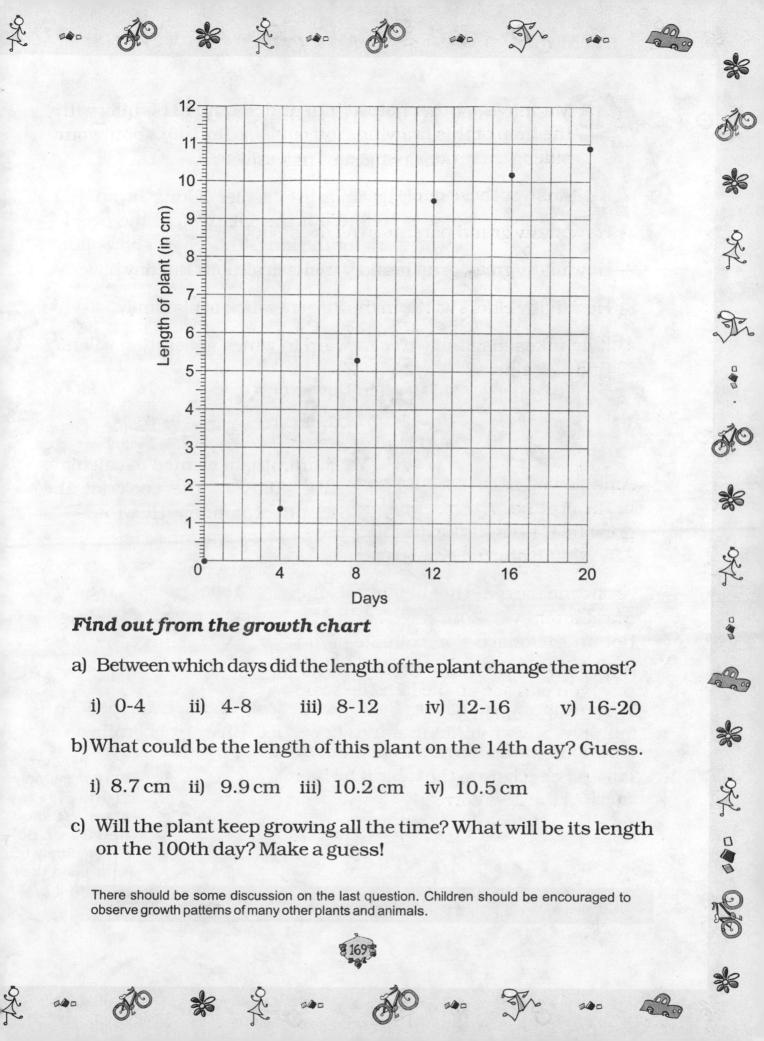

Find out from the growth chart

a) Between which days did the length of the plant change the most?

   i) 0-4   ii) 4-8   iii) 8-12   iv) 12-16   v) 16-20

b) What could be the length of this plant on the 14th day? Guess.

   i) 8.7 cm   ii) 9.9 cm   iii) 10.2 cm   iv) 10.5 cm

c) Will the plant keep growing all the time? What will be its length on the 100th day? Make a guess!

There should be some discussion on the last question. Children should be encouraged to observe growth patterns of many other plants and animals.

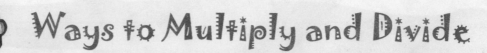

⑬ Ways to Multiply and Divide

Maniratnam – The Cashier

Maniratnam is the cashier of king Jayan. His job is to find out the salary of all the people who work for the king. This chart shows how much salary each person gets in a day.

Person		Salary in a day
Minister	—	Rs 195
Horse rider	—	Rs 76
Cook	—	Rs 65

Maniratnam wanted to calculate the salary of the cook for the month of January. He wrote —

	60	5
30	60 × 30 **1800**	5 × 30 **150**
1	60 × 1 **60**	5 × 1 **5**

Rupees 1800 + 150 + 60 + 5 = Rs _____

Maniratnam's daughter Bela has learnt another method to multiply. She wrote like this and showed it to Bhanu, her brother.

Akka, how did you do this?

$$
\begin{array}{r}
65 \\
\times 31 \\
\hline
65 \\
+1950 \\
\hline
\end{array}
\quad
\begin{array}{l}
(65 \times 1) \\
(65 \times 30)
\end{array}
$$

We can multiply 65 with 31 in two steps. We know 31 is 30 + 1. So, first multiply 65 with 1 and then with 30.

Now Bhanu tried to find the salary of a minister for the month of January. He wanted to multiply 195 × 31.

```
    195
  × 31
  ───────
    195      (195 × 1)
+ ___0       (195 × 30)
  ───────
```

To multiply by 30 I first write a zero here. Then I only have to multiply by 3.

Practice time

1) Use Bela's method to multiply these numbers.

   a) 32 × 46

   b) 67 × 18

```
     32
   × 46
   ───────
    192      (32 × 6)
+  ─────     (32 × 40)
   ───────
```

```
     67
   × 18
   ───────
    ───       (67 × 8)
+  670       (67 × __)
   ───────
```

2) Do these in your notebook using Bela's method.

   a) 47 × 19   b) 188 × 91

   c) 63 × 57   d) 225 × 22

   e) 360 × 12   f) 163 × 42

Shantaram a Special Cook

✳ Shantaram is a special cook who comes only on party days. Last year he was called for only 28 days. For each day he has to be paid Rs 165. Find out how much money he will get in all.

✳ If he is called for all days of the year, how much salary will he get?

```
     1 6 5
   × 3 6 5
   ─────────
     - - -      (165×5)
   - - - -      (165×60)
 + 4 9 5 0 0    (165×300)
   ─────────

   ─────────
```

✳ Now find the salaries of the minister and horse rider for 1 year.

Years and Years

a) Sohan drinks 8 glasses of water every day.

✳ How many glasses will he drink in one month? _____

✳ How many glasses will he drink in one year?

✳ If 125 people living in a colony drink 8 glasses of water in a day, how much water will they drink in a year?

Can you guess how many glasses of drinking water are used in a day in your colony?

b) If Soha's heart beats 72 times in one minute, how many times does it beat in one hour?

Guess how many times it beats in one year.

✳ Now find out how many times it beats in one day.

✳ Count your own heart beats to find out how many times your heart beats in one week.

c) A baby elephant drinks around 12 L of milk every day. How much milk will it drink in two years?

d) A baby blue whale drinks around 200 L of milk in one day. Just imagine how much milk that is! Find out in how many days your family would use 200 L milk. How much milk would the baby blue whale drink in eight months?

Karunya — The Landlord

Karunya bought three fields.

27 m
28 m
Field (A)

36 m
12 m
Field (B)

27 m
19 m
Field (C)

* Find the area of all the three fields.

Field (A) _____ square metre.

Field (B) _____ square metre.

Field (C) _____ square metre.

Hum, did he spend more than a lakh of rupees!

He bought field (A) at the rate of Rs 95 for a square metre, field (B) at Rs 110 for a square metre and field (C) at Rs 120 for a square metre.

* Find the cost of all three fields.

Thulasi and her husband work on Karunya's farm. The Government has said that farm workers should be paid at least Rs 71 for one day's work. But he pays Rs 55 to Thulasi and Rs 58 to her husband.

If Thulasi works for 49 days, how much money does she get? _____

If her husband works for 42 days, how much money does he get? _____

Find the money they earn together _____

Oh! He does not give them the **minimum** wage?

And why does he pay less to Thulasi and more to her husband? Discuss.

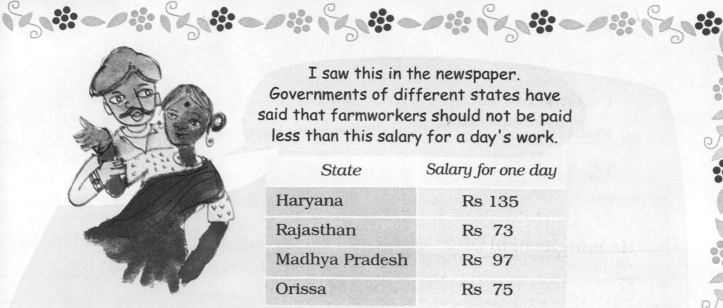

I saw this in the newspaper. Governments of different states have said that farmworkers should not be paid less than this salary for a day's work.

State	Salary for one day
Haryana	Rs 135
Rajasthan	Rs 73
Madhya Pradesh	Rs 97
Orissa	Rs 75

The table shows the amounts fixed by four states.

a) For farm work which state has fixed the highest amount? Which state has fixed the lowest?

b) Bhairon Singh is a worker in Rajasthan. If he works for 8 weeks on the farm, how much will he earn?

c) Neelam is a worker in Haryana. If she works for 2½ months on the farm, how much will she earn?

d) How much more will a farm worker in Madhya Pradesh get than a worker in Orissa after working for 9 weeks?

Farmers in Vidarbha (Maharashtra)

Vidarbha is facing a very serious problem. There was no rain and crops failed. Many farmers were unhappy. Some farmers even ended their own lives. A newspaper reporter went around the area and spoke to the people. He wrote these two reports.

Satish's story

Satish is a 13 year old boy. His father had taken a loan for farming. But the crops failed. Now Satish's mother has to pay Rs 5000 every month for the loan.

Satish started working — he looked after 17 goats of the village.

He earns Rupee 1 everyday for one goat.

✳ How much will he earn in one month?

✳ Does he earn enough to help pay the loan every month?

✳ How much will he earn in one year?

Kamla Bai's story

To help farmers the State Government gave cows. Kamla Bai Gudhe also got a cow. The cost of the cow was Rs 17,500. She had to pay Rs 5,500 and the government spent the rest of the money.

✳ How much did the government spend on the cow?

✳ If 9 people from her village got cows, how much did the government spend in all?

But Kamla Bai was not happy. She had to spend Rs 85 everyday on the cow. She made some money by selling the milk. But still she wanted to sell the cow.

✳ If Kamla Bai spends Rs 85 a day, find out how much she will spend in one month.

✳ The cow gives 8 litre of milk everyday. How much will it give in one month?

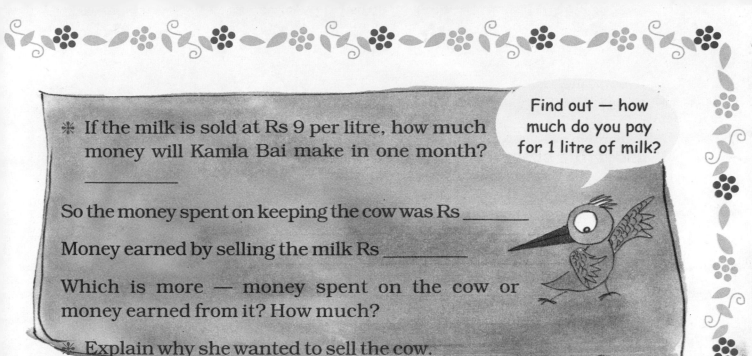

✳ If the milk is sold at Rs 9 per litre, how much money will Kamla Bai make in one month? _____

Find out — how much do you pay for 1 litre of milk?

So the money spent on keeping the cow was Rs _____

Money earned by selling the milk Rs _____

Which is more — money spent on the cow or money earned from it? How much?

✳ Explain why she wanted to sell the cow.

Practice time

a) Sukhi works on a farm. He is paid Rs 98 for one day. If he works for 52 days, how much will he earn?

b) Hariya took a loan to build his house. He has to pay back Rs 2,750 every month for two years. How much will he pay back in 2 years?

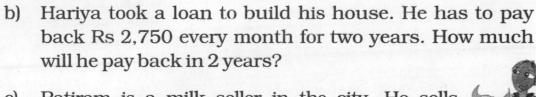

c) Ratiram is a milk seller in the city. He sells 13 litres of milk everyday at Rs 23 per litre. How much does he earn?

d) A farmer sells 1 litre of milk for Rs 11. In one month he sells 210 litres of milk. How much does he earn in a month?

e) A company sells 1 litre of packed water for Rs 12. A shopkeeper buys 240 litres of packed water. How much does he pay?

Oh God! Water costs more than milk!! In the city people buy water for Rs 12 per litre!

Fun with multiplication

A) Look for the pattern and take this forward.

$$(0 \times 9) + 1 = 1$$
$$(1 \times 9) + 2 = 11$$
$$(12 \times 9) + 3 = 111$$
$$(123 \times 9) + 4 = \underline{\hspace{2cm}}$$
$$(1234 \times 9) + 5 = \underline{\hspace{2cm}}$$
$$(12345 \times 9) + 6 = \underline{\hspace{2cm}}$$

B) Each letter a, b, c here stands for a number.

```
      a a a
  ×   a a a
  _____
      a a a
    a a a 0
  a a a 0 0
  _____
  a b c b a
  _____
```

Take a = 1, then find what the numbers b and c will be.

C) Tricks with your age.

Write your age _____

Multiply it by 7 _____

Again multiply the answer by 13 _____

Multiply again that answer by 11 _____

Now look at your last answer. Can you find your age in that answer? How many times does your age show in the answer?

Now try this trick with other people.

D) Going round and round!

142857	142857	142857	142857	142857
×1	×2	×3	×4	×5

Do you find a pattern in all these answers? Discuss this with your friends.

Division

Dolma took a loan from a friend to buy a moped for Rs 9,588. She has to pay it back in equal amounts every month for six months.

✳ How much will she have to pay every month? She asked her children to calculate.

Her daughter did it this way.

$$500 + 500 + 500 + 90 + 8$$

$$
\begin{array}{r}
6\,)\;9588 \\
-3000 \\
\hline
6588 \\
-3000 \\
\hline
3588 \\
-3000 \\
\hline
588 \\
-540 \\
\hline
48 \\
-48 \\
\hline
\times
\end{array}
$$

Her son started this way. Now you complete it.

$$1000 +$$

$$
\begin{array}{r}
6\,)\;9588 \\
-6000 \\
\hline
 \\
\hline
 \\
\hline
 \\
\hline
 \\
\end{array}
$$

Will both of them get the same answer? Discuss.

Practice time

Try to solve these using as few steps as you can.

a) $4228 \div 4$ b) $770 \div 22$ c) $9872 \div 8$

d) $672 \div 21$ e) $772 \div 7$ f) $639 \div 13$

How Many Times?

976 children are going on a picnic. They will be taken in mini buses. If 25 children can go in one bus, how many buses do they need?

✳ Two children have solved it. Check if they have made a mistake — correct it. Discuss.

$$
\begin{array}{r}
25\,\overline{)\,976\,}\quad 5 + 10 + 10 + 10 + 4 \\
-125 \\ \hline
851 \\
-250 \\ \hline
601 \\
-250 \\ \hline
351 \\
-250 \\ \hline
101 \\
-100 \\ \hline
\times
\end{array}
$$

Ans. We need 39 buses.

$$
\begin{array}{r}
25\,\overline{)\,976\,}\quad 20 + 10 + 9 + 1 \\
-500 \\ \hline
476 \\
-250 \\ \hline
226 \\
-215 \\ \hline
11
\end{array}
$$

Ans. We need 40 buses.

Giving children the opportunity to find and discuss the errors in these examples will help their own understanding about the different steps for division. In A) a very common error has been given in which children either forget or do not understand the remainder. In B) there is a simple error of multiplication but there is also a more interesting question of whether the child has shown one extra bus for the remaining children.

How Much Petrol?

Isha has Rs 1000 with her. She wants to buy petrol. One litre of petrol costs Rs 47. How many litres can she buy?

Money with Isha = Rs 1000

Cost of 1 litre = Rs 47

Litres of petrol she can buy = Rs 1000 ÷ Rs 47 = ?

Isha can buy _____ litres of petrol.

Find out

If Isha comes to your city, how much petrol can she buy with the same money?

Children's Day

Children are happy today. They are celebrating Children's Day. Each child will be given 4 coloured pencils from school. The school has got 969 pencils. To find out how many children can get pencils the teacher asks them to divide.

Iru's Way

$$4\overline{)969}\ 100+$$
$$-400$$

Sreeni's Way

$$4\overline{)969}\ 200+$$
$$-\underline{}$$

Complete Iru's and Sreeni's way of division. What is the answer you get?

Shivangi did it by a shortcut way.

Shivangi's Way

Practice Time

* 576 books are to be packed in boxes. If one box has 24 books, how many boxes are needed?

* 836 people are watching a movie in a hall. If the hall has 44 rows, how many people can sit in 1 row?

* A gardener bought 458 apple trees. He wants to plant 15 trees in each row. How many rows can he plant?

  How many trees would be left over?

Brain Teaser

* Shyamli bought a battery. She read on it 'Life: 2000 hours'. She uses it throughout the day and the night. How many days will the battery run?

More with Multiplication and Division

* A tank is full of 300 L of water. How much water will be filled in 25 tanks? If 15 buckets can be filled with one tank of water, how many buckets in all can be filled with the water in 25 tanks?

* There are 28 *laddoos* in 1 kg. How many *laddoos* will be there in 12 kg? If 16 *laddoos* can be packed in 1 box, how many boxes are needed to pack all these *laddoos*?

* There are 26 rooms in a school. Each room has 4 plants. If each plant needs 2 cups of water, how much water do we need for all the plants?

Make the Best Story Problem

Each line gives a story. You have to choose the question which makes the best story problem. The first one is already marked.

1) *A shopkeeper has 50 boxes. There are 48 fruits in one box.*

Tick the one question which matches with the given problem.

a) How much will the shopkeeper pay in all?

b) How many fruits are there in all? ✔

c) How many more boxes will he need?

Explain why (a) and (c) are not good choices.

2) *352 children from a school went on a camping trip. Each tent had a group of 4 children.*

a) How many children did each tent have?

b) How many tents do they need?

c) How many children in all are in the school?

3) *A shopkeeper has 204 eggs. He puts them in egg trays. Each tray has 12 eggs.*

a) How many more eggs will he need?

b) How many fresh eggs does he sell?

c) How many egg trays does he need?

Such exercises will help children understand the strategies to make questions related to the concepts of division and multiplication.

4) The cost of one book is Rs 47. Sonu buys 23 books.

   a) How much money does she have?

   b) How much money does she pay for the books?

   c) What is the cost of 47 books?

Cross Check for Harisharan

Harisharan wanted to divide Rs 2,456 amongst his 4 sons. He asked his eldest son to tell him how much money each one will get.

Papa, each of us will get 2456 ÷ 4 = Rs 624.

When Harisharan started giving Rs 624 to each son, he was left with less money for the youngest one.

It seems you have made some mistake in the calculations. Let me check.

Harisharan multiplied 624 with 4.

He got = Rs 2,496.

Hum! This shows you have done the division wrong.

The son did the division again 2456 ÷ 4 = 614.

Before telling his father he checked on his own.

614 × 4 = 2456.   Now, it is correct. Each one will get Rs 614.

Practice Time

1) Do these divisions. Check your results by multiplication.

   a) $438 \div 9$

   b) $3480 \div 12$

   c) $450 \div 7$

   d) $900 \div 10$

   e) $678 \div 6$

   f) $2475 \div 11$

2) Solve the given sums and colour the answers in the grid given below. See what you find.

21×16	15×7	93×2	17×5	10×10	
26×26	77×10	50×10	11×11	59×7	31×19
85×30	64×42	$3200 \div 40$	19×3	$248 \div 8$	
$432 \div 18$	$729 \div 9$	$825 \div 5$	$221 \div 13$	$576 \div 12$	
$288 \div 4$	$869 \div 11$	$847 \div 7$	$981 \div 3$	$475 \div 19$	

545	110	434	642	709	623	919	341	12	168
984	16	561	608	236	413	529	62	259	905
709	907	367	632	336	121	492	178	431	25
166	806	584	186	100	589	72	717	248	676
624	82	105	24	165	17	85	770	327	500
247	997	485	2688	81	80	48	901	126	121
742	427	756	531	79	2550	347	1001	314	57
945	1000	687	854	1200	31	124	3126	918	53
109	799	845	1999	864	955	123	1234	678	56
549	459	614	1864	834	559	900	1111	268	171

14 How Big? How Heavy?

Sarika collects things like marbles, coins, erasers etc. She takes some water in a glass and marks the level of water as '0'.

If I drop 5 marbles in this glass, can you guess what will be the level of water?

I think this much.

She drops 5 marbles in the glass. She marks the new level of water as 5 marbles.

*Oh, how did you guess! Do you know the **volume** of a marble?*

I just made a guess about how much water will be pushed up by the marbles. How do you find the volume?

See, each marble pushes up some water. Right? That is because it takes up some space which is its volume.

Children will need more exercises to compare the volume of solid bodies by guessing and by informal measurement (using marbles, coins, matchboxes, etc.) before they begin to use formal measures such as litres and cubic centimetres.

Your Measuring Glass

Now make a guess. Do you think the volume of 10 five-rupee coins will be more than that of 10 marbles?

Guess the volume of each of these:

* A ball is nearly _____ marbles.

* An eraser is nearly _____ marbles.

* A lemon is nearly _____ marbles.

* A pencil is nearly _____ marbles.

* A potato is nearly _____ marbles.

Now make your own measuring glass using 35 marbles.

Take a glass of water and mark the level of water as '0'. Then put in 5 marbles and mark the level of water as 5 M.

Again drop 5 marbles and mark the level of water as 10 M. Likewise make the markings for 15 M, 20 M, 25 M, 30 M and 35 M.

Now put each thing in the measuring glass and check your guess.

Try with different things like a matchbox, a stone, etc. and fill the table.

The matchbox floats. How do I find its volume?

Let's fill it with sand or nails.

Name of the thing	Its volume (nearly how many marbles?)

Children can paste a paper strip on the glass and mark the level of water using a pen or a pencil. The aim is to develop a sense of the concept of volume through examples and hands on activities without giving a definition of volume. Comparing things on the basis of volume is more abstract then comparison in terms of length or area.

Which has More Volume?

In Class IV you made a measuring bottle for 250 mL.

Can you think of ways for making a measuring bottle which can measure 10 mL, 20 mL, 30 mL, ..., 60 mL? Discuss with your friend.

Tariq and Mollie made their measuring bottles.

Tariq had an injection. He used it to make his measuring bottle. Mollie used an empty medicine bottle.

Mollie used her measuring bottle to find the volume of five-rupee coins. She found that **9 five-rupee coins push up 10 mL of water**. So you can also use 9 five-rupee coins to make your measuring bottle! Go ahead!

Use your measuring bottle to find out:

a) What is the volume of 6 marbles? _____ mL.

b) What is the volume of 16 one-rupee coins? _____ mL.

Now solve these in your mind.

c) The volume of 24 marbles is _____ mL.

d) The volume of 32 one-rupee coins? _____ mL.

e) Mollie puts some five-rupee coins in the measuring bottle. How many coins has she put in it:

　❋ if 30 mL water is pushed up? _____

　❋ if 60 mL water is pushed up? _____

First guess and then use your measuring bottle to find out the volume in mL of some other things.

Thing	Its volume (in mL)

Guess how many litres of water your body will push up?!

How Many Can Fit In?

1cm
1cm

This is a cube whose sides are of 1 cm each. See, your Math-Magic book is 1 cm high. So guess how many such centimetre cubes will take the same space as your Math-Magic book?

To make a measuring bottle, make children use a wide-mouthed and transparent bottle so that markings can be made easily. The activity aims to develop measurement skills in children and involves both making and handling apparatus (such as measuring bottle) in the mathematics classroom.

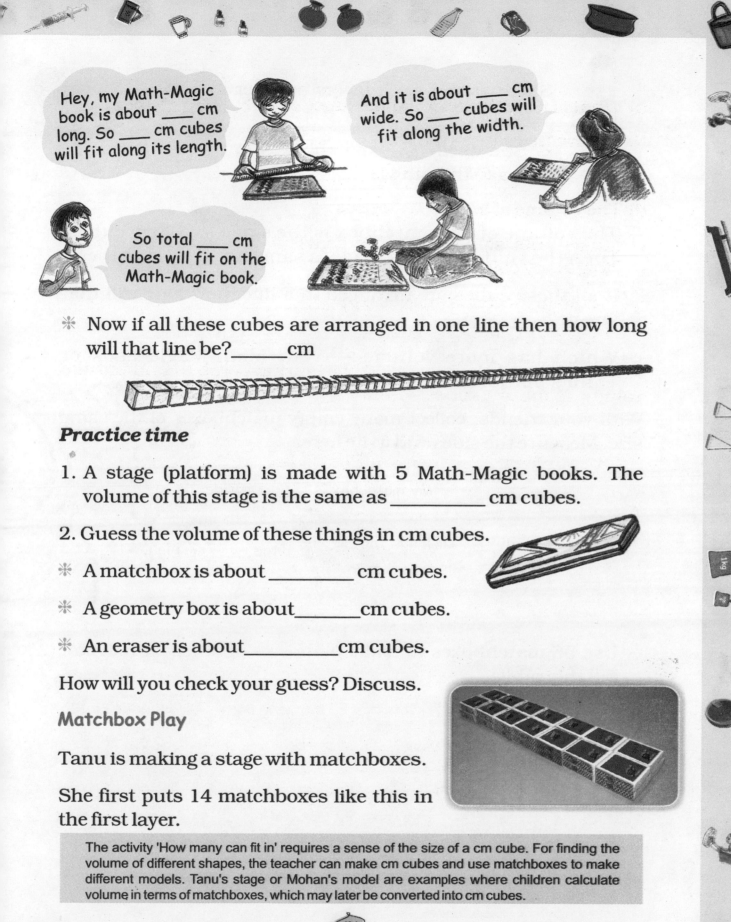

Hey, my Math-Magic book is about ____ cm long. So ____ cm cubes will fit along its length.

And it is about ____ cm wide. So ____ cubes will fit along the width.

So total ____ cm cubes will fit on the Math-Magic book.

✳ Now if all these cubes are arranged in one line then how long will that line be?_____ cm

Practice time

1. A stage (platform) is made with 5 Math-Magic books. The volume of this stage is the same as _____ cm cubes.

2. Guess the volume of these things in cm cubes.

✳ A matchbox is about _____ cm cubes.

✳ A geometry box is about _____ cm cubes.

✳ An eraser is about _____ cm cubes.

How will you check your guess? Discuss.

Matchbox Play

Tanu is making a stage with matchboxes.

She first puts 14 matchboxes like this in the first layer.

The activity 'How many can fit in' requires a sense of the size of a cm cube. For finding the volume of different shapes, the teacher can make cm cubes and use matchboxes to make different models. Tanu's stage or Mohan's model are examples where children calculate volume in terms of matchboxes, which may later be converted into cm cubes.

She makes 4 such layers and her stage looks like this.

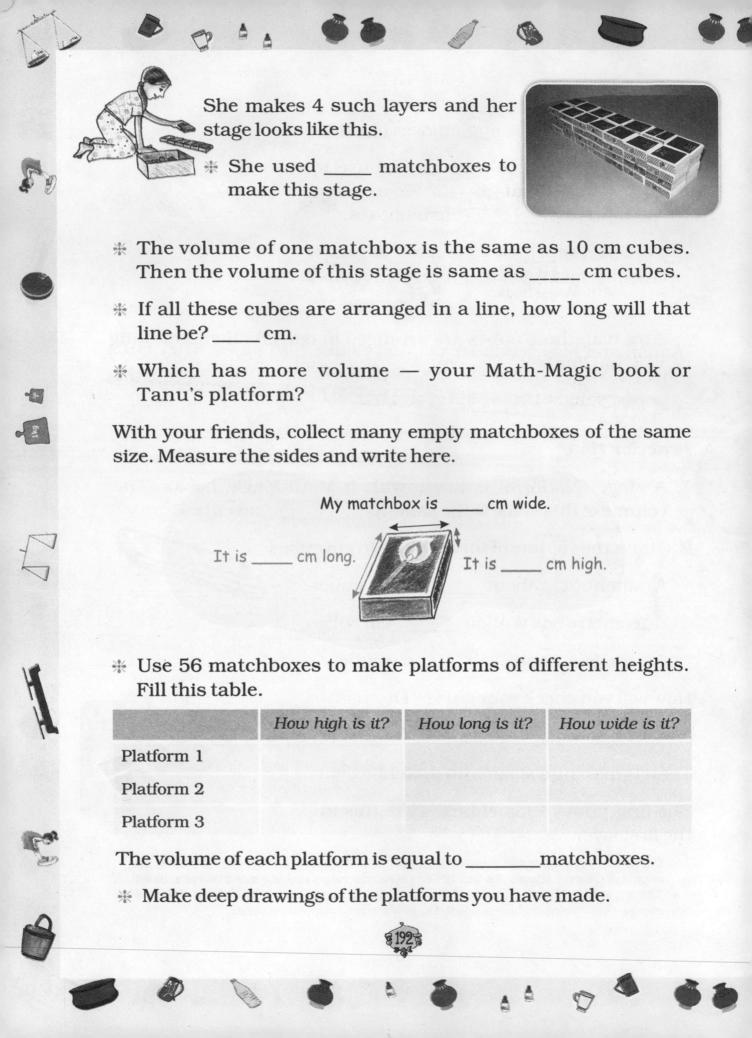

❋ She used _____ matchboxes to make this stage.

❋ The volume of one matchbox is the same as 10 cm cubes. Then the volume of this stage is same as _____ cm cubes.

❋ If all these cubes are arranged in a line, how long will that line be? _____ cm.

❋ Which has more volume — your Math-Magic book or Tanu's platform?

With your friends, collect many empty matchboxes of the same size. Measure the sides and write here.

My matchbox is _____ cm wide.

It is _____ cm long.

It is _____ cm high.

❋ Use 56 matchboxes to make platforms of different heights. Fill this table.

	How high is it?	*How long is it?*	*How wide is it?*
Platform 1			
Platform 2			
Platform 3			

The volume of each platform is equal to _____matchboxes.

❋ Make deep drawings of the platforms you have made.

Practice time

Mohan arranged his matchboxes like this.

❋ How many matchboxes did he use to make it? What is its volume in matchboxes? _____ matchboxes.

❋ Collect empty matchboxes. Arrange them in an interesting way. Make a deep drawing of it.

Making a Paper Cube

Aanan and his friends are making a cube with paper. They cut a sheet of paper into a square of 19.5 cm side. They cut 6 such squares. Follow these photos to make your paper cube.

1. Fold the paper into four equal parts to make lines like this.

2. Fold the top **left** corner and the corner opposite to it like this.

3. Fold the top and the bottom edges to meet the centre line. Now fold corner P...

4. So that the paper looks like this.

5. Fold corner Q in the same way. The paper will look like this now.

6. Lift corner P and slip it under the folded paper like this.

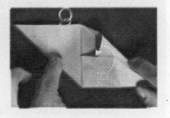

Encourage children to make different shapes of the same volume using identical units, for example, bricks or matchboxes. To calculate the sides of the platform, lengths can be rounded off to the nearest centimetre.

7. Do the same for corner Q. The paper will look like this.

8. Turn the paper and fold it to make lines like these.

9. Each child should make one such piece. Six children will take their pieces and put one inside another to make this paper cube.

Note: Remember to begin with a square paper of side 19.5 cm. Also, in step 2 you must all start by folding the **left** corner.

How Big is Your Cube?

How many cm cubes in all do I need to make a platform as big as the paper cube?

1. a) How long is the side of your cube? _____

b) How many centimetre cubes can be arranged along its:

 ✳ Length? _____

 ✳ Width? _____

 ✳ Height? _____

Thimpu

c) Answer Thimpu's questions:

To make the first layer on the table how many cm cubes will I use? _____

How many such layers will I need to make a paper cube? _____

d) So the total cm cubes = _____

e) The volume of the paper cube is same as _____ cm cubes.

If we begin with square paper of side 19.5 cm, then we get a cube of side 7 cm.

2. Anan made a big cube having double the side of your paper cube.

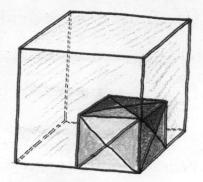

How many of the your paper cubes will fit in it? Try doing it by collecting all the cubes made in your class.

Packing Cubes

Ganesh and Dinga want to pack 4000 centimetre cubes in boxes. These are to be sent to a school. There are three different boxes available for packing.

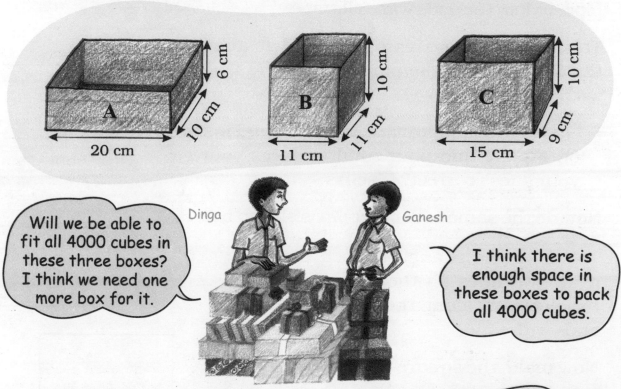

Will we be able to fit all 4000 cubes in these three boxes? I think we need one more box for it.

I think there is enough space in these boxes to pack all 4000 cubes.

* What is your guess? Who is right?

* How can Ganesh and Dinga test their guesses before packing the cubes in the boxes? Discuss with your friend.

Look at Box A. In the first layer we can arrange 20 × 10 = 200 cubes. And 6 such layers can be packed. So in box A we can arrange 200 × 6 = 1200 cubes.

Use Ganesh's method and write:

✳ _____ centimetre cubes can be arranged in box B.

✳ _____ centimetre cubes can be arranged in box C.

✳ So _____ centimetre cubes in all can be packed in the three boxes.

Which Pipe Fills More?

Collect some old postcards. You can also use thick paper of size 14 cm × 9 cm.

Fold the postcard along the **width** to make pipe-1. Join the ends with cello tape.

Take another postcard and fold it along the **length** to make pipe-2. Join the ends with tape.

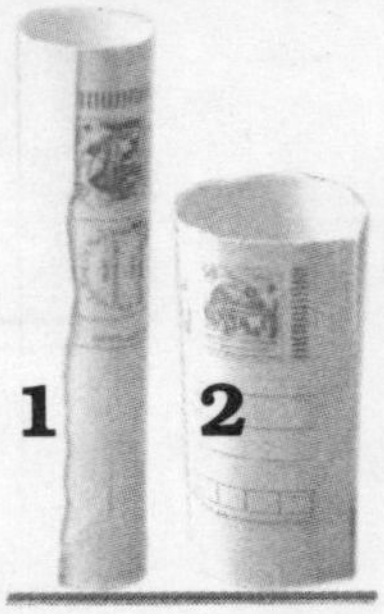

✳ Guess which pipe can take more sand inside it. Hold it on a plate and pour sand to check your guess. Was your guess correct? Discuss.

Now do the same with other pipes shown here.

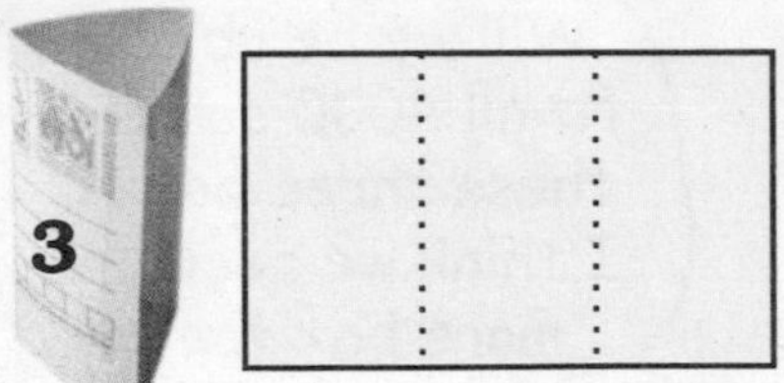

To make the triangle-shaped pipe-3, draw two lines on the postcard. Fold the postcard along the lines. Join the ends with tape.

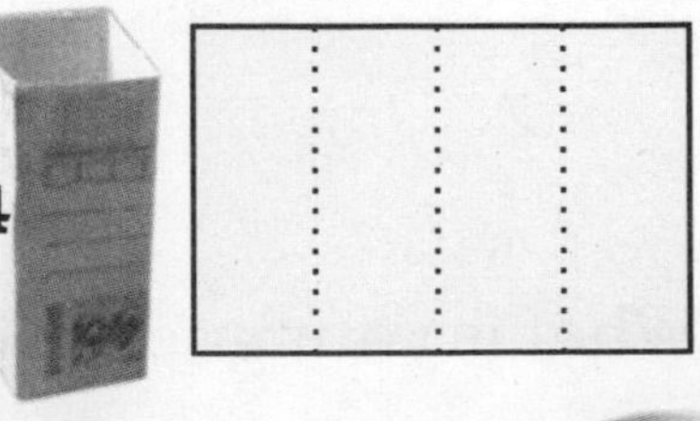

Now make the square-shaped pipe-4.

Find out which pipe can take the most sand inside it. So which pipe has the most volume?

Remind children of the thread activity on page 155 where they may have seen that out of the shapes they made with a fixed perimeter, the circle had the biggest area. Here they will be looking for the shape with the biggest volume while they keep the area of the paper fixed.

Trek to Gangotri

The students of Class XII are going on a trek to Gangotri. They have to pack their bags for six days and keep them light. They also have to take things that do not take too much space. So they will look for things that have both less volume and less weight. After all, they will carry their own bags while climbing the mountains!

They even dry the onions and tomatoes to make them light. One kg of onions or tomatoes becomes 100 g when the water inside dries up.

The list of food each person will need for **one day**:

- **Rice**: 100 g

- **Flour (*Atta*)**: 100 g

- **Pulses (*Dal*)**: $\frac{1}{3}$ the weight of rice and flour

- **Oil**: 50g

- **Sugar**: 50g

- **Milk powder**: 40g (for tea, porridge, and hot drink)

- **Tea**: Around 10g

- **Dalia**: 40g for breakfast.

- **Salt**: 5 g

- **Dried onions**: 10 g

- **Dried tomatoes**: 10 g

a) For 6 days, each person will need

- Rice and flour – _____ g
- Pulses – _____ g
- Dried onions – _____ g

b) How much of fresh tomatoes should be dried for 6 days for 10 people?

c) What is the total weight of food (for 6 days) in each person's bag?

Even one gram extra can make the trek tough!

Guess how many of us together weigh one gram! About 100?

How Heavy am I?

Do you remember the story of how Vaidika's daughter found the weight of an elephant? (Math-Magic Class IV Page 143)

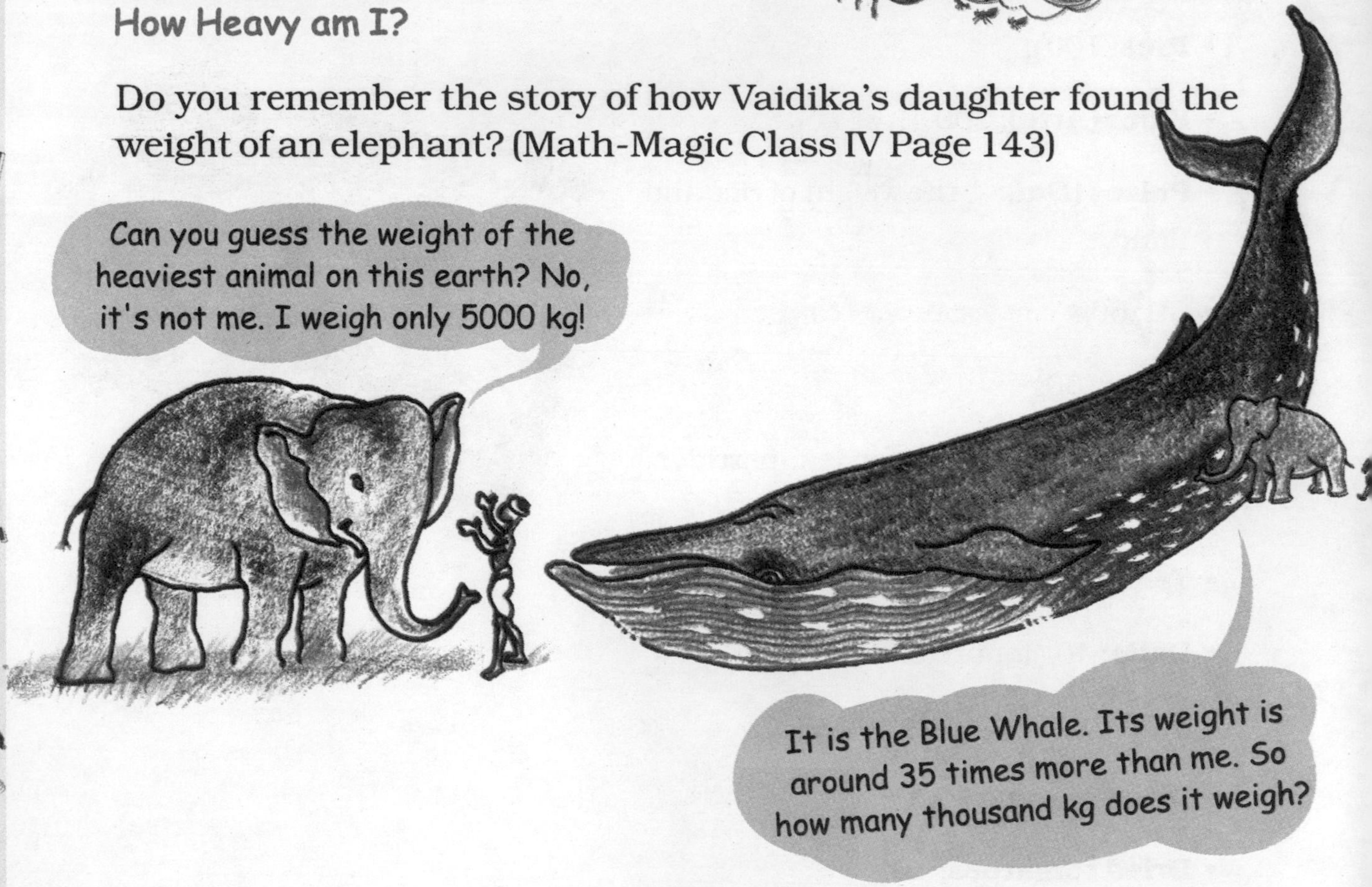

Can you guess the weight of the heaviest animal on this earth? No, it's not me. I weigh only 5000 kg!

It is the Blue Whale. Its weight is around 35 times more than me. So how many thousand kg does it weigh?

✳ Guess how many children of your weight will be equal to the weight of an elephant of 5000 kg.

✳ At birth, a baby elephant weighs around 90 kg. How much did you weigh when you were born? Find out. How many times is a baby elephant heavier than you were at birth?

✳ If a grown up elephant eats 136 kg of food in a day then it will eat around _____ kg in a month.

Guess about how much it will eat in a year.

Shahid Saves the Bank!

Shahid works in a bank. He sits at the cash counter. Whenever there are too many coins he does not count them. He just weighs them.

Weighing is so much easier! The weight of a 5-rupee coin is 9 g. Tell me the weight of the sack and I will tell you the number of coins in it.

Can you hold these coins and say which is the heaviest?

My bag of 5 rupee coins weighs 9 kg. So how many coins does it have?

One kg is equal to 1000g so 9 kg is equal to 9000 g. If one coin weighs 9 g, then the bag weighing 9000 g has 9000 ÷ 9 = _____ coins in it. Easy!

✳ How many coins are there in a sack of 5 rupee coins if it weighs:

a) 18 kg? _____   b) 54 kg? _____

c) 4500 g? _____   d) 2 kg and 250 g? _____

e) 1 kg and 125 g? _____

> 2250 g can also be written as 2 kg and 250 g. Can you explain why?

✳ A 2 rupee coin weighs 6 g. What is the weight of a sack with:

a) 2200 coins ? _____ kg _____ g   b) 3000 coins? _____ kg

✳ If 100 one rupee coins weigh 485 g then how much will 10000 coins weigh? _____ kg _____ g

With your eyes closed, can you tell which is heavier — a 100-rupee note or a 50-rupee note? This may be difficult to say, but Shahid, who cannot see, has a better sense of touch than most people.

Once Shahid noticed that a bundle of notes which came to the bank felt different and heavier. He asked the manager to check. Others looked at it but found no problem. He insisted and so a machine was brought to weigh it. It showed that the notes were fake, not real ones. "Oh Shahid! You really saved the bank!" said everyone.

Find out and discuss

✳ How do people who cannot see make out different notes and coins? (Hint: Look for a shape ▲, ■, ●, ▬ etc. on notes of Rs 20, 50, 100, 500 etc. and feel it.)

✳ What should we look for to check if a 100-rupee note is real or fake?

During the discussion on checking a note as fake or real, different things can be observed. A fake note may differ in size, quality of paper and printing or the style in which numbers are written. The watermark (the white area with Gandhi's image) and the words 'भारत' and 'RBI' written on the shiny security thread are meant to prevent people from printing fake notes.

A Page to Cut Out

Angles

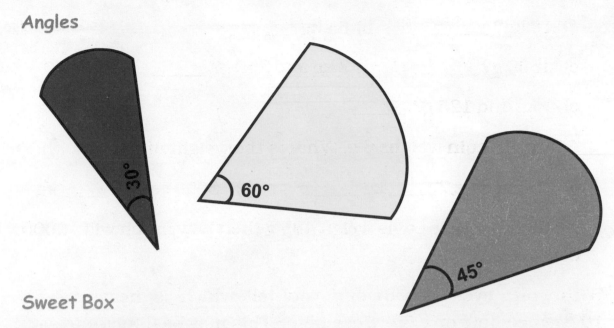

Sweet Box

Cut along the dark lines. Paste the shape on a thick paper. Fold along the dotted lines to get a sweet box as shown on page 126.